AMONG THE FIRSTS: LIEUTENANT COLONEL GERHARD L. BOLLAND'S UNCONVENTIONAL WAR

D-Day 82nd Airborne Paratrooper,
OSS Special Forces Commander, Operation *Rype*

MATTHEW T. BOLLAND

CASEMATE
Philadelphia & Oxford

Published in the United States of America and Great Britain in 2022 by
CASEMATE PUBLISHERS
1950 Lawrence Road, Havertown, PA 19083, USA
and
The Old Music Hall, 106–108 Cowley Road, Oxford OX4 1JE, UK

Hardback Edition: ISBN 978-1-63624-121-0
Digital Edition: ISBN 978-1-63624-122-7

A CIP record for this book is available from the British Library

Printed and bound in the United Kingdom by TJ Books

Typeset in India by Lapiz Digital Services, Chennai.

For a complete list of Casemate titles, please contact:

CASEMATE PUBLISHERS (US)
Telephone (610) 853-9131
Fax (610) 853-9146
Email: casemate@casematepublishers.com
www.casematepublishers.com

CASEMATE PUBLISHERS (UK)
Telephone (01865) 241249
Email: casemate-uk@casematepublishers.co.uk
www.casematepublishers.co.uk

Dedication

To Nancy, my wife, soulmate and love of my life. Ever since we took our wedding vows on August 9, 1980, she has been my constant companion throughout this adventure we call "life." She also shares a deep appreciation for our parents' generation who lived through the scourges of World War II. Her own father served in the navy on the escort carrier USS *Croatan* (CVE-25). Besides being my companion on many trips to various veterans' gatherings and research facilities, she also spent many meticulous hours typing up the original handwritten works of my father's manuscript. In the truest sense, the "two became one" when taking on the task of writing of this book.

Contents

Foreword		ix
Introduction		xiii
1	A Changing Scene	1
2	The Making of a Paratrooper	5
3	Battle Experience, D-Day Invasion with the 82nd Airborne	21
4	The British Temperament	45
5	The Norwegian Temperament	49
6	Norwegian–American Roots of the Bolland Family	63
7	German Subterfuge	67
8	Norwegian Resistance	71
9	OSS Beginnings, Background and History	81
10	Prelude to a Mission	97
11	The Scandinavian Section, OSS London	101
12	The Inception and Importance of Operation *Rype*	103
13	Meeting the NORSO Group Personnel	113
14	NORSO Beginnings	123
15	Operation *Rype* Preparation	127
16	Carpetbaggers	153
17	Operation *Rype*	157
18	Spies through Sweden	205
19	Impending Victory	215
20	Capturing the German Airfield at Trondheim Fjord	227
21	NORSO's Final Days	231
22	Liberation	235
23	Bon Voyage, Back to the United States	257
24	Closing Military Endeavors—Korea and Japan	263
Conclusion		277

Epilogue: Congressional Gold Medal   287
Appendices   289
Bibliography   353
Index   359

Foreword

The great conflict, World War II, saw many changes in military strategy from nations around the world. The United States was no exception. New methods of warfare emerged as nations sought an advantage over their foe.

Among these "firsts" in unconventional warfare tactics were soldiers that jumped out of airplanes via parachute, landed on the ground and conducted military operations. These "paratroops," as they were first called, were a daring bunch. Sometimes they engaged the enemy in immediate combat; sometimes they parachuted in the dead of night to setup and prepare for long-term sabotage operations. Either way, paratroopers as they were later designated, proved to be a vital part of successful modern warfare.

Another "first" was the creation of a government intelligence gathering and covert operations branch. Until then, the United States had no such formal capacity to carry out such functions. Before World War II, there were no British or American central clearing houses to interpret intelligence gathered on aggressor nations. Thus, the United States and Britain were caught by surprise when Hitler invaded Poland in 1939 and Denmark and Norway in 1940. Only fragmented Allied agencies existed that indicated Germany might do so. The British were the first to develop their intelligence agencies and begin covert operations behind enemy lines. The Americans took longer, mainly because the Federal Bureau of Investigation resisted the idea and, within the United States itself, the popular notion was that covert activities were not the American way to conduct business. As far back as 1929, under the Hoover administration, when a deciphered Japanese message landed on his desk, then Secretary of State Henry Stimson infamously remarked, "Gentlemen, do not read each other's mail." He considered such activities to be underhanded and shut down the Black Chamber, a cryptographic service that was cracking Japanese codes at the time. Fortunately, the military still pressed on with code-breaking efforts.

Under the orders of President Roosevelt, such a top secret agency was eventually created. Spies, if you will, spread throughout foreign lands as well as here at home. General William Donovan headed up this effort. He had no time to build his organization with reliable people in the normal way. He went to friends and colleagues for recruitment of the immediately needed talent. The head of the Library of Congress, Archibald MacLeish, helped Donovan organize the scholars for the new American worldwide intelligence service. They included historians, political scientists, economists, and others hired for research in the Library of Congress. Donovan thought the best way to beat the Germans and other aggressor nations was at their own game. He wanted as much information as possible, especially on the German war machine. His new organization would have strategic study centers filled with reports and analyses of political, economic, psychological, and financial data. In the German *Wehrmacht*, the world faced the most modern conventional army to date. Until the United States could match German strength, unconventional methods had to be developed.

The result was the creation of the Office of Strategic Services (OSS). The OSS was the forerunner to today's Central Intelligence Agency that later formed in 1947. In all, there were about 13,000 elite OSS members operating under the strictest secrecy during the war. In fact, many notable individuals were part of the OSS, unbeknown to the American public. Among them was the famous chef Julia Child. Her husband, Paul Child, had already joined the OSS while stationed in Kandy, Ceylon (now Sri Lanka), where he met the (then) Julia McWilliams who was working for the OSS as a file clerk. They eventually married on September 1, 1946, in Lumberville, Pennsylvania. Other notables included the movie director John Ford, actor Sterling Hayden, actress Marlene Dietrich, Arthur Schlesinger Jr., John Hemingway (son of author Ernest), Supreme Court Justice Arthur Goldberg and Boston Red Sox catcher Mo Berg. General Donovan referred to OSS members as "Glorious Amateurs."

My father, Lieutenant Colonel Gerhard L. Bolland was also among both of these "firsts." His military career was a rather storied one. Beginning in 1926, as part of the Minnesota National Guard, serving with I Company, 135th Infantry, he was later accepted into West Point, getting in solely on merit rather than by political appointment, as was usually the case back in those days. He graduated as a second lieutenant with a B.S. degree in Military Engineering. After spending time as a student officer at the Air Corps' Randolph Field Flying School in Texas, he was then assigned as Platoon Commander of the 21st Infantry in the then territory of Hawaii. On June 12, 1937, he was promoted to first lieutenant and spent the fall, winter and spring of 1937–38 as a student infantry officer at Fort Benning, Georgia. On November 1, 1938, he was assigned Company Commander of the 16th Infantry at Fort Jay, New York. He returned to Fort Benning, Georgia, to complete his training course and became a qualified parachutist on July 4, 1942. On August 26, 1942, he was promoted to major. From July 20, 1942, to January 15, 1943, he was Base Commander of the 506th Parachute Infantry. His final promotion to lieutenant colonel came on May 17, 1943. After graduating Command and General Staff School at Fort Leavenworth, Kansas, he was Regiment Executive Officer of the 507th Parachute Infantry from May 28 until November 24, 1944.

On D-Day, June 6, 1944, he jumped into battle behind enemy lines out of the 82nd Airborne's lead aircraft with General James Gavin and fought for 33 days straight. After returning to England, he served as Base Commander for the Parachute Infantry Unit until he volunteered for service in the Scandinavian Section, Special Operations Branch of the OSS. King Haakon VII and Prince Olav of Norway, who were exiled in England for five years during the Nazi occupation, were looking for Norwegian-speaking military men to work with the Norwegian Resistance. The operation was code-named *Rype* (pronounced "Ree-pah"), the Norwegian word for grouse, and Bolland became the Field Commanding Officer. The main objective of *Rype* was to prevent German troops from getting to the European Continent by destroying the railroad lines used to transport them. There were at least 17 German divisions, if not more, stationed in Norway at the time. Had they been able to reach Europe in full force after the D-Day invasion, it very likely could have changed the outcome of the war.

When the war ended, Bolland returned to the Air Training Command at the Randolph Field Sub-Base in San Marcos, Texas, where he became a liaison pilot, graduating on April 5, 1947. Later in his career, he was assigned Commander of the 2nd Battalion, 31st Infantry in Korea. Afterwards, he was sent to Japan to command the 17th Infantry Regiment, AIO 7 Unit 1, during the post-war rebuilding of that country. Due to a disability, he eventually retired from active military service on May 31, 1951.

My father wrote a detailed manuscript back in 1966 regarding OSS's Operation *Rype*. He also kept several documents, photos, memoirs and military records describing his paratrooper experience as well as what led up to *Rype*, its execution, and the effect upon the war effort. This book is derived from his manuscript and those records. Other sources and documents were obtained and researched for clarity, accuracy and additional historical details.

This is not the first book to be written about OSS Operations or the 82nd Airborne's assault during D-Day. For example, William Colby, whom my father put in charge of the first Norwegian Special Operations Group (NORSO I) wrote *Honorable Men—My Life with the CIA*. He also contributed heavily to a book by Bruce Heimark entitled *The OSS Norwegian Special Operations Group in World War II*. Later in life, my father visited William Colby in 1974 while the latter served as Director of the CIA. Further letters were exchanged between the two, which my father kept as part of his documents.

Other books have also been written about the 82nd Airborne. An extensive account was written by Phil Nordyke in his book *All American All the Way—The Combat History of the 82nd Airborne Division in World War II*.

Since D-Day was such a significant historical event, it has been well documented by several other historians in their various books and publications as well.

In 1980, while his health was declining, my father entrusted me with his handwritten memoirs regarding his paratrooper experience and OSS involvement. This is referenced in the bibliography under "Bolland, Lt. Col. Gerhard L, Personal Memoirs, Transcribed 1966." Throughout the text, these personal accounts are referred to him as speaking in the first person and embedded into chapters 1–23 where appropriate. Several official military documents are also embedded into the text. Many consist of communications between headquarters and soldiers in the field. These were duplicated verbatim, including the use of capital letters, misspellings and improper grammar in order to faithfully replicate the original.

Being the soft-spoken man I knew my father to be, he never did get the chance to tell his side of the story. Since his disability limited his mobility, and unbeknown even to my five siblings until now, I used to sit with him for countless hours as he relayed story upon story of his war experiences: some of them intriguing, some with tragic outcomes, some with historical significance, and some even downright humorous. After he passed away on November 12, 1999, I retain that perspective of his life that I will always cherish.

So here's to you, Dad, your story and your legacy. On behalf of my late father, I sincerely hope this book accomplishes that goal.

Matthew T. Bolland

Introduction

Early in 1966, on magazine racks throughout the United States of America, there appeared a pulp edition book entitled *Selective Service Draft Deferment Test*; very popular around college bookstores, especially for those seeking a way out. The evasion of a man's civic duty in our democracy no less! Instead of fighting a war with the "sons of slum and gravy," as the West Point song goes, certain individuals are by virtue of birth and circumstance to be most sacrosanct and not exposed to the horrors of war; a breed to be set apart.

This brings to attention a situation which developed in G Company, 16th Infantry of the "Big Red One" 1st Division in Fort Devens, Massachusetts. After our first batch of Selective Service men arrived at the unit in the fall of 1940, it was obvious something was amiss. They were a true cross-section of American manhood. Some were college men, others high school graduates and still others less fortunate in scholastic achievements. The company lacked cohesion. To further complicate matters, the solid core of the company had been through very trying and vigorous maneuvers for almost a year. Some of the old timers were very real fine soldiers, tried, conditioned and disciplined, but, again, not of too high an educational level.

Cliques were forming. This bothered the first sergeant, but he had a solution. One morning at police call, "Sarge" booms out, "Fall out for police call." With a blast of the whistle, out come the men, promptly assembling in the company formation. He barks, "Men, form in three ranks. College men first rank, high school graduates second rank, grade school third rank. You'll sweep through the company area. First rank pick up all cigarette butts, cigars, paper wrappers and loose paper. Second rank, pick up anything the first rank missed, and you dumb *#@&s in the third rank just follow along behind and find out how it's done." They all got the message. That was the beginning of a tight-knit organization that was later to go through the hell of Africa, Normandy, the rest of France, and central Europe; each man truly his brother's keeper. Angry bullets never consider scholastic achievements.

The currency of the United States bears the inscriptions "*E Pluribus Unum*," meaning "one from many," and "In God We Trust." Therein lay the strength of a nation. The war was not a brush fire by any means, but a maximum effort. It was considered worthy of our best, which were given, and the job was done.

CHAPTER I

A Changing Scene

Even before the war began, and after Hitler was appointed chancellor on January 30, 1933, there were events on the world stage warning Germany was heading towards a major conflict. On May 20 of the same year, Sir William Stephenson witnessed the Nazi burning of books. In August, Winston Churchill was jeered when he warned of Germany's rearming. April 1, 1934, saw Hitler's organized persecution of the Jews begin. Benito Mussolini's Italian fascist forces then invaded Abyssinia on October 2, 1935. On March 7, 1936, Germany began its occupation of the Rhineland and on October 25 the Rome–Berlin Axis was established. In November 1937, Stephenson was able to obtain a copy of German High Command secret briefings revealing plans for the conquest of Europe and control of the British Empire. Then, of course, on March 11, 1938, Germany marched into Austria.

World War II was the biggest and deadliest war in history; a global military conflict fought between the Allied powers of the United States, the United Kingdom and the Soviet Union, along with other countries, against the Axis powers of Germany, Italy and Japan. More than 60 million people, the majority of them civilians, lost their lives.

It officially began on September 1, 1939, when Germany invaded Poland. On September 3, Britain, France, and the members of the Commonwealth declared war on Germany. They could not help Poland much and only sent a small French army to attack Germany from the west. Soon afterwards, the Soviet Union invaded eastern Poland and, by September 17, Poland was divided.

Germany then signed an agreement to work with the Soviet Union. The Soviet Union forced the Baltic countries to keep Soviet soldiers in their territories. Finland did not accept the Soviet call for its land, so it was attacked in November 1939. France and Britain had thought the Soviet Union might enter the war on the side of Germany. As a result, they were successful in driving the Soviet Union out of the League of Nations. After Poland was defeated, British soldiers were sent to the Continent. Initially, there were no big battles between the two sides. Then, in April 1940, Germany decided to attack Norway and Denmark in order make it safer to transport iron ore from Sweden. The British and French sent forces to counter the German occupation but had to leave when Germany invaded France. On May 10, Germany invaded France, Belgium, Holland and Luxembourg and quickly defeated them by using blitzkrieg tactics. The British were forced to retreat from mainland Europe at Dunkirk. On June 10, Italy invaded France, declaring war on France and the United Kingdom. Soon after, France was divided into occupation zones. One was directly controlled by Germany and Italy, and the other was unoccupied and known as Vichy France. This was the government set up by the Germans in southern France in 1940. It was led by Philippe Pétain, notable for helping to win World War I. The Vichy Government, a satellite state of Germany, controlled the southern half of France until 1942. The Germans ran the northern half.

Thus, by mid-1940, it became apparent Hitler's scheme of world domination would be carried out by terror, deceit and conquest. It was undeniably underway. Roosevelt recognized that, if Hitler could conquer embattled Britain, this would eventually lead to an attack upon the United States. The British Security Coordination, a relatively innocuous sounding organization headquartered in New York, was, in fact, a hub for all branches of British Intelligence and supplied Roosevelt with critical information.

By June 1940, the Soviet Union moved its soldiers into the Baltic States and took them, followed by Bessarabia and Romania. Although there had been some collaboration between the Soviet Union and Germany earlier, this made it serious. Later, when the two could not agree to work more closely together, relations became worse.

Then, on June 22, 1941, the European Axis countries turned against the Soviet Union. During the summer, the Axis quickly captured Ukraine and the Baltic regions from the Soviets. Britain and the Soviet Union formed a military alliance in July. Germany had now created an eastern battle front for itself. Although there was great progress in the previous two months, when winter arrived, the tired German army was forced to delay its attack just outside Moscow. It showed that the Axis had failed to secure its main targets, while the Soviet army was still not substantially weakened. This marked the end of the blitzkrieg stage of the war. Later on, with the impending D-Day invasion, Germany would battle on two fronts. The war dragged on for six bloody years until the Allies finally defeated Nazi Germany and Japan in 1945.

When Hitler invaded Norway, of the six army divisions Norway could mobilize, four were essentially destroyed; their soldiers either killed, wounded or imprisoned. This amounted to approximately fifty thousand men. All the towns of Østerdalen, Gudbrandsdalen and the northern Trondheim area were severely bombed and most of them were completely destroyed. Airfields, railroads, bridges, roads, and lines of communication also took tremendous tolls. These had been built with the blood, sweat and tears of the Norwegian people through a span of about a century.

***

Now to Lieutenant Colonel Bolland's story. It goes like this.

Opening scene:

The timeline is rewound back to the United States a year after Pearl Harbor. Then Captain Bolland was taking a "get rich quick" course on "How to become a Battalion Commander and Staff Officer" in 13 weeks of accelerated training. Little did I realize this would be my first encounter with someone who had first-hand knowledge about the conditions in Norway.

Into sharp focus come the efforts of one Major Axel Petersen, a Norwegian. He was assigned the task of helping the U.S. Army develop equipment for use in the snow and cold of the mountains. My first meeting with him occurred in the Officers Mess at Fort Benning, Georgia, in January 1942. I noticed this lonely-looking major of the Norwegian Army having dinner a few tables from me. We were both alone so, having finished my entrée, I picked up my coffee cup and moved over to his table and introduced myself in Norwegian. This surprised him and the far-away look in his eyes faded into a pleasant smile. The patch spelled out "NORGE" on his tunic and the pips on his shoulders denoted the rank of major. This gave me a sense he had an adventurous tale to tell. He said, "I am Major Axel Petersen, just in from Camp Hale, Colorado, where I've been working up equipment for the 99th Mountain Battalion, special items such as ski equipment, rucksacks, parkas and the like." Little did I know then that the equipment he had worked up would be playing a part in my operation three years later. He went on to explain how he escaped from Norway. He had skied deep into Russia, boarded the Trans-Siberian Railroad, proceeded by way of Japan, the Philippines, and eventually to our west coast, and then to the Norwegian Embassy in Washington, D.C.

We settled down into a real bull session about the conditions in Norway. Our conversation turned to the fate of the Norwegians under Nazi domination. At that time there was a question in many minds as to which way Norway would go, with Vidkun Quisling the traitor, or with the exiled King Haakon VII. He quickly dispelled any doubts I may have had. I listened to a long list of things the Germans had done and were doing to the intense displeasure, even hatred, of the populace as a whole. As he spoke, I could only agree that this was bad or that was bad. In fact, there was nothing the Germans had done or were doing that was good for the citizens. He convinced me of that. This went on for quite some time until suddenly his countenance became deadly serious and foreboding, almost emotional. His next statement did it. "Do you realize that in Norway today, you can't even get a cup of coffee?" It couldn't be! Denying Norwegians coffee was a *cause célèbre* if there ever was one. Norwegians the world over would now rally against the Germans. Anyone so stupid as to stop the coffee trade from South America to Norway had to lose the war. My reaction? How do you get into this war and quickly? Sign me up right now! Coffee, that's just plain good ol' Norwegian gasoline. Another cup and away you go! My Norwegian roots now kicked into high gear. Enough had been said. Bolland would like to go overseas immediately!

Fast forward to the East Coast where I found myself with 300 men, some from the 99th Battalion, in the pipeline of replacements leaving Boston and bound for Glastonbury, England. Glastonbury served as a replacement depot. The trip over was, for the most part, uneventful and crowded. We sailed on the British ship *Cynthia* which had some difficulty feeding us palatable rations. Many of us found ourselves trying our K-ration packets, although they were supposed to be our sustenance upon disembarking at the replacement depot. We were in a convoy. The monotony of the voyage was occasionally interrupted by a submarine scare followed by depth charge releases and explosions that sent up large spouts of water, hopefully fending off submarine attacks, real or imagined.

CHAPTER 2

The Making of a Paratrooper

Modern warfare had become three-dimensional. No longer would enemies be subverted on a flat battlefield. We would be the first to descend from the skies into any part of the interior of enemy-occupied territory in an effort to destroy its capabilities.

Before the Norwegian Special Operations Group (NORSO) and the Office of Strategic Service's Operation *Rype* became a part of my military endeavors, I first saw action in France, dropping in behind enemy lines as a paratrooper with the 82nd Airborne. We were the force needed to take the high ground during D-Day on June 6, 1944. Of course, before all of this, the military makes for a well-prepared soldier, especially those jumping from airplanes into battle behind enemy lines. Consequently "paratroops" were a little-known outfit and relatively new at the time to modern-day warfare.

My own paratrooper training began at Fort Benning, Georgia, in 1942. Located just outside of Columbus, it is abundant with tall green pine trees, swamps, streams, and rivers. The only exception was the sand; hardly any grass at all, just sand. It seemed so out of place. There was also a place called Cactus Hill. It was appropriately named as some paratrooper trainees had the unfortunate luck of landing in it and being dragged by their chutes across its prickly terrain, adding further misery to the occasional broken legs, wrenched backs and sore muscles.

Fort Benning consisted of 180,000 acres of rolling pine-covered hills along the Chattahoochee River in western Georgia. It was called "the most complete Army Post in the continental United States" at the time. About a thousand new lieutenants were produced each week and shipped off to combat platoons at the front. They lived in small, unpainted barracks in orderly rows. There was also a large tent city set up on the west side. There were no glass windows in the barracks. Instead, large wooden shutters jutted out over screened openings and were let down during rainstorms. The buildings rested on short posts, or footings, and there were two steps up to a door located in the center at the front. If you were one of the lucky ones, you got assigned to a barrack that even had a door on the door opening. Two rows of barracks faced each other, creating a sort of street between the two. Located at one end were the mess halls, placed at right angles to the Company Street, forming a large "T." The latrines were located at the other end, apart from the Company Street. Located further down the hill and closer to the blacktop road was the post exchange. Inside were "one-armed bandit" gambling machines where many a trainee frittered away their basic pay during leisure time.

Training began with the sergeant in command of our group spelling out some basic rules. "We're going to do everything we can to make you quit the paratroops," he said. "We're going to be tough on everyone here. Don't expect any sympathy from us." He then briefed us on a few unwritten rules we were expected to follow while in camp. The cadre of sergeants were the ultimate bosses, law and order. No one was to question that. Rank meant nothing in jump school. Officers and regulars were mixed. In fact, most of the time we were stripped to the waist removing all evidence of official rank. At no time was a trooper allowed to sit down, lean against anything or stand in a resting position when he was outside the confines of his own barracks. In addition, no trooper was allowed to walk from one point to another unless ordered to do so. He must instead run, on double-time at that. This included falling out and into formation. He was only allowed two walking steps to get into ranks. Failure to do so meant an automatic 25 pushups the first time, 50 for the second, 75 the third, and so on.

Our first living quarters consisted of weather-beaten tents until we were assigned barracks. We unloaded our gear and then were marched around the camp and down the road overlooking the airfield.

The next morning we fell out at five o'clock and stripped down to the waist to begin our first day of training as paratroopers. This was to be our regular routine, wearing only jump boots and pants. It was still dark when we answered roll call. After everyone was accounted for, the process began to separate the men from the boys. The sergeant started us on a run with him setting the pace. We headed down the sandy road and onto the blacktop road towards the ferryboat landing on the Chattahoochee River. After a mile so or we were all expecting a quick break with the pace slowing to a march. Not so. This may be true in the regular infantry but not in paratrooper school. We made a wide circuit in the countryside before eventually heading back. The entire run that first day was six miles. I heard reports of men staggering and then passing out in the heat of the sun. The sergeants would order the men to pay no attention to them but keep going. Men behind them spread out on either side and ran around them. I later learned these were left to their own devices to find their way back to camp. Some showed up later in the evening only to be booted out of paratrooper school the next day. They ended up going to the military police. Nothing more was ever heard or said about them. After the six-mile run, we immediately formed ranks to begin calisthenics to cool down, starting with side-straddle hops then pushups and then onto other exercises. Double-timing back to the company area, we fell out for breakfast which consisted of cornflakes and black coffee. Half the coffee was poured over the cornflakes to make them soft. After breakfast we headed down the same road but then veered onto a trail to cut through the woods and across a creek.

Jumping from rock to rock, we scrambled up the opposite bank and re-formed. We continued double-time, came out of the woods and onto a road that encircled the Air Force barracks. The Air Force was just falling out for reveille.

When we reached the point where we began the "A" stage of our training, an instructor told us we weren't volunteering for any picnic and that most of us would die in combat. To emphasize the point he said, "In fact, if any man lives through three missions, the Government will fly that man home and discharge him. You know as well as I do that Uncle Sam never discharges anyone during wartime. So now you know what your odds are of living through this war. You don't have a chance!"

As training progressed, we were taken to the packing sheds to learn how to fold and pack parachutes. We would pack our own chutes for our first five jumps, quite an incentive to get it right! Four men each were assigned to long tables. These tables were highly polished to prevent any tears in the parachute fabric during packing. Standing at rigid attention the order was given. "Stow … equipment!" At the first word we took hold of our caps with our right hands. At the second word we slapped the tables hard with them. Our shirts came off next, folded neatly and stored on shelves underneath the tables. Next came the task of familiarizing ourselves with the type of 'chute used to jump. The T5 assembly consisted of a 28-foot canopy and the same number of panels. Each panel was made up from four sections. The center apex of the canopy had an 18-inch hole to let surplus air escape. This was supposed to keep the 'chute from oscillating, although that did not always work. Twenty-eight suspension lines, each 22 feet long, ran from the canopy to four cotton web risers. These suspension lines were attached, seven to each riser, by metal ring connector links. The risers were actually the ends of the harness. They were constructed in such a way to loop around the body, pass through the crotch and back up to the shoulders. This T5 type of 'chute was designed to open in the prop blast which created an opening shock of approximately five Gs.

The harness itself had a unique construction. Much like Chinese finger cuffs, under strain it had a tightening effect around the body to absorb the shock rather than yanking up through the crotch. Bless the man who came up with that design! It also had a band around the mid-section that held the smaller reserve 'chute in the front. The wide part that fit the seat was appropriately called the saddle. The pack tray, as it was called, consisted of a canvas-covered rectangular wire frame worn on the back that contained the canopy, suspension lines and risers. When jumping, a 15-foot static line was attached to a cable inside the plane and ripped the pack cover off as the trooper jumped free of the airplane, pulling the entire works out of the pack tray. The prop blast did the work of blowing the 'chute open and snapping the break cord tied between the static line and the apex of the canopy. The opening time for this 'chute was not more than three seconds. This allowed paratroopers to make mass jumps at low altitudes.

After an hour or so of practicing packing chutes, we fell out for more calisthenics. The afternoon exercise session was pretty much a copy of the morning routine with the day ending at five in the evening. As time went on, besides ramping up our regular fitness training, our six-mile morning runs eventually stretched into nine-mile runs. We were becoming highly fit for combat duty as an elite class of paratrooper soldiers. For sure, a few more had left our ranks, but those that remained were bound and determined to see this through.

Stage B of our training was designed to get us familiar with getting out of a plane and controlling the chute in order to land without getting hurt. There were platforms and towers of various heights available for this. The harness test was conducted on a low-level platform by attaching our regulation parachute harness to hoops that looked like wagon wheels. The men would mount the steps to the top of the platform, get into the harness which was suspended about 15 feet above the ground and, at the command of the sergeant, jump off the platform and hang suspended with their feet about three feet off the ground. From this position we were taught how to guide a chute by pulling on the risers and how to assume a body position best suited for landing. Due to the high pace of this exercise, there was no time to adjust the harness for individual fit. Needless to say, many men were not eager to put their manhood through this more than once.

Falling into formation. (Author's collection)

Equipment preparation. (Author's collection)

Landing practice via chute drag. (Author's collection)

Suspended trainee attempting to master the proper technique. (Author's collection)

Stage B also had us wearing dummy 'chutes filled with sawdust and jumping off platforms from four to eight feet in height. We practiced landing correctly and doing a right or left frontwards tumble, whichever the instructor commanded. Jump, hit the ground, roll over headfirst on either the right or left shoulder, complete the roll across the back then onto the buttocks and come to a complete standing position and remain there until an "as you were" order was given. We had to recover without taking a step to halt our forward momentum. To do otherwise meant automatic pushups. Over and over again we practiced this. Jump off a right-footed platform, do a right front tumble, run around to get in

Tower jumping practice. (Author's collection)

line and jump off a left-footed platform with a left front tumble then backwards both ways.

Our first test with any significant height was on a 40-foot tower with a mock-up plane door. Even though this does not sound high, many men voiced they would rather jump out of a plane than go off this short jump. There is a profound psychological effect that goes through the mind when jumping off something that you can see is physically attached to the ground. A cable ran from the mock-up door down at an angle to the ground. A pulley wheel rode on the steel cable and attached to it were two long risers that fastened to the jumper's parachute harness. This allowed the jumper to free fall to within a few feet of the ground before being jolted in an abrupt halt and then sliding down the cable until his feet touched the ground. He then detached his harness from the risers and grabbed a long rope attached to the pulley to tow it back up the tower for the next man.

The first morning of our "C" stage found us back in the packing sheds for more practice. The last table to finish had to stay and sweep out the entire shed while the rest lounged outside for a short break. Occasionally, during the final stages of the packing process, the entire works would squirt out of the pack tray and you had to start over.

Training eventually progressed to putting on a parachute, lying on the ground and being blown across the field by the slipstream of a ground-bound airplane engine and propeller. After skidding on our bellies or backs (or both), the instructor would order what type of recovery and 'chute collapse he wanted. The trooper had to get it right. Otherwise, he would be blown across the field again and again until he did get it right. Some ended up with large holes in the knees and elbows of their fatigues. Sometimes you could see through those holes that patches of skin were missing.

Next came drops from the 250-foot towers. The troopers put on parachutes and hooked the open canopies into large rings. They were hoisted three at a time to the top of the towers. They were released and floated to the ground one at a time. The instructor then ordered them to slip right, slip left or make a body turn. Donald Burget records in his book *Currahee* that, on one occasion, while he was at the top of one of these towers, he saw a large caravan of automobiles approaching the camp. The cars came to a stop between the jump towers. Just about then the sergeant ordered him to jump. Later on, a noncom told him it was a good thing he didn't mess up because it was President Roosevelt on an inspection tour!

The final practices we had off the 250-foot towers involved night jumps. Everyone was getting pretty excited now, because we knew training was almost complete, as we would be making actual jumps out of airplanes soon. At nightfall, we assembled at the base of the towers and awaited our turn. A sergeant was calling out

(Above and overleaf) "C" Stage: Preparing to be hoisted up 250-foot tower; open chute drop; preparing to drop; open chute drop; drop in progress. (Author's collection)

names and checking them off. We were told there would be a man with a flashlight on the ground a short distance from the tower. He would give a quick flash toward the trooper and then turn it off. The trooper then would have to guide his chute toward the point where he last saw the light. This, among other things, was to keep the wind from blowing him into the tower girders. As in the day exercise, three men at a time were lifted to suspend 250 feet in the air until the instructors were ready to release them. We finally finished two jumps each and headed back to the barracks for a few hours' sleep.

Finally, after passing "C" stage, our time had come. May 30, 1942,

was the day of our first jump from an actual aircraft. We drew our 'chutes, put them on and waited in the sweat sheds until called to load the plane. This first jump would be at 1,200 feet.

Before qualifying as official paratroopers, we would eventually make jumps at 1,000 feet, 800 feet, and night jumps at 1,000 feet as well. When our group finally moved outside to the runway for this initial jump, a sergeant came down the ranks to check our harnesses, static lines and break cords.

The C-47 was finally loaded and we all took our seats. Stomach butterflies, nerves and twitching muscles were commonplace, as could be expected with a bunch of new paratroopers about to put it all on the line. The pilot ramped up the

Leg injuries. (Author's collection)

throttle and the plane sped down the runway. We started singing the trooper's song, *Blood Upon the Risers*, partly out of tradition but mostly, I think, to calm nerves. It was written to the tune of the *Battle Hymn of the Republic:*

"Is everybody happy?" cried the sergeant looking up;
Our hero feebly answered "yes," and then they stood him up.
He leapt right out into the blast, his static line unhooked;
He ain't gonna jump no more.

Captain Gerhard L. Bolland tower jumping with a broken rib. (Author's collection)

Just before my first jump – May 30, 1942

Captain Gerhard L. Bolland, first jump, May 30, 1942. (Author's collection)

Chorus:
Gory, gory, what a helluva way to die;
Gory, gory, what a helluva way to die.
Gory, gory, what a helluva way to die;
He ain't gonna jump no more.

He counted long, he counted loud, he waited for the shock;
He felt the wind, he felt the clouds, he felt the awful drop.
He jerked his cord, the silk spilled out and wrapped around his legs;
He ain't gonna jump no more.
(chorus)
The risers wrapped around his neck, connectors cracked his dome;
The lines were snarled and tied in knots, around his skinny bones.
The canopy became his shroud, he hurtled to the ground;
He ain't gonna jump no more.
(chorus)
The days he lived and loved and laughed, kept running through his mind;
He thought about the girl back home, the one he left behind.
He thought about the medics and wondered what they'd find;
He ain't gonna jump no more.
(chorus)
The ambulance was on the spot, the jeeps were running wild;
The medics jumped and screamed with glee, they rolled their sleeves and smiled.
For it had been a week or more since last a chute had failed;
He ain't gonna jump no more.
(chorus)
He hit the ground the sound was "splat," his blood went spurting high;
His comrades then were heard to say, "A helluva way to die."
He lay there rolling round in the welter of his gore;
He ain't gonna jump no more.
(chorus)
There was blood upon the risers, there were brains upon the chute;
Intestines were a-dangling from his paratrooper's boots.
They picked him up still in his chute, and poured him from his boots;
He ain't gonna jump no more.
(chorus)

We had just passed over the Chattahoochee River and turned to head back over the drop zone. The jump master was standing in the doorway and gave the order, "Stand up and hook up." This was it, the moment we have all been waiting for! He barked out the next order, "Check equipment." We went through the process of checking our own equipment as well as the man ahead of us. No turning back now. "Sound off." The man in the back yelled, "Twelve okay" and slapped the man ahead of him. "Eleven okay." The slaps and sound offs continued down to the first man standing in the doorway. The jumpmaster yelled, "Stand in the door. Close it up tight." The first man pivoted into the doorway, placed his hands on either side of the opening and extended his left foot forward. The next man put his right foot against the first trooper's right foot and his left behind him. That way he would be ready to pivot to his left foot into the door as soon as the first man jumped. The jump master was kneeling by the right side of the door. "Everybody happy?," he yelled. "Yeah!" came back the resounding chorus reply.[1]

The jump master tapped the first man on the calf of his right leg, which was the signal to go. The man shot through the opening. His static line snapped taut and the cable line inside the plane that we were hooked up to vibrated. The next man did a quick left foot pivot and positioned into the doorway. Another tap on the calf. I found myself whispering a "go" command under my breath each time. The men moved forward keeping their right foot forward and the left behind. The wind whistling by the door became louder. The man in front of me jumped. Immediately I kicked into autopilot recalling the ground instructor's words: "Keep your fingers outside the door. Don't look down, watch the horizon." I felt the tap and unleashed like a spring, out into nothing. The next few seconds can only be described as the most exciting in my life. There was no sensation of falling, not even like one experiences in an elevator. One thousand, two thousand, three … I could hear the canopy crackling overhead as the prop blast caught it. The connector links whistled past and then, pow! The opening shock jolted every part of my body. Travelling forward with the momentum of the plane at about a hundred miles an hour and then to be thrown back by the prop blast at the same rate of speed, you experience everything, from your cheeks pulling out and away from your teeth to feeling like your boots are going to tear off your feet. I must have initially tumbled because the ground that first appeared above me, then in front of me, finally settled underneath me. A crazy few seconds of feeling suspended in air while everything else moved around me. With the 'chute open, I started a normal descent, only oscillating mildly. As trained, I opened the risers and looked up at the canopy. No blown panels or broken, snarled lines. I looked at other 'chutes around me. None were going up or down in relation to my own descent, which meant my rate of descent was normal. Looking down, I checked my boots in relation to the movement of the ground to measure wind drift. I turned my back to the wind by crossing the risers behind my neck and gently pulling outward on them. This would put me in a position for a forward-facing landing. I took up what I thought was a good body position, floated down and hit the ground. Even though we had gone through training back at the towers, the impact of the landing still surprised me. I rolled as we had been taught, albeit rather awkwardly, stood up, collapsed the chute and unbuckled the harness. I did it! I made my first jump! Feeling jubilant I walked back to retrieve the canopy, rolled it up and fastened it to my pack tray

---

1   While attending the Experimental Aircraft Association's Airventure on July 28, 2018, in Oshkosh, Wisconsin, the author met an active jumpmaster who took his training at Fort Benning, Georgia. He related the jump tactics taught to paratroopers today are basically the same as back in 1942. There were also four C-47s on display. The author was able to tour "That's All—Brother" (tail number 42-82947), one of the aircraft involved in the D-Day invasion.

with the belly band. The truck pulled up to take us back to the packing sheds. I was fully expecting a hearty congratulations from the sergeant for successfully completing my first jump. Not so. All he said was, "I see you've recovered your 'chute properly. Get on board." We returned to the packing sheds to repack our 'chutes for the next day's jump.

My first jump was successful; a reason to feel a little puffed up in the chest. However, a few initial jumps did not go so well for some others and a few casualties resulted along the way. There was one particular training jump that went horribly wrong as witnessed by Donald Burget. Two 'chutes bumped together in mid-air and the men became entangled in the suspension lines. One 'chute collapsed but the other one held. This may have been enough to save them but the man hanging below the other pulled his reserve 'chute. In one sense, a reserve 'chute can be a false sense of security. This is something we were specifically instructed not to do. The only time a reserve 'chute is any good is when the main doesn't open at all or has a serious malfunction. The main is then cut away and the reserve deployed. Sadly, by deploying his reserve it became entangled and collapsed the remaining 'chute and both men fell to their death. They landed with such a force that they actually bounced a couple of feet into the air. Ambulances raced to the scene. One of the sergeants hurriedly drove his jeep to the spot and leapt out. He busied himself over the bodies for a few minutes and then he returned to the group. He climbed out of the jeep with two pairs of bloodied jump boots. "Now, does anyone want to quit?" He then handed to boots to the first man and told him take a look and pass them on. When they got to Burget, he took a close look. A sliver of white bone protruded through one of them and the blood had not yet coagulated. After everyone had a turn, he asked again. "Does anybody want to quit?" No one stepped out of line. It was a somber lesson for all who witnessed it.

As jump training progressed, our first night jump was approaching quickly under the "D" stage. We knew this was the last step to becoming full-fledged qualified parachutists. At long last the wait was over and we found ourselves loaded onto a plane at nightfall. The C-47 taxied in front of the hangars and then moved in a zig-zag pattern to the end of the runway. The plane bounced a little and soon we were airborne. It was dark inside the plane and we could see the long tongue of flame from the exhaust port of the engines. We got the orders to stand up and hook up. We got the green light and went out the door. By this time the jumps were easier since we mostly knew what to expect.

I am reminded of a practice jump later in England while we were training the NORSO men for the *Rype* operation. We were making jumps from 1,000 feet. The man in front of me hesitated at first. He then sat down at the door before pushing out. I burst into laughter. Instead of making it a 1,000-foot drop, he was going to make it a 994-foot drop! My jump turned out to be one of the smoothest ever since I was so relaxed from laughing.

My paratrooper training at Fort Benning, and the long weeks of "A," "B," "C," and "D" stages, finally came to a close, along with the exercises, humiliations and punishments. We officially became qualified parachutists on July 9, 1942. Shortly thereafter, the 507th Parachute Infantry Regiment (PIR) was activated on July 20, with Colonel George V. Millet, Jr. in command. The new regiment insignia was created by Sergeant Kenneth Jenkins of the regimental intelligence section and bears a parachute and a lightning bolt:

Later, on January 14, 1944, the 507th PIR would become attached to the 82nd Airborne Division. The men walked down the Company Street with sort of a swagger, occasionally singing and giving out yells of victory. We were qualified paratroopers at long last! We toasted our impending departure. "Here's to the last one. Here's to the next one. Here's to the ones we left behind."

The 507th PIR motto is *Descende Ad Terram* which means *Down to Earth*.

CHAPTER 3

Battle Experience, D-Day Invasion with the 82nd Airborne

After arriving at Glastonbury, we found ourselves quartered about half a mile from the depot proper in an old brick house with no heat and no hot water. About eight officers used two small rooms. We walked to and fro for our meals and orders, expecting any day to be assigned to our combat units. As the days passed, we became increasingly anxious knowing the big event was not too far off. Each day started with cold showers and a brisk dressing. One day, I laboriously sharpened my straight-edge razor because it was giving me considerable discomfort. I finally finished shaving and with an "Ahem" gesture brought both hands down sharply. The only difficulty was the razor was stopped by my ring finger. It wasn't a serious wound as far as wounds go. The bone stopped it from going completely through; a self-inflicted wound no less and quite embarrassing to say the least. The bleeding refused to stop so I high-tailed it the half mile by foot to the aid station. After treatment, I retreated, quite subdued, to the gentle ribbing of my roommates. This cut was to give me considerable difficulty later on in combat.

Of course, on everybody's mind was that D-Day was on the horizon. An historic event that would change the course of the war, the Western Allies—American, British and Canadian forces—were about to invade the European continent to retake it from Nazi occupation. The German Navy and Air Force had already been weakened considerably. Now the time was at hand for the German Army to experience the same. Germany would surrender a mere eleven months later.

The codename for the overall invasion was Operation *Overlord*. After extensive aerial and naval bombardment, the amphibious landings, code-named Operation *Neptune*, were to take place. This amphibious effort would fill the English Channel with more than 3,500 ships. Three thousand were landing craft and 500 were warships that, soon after 5 o'clock in the morning, began deluging the coastline and its hinterland with a rain of shells. Ten thousand German soldiers who had gone to sleep beside an empty English Channel saw, at first light, a sea filled from horizon to horizon with ships.

Historians love to dwell on the military hardware. They describe in detail the equipment—the landing craft, the artillery, the tanks, planes, ships and even the individual arms each soldier carried ashore. Battles tend to become red and blue arrows on maps, painting the successes and failures of divisions, battalions, and corps of armies. D-Day can certainly be viewed in this manner, showing the "big picture." In fact, one might say this was the moment the United States became a superpower, demonstrating it could organize a military force just about anywhere in the world. Along with their British and Canadian counterparts, U.S. forces launched a massive liberation campaign into the heart of Nazi-occupied Europe.

In reality, however, wars are won on the human level. The decisions by commanders all the way down to the foot soldier are replete with frailties, subject to chance, surprise and mistakes. Some were good decisions, resulting in major victories and acts of bravery. Some were poor decisions, resulting in tragedy. In other words, the Allied difference was not in the weaponry. The Germans held the high ground, especially on the beaches of Omaha. Rather, small numbers of brave GIs and officers refused to knuckle under; men who refused to admit defeat, men who soldiered on.

On June 6, 1984, on the 40th anniversary of D-Day, President Ronald Reagan spoke of one such group in Normandy, France, as he stood at the Pointe du Hoc Ranger Monument overlooking Omaha Beach. This, perhaps, was one of the finest speeches of his presidency. The 1,850-word address, penned by gifted speechwriter Peggy Noonan, cemented Reagan's legacy as one of the great orators of all time. In it he described the near-impossible task assigned to one particular group, 225 U.S. Army Rangers:

> Their mission was one of the most difficult and daring of the invasion. To take out the enemy who were shooting down at them with machine guns and throwing grenades.
>
> And the American Rangers began to climb. They shot rope ladders over the face of these cliffs and began to pull themselves up. When one Ranger fell, another would take his place. When one rope was cut, a Ranger would grab another and begin his climb again. They climbed, shot back, and held their footing. Soon, one by one, the Rangers pulled themselves up over the top, and in seizing the firm land at the top of these cliffs, they began to seize back the continent of Europe.

As Reagan continued, those who survived, now in their sixties, looked down at the straight drop into the crashing waves below. Understandably, some were overcome with emotion recalling that day 40 years earlier. Indeed, more than half were killed. Ordinary men, many still in their teens at the time. Reagan then asked and answered the same questions:

> Why did you do it? What impelled you to put aside the instinct for self-preservation and risk your lives to take the cliffs? What inspired all the men of the armies that met here? We look at you, and somehow know the answer. It was faith and belief. It was loyalty and love.

These Rangers, along with countless others, saved the world from tyranny and preserved our system of democracy and freedoms. They exhibited the very bravery human beings can have on behalf of a noble cause.

There was some question in the beginning as to who would be supreme commander of the Allied forces for this massive invasion. Winston Churchill long thought General Sir Alan Brooke should lead the forces. He accompanied Churchill to Quebec in early August 1943, to meet with the Americans, where he met stiff opposition. The Americans were insistent the appointment should go to an American. Henry Stimson, then Secretary of War, conferred with President Roosevelt ahead of the Quebec conference and voiced his strong opinion about this. Churchill eventually came around and agreed that an American should run the operation. He informed Brooke of his decision on August 15. Brooke took it hard. He wrote in his diary: "I felt no longer necessarily tied to Winston and free to assume this Supreme Command which he had already promised on three separate occasions. It was a crushing blow to hear from him that he was now handing over his appointment to the Americans."

General George Marshall was the initial choice by Roosevelt. However, with the end of summer and the Quebec conference behind him, Roosevelt felt Marshall should remain in Washington as he would be invaluable to the war effort there. At a conference in Cairo in December 1943, Roosevelt proposed General Dwight Eisenhower lead the operation. Churchill agreed and moved Field Marshal Bernard Montgomery to London where he would command the 21st Army Group and the land battle during the Normandy invasion. Thus, Montgomery would command all the ground troops in the Normandy assault. President Roosevelt stopped off in Tunis on his way back from Cairo to inform Eisenhower of his decision. This came as quite a surprise to the general. Eisenhower did, however, have some British commanders on his staff. Most notable were Admiral Bertram Ramsay as naval commander-in-chief and Air Marshal Sir Trafford Leigh-Mallory as air commander-in-chief.

In the weeks before the D-Day invasion, the Supreme Headquarters Allied Expeditionary Forces temporarily halted strategic bombing of targets inside Germany. Instead, Allied air resources hit France. This affected the Germans' daylight maneuverability. All methods of transportation—rail lines, roads and so forth—were under constant attack. Unable to stop these fierce attacks, Germany had another big problem. In the summer of 1943, the *Wehrmacht* had launched a final offensive on the Eastern Front with the aim of stunning the Russian Army at Kursk. This failed miserably and the Russians were undeterred by heavy casualties. The Russians started pressing westward with the largest army (at the time) in history. As it approached East Prussia, the Germans were anxious to slow its advance. These fierce battles started to drain Germany of reserve manpower on the Western Front and it thinned out considerably. Many units in France were relocated to the Eastern Front. Normandy was ripe for invasion.

General James Gavin was to lead the 82nd Airborne paratroopers into battle. From previous experience he had seen how lightly armored paratroopers struggled against enemy tank units. That led Gavin to seek General Omar Bradley's input, since Bradley would be commanding the landing forces on Utah Beach. Bradley was a strong proponent of airborne operations and, in him, Gavin found an ally. Together they created a plan that helped Gavin immensely. Studying the maps, they realized that, because the area behind Utah Beach contained a lot of marshland, troop movements would be channeled by available terrain. Even if the beach was quickly taken, the maze of obstacles, irrigation canals, swamps, streams and bridges might make troops more vulnerable and could prove more costly than the beach assault itself. Thus, Bradley was insistent that no Utah Beach landing would take place unless a substantial airborne assault landed behind enemy lines to assist in taking hold of critical transportation points and bridges. Paratroopers would also block German advances in attempts to retake the beach. Once landed, these paratroopers could actually use the honeycombed countryside of marshes, canals and rivers to their advantage. German armor on the move would be forced onto roads and bridges, making enemy tanks less mobile and thus, easier to avoid. Bradley's plan also enlarged the drop zone Gavin felt was favorable, terrain wise, for both the 101st and 82nd.

Gavin also studied a pamphlet, *What Every Soldier Should Know About Airborne Troops*, published by German commanders that found its way into his hands. It described how to best to fight against paratroopers and described their weaknesses in detail. He thought the pamphlet was excellently written.

In mid-May, Field Marshal Erwin Rommel, commander-in-chief of Army Group B, the most powerful force in the German West, moved another division, the 91st Infantry, into the area of the projected 82nd Airborne landings. Rommel, the celebrated *Afrika Korps* commander, had been in France since November 1943. He thought there was only one way to defeat the Allied attack and that was to meet it head on. There would be no time to bring up reinforcements. Everything, in his view, from troops to *Panzer* divisions, had to be held ready at the coast or just behind it. Rommel was also fascinated with mines as a defensive weapon. On one inspection trip with the field marshal, Major General Alfred Gause, Rommel's chief of staff before Major General Dr. Hans Speidel took the position, pointed to several acres of spring wildflowers and said, "Isn't that a wonderful sight?" Rommel responded, "You might want to make a note, Gause, that area will take about one thousand mines." On yet another occasion, when they were en route to Paris, Gause suggested they visit the famous porcelain china works at Sèvres. Gause was surprised when Rommel agreed but he was not interested in the works of art he was shown. He walked quickly through the display rooms and, turning to Gause, said, "Find out if they can make waterproof casings for my sea mines."

Tom Brokaw, in his book *The Greatest Generation*, talks about the Allied assault on the beaches of Normandy. The soldiers that had gone in first reached the hillside and tried to locate where the mines were. Many did … with their own bodies. Men were left lying on the hillside with their legs shattered and other mortal wounds. Gino Merli—a sergeant with the 2nd Battalion, 18th Infantry Regiment, 1st Infantry Division that went ashore at Omaha Beach on D-Day and Medal of Honor recipient—gave an account of that day:

> They'd shoot themselves up with morphine and they were telling us where it was now safe to step. They were about twenty-five yards apart, our guys, calmly telling us how to get up the hill. Human markers if you will, knowing they were going to die, but directing others around the lethal charges as long as they could.

Captain Helmut Lang, Rommel's 36-year-old aide, remembered a day when Rommel had summed up his strategy regarding a beach assault by the Allies. They had stood on a deserted beach and Rommel, a short, stocky figure in a greatcoat, stalked up and down, waving his marshal's baton. As quoted in Ryan's *The Longest Day*, Rommel pointed to the sands and said:

> The war will be won or lost on the beaches. We'll have only one chance to stop the enemy, and that's while he's in the water, struggling to get ashore. Reserves will never get up to the point of attack, and it is foolish even to consider them. Everything we have must be on the coast. Believe me, Lang, the first twenty-four hours of the invasion will be decisive. For the Allies, as well as Germany, it will be the longest day.

Rommel laced the shoreline with trenches, pillboxes and land mines. Adolf Hitler, however, expected the main attack would be on Calais, where the English Channel was its narrowest.

To give further perspective, consider the vast amount of resources and manpower amassed in England to prepare for the invasion. General Eisenhower, from his house trailer near Portsmouth, commanded almost three million Allied troops. More than half of this immense array were Americans, roughly 1.7 million soldiers, sailors, airmen and coast guardsmen. British and Canadian forces together totaled around one million and, in addition, there were Free French, Polish, Czech, Belgian, Norwegian and Dutch contingents. Never before had an American commanded so many men from so many nations or shouldered such an awesome burden of responsibility. Even before the invasion plan reached its final form, an unprecedented flow of men and supplies began pouring into England. Soon there were so many Americans in the towns and villages that the British were often outnumbered. By May 1944, southern England looked like a huge arsenal. Hidden in the forests were mountains of ammunition. Stretching across the moors, bumper to bumper, were tanks, halftracks, armored cars, trucks, jeeps and ambulances, more than fifty thousand of them. In "cities" of huts and tents, men slept in bunks stacked three and four deep. Chow lines were sometimes a quarter mile long. There were so many troops that it took some 54,000 men, 4,500 of them newly trained cooks, just to serve American installations.

Yes indeed, this was the grandiose scheme of the invasion if all went according to plan. In the last week of May, troops and supplies began loading onto transports and landing ships. General Eisenhower and his commanders had done everything possible to ensure the invasion would have every chance to succeed at the lowest cost of lives, but now, after months of planning, Operation *Overlord* had one more obstacle to contend with. That obstacle was the weather. The invasion was originally scheduled for June 5. However, high winds, clouds and rough waters forced Eisenhower, on Sunday morning, June 4, to postpone the invasion another 24 hours.

At 9:30 that night, Eisenhower's senior commanders gathered in the library of naval headquarters at Southwick House. A preamble was not needed. Everybody knew the seriousness of the decision that had to be made. Three senior *Overlord* meteorologists, led by Group Captain J.M. Stagg of the Royal Air Force, came into the room. There was a hush as Stagg opened the briefing. He sketched the weather picture, then spoke quietly. "Gentlemen, there have been some rapid and unexpected developments." All eyes were on Stagg now as he presented a slender ray of hope. A new weather front had been spotted which, he said, would move up the Channel within the next few hours and cause a gradual clearing over the assault areas. These improved conditions would last throughout the next day and continue into the morning of June 6. After that, the weather would deteriorate again. During this period of improved weather, winds would drop appreciably and the skies would be clear enough at least for airplanes to operate on the night of the 5th and the morning of the 6th.

In short, Eisenhower was being told that a barely tolerable period of fair conditions would prevail for a little over 24 hours. For the next 15 minutes, Eisenhower and his commanders deliberated. It was then up to "Ike" to make the fateful decision. There was a long silence and then he spoke. "I don't like it, but there it is. I don't see how we can do anything else." Also weighing heavily on Eisenhower's decision was that June 6 was the last opportunity for favorable tidal conditions. The next opportunity would not come until the 19th. That afternoon, Eisenhower and his aides drove to the 101st Division's headquarters. He had originally planned to visit the 82nd but Gavin asked him not to come as he felt it would be a distraction to his men.

Night parachute drops, including over 13,300 American paratroopers, were a critical part in breaching Hitler's "Atlantic Wall," as Eisenhower called it. This was to be the largest paratroop drop in history with two waves of more than 800 C-47 aircraft. Two American airborne divisions, the 82nd and 101st, were to drop into the Cotentin Peninsula in Normandy, France. Their mission was multi-purpose: to block reinforcements by German troops in the vicinity of the amphibious landing at Utah Beach, to capture causeway exits off the beach, to establish crossings over the Douve River at Carentan, and to assist U.S. troops emerging from the two beachheads at Utah and Omaha.

Surprise!

In another day and in another war, there was a general who believed that taking the other fellow by surprise was half the battle. He was the immortal Stonewall Jackson. His gaunt, gray legions marched so fast and so far—struck so swiftly and so unexpectedly—that they were known everywhere as "Jackson's foot cavalry."

In this day and in this war, "surprise" is no less a factor. But, today, it's not the "foot cavalry" that does the surprising . . . it's the air-borne infantry. Swooping down behind enemy lines in huge, *Waco* designed gliders with jeeps and field guns, these tough fighting men strike as quickly and as quietly as lightning at key air fields, ports and gun emplacements . . . and with all of lightning's deadly effect.

That's the way it happened in Sicily—*remember!*—and, very likely, that's the way it will be happening soon all along the road to Berlin and Rome and Tokio.

Against that day, we're right up to our ears in glider construction here at *Waco* . . . and the same goes for the fifteen other widely scattered manufacturing plants which are building these *Waco* designed gliders under *Waco* engineering supervision.

<u>ALL</u> ARMY CARGO-TRANSPORT GLIDERS ARE WACO DESIGNED

THE WACO AIRCRAFT COMPANY • TROY, OHIO • U. S. A.

Waco Glider advertisement, October 1942. (Author's collection)

By May 1944, the IX Troop Carrier Command, U.S. Army Air Force, stationed in England had amassed 1,207 Douglas C-47 Skytrain troop carrier aircraft (Dakotas as they were called by the Royal Air Force), 1,118 CG-4A Waco gliders (called Hadrians by their allies), and British Airspeed Horsa gliders. The Horsas were actually used in greater numbers by the U.S. Army during the D-Day invasion since they had greater carrying capacity. They were able to carry a jeep and a small anti-tank gun, as well as up to 25 troops, and were extremely maneuverable. The American Waco, by comparison, could only carry 13 soldiers. A large number of the Horsas were supplied on a Lend-Lease basis to the U.S. Army during the war, which seemed rather unusual since they were intended for a one-way trip into a war zone.

It is estimated a full three-quarters of the flight crews had never been under fire. This was quite significant considering in 1939, at the start of the war, the U.S. Army Air Corps, as it was then known, was still a fledgling organization. As the Germans bombed their way from Warsaw to London, however, military commanders took decisive action then to meet that new threat head on. By the end of the war, the United States Army Air Force was well on its way to becoming an official, separate branch of the military (the United States Air Force). It had amassed 30 times the number of aircraft and 85 times the number of pilots and support crew compared to just six years earlier.

It was feared thousands of Allied aircraft flying on D-Day would break down the system and make it impossible to identify friendly aircraft. To assist with recognition, orders were given on May 17, 1944, to apply markings to all tactical aircraft (not strategic bombers). However, to maintain security, the final orders were not given until just three days before the invasion. This gave ground personnel very little time to paint black and white stripes, commonly called invasion stripes, onto hundreds of aircraft involved in the initial assault. This meant hand painting with anything available. Military supplies and local paint stores were depleted of supplies. Even some hardware stores were broken into to get the necessary paints. The result was less than perfect stripes.

The orders finally came. We were ordered to report to our units. Some were ordered to the 101st. Others, including myself, reported to the 82nd Airborne Division north of London. The operation was divided into two simultaneous parts. Mission *Albany* was made up of 432 C-47s carrying 6,928 paratroopers of the 101st Airborne Division. Mission *Boston* consisted of 378 C-47s carrying 6,420 paratroopers from the 82nd Airborne Division.

Just before each man boarded a plane, he was given a letter from General Dwight Eisenhower, Supreme Commander of the Allied Expeditionary Force:

> Soldiers, Sailors and Airmen of the Allied Expeditionary Force!
> You are about to embark upon the Great Crusade, toward which we have striven these many months. They eyes of the world are upon you. The hopes and prayers of liberty-loving people everywhere march with you. In company with our brave Allies and brothers-in-arms on other

fronts, you will bring about the destruction of the German war machine, the elimination of Nazi tyranny over the oppressed peoples of Europe. And security for ourselves in a free world.

Your task will not be an easy one. Your enemy is well trained, well equipped and battle hardened. He will fight savagely.

But this is the year 1944! Much has happened since the Nazi triumphs of 1940-41. The United Nations have inflicted upon the Germans greats defeats, in open battle, man-to-man. Our air offensive has seriously reduced their strength in the air and their capacity to wage war on the ground. Our Home Fronts have given us an overwhelming superiority in weapons and munitions of war, and placed at our disposal great reserves of trained fighting men. The tide has turned! Free men of the world are marching together to Victory!

I have full confidence in your courage, devotion to duty and skill in battle. We will accept nothing less than full Victory!

Good luck! And let us beseech the blessing of Almighty God upon this great and noble undertaking.

Dwight D. Eisenhower

Only Eisenhower could give the order to attack. The vast power of the Allied forces lay coiled in England, ready to spring across the channel into German-occupied France. If this war was to be considered this century's turning point, then the turning point for this war was D-Day.

To be sure, at the onset, almost nothing went right for the Americans, especially at Omaha Beach which quickly became a meat grinder. Allied air and naval bombardments had failed to completely knock out the German defenses. As they approached the shore, flat-bottomed landing craft were pushed off course by a strong current and landed in the wrong places. Struggling through heavy surf, the first assault teams walked into the Germans' carefully planned fields of fire and suffered nearly 50 percent casualties. Many of the more than 2,000 Americans killed on that stony coast died without firing a shot. "Omaha Beach was a nightmare," Lieutenant General Omar Bradley, the U.S. field commander, wrote later. Some of the GIs thought the landing had failed, and so did some of the Germans, but individual Americans took the initiative. They improvised new plans and fought their way up the dunes. Eventually, they broke though the defenders and the invasion ended in success.

After those first tense 24 hours, the Allies knew they had reached the beginning of the end. Winston Churchill, whose anxiety about the attack never actually completely subsided, was jubilant after reports came in that the Allies had established beachheads and were making advances towards the interior of France. "What a plan!" he raved to parliament. Even the Soviet dictator, Joseph Stalin, who had been demanding the opening of this second front for years, paid tribute: "The history of warfare knows no other like the undertaking from the point of view of its scale, its vast conception and its mastery of execution."

The same extraordinary undertaking reverberated into American politics, securing the reputation of an indifferent student from Kansas as a great military leader and propelling him eight years later into the White House. This was Eisenhower's invasion. The one he had planned and argued for and believed in wholeheartedly.

By any measure, the D-Day story is an epic one, starring a cast of thousands. Waves of fighting men rushing onto the beaches and into the fire of the enemy, many falling but few giving up. It is a story of two massive military machines clashing in a showdown of worldwide implications.

Even to this day, the struggle to win a toehold on the western beaches of the 50-mile invasion front, is etched forever in American memories with the words "Omaha" and "Utah." Similarly, for the 83,000 British, Canadian, Free French, Czech and Polish troops, "Gold," "Juno" and "Sword" continue to reverberate.

Before the actual invasion, an elite group of paratroopers known as the "Pathfinders" were the first into Normandy, the first to break the Atlantic Wall. They parachuted into France an hour ahead of the main airborne assault and approximately six hours before the amphibious forces hit the beaches. General James Gavin is often credited with helping pioneer the Pathfinder concept. He helped train them in infiltration tactics and signaling devices such as flares, smoke canisters, lanterns and radio beacons. The British also had their own pathfinder group, the 21st Independent Parachute Company.

Twenty-six paratroopers from the 504th, 507th and 508th Parachute Infantry Regiments (PIR) made up the Pathfinder teams. Four from the 504th would accompany each of the six battalion Pathfinder teams of the 507th and 508th. Lieutenant Thomas A. Murphy with Headquarters Company, 3rd Battalion, 504th, would jump with the 2nd Battalion, 508th team. Lieutenant James H. Goethe with Company A, 504th, would jump with the 3rd Battalion, 507th team.

As the name implies, the Pathfinders' missions were to mark the drop zones and use special radio sets and signal lanterns to guide Allied aircraft to the target areas. Each Pathfinder group was assigned a specific landing zone to capture and mark. American drop sites were located only a few miles to the west and inland from Utah Beach. The British drop sites were located to the east of Sword Beach. The Pathfinders used top secret, portable radio transponders called *Eurekas*. These sent electronic pulses picked up by short-range air navigation systems installed on the incoming aircraft. Yagi antennas provided the aircraft with distance and directional information to help the crew navigate to the transponders set up in the drop zones. The system was ineffective once the aircraft approached within a two-mile radius of the transponder. This prevented the enemy from determining its exact ground location. Within that range, the aircrew had to switch to visual or airspeed timing to locate the drop zone.

As the aircraft closed in on their intended drop zones, visual signals, such as Holophane lanterns, helped pinpoint the landing zones. Pathfinder teams, or "sticks" as groups of paratroopers were known, were usually made up of eight to twelve men, including six "bodyguards" to protect the remaining Pathfinders while they set up their equipment. Jumping ahead of the main force and in small groups gave them the element of surprise and meant they would encounter less resistance. Once the main body landed, the Pathfinders then joined their original units and fought as standard airborne infantry.

The Germans also flooded fields and placed concrete protrusions hidden in cornfields and other places which later proved detrimental to the gliders attempting to bring in support troops and equipment. These were deadly, stout poles approximately 12 feet high. Thousands were dug in on potential drop zones. Some were connected by wires that activated mines. These became known as "Rommel's asparagus." Pre-invasion intelligence was able to identify some, but not all, through study of aerial photographs. This told Gavin the Germans were not only aware an airborne assault would take place, but that the enemy had trained and prepared to meet it. Drop zones were adjusted accordingly but this, Gavin knew, gave an advantage to the enemy. It forced the attackers away from the most favorable areas. Incidentally, each glider carried two passenger pigeons. The thought was that once the glider landed, the pigeons would be released to make it back to their home base to let headquarters know that particular glider had made it. In reality, however, many of the personnel on board were killed when the glider crashed; the pigeons, if they survived, could fly back and give a false sense of a successful landing.

On June 5, 1944, a group of about 120 Pathfinders took off at 9:30 pm to prepare drop zones for the 82nd and 101st Airborne Divisions. Their mission was to mark drop zones in a 50 square mile area of the peninsula behind Utah Beach for the full-scale U.S. paratrooper and glider assault that would begin an hour later. "When you land in Normandy," Gavin told them, "You will have only one friend … God." Low clouds and anti-aircraft fire scattered the planes. Only 38 of the 120 men landed on their targets. Many were not able to locate their assigned zones. Some of the zones were heavily defended. Even though off course and widely scattered, the Pathfinders set up their equipment. Their radar beacons worked somewhat effectively but the lights proved ineffective due to the low clouds. Many sticks of follow up paratroopers landed in clusters near these beacons. Even with the mis-drops, however, the overall airborne drop turned out to be successful for the following reason: the misplaced and scattered airborne forces deceived German High Command. They thought there were far more American paratroopers present in France than there actually were. Reports of parachute landings came to German headquarters from so many points that it was impossible to coordinate countermeasures.

One Pathfinder, Private Robert Murphy of the 82nd, landed in a garden in the quiet village of Sainte-Mère-Église. As he headed out of the garden toward his drop zone, he heard a burst of firing. He was told later that his buddy, Private Leonard Devorchak, had been shot at that moment. Devorchak, who had sworn to "win a medal today just to prove to myself that I can make it," may very well have been the first American to be killed on D-Day.

The grand mission of the 82nd Airborne was to immediately follow the Pathfinders and drop south of the strategic port of Cherbourg in the Cotentin Peninsula near the town of Saint-Sauveur-le-Vicomte. From there they would create confusion within the German defenses, divert reinforcements and seize bridges. Ideally, they could also divide the defenders, driving some of them to the tip of the peninsula near Cherbourg where they would be isolated. Meanwhile, the 101st would land closer to the beaches near Sainte-Marie-du-Mont. It would attack and secure the routes leading inland so Bradley's forces on Utah Beach could advance. Each force would help the other with Allied reinforcements of tanks and other artillery pouring in from the beaches to link up with the paratroopers fighting and holding down strong points behind enemy lines. The 82nd would further cut off Cotentin from the main German forces. This would make it easier for the Allies to take Cherbourg, an important location to sustain further operations.

To say the least, D-Day was a day when many soldiers experienced their first real wartime battles. For the men of the 507th and 508th, it would be their first combat jump. They would be dropping into a heavily defended continent as part of the largest amphibious and airborne invasion the world had ever seen. A huge bomber armada was to saturate Normandy, the navy was to shell the coast, soldiers were to wade ashore and paratroopers were to float downward into the heart of German defenses.

For the main airborne assault, I was assigned to the same plane as General James Gavin. General Gavin was, without doubt, a legendary World War II leader. He led the 505th Parachute Infantry Regiment on airborne drops into Sicily and Salerno before he led the entire 82nd Airborne Division on the Normandy and *Market Garden* jumps. All of this earned him the nickname the "Jumpin' General."

The day had come. Airfields throughout southern England were loaded with C-47s carrying the finest of British and American youth, paratroopers of the 82nd, 101st and British 6th Airborne Divisions. The scene outside the window of the plane was very moving. Hundreds of people, both American and British, literally lined the runway two and three deep. Cooks, office girls, clerks, ground crews, no one moved. They just stood silently and stared at the aircraft, offering perhaps a profound salute and prayers. Those inside our plane could feel the hope and spirit of all those people as the pilot released the brakes and we surged forward. The Pratt & Whitney R-1830 Twin Wasp engines at full power were shaking the plane violently as we rolled down the runway and into a long formation on our way to France. Over the English Channel, all the ships at sea, all the buildings, and anyone who could make a light without breaking their blackout codes, were blinking three dots and a dash, the "V" for victory sign. The invasion was underway.

The 378 planes of the 82nd Airborne Division parachute element flew in nine plane waves arrayed in a vee-of-vees formation. The nine plane waves were further grouped into 36 to 45 plane serials, each serial carrying a battalion.

We approached Normandy from the west at 500 feet to avoid German radar. A stationary marker boat, code-named *Hoboken*, sent a transmission and then a quick

SECRET - (when filled in)

FORM 'B' LOADING MANIFEST (PARACHUTE)

Exercise/Operation _____

Date May 30, 1944

A/C No. (Tail No.) 43-3065   Chalk No. 43

PERSONNEL

Drop Order	Army Serial Number	Rank	Full Name	Remarks
1	017676	Brig. Gen.	GAVIN, JAMES M.	
2	01204562	1st Lt.	OLSON, HUGO V.	
3	6902172	S/Sgt.	DALTON, DAVID G.	
4	01698814	1st Lt.	WITCHER, EARL W.	
5	34435056	Pfc.	WOOD, WALKER E.	
6	01292058	1st Lt.	PRICE, CARL M.	
7	01529127	2nd Lt.	DEVINE, JAMES H.	
8	0-225745	Cpl.	WALTON, Wm.	
9	58090303	Pvt.	CREEL, JOHN J.	
10	37661800	Pvt.	Auge, Kenneth J.	
11	35999572	Pvt.	Moderelli, Paul	
12	35266855	Pfc.	Wolk, Morton S.	
13	01018616	2nd Lt.	Miller, Carl O.	
14	19045953	Sgt.	Pearson, Jesse L.	32728693- T3 FRYDMAN, SZAJKO
15	35485090	Pfc.	Walker, Kendall A.	
16	36419670	Pvt.	Brozovich, George J.	
17	01289298	1st Lt.	Graham, Thomas W.	
18	0995974	Capt.	Harrison, Willard E.	
19	019565	Lt Col.	BOLLAND, GERARD L.	
20				

CONTAINERS

Rack No.	Type	Contents(general)	Gross Weight	Pilot color/light
		NO BUNDLES		

Inspection Completed _____   Signed _____

FORM 'B' LOADING MANIFEST (PARACHUTE)

SECRET - (when filled in)

(Above and overleaf) Loading manifest for the lead aircraft, 82nd Airborne (C-47A, tail number 43-30651, of Serial 21): Brig. General James M. Gavin; 1st Lt. Hugo V. Olson, Gavin's aide; S/Sgt. David G. Dalton, Gavin's guard (Gavin was told that he must have a personal guard with him, Dalton jumped right behind Gavin and Olson. They never saw Dalton again and never heard if he survived the drop into Normandy); 1st. Lt. Earl W. Witcher; Pfc. Walker E. Wood; 1st Lt. Carl M. Price; 2nd Lt. James H. Devine; Cpl. William Walton, correspondent for *Time* magazine; Pvt. John J. Creel; Pvt. Kenneth J. Auge; Pvt. Paul Moderalli; Pfc. Morton S. Wolk; 2nd Lt. Carl O. Miller; T3 Szajko Frydman; Pfc. Kendall A. Walker; Pvt. George J. Brozovich; 1st Lt. Thomas W. Graham; Capt. Willard E. Harrison; Pilot Lt. Col. Glen A. Myer; Lt. Col. Gerhard L. Bolland; Co-Pilot 1st Lt. Gene E. Hill; Crew Chief S/Sgt. Coner Goodwin; Radio Operator Sgt. Alexander W. Hastings; Navigator 1st Lt. Gaston E. Heffington; Navigator 1st Lt. Herbert Pluemer; Radar Operator S/Sgt. Joseph Bobo.

SECRET - (when filled in)

FORM 'B' LOADING MANIFEST (PARACHUTE)

Exercise/Operation   Date

Details of Aircraft

Squadron _50 TH_   A/C Type _C-47A_ Tail No _43-30465_/chalk No _44_   43

Aircrew

PILOT MYER, GLEN A.   LT. COL   O-381232

Co-Pilot - HILL, GENE E.   1ST LT   O-231983

Crew Chief- GOODWIN, HOMER   S/SGT   34168207

RADIO OPR - HASTINGS, ALEXANDER   SGT   1215 3113

NAVIGATOR- HEFFINGTON, GASTON   1ST LT   O-680735

    "   - PLUCHER, HERBERT   1ST LT   O-792905

RADAR   - BOBO, JOSEPH L   S/SGT   15330920

FORM 'B' LOADING MANIFEST (PARACHUTE)

(OVER)

SECRET - (when filled in)

dot-dot-dot-dash victory sign. We banked sharply to the left and flew between the Channel Islands of Guernsey and Alderney. We proceeded to Flamanville, France, code-named *Peoria*, while the 101st proceeded to Portbail.

On the night of June 6, 1944, President Franklin Roosevelt addressed the nation in a radio broadcast.

Last night, when I spoke to you about the fall of Rome, I knew at that moment that the troops of the United States and our Allies were crossing the Channel in another and greater operation. It has come to pass with success thus far. And so, in this poignant hour, I ask you to join me in prayer:

Almighty God: our sons, pride of our Nation, this day have set upon a mighty endeavor, a struggle to preserve our Republic, our religion, and our civilization, and to set free a suffering humanity. Lead them straight and true. Give them strength to their arms, stoutness to their hearts, steadfastness to their faith. They will need Thy blessings. Their road will be long and hard. For the enemy is strong. He may hurl back our forces. Success may not come with rushing speed, but we shall return again and again: and we know that by Thy grace, and by the righteousness of our cause, our sons will triumph.

On our way to the drop zone, most of the paratroopers did a lot of smoking, some squirmed quite a bit, checking and re-checking their equipment. Others sang quietly to themselves. Each man dealt with the high tension and jittery nerves in his own way. Although many paratroopers jumped into Normandy with their Garand rifles disassembled and stored in a padded case, known as a Griswald bag, my own regiment, the 507th, did not. Instead, we jumped with the rifle assembled and slung over our shoulders with the belly band of the parachute over it, securing it in place. Also, in addition to the bayonet and trench knife, a backup switchblade was carried into battle, partially inserted into the placket pocket of the M2 jump jacket. There was an assortment of these knives the soldier could choose from. I selected a 7-1/4" Presto M2 with textured grips. All in all, the average paratrooper was loaded down with about 85 pounds of equipment.

About 20 minutes before we were to hit the drop zone, the plane's door was removed. The cool air that billowed in felt good. Our first glimpse of France was filled with flak flashes and tracer lines streaking across the darkened sky. Seven-and-a-half minutes before we were to drop, the red light flashed on and we stood up and hooked up. This was General Gavin's standard operational procedure. As soon as we crossed into enemy territory, he had his men ready to jump. That way, if our plane was hit by enemy fire, we could bale out at a rapid pace. Since I was in the back of the plane, I started the sound off for equipment check. "Nineteen OK," then slapped the next man in front of me on the shoulder, "Eighteen OK," and so forth. Bullets were hitting the plane at this point and I'm sure each man wondered whether he would get hit even before he reached the ground? An entire lifetime of thoughts can pass through your mind between the time the red light flashes until the green jump light comes on.

Suddenly, we entered a dense cloudbank that was so thick you could not see the wing tips of the plane. The aircraft were flying in close formation, so this became a dangerous situation. Gavin thought it may have been a smoke cloud put up by the Germans. One always attributes anything unexpected in combat to the cleverness and guile of the enemy.

In an instant, the command was given by the jumpmaster, "Go!," followed by Gavin yelling "Let's Go!" as he jumped out the door. The men baled out rapidly. Into the night sky, jumping straight down Hitler's chimney. Because of the pilot's apprehension with the density of flak around us, and the sight of burning planes going down, he was flying at a much higher speed and the initial prop blast shock was much more violent. Actually, exiting the plane was quite dangerous since each paratrooper was weighed down quite heavily with equipment. We carried a loaded M-1 rifle, 156 more rounds of ammunition, a pistol with three loaded clips, an entrenching shovel, a knife, a water canteen, a first aid packet, four grenades, reserve rations, maps, and a raincoat. There was little time to worry about the dangers of the undertaking, however.

The red, green and white pencil lines of tracer bullets were visible everywhere. The Germans were throwing everything at us. Search beams crisscrossed the sky looking for flak targets. Burning planes lit the countryside. The Germans were trying to kill us as we floated to the ground. You could hear the bullets whizzing by. I pulled down on the front risers of my 'chute to collapse it a bit, also called a 'chute slip, a common practice we were taught in paratrooper school. This allowed me to drop at a greater rate of speed. I held this until I feared I was getting too close to the ground. Easing back on the risers, I slowed my descent to a normal rate. In the dark it is hard to estimate how close you actually are to the ground. I unfastened my reserve 'chute and let it drop since the main chute had deployed successfully and it was no longer needed. Within about five seconds after that, splash! I hit water and went completely under. After the initial shock, the struggle to reach the surface took every ounce of strength I had because of the sheer weight of my equipment. The wind and the current pulled the collapsed 'chute and dragged me forward, face down. The water was too deep to stand. Still in a state of shock, I instantly recognized the seriousness of my situation. I struggled to get out of my 'chute right away by grabbing my M3 trench knife and cutting away the harness. That was a mistake. Desperation started to set in. My lungs felt like they were going to burst. I felt myself becoming light-headed and was to the point of going unconscious. I had a few quick words with the Lord and, despite what atheists may claim, I heard, in a very audible voice, "Roll over onto your back." As soon as I did, the 'chute that was drowning me by dragging me face down, was now planing me along the top of the water, keeping my head up so I could breathe. My heart was pounding, but I was alive! Half gasping and half choking, I coughed up some of the water that had gotten into my lungs. Once I realized my head would remain above water, I slowly began to retain my composure. I paddled and kicked my way towards the shoreline until I could feel my feet touch. Once able to stand, on very shaky legs no less, I dragged my soaked and tired, but very grateful, body to the river's edge and unlatched my 'chute.

Sitting there alone catching my breath, I could hear the artillery and gunshots going off all around me. For the first time in my life I offered a sincere prayer of thanks to the Lord for sparing my life. At one point, a piece of shrapnel hit the ground and rolled within arm's reach. "Well," I thought, "that would make for a nice little souvenir to remember my first night into battle." "Ouch!" The shrapnel lasted only about a millisecond in my hand. Today's lesson learned. Shrapnel fresh from an explosion is still very hot!

I removed my equipment and began to get out as much water as I could to lessen the weight. I poured out my boots and squeezed as much water as I could out of the clothing. When I got to my mess kit, there was a minnow swimming around inside the container.

I learned afterwards I had landed in the Merderet River. The Cotentin Peninsula itself is abundant with marshes and hedgerows. To make matters worse, portions of land surrounding the river had been flooded by the Germans to hinder airborne operations. Much of the surrounding area had been hidden from aerial reconnaissance because of high grass. It was disguised as solid ground. What should have been a smaller shallow river was now much deeper and turned into a thousand-yard-wide lake. Many other paratroopers were not so lucky. They drowned under the weight of their equipment when they hit the flooded waters in the dark. One of the men in our group landed in a German gun emplacement and fought his way out. After surviving the anti-aircraft fire on the way down, the actual landing for many paratroopers was just as dangerous.

As is well known, the 507th was spread out over a greater area than any other parachute infantry regiment, from Cherbourg to Carentan, over 60 square miles by some estimates.

Much as other units had suffered from disorganization and dislocation, we paratroopers of the 82nd dealt with our problems and proceeded to accomplish our missions to the best of our abilities. The feeling was the Germans had their chance while the paratroopers were on their way down. Now it was the Americans' turn.

Lt. Colonel Charles Timmes ended up on the west bank of the Merderet and east of Amfreville. Since he was the Commanding Officer of the 2nd Battalion, he was anxious to find out where the rest of the regiment had landed. He desired to coordinate with Colonel George V. Millett Jr. but had no radio to communicate. He, and about thirty other paratroopers headed towards Amfreville. They could hear the fighting going on there, which happened to be Colonel Millett's undertaking. However, the German defenders were strong and Timmes and his men were forced to pull back. They retreated and ended up in the apple orchard near Le Motey, the same orchard where General James Gavin had landed. Timmes immediately organized a defense perimeter using the flooded Merderet River as a backstop.

Allied gliders were coming in and providing reinforcements and supplies. The CG-4A gliders could carry men, a jeep, a small artillery piece or even a baby bulldozer. When fully loaded they weighed around seven thousand pounds. On takeoff the gliders cleared the ground first. It was all a C-47 could handle reaching a minimum airspeed of one hundred ten miles per hour towing a loaded glider. The C-47s had to remain at full throttle for the duration of the flight with the nose tilted upwards, powered along by the props. Gavin had patrols retrieve equipment from these gliders, but not without difficulty. Some landed in swampy areas. 57mm AT guns and a

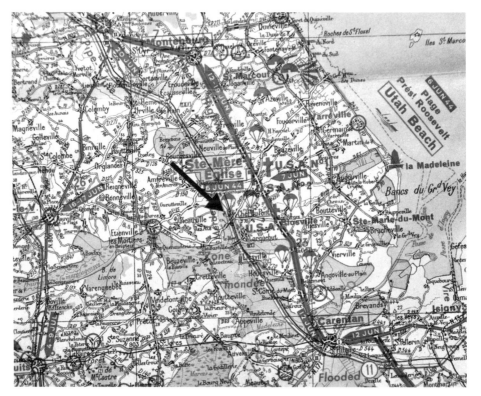

The original drop zone (DZ) for Gavin's plane was designated with the letter "N." It was located on the west side of the Merderet River, north and east of the town of Picauville. According to Gavin's book *On To Berlin*, he became aware he was overtime for DZ "N" and, based on visual observation, he figured out they were off course. He described seeing a rail line which most likely was the one that ran north-south between Amfreville and Sainte-Mère-Église. In the seconds he had to make a decision, and based on what he saw out the door, he decided to jump and "come what may." As it turned out, he landed almost squarely on DZ "T," which was the objective of the 507th PIR about three miles from where he was supposed to land. He landed rather close to le Château, also called Gray Castle, which was the headquarters of the German 1057th Grenadier Regiment, near the town of Amfreville. Based on the narratives of the other people in the plane, Gavin landed in the fields east of Amfreville. Extending the line of flight and interpolating a sequence of the drop, with my father as last man out, he landed either in the flooded marshy area of the Merderet or on the La Fière/Sainte-Mère-Église side of the river. This area is still prone to flooding. Given this information, the highly probable line of flight, when the paratroopers jumped out of Gavin's plane, is indicated by the black arrow on the map above. (Author's collection)

couple of jeeps were retrieved which helped immensely. He also had the men pick up all usable, German small arms.

C Company Commander, Captain Floyd Schwartzwalder ended up with a group of about forty-five paratroopers. They headed south along a set of railroad tracks of the Cherboug–Sainte-Mère-Église railroad and reached a road that led into La Fière.

His force was assigned a sector on the other side of the river. Schwartzwalder's group ended up joining forces with the 505th PIR and Colonel Roy Lindquist's 508th PIR. They had already been fighting Germans that were defending the Manoir de La Fière for several hours when Schwartzwalder's group arrived.

The 507th eventually regrouped as much as we could but without Colonel Millet, Jr. We pushed southward towards the bridge at the Chef-du-Pont causeway. This bridge was anchored in the middle of an island and alive with German machine guns and artillery. About ten miles away we were aware that the major waterborne assault was underway.

By D+1, June 7, the 82nd Airborne Division occupied an area roughly in the shape of a triangle, about five or six miles on a side, on the English Channel side of the Merderet River. Just to the east was the town of Sainte-Mère-Église where several paratroopers had landed and were killed. One trooper dangled from one of the spires on a church and saved himself by feigning death. Shortly before daylight the 3rd battalion of the 505th moved in and drove the Germans out. The 2nd battalion of the 505th that was under the command of Lieutenant Colonel Ben Vandervoot moved towards occupying Neuville-au-Plain to block any attempts by the Germans to move southward.

The Germans however got reinforced as well by elements of the Grenadier-Regiment 1057. They made an attempt to charge and seize the bridge at the Chef du Pont causeway. Five of them were shot down at point-blank range. Little by little, the shots stopped in intensity, which allowed the Americans to reorganize. The Germans retired at nightfall. Twenty-five paratroopers were injured with no means of transport. Towards midnight advanced elements of Company K of the 8th Infantry Division from the Forges established liaison with the paratroopers, to their great relief. The Americans held Chef-du-Pont but the Germans were not far away, they still held Carquebut just 1,000 meters to the southeast.

The day of June 7, 1944 found the Americans continuing to defend the approaches to Chef-du-Pont. They are eventually reinforced by the 3rd Battalion of the 325th Glider Infantry Regiment. The 3rd Battalion of the 508th under the command of Lt. Colonel Louis G. Mendez Jr. reorganized itself the following day and took control of the area. The Germans still controlled the west bank of the Merderet. The 90th Infantry Division, which was reinforcing the paratroopers, went on the offensive. The 1st Battalion of the 358th Infantry Regiment crossed the bridge in a westerly direction under enemy fire and engaged the Germans on the other side of the Merderet. At approximately 5:30 am, they had permanently removed the threat to the bridge and to the 82nd the span over the Merderet became known as "Kellam's Bridge." Major Fred Kellam from Jennings, Louisiana, 1st Bn, 505th, his executive, Major Jim McGinitry and the next two senior officers were killed in defense of the bridge. Lt. Colonel Herbert Batchelor from Minneapolis, Minnesota, a 508th Battalion Commander was also killed. Two bazooka teams were able to destroy five tanks and were awarded Distinguished Service Crosses for their gallant stand at the bridge.

In the middle of the morning, General Gavin, ordered Lt. Colonel Arthur A. Maloney commanding the 3rd Battalion of the 507th Parachute Infantry Regiment to survey the bank of the Merderet in the direction of Chef-Du-Pont in search of another crossing point. To this end, he was accompanied by 75 paratroopers from his unit. A bridge at La Fière was located and Gavin was informed that the approaches to the bridge were not guarded. He then decided to seize it and ordered Lieutenant Colonel Edwin J. Ostberg, Commander of the 1st Battalion of the 507th PIR, to complete this mission with a hundred paratroopers, from both the 507th and the 508th PIR. Around 10 o'clock, Ostberg and his men reached the station in the center of the village. A battle group is sent to secure the northern part of Chef-du-Pont causeway, which it does without incident. Other elements follow Lt. Colonel Ostberg through the village towards the La Fière Bridge. The Germans opened fire from several buildings, hitting four paratroopers and forcing others to stop. During the next two hours, Ostberg secures Chef-du-Pont and the Germans retreated towards the bridge. The paratroopers then ran at full speed towards this structure to prevent their opponents from reorganizing. But when they reached the bridge, an officer was killed and Lt. Colonel Ostberg was wounded. Ostberg was leading from the front when a bullet found him and he collapsed near the edge of the bridge, and tumbled into the Merderet. Captain Roy E. Creek, unit Commander of company E of the 507th and one other paratrooper ran down the riverbank and pulled Ostberg out of the water. Ostberg had survived but was out of action for the duration. This left Creek as the next highest Commanding Officer in charge. The Germans were entrenched on both sides of the bridge, installed in battle stations. A few minutes later Lt. Colonel Maloney with his seventy-five men arrive as reinforcements. The Americans manage to seize the east bank of the Merderet but they failed to hold the position very long. Only one section was left to hold the bridge. The thirty-four paratroopers who remained were under the orders of Captain Creek. These few paratroopers are quickly taken to task by the Germans along the western shore which are supported by a cannon causing additional losses in the American ranks and reducing the section to only 20 able-bodied soldiers. In addition, some fifty Germans are still in Chef-du-Pont and begin fighting there. Creek urgently requests reinforcements. By a miracle, a Douglas C-47 appears in the sky parachuting weapons, especially a 60 mm mortar and ammunition, near the positions held by the Americans. Thirty minutes later, an officer and a hundred soldiers came to reinforce Captain Creek. They were equipped with a 57 mm anti-tank gun that they retrieved from a Waco Glider that had just landed nearby. This was used immediately used to silence the German artillery piece on the west bank.

In the end, the battle at the La Fière Bridge was a costly one. At times the battle stalled. Reinforcements were necessary. On June 9th, Gavin's attack plan finally succeeded on the five-hundred and seventy-four-yard-long causeway. Yet, at the end, approximately five hundred men lost their lives.

The 507th advanced on to take La Graignes, about twenty miles south of La Fière and drove the occupying German forces out. The French people in the town were wonderful, providing food, medicine and transportation. They were grateful for the Allies liberating their town. The local church was used as a staging area for our wounded. However, this only lasted three days. The Germans counter attacked with about 2500 troops from their 17th SS Waffen Panzergrenadier Division. The Allies set up guns in a crisscross fashion that the Germans ran directly in to. They were able to kill an astonishing amount, about 1250 before running out of ammunition and being overwhelmed. The remaining men of the 507th had to flee into the swamps and did not even have time to evacuate the wounded from the church. Later, it was learned the Germans shot all the wounded, killed the two priests and butchered townspeople for helping the Allies.[1]

In the days following, with reinforcements at hand, the Allies once again began to advance and push back the German forces. Some 30 years later, in 1974, Lieutenant Colonel Bolland wrote to retired General James Gavin recounting his final actions with the 507th:

> When we advanced to Porterie Ridge I was present when General Omar Bradley pinned the Distinguished Service Cross Medal on General Gavin at a front-line presentation. The Ridge had just recently been captured and was hopefully secure. This same Ridge was to become the final mark of my service in Normandy. I had the privilege of conducting the last attack of the 82nd in Normandy which captured the last half-mile from Porterie Ridge to the road, thus cutting off the last remaining road for the Germans from Cherbourg to Saint-Lô. Since we were decimated, I was given extra personnel from Lt. Col. Smith's 3rd Battalion which made it a composite effort of two battalions. I heard the glider regiment was pulling out of the line so I latched onto all of their 81mm mortar ammunition which was very effectively used by Lt. Young. The objectives were captured without a single casualty and the enemy was propelled with sufficient velocity so as to not make a meaningful stand until they reached the Saint-Lô area. When I met Col. Raff he was profusely laudatory of our successful attack. After the night attack, we received orders on July 12th to pull out of action and return to Utah Beach to be sent back to England to retrain. An amphibious Landing Ship, Tank [LST] was waiting for us.[2]

Although a huge calculated risk was taken by Eisenhower and the Supreme Allied Command, the D-Day invasion eventually proved to be one of the greatest military victories of the 20th century. Beginning on the night of June 5/6, both British and American airborne troops succeeded in consolidating strong positions which the Germans failed to overwhelm. They also failed to drive the seaborne attackers back into the sea to prevent them from establishing well-defended footholds. It is

---

1 This section drew on the excellent accounts of the initial fighting by the 82nd Airborne during those first few critical days by Phil Nordyke, in his book *All American All the Way*, and General James Gavin, in *On to Berlin*.

2 The entire letter transcript and General Gavin's reply letter are located in Appendix 4.

recorded that, late in the afternoon of the invasion, one German tank division, the *21st Panzer*, drove to within three miles of the sea. It was stopped by a line of Allied tanks and anti-tank guns lining a ridge in its path. In the gun duel that followed, 19 German tanks were destroyed and the survivors withdrew. No German unit ever again got so close to the beaches. It could be said the eventual defeat of Hitler's Reich could be dated from that hour.

When the 82nd Airborne Division finally pulled out of the front lines to return to England, 16 of its 21 regimental and battalion commanders had been killed, captured or wounded. The Allied paratroopers landing in the dead of night did not have the advantage of a gigantic supporting cast just enumerated, nor the thousands of ships and aircraft spewing fire. They were on their own; small groups of courageous men, armed with little more than their rifles, dropping directly onto German defenses.

In Normandy, I had the privilege of serving under the proud banners of the 82nd Airborne Division. It gave richly of its strength and fought hard against the enemy. We fought for 33 days straight without let up or reinforcements. In fact, from D-Day until D+33, it had ground up two German divisions which were never to fight as units again. The price was high. I can still see the morning report figures of those that remained and were present for duty from my own regiment, the 507th PIR. We dropped into Normandy 15 percent over strength (more than 2,500 men). Only 733 remained the day we went out.

Severe losses like these have paralyzed many divisions, but throughout the Normandy campaign, the 82nd never lost combat effectiveness. The division's infantry companies did most of the bleeding during desperate night actions and bloody slogs through hedgerows. Their dead lay strewn from Sainte-Mère-Église to Amfreville to La Haye-du-Puits. Their deeds and bravery captured the hearts of Americans as their D-Day assault, at the time, was one of the nation's greatest successes. General Gavin had long been known to High Command, but now the press took to him and he became a public figure.

The 507th was awarded the Presidential Unit Citation for its assault crossing the Merderet River, holding positions on the west side and stymieing large German forces. We knew the fighting forces of the Third Reich were not the supermen they thought they were. They could be beaten.

On our return to England, we had to start all over again, filling our ranks, retraining and preparing for our next task. Later, after an abort on a flight into the Netherlands, things looked quiet in Andover, England, where we were completing our retraining maneuvers. In fact, it looked like our next mission would be to lay down an airborne carpet over the rivers of the lowlands in the spring, especially since we were pulled from the 82nd and assigned to a new division, the 17th Airborne, which was just arriving in England from the U.S.

James Gavin was promoted to major general in October 1944. "Slim Jim," as his men called him, now got another nickname, the "Two Star Platoon Leader." Being

COMPANY MORNING REPORT — ENDING 2400 28 June 1944

STATION Leicester 1½ mi SE WF0822 England
ORGANIZATION Hq & Hq Co 504th Prcht Inf Inf

SERIAL NUMBER	NAME	GRADE	CODE
01288472	Voss Vincent E	1st Lt	
Fr 5-day lv to dy 21 June 44			
019565	Bolland Gerhard L	Lt Col	
Reld fr atchd-unasgd to Co 18 June 44			
0481347	Kozak Edwin J	Capt	
Fr DS Cheltenham, England to dy 23 June 44			

OFFICER STRENGTH	FLD O & CAPT PRES	ABS'T	1ST LT PRES	ABS'T	2D LT PRES	ABS'T	WO PRES	ABS'T	FLT O PRES	ABS'T
	12	6	2	2	1	1				
ATCHD	2									
TOTAL	14	6	2	2	1	1				

AVIATION CADETS PRESENT	ABSENT	ENLISTED MEN PRESENT FOR DUTY	PRESENT NOT FOR DY	ABSENT	PRESENT AND ABSENT
		149	1	8	158
				1	1
		17		1	18
		166	1	10	177

ESTIMATED NUMBER OF RATIONS REQUIRED FOR DAY OF WEEK Sat DATE 1 July 44 NUMBER 189

MESS ATTENDANCE FOR DAY OF THIS REPORT: BREAKFAST 183 DINNER 183 SUPPER 183 TOTAL 549 ÷ 3 AVERAGE 183

MEN PRESENT 167 LESS 1 NET 166 PLUS 23 TOTAL 189

PAGE 1 OF 1 PAGES

SIGNATURE W H DAVIDSON 1ST LT INF

Company morning report June 28, 1944.

the first out of the plane on all four combat jumps, the general specialized in close contact with his men.

An interesting nickname, that came out of a battle at Anzio, Italy, was given to paratroopers. A German officer wrote in his diary, "Enemy patrols in baggy pants are 100 meters from my OP. We don't know who they are or from where they come. Seems like black devils (troopers blackened their faces for patrol missions) are all around." Thus, the nickname "Devils in Baggy Pants" was born.

The official march song of the 82nd Airborne Division, *The All American Soldier,* goes like this:

> We're all Americans, and proud to be;
> For we're the soldiers of liberty.
> Some ride the gliders thru the enemy;
> Others are sky par-a–troop–ers.
> We're all Americans, and fight we will;
> til' all the guns of the foe are still.
> Airborne from skies of blue, we are coming thru;
> Let's go. Put on your boots;
> your par-a-chutes.
> Get all those gliders ready to attack to–day;
> For we'll be gone;
> into the dawn;
> To fight 'em the eighty-second way.

At war's end, in September 1945, those from the 507th that survived boarded the steamship SS *Mariposa* and headed back to Boston.

CHAPTER 4

The British Temperament

Of course, before D-Day, the battle for England was in high gear. German and British air forces were locked in bloody battles over the skies of the United Kingdom in 1940. England experienced the largest sustained bombing campaign to date. The Battle of Britain received its name after France capitulated on June 17, 1940, and signed an armistice to quit the war. Hitler had conquered most of Western Europe in less than two months. His next logical step in global conquest was the British Isles; Britain stood alone against what seemed insurmountable odds. In a speech to the House of Commons on June 18, 1940, Winston Churchill, who became prime minister of Great Britain on May 11, replacing Neville Chamberlain, stated, "The Battle of France is over. I expect the Battle of Britain is about to begin." The name stuck.

The Battle of Britain proved to be a significant turning point in the war. The mighty and powerful German *Luftwaffe* failed to gain air superiority over the Royal Air Force (RAF) in the first all-air battle in history. This, despite months of attacking Britain's air bases and military posts. The initial air strikes did do substantial damage to coastal convoys and radar sites. However, around August 13–15 the Germans abandoned that avenue and turned to attack RAF bases directly. This probably would have been successful had it continued since the RAF was almost at breaking point. Instead, however, Hermann Göring's *Luftwaffe* changed tactics again and started raiding London in an effort to demoralize its civilian population. This proved to be a major tactical error on the part of the Third Reich. The British military and RAF were now able to rebuild and recover and thwart the Germans' efforts to gain air superiority. The first bombing attack on London happened on September 7, 1940. It was successful from the German standpoint. However, the second attack on September 15 resulted in heavy losses and led to a collapse in morale among the German bomber crews. Revitalized, RAF fighters continued to engage German formations in large numbers. The Germans were depending on the *Luftwaffe* to defeat British air defenses so its attention could then be turned to, among other things, engaging the powerful Royal Navy once the seaborne invasion from France commenced. In addition, the German Army was relatively unprepared and under-resourced for any sort of amphibious invasion.

There is a bulldog tenacity that comes to the fore so splendidly when the British are under pressure. It showed up in their countenances. The weary lines in their faces became deepened, etched character lines. Through them, their eyes shone an inner beauty that one could not help but admire and love. So different from the rapid, self-centered, well-rested and properly nourished faces of those in distant, safer lands. The two were worlds apart.

Britain's decisive victory in the Battle of Britain saved the country from a ground invasion and occupation by German forces, but attrition had taken its toll on both sides.

Hitler was forced to give up invading the British Isles and suspended the Battle of Britain. The effective air defense system, first-rate fighter pilots, and a great military leader in Air Chief Marshal Hugh Dowding, led Germany to its first defeat in World War II; proof that a major battle could be won by air power alone. It was then and there that the magnificent RAF fought the bloody battles of the skies over England and Churchill found the words to express their gallantry: "Never in the field of human conflict was so much owed by so many to so few."

Out of necessity, England found itself in need of an intelligence branch of its own. By June 1940, the Third Reich had invaded and occupied Poland, Norway, Denmark, Belgium, Holland, Luxembourg and France. Germany would also soon sign the Tripartite Pact with Italy and Japan. Since the United States still had an isolationist stance at the time, Britain and its empire pretty much stood alone. Due to the massive scale of the German military and the territory now under its control, there was no way Britain could conduct a large military invasion and carry out a conventional war. Thus, unconventional warfare became the only alternative. Winston Churchill held secret meetings in July 1940 at 2 Caxton Street, in Westminster, with Hugh Dalton, his Minister for Economic Warfare, to discuss the possibility of creating an organization to carry out sabotage and subversive operations, and to organize resistance groups in enemy-held Europe.

Thus, Britain took the combined operations of its Royal Navy, Royal Air Force and the Secret Intelligence Service and created the Special Operations Executive (SOE). This became official when the War Cabinet approved this new operation on July 22, 1940. The Minister of Economic Warfare was responsible for the SOE and, over the next five years, deployed great numbers of agents throughout Occupied Europe (and, later, the Far East). In addition to the SOE, the Government Code and Cypher School (GC&CS), as well as the Security Service, also aided Resistance fighters. The GC&CS, for example, after obtaining German cypher equipment and codes smuggled out of Norway, were able to decipher *Abwehr* (German Intelligence) transmissions and this enabled the Security Service to arrest a good number of Norwegians the *Abwehr* had sent into England as spies.

The nationals of the oppressed countries would carry out resistance operations and this new organization, the SOE, coordinated and assisted with these efforts. Absolute secrecy was paramount as was a willingness to work with people of different nationalities who were politically reliable. Brigadier Colin Gubbins came on board as director of operations. Resistance activity was to use all means possible, including deception, bribery, blackmail, black propaganda, forgery, burglary, sabotage, guerrilla warfare, murders and assassinations. It was also responsible for running escape and evasion lines which were of particular use for shot-down Allied airmen trying to avoid capture.

Sometimes, agents were delivered by sea, using both submarines and surface vessels. Westland Lysander and Lockheed Hudson aircraft, flying at night, delivered agents to, and picked them up from, pre-arranged locations in Occupied France. This was one of the more common practices. A variety of RAF bombers were also used to parachute agents into Europe. The RAF also delivered arms, ammunition and other supplies by parachute to pre-determined drop zones. Much of the specialized equipment required for undercover warfare was designed and manufactured at Aston House in Stevenage. This was only known as Station XII. Churchill's famous instructions to Hugh Dalton were, "Now set Europe ablaze!"

CHAPTER 5

The Norwegian Temperament

The official government of Norway is a constitutional monarchy and has been since 1805. The last war it had known was in 1814 when, as part of Denmark, it had participated in the Napoleonic Wars. In 1814, the Treaty of Kiel made Norway and Sweden a single union, but by 1905 Norway successfully achieved its independence. Norway, Sweden and Denmark all managed to stay out of World War I by adopting a policy of strict neutrality. When World War II broke out, Norway thought this policy would again keep it out of war, but Germany and Great Britain had other ideas. Both were interested in the military occupation of Norway's harbors and airfields and each desired to deny the other use of Norway as a pipeline for Swedish exports.

Eleanor Kittredge, a columnist for *The New York Times*, wrote a book review in 1941 regarding Dr. Halvan Kohlt's *Norway, Neutral and Invaded.* Kohlt was the former foreign minister of Norway. In her article, Kittredge discusses Kohlt's explanation of why Norway was reluctant to get involved in the war. Kohlt wrote that Norway had not considered that its membership in the League of Nations might eventually involve it in foreign wars. After all, this was a country that believed in neutrality and that "butter rather than guns" was money better spent to raise civilian standards of living. Together, with other Scandinavian nations, the country had helped from the start to make military obligations of the League as non-committal as possible. In the royal address opening of the Storting (the Supreme Legislature of Norway, i.e., their parliament) on January 12, 1938, it was stated that it ought to be the principal task to keep Norway out of all warlike entanglements. Furthermore, Norway would maintain perfect neutrality in all wars it did not regard as actions on the part of the League of Nations. A proclamation virtually supporting the same principle was issued by a meeting, in Copenhagen on July 27, 1938, of the foreign ministers of the "Oslo Powers"—Finland, Sweden, Denmark, and Norway, and Belgium, Netherlands and Luxembourg (the three lower countries).

To counter this, on Friday evening of April 5, 1940, Dr. Kurt Bräuer, the German minister in Oslo, invited a body of distinguished guests, including members of the government, to see a German film. This chilling bit of ritual hospitality had been ceremoniously repeated in various capitals on the eve of invasions. With full diplomatic courtesy and protocol, the prospective victims were invited to watch a flickering horror of the conquest of Poland and the bombing of Warsaw. Thus, responsible officials, still maintaining "correct personal relations" with other diplomats, were expected to sit in civilized delegation rooms wearing white ties and watch the spectacle of what would befall their country and their children if they were to resist. While this film showing happened on a Friday evening, by three o'clock in the morning of the following Tuesday, Dr. Bräuer was no longer a host of his delegation, but a man delivering an ultimatum to the Norwegian Government.

The stage was now being set for the invasion of Norway by Germany. The Nazi invaders came like thieves in the night. The Norwegian people were never to forget the dastardly sneak attack and subsequent invasion.

On April 8, 1940, the Oslo forts came under fire and the Norwegians sounded an air raid alarm. Lieutenant Colonel R. Rosher Nielsen, Chief of the Operations Section, was awakened by the Army's chief of staff and told the Germans had attacked fortresses at the mouth of Oslo Fjord. Oslo began a blackout in anticipation of air raids.

On April 9, 1940, the cabinet learned the Germans had seized Narvik, Trondheim, Bergen, Stavanger and Kristiansand, including all the important airfields. At 9:30 am, on April 9, 1940, a special train left for Hamar with King Haakon VII, his family, and members of the government and the Storting on board.

At the same time, 20 trucks transported the gold of the Bank of Norway and the secret papers of the Foreign Office to Hamar. Bräuer delivered the ultimatum demanding immediate surrender to the Norwegian Government in Hamar. The Norwegians rejected it, even though Bräuer's message suggested the Germans came as friends.

The Germans knew if they could capture the King, they could force his government to persuade the populace to fall in line. Thus, on April 9, German naval and air forces raced towards Oslo. The naval force was opposed by the Oscarsborg Fortress. The fortress fired at the invaders, damaging the pocket battleship *Lützow* and sinking the heavy cruiser *Blücher*, with heavy German losses that included many of the military, *Gestapo* and administrative personnel who were to have occupied the Norwegian capital. This led to the withdrawal of the rest of the German flotilla, preventing the invaders from occupying Oslo at dawn as had been planned. The German delay in occupying Oslo, along with swift action by the President of the Storting, C. J. Hambro, created the opportunity for the Norwegian Royal Family, the cabinet and most of the members of the Storting to make their hasty escape by train. A handful of Norwegian army and navy personnel kept the German fleet out of Oslo for most of the day and made the King's escape to England possible.

The next day, Dr. Kurt Bräuer demanded a meeting with King Haakon to accept Hitler's demands to end all resistance and appoint Vidkun Quisling, the leader of Norway's fascist party, the Nasjonal Samling, as prime minister, thus creating a German puppet government. Bräuer suggested that Haakon follow the example of the Danish Government, and his brother Christian X, which had surrendered almost immediately after the previous day's invasion, and threatened Norway with harsh reprisals if it did not surrender. In order to buy time, King Haakon told Bräuer he could not make the decision himself, but only on the advice of the Government. In reality, the King would have been well within his rights to make such a decision on his own authority since declaring war and peace was a part of the royal prerogative. Even at this critical hour, however, he refused to abandon the convention that he must act only on Government advice.

In an emotional meeting in Nybergsund, the King reported the German ultimatum to his cabinet. He knew he could use his moral authority to influence their decision. Therefore, he told the Cabinet:

> I am deeply affected by the responsibility laid on me if the German demand is rejected. The responsibility for the calamities that will befall our people and country is indeed so grave that I dread to take it. It rests with the government to decide, but my position is clear.

King Haakon VII and his son Prince Olav V fleeing the German attack on April 9, 1940.

> For my part, I cannot accept the German demands. It would conflict with all I have considered to be my duty as King of Norway since I came to this country nearly thirty-five years ago.

He went on to say that he could not appoint Quisling as prime minister because he knew neither the people nor the Storting had confidence in him. Nils Hjelmtveit, Minister of Church and Education, later wrote:

> This made a great impression on us all. More clearly than ever before, we could see the man behind the words; the king who had drawn a line for himself and his task, a line from which he could not deviate. We had through the five years (in government) learned to respect and appreciate our king, and now, through his words, he came to us as a great man, just and forceful; a leader in these fatal times to our country.

Inspired by Haakon's stand, the Government unanimously advised him not to appoint any government headed by Quisling. Within hours, it telephoned its refusal to Bräuer. That night, NRK (the Norwegian Broadcasting Corporation) broadcast the Government's rejection of Germany's demands to the Norwegian people. In that same broadcast, the Government announced it would resist the invasion as long as possible and expressed its confidence that Norwegians would lend their support to the cause.

The following morning, April 11, 1940, in an attempt to wipe out Norway's unyielding king and government, *Luftwaffe* bombers attacked Nybergsund, destroying the small town where the Government was staying. The King and his

ministers took refuge in the snow-covered woods and escaped harm, continuing farther north through the mountains towards Molde on Norway's west coast. As the British forces in the area lost ground under *Luftwaffe* bombardment, the King and his party were taken aboard the British cruiser HMS *Glasgow* at Molde and moved 620 miles further north to Tromsø, where a provisional capital was established on May 1. King Haakon and Crown Prince Olav took up residence in a forest cabin in the Målselvdalen valley in inner Troms County, where they stayed until evacuated to the United Kingdom. While at Tromsø, the two were protected by the local rifle association members armed with ubiquitous Krag–Jørgensen rifles. Finally, on June 7, 1940, King Haakon and most of his government left Tromsø for Britain on HMS *Devonshire*.

The Norwegian party arrived in Britain as the Battle of Britain got into full swing. The Government, now in exile, determined to train its existing pilots,

The King's monogram was a symbol of resistance throughout the war.

and new recruits, in North America, eventually settling on an airfield on Toronto Island in Canada (a base that soon became known as "Little Norway"). Some of these flyers eventually formed Norwegian squadrons within the RAF.

As for myself, Lt. Colonel Bolland, I had the pleasure of seeing Lieutenant Colonel Ole Reistad, Little Norway's commander, at Carnegie Hall where Crown Princess Martha also graced our affair, raising funds for the base. How strange to find out Lieutenant Commander G. Unger Vetlesen of the United States Naval Reserve (USNR) organized the entire affair. Little did I know that fate would throw us together later in England. "*Jore Din Plight, Krave Din Rett, Freihet, Leighet, Broderskapp.*" Those were the words emblazoned on a framed poster in my grandfather's living room. The translation is "Do your duty, and demand your rights, freedom, enlightenment, brotherhood." That probably would be the closest motto to crystallize the Norwegian way of thinking and living.

Norwegians are a proud people and quite self-sufficient, especially throughout their lives in the rugged mountains of their country; an environment very inhospitable to a livelihood and a real challenge to living a life of decency and independence in a troubled world. The Norwegians had depended upon their merchant fleet for years, plying the routes of commerce with their ships and hauling the world's cargo from one part of the world to another. Now they found themselves embroiled in a war, one they tried desperately to avoid. Neutrality was impossible with all the powerful forces around them demanding their attention and help. Norwegians found themselves on an extreme flank of the European front, not by their choosing but merely by their geographical location. The German High Command had evidently thought it advisable to secure the right flank all the way to the Arctic Ocean. That entailed the conquest and domination of Norway.

Now, to be honest, the Norwegians were by nature quite sympathetic to the German people. Way back in time, Norwegian roots were probably Germanic with the language probably of a Germanic origin. The words in the language are quite similar. For example, "*autobahn*" is the German word for highway. In Norway, we have "*jernbane*," which is the word for railroad. Even my name, Gerhard, is quite German if you put a "t" on the end of it.

On March 12, 1940, a ceasefire was forced on Finland after their incredibly heroic resistance to Soviet aggression in the Winter War. Their white-clad soldiers on skis stopped the invading armored columns deep in the pine forests, but they were too few to hold out. Volunteers did come from other Nordic lands. Colonel Bernt Balchen, a crack pilot, was actually involved in flying these volunteers in to help with the resistance. "Sublime Finland," to quote Winston Churchill, could not stand up to its giant neighbor.

It must be noted that Denmark was also attacked the same day as Norway. It is remembered as one of the most painful of dates in Danish history. Their pacifist, defeatist government naively banked on Adolf Hitler's usual non-aggression pledges.

It was forewarned of the attack but refused to order mobilization or join forces with the other intended victim, Norway. Thus, Hitler captured Denmark and was free to use Danish ports and air bases as springboards to the north. King Christian X, the older brother of King Haakon of Norway, remained in his occupied capital of Copenhagen for the duration. The Danes' instant capitulation ruled out any chance of halting or even delaying the German advance northward in the face of determined Norwegian resistance. Nor did it give the British and French forces, especially the Royal Navy, time to intercede while Norway might still have been saved. The winds of war were blowing hard.

The Norwegians approached April 9 with a much purer conscience. The vast majority agreed with their King that it was their self-evident duty to join the battle.

As a prelude to the invasion, Hitler even sent an advanced party of spies. These were the former hungry, helpless German orphans from World War I whom the Norwegian people had taken into their homes, raised, fed, clothed, nurtured, and sent back to the Fatherland as healthy, wholesome, well-adjusted citizens, only to have them return years later loyal to the Third Reich. How despicable was that?

German High Command struck in 80 different places simultaneously. General Nikolaus von Falkenhorst was commander of all German forces in Norway. The might of the Third Reich was supposed to subjugate Norway by noon of the invasion day. This was a most optimistic view and did not meet with the concurrence of the Norwegian people. As a matter of fact, Norway, instead of being a successful invasion, turned out to be flypaper for the Germans, and very, very sticky flypaper at that!

Probably the biggest impact upon the Norwegian population was the forced exile of their King to England. Their beloved King and Royal Family were lost to them for five long, hard years. At one point, the people even purchased a yacht for him through voluntary contributions.

Reidar Claffy, an American news reporter of mixed Norwegian and Irish descent educated partly in Norway and the United States, was in Oslo at the time and gave an account of the invasion:

> News was received that an hour earlier the Royal Family and the entire membership of Parliament had left Oslo. The city was given over to Police Commissioner Welhaven with instructions to surrender Oslo to the Germans, if demanded. This would spare the population from the horrors of bombardment. Gas masks, helmets and other equipment were dispersed. Not long afterward the terrible blasts from air raid sirens were heard throughout the city. Less than ten minutes later the first German bombers appeared in the blue sky. They came in groups of threes and fives, flying at different altitudes. Some so low that the taller buildings were nearly scraped. Simultaneously, a few British and Norwegian fighting planes came into sight and engaged the enemy bombers while the ground defense let loose with everything they had, machine gun and anti-aircraft batteries. These batteries forced the German bombers into higher altitudes, thus causing the enemy to drop bombs without much effect. Three German bombers were shot down in this first encounter; one inside the city, one in the harbor and one went down in flames on the outskirts. This first wave was driven off but returned a few minutes later, spraying the city with machine gun bullets. Traffic stopped and people sought shelter in improvised locations as

bullets spattered in the streets. Some stood defiant, cursing and damning the brutal Germans. An ambulance and open truck came rushing by loaded with bleeding and wounded people. More cursing and damning of the Germans overhead as other streets and open squares were plastered with German bullets killing scores of innocent people. In the face of all this people kept trying to reach their jobs and places of work by jumping and dodging from doorway to doorway. Some brave souls kept walking as if nothing had happened. The courage and stamina of these citizens was amazing to watch.

The bombing attacks kept on until about 10am, when an ultimatum to surrender was given. Thanks to the stubborn defense of the ground forces, the enemy never managed to come low enough to score direct hits. Most of the bombs were duds anyway and invariably fell well off their marks. However, after it was confirmed that airports, coastal cities, and fortresses had been overpowered and were in the hands of the Germans, it was decided by the civil authorities to hand over the city. This was the only thing to do, since further resistance would have been futile and a needless sacrifice of lives and property.

The attacks finally ceased and the nerve-racking bedlam died down. It was noon hour and people poured out into the streets, taking stock of what had happened. Some appeared with luggage, preparing to evacuate. There was calm everywhere, no sign at all of panic or hysteria.

Eventually the first truckload of a dozen German soldiers appeared. Their guns were not dangling carelessly, as reported by other correspondents. They sat in the truck, probably more scared than the amazed people in the streets, but ready for action. Later in the afternoon several companies of German infantry came marching into Oslo. The residents of Oslo did not, as reported by the world press, watch the entrance of soldiers in a state of stupor and bewilderment. On the contrary, they were very much alive and kicking. It is likewise untrue that, as reported, tens of thousands of Oslo people stood lined up to stare at the invaders and that most of them were able-bodied young men. There was plenty of room on Karl Johan Street and no one needed to battle his way through the crowds. There did happen to be more people than usual in the street because the subway tunnel nearby had provided shelter during the air raid. The Oslo people received the Germans with utter contempt written of their faces.

After the official surrender, the broadcasting station still under Norwegian control, repeatedly urged people to remain calm. The Oslo radio announcer stayed at his post up to the last minute. When the clanking of German boots was heard on the front stairway, he ran down the back stairs, entered a waiting automobile and drove out of the city, thus severing Oslo's last tie with the old administration.

The civil authorities left behind to care for Oslo were trying to keep the populace in check so that no unhappy incidents would occur to incite a wholesale massacre, which the Germans had threatened as reprisal should the citizens rebel. However a subtle reign of terror had begun. German troops bivouacked in the Parliament building and the National Theatre. For lack of bedding they filled the places with hay. Norwegian bus and truck drivers were pressed into service at the point of a gun. The Germans requisitioned right and left, indiscriminately. The day after the occupation all oranges and most other fruit disappeared from the market. During the following weeks the Germans put their hands on everything from medical supplies to gasoline. As more troops arrived, the shortages became more acute. Milk, bread and other vital foods were now rationed on cards. It was forbidden to leave the city and proclamations were glued up all over the city offering high monetary rewards to all informers.

Having little in the way of ammunition and weaponry, the Norwegian soldiers fought valiantly. On at least two separate occasions, they were able to delay the Germans while protecting their King and Crown Prince's escape route. They were also able to delay the German forces at Bodø and, with the help of British forces, they regained the port city of Narvik. This was extremely important as this port was used to ship much needed Swedish iron ore to Germany. The iron ore came from the Swedish port city of Luleå, which lies in the Gulf of Bothnia and is impassable in the winter due to ice. As a consequence, a railroad was built between Luleå and Narvik. Unfortunately, with the invasion of France and Belgium by Germany, British forces were withdrawn completely from Norway and Narvik was soon back in German hands.

King Haakon and Prince Olav moved northward and left Norwegian soil on June 7, 1940. Crown Princess Märtha, who also worked tirelessly for Norway, lived with her children—Princess Ragnhild, Princess Astrid and Prince Harald—in the U.S. after they had to leave Norway. Crown Prince Olav visited them every year during the war. President Roosevelt became a personal friend and was very supportive of Norway's war efforts. He gave his famous "Look to Norway" speech in 1942. These are the opening lines:

> If there is anyone who still wonders why this war is being fought, let him look to Norway. If there is anyone who has any delusions that this war could have been averted, let him look to Norway. And if there is anyone who doubts the democratic will to win, again I say, let him look to Norway. He will find in Norway, at once conquered and unconquerable, the answer to his questioning.

General Otto Ruge was appointed commander-in-chief on April 11. It fell to his lot to re-establish order out of the initial chaos. He led the desperate fighting of the small Norwegian forces during the three weeks while they were retreating northward through the central valleys of Norway. When the invasion took place, the sea defenses, ships and coastal batteries were mobilized. Unfortunately, the mines had not been laid. In the case of land defenses, the situation was quite different. Apart from a few battalions that functioned as a neutrality guard, the army as a whole had not been mobilized. Even when the order came to mobilize, it did not reach all divisions. The only indication regarding mobilization which reached the country was a remark in a radio speech by the foreign minister to the effect that mobilization had begun. This, however, was denied afterwards by Oslo radio, which had been quickly seized by the Germans.

While this went on, the Germans had taken over all the arsenals in southern Norway and many of the mobilization centers with their supplies. They had occupied broadcasting stations and broken off all important telegraph and telephone connections. Norway had only six army divisions. One of those was in the north. The commanders of the five southern divisions, as well as a number of regimental staff, had been removed from their quarters and their mobilization files were in the hands of the Germans, making a systematic mobilization impossible. Only in Romsdal and Voss could a fairly normal activation be carried out. Otherwise, everything had to be improvised. Groups or individuals who were not already under German control started to get together, fighting as they went.

Among the heroic efforts of these early stages, special mention ought to be made of the battle to the death of the aviators at Fornebu airfield, Oslo. Another heroic act of special note took place at Midtskogen, near Elverum, where military laborers were given guns. Some of them had never held a gun before and were rather surprised to find themselves soldiers. This hastily assembled group of guard recruits, laborers and volunteers stopped a German motorized force, but they paid the ultimate sacrifice. Other acts of heroism took place throughout Norway. The railway station at Dombaas was bombed regularly and laid waste. Workmen, in great danger to their lives, would work, night after night, repairing broken telegraph connections sufficiently to be used. The so-called Sørkedal Ski Company consisted of men who had escaped from Oslo and met in the ski hills of Nordmarka outside the city where they evolved into a well-established fighting unit. Norwegian flyers, in their old Moths and Fokkers, continued to fly communications flights, darting in and out among the fast German planes at great risk. Hegra, an old, abandoned fort, held out for a month manned by casually assembled people who simply would not give up.

It was a hard three weeks for the small Norwegian forces who fought without respite, day after day, night after night, without reserves, always on the front line against heavy artillery, tanks and an overwhelming number of German bombers.

Never let it be said the Germans did not try to win over the population. After all, they had strict orders to try to do so, and the Germans held a rigid code of discipline that was inviolate and, I might add, inflexible. There began a drain on Norwegian lives to feed the Nazi war machine. Attempts to "nazify" Norwegian organizations, such as the sports federation, the federation of labor and business, and professional associations, were met by wholesale resignation from these organizations. Pressure on the clergy and teachers to try to make them minister and teach more in accordance with the "new order" under which Norway was expected to live only stiffened resistance. The Germans were soon made to realize the majority of the population did not see them as "friends and protectors." Quisling met solid opposition from an overwhelming majority of the fourteen thousand teachers. At his request, the Germans put approximately 1,300 of them in concentration camps in Norway where they were badly mistreated. Later, hundreds of them were sent north to do hard labor under absolutely gruesome conditions. The teachers' solidarity was such that Quisling and the Germans gave up on the plan to nazify Norwegian school children and young people.

In addition to the solidarity of the teachers, there was another factor involved that created a dilemma for the Germans. According to the racial myth of Nazi ideology, Norwegians were exemplars of the Aryan super race of people destined to be rulers. It would not enhance that racial ideology to have all the schools of supposedly Aryan Norwegian pupils and teachers closed permanently by the occupying Aryan Germans, who claimed to have come to Norway as friends.

A climax of Norwegian open and strong opposition came when the bishops and all Supreme Court justices resigned their positions, along with almost all of the leaders of 43 major organizations including professional groups, labor unions and sporting organizations.

Quisling desperately tried to get them to fall under Nazi rule, especially with regards to the Church. He passed new laws stating the Church had to teach certain Nazi principles during weekly services. In the process, the Nazis would also take over the control of religious broadcast programs. He demanded an alteration be made in the Common Prayer of the service book. The paragraph in the prayer referring to the King, Parliament, and Government was to be taken out and a prayer for the new Nazi authorities was to be inserted. What Quisling did not anticipate was that bishops and priests would refuse to comply. Although they were threatened by the new Quisling government and their pay was stopped, the bishops and priests held fast. Members of the congregation did what they could to keep the bishops fed, housed and clothed. Quisling had several church leaders arrested but to no avail. Of the 699 clergymen in the Church of Norway, 645 resigned. One hundred and fifty-one of the 155 ordained priests followed suit. In the end, the bishops and priests continued their services with overcrowded audiences outside the church walls and refused to preach the Nazi ways. Another prime example of Quisling's failed attempt to rein in the populace and having his ineptness show through instead. When the Nasjonal Samling, supported by Josef Terboven, the Reichskommissar for Norway, attempted to take control of the Church of Norway, the bishops directed the following "Order of the Church" on December 15, 1941. This classic confession and testimony, along with the King's historic "No," were the most lethal blows to Nazi tyranny during the entire occupation. On April 5, 1942, in churches all over the country, a declaration was read making the stand of the Church clear to the nation:

> The Church is an organization whose great calling is to spread the Gospel and unite all believers in a way of life in accordance with the will of God. Outwardly the Church is a worldly organization, heavy with human shortcomings and sufferings, from the fact that we, who are the instruments of the Church, are sinful men. Even so, or Lord has called such men to be His servants from the very days of the Apostles and has promised them the mercy and the power by which He himself leads His children.
>
> The Christian congregation has its roots in a living spiritual communion, founded by Jesus Christ who is their Lord and Savior. The Church, therefore, belongs to God, and shall fulfill its mission freely and fearlessly because God's Word and God's Will are above all else in the world.
>
> The mission of the Church is identified with the very life of the people and is charged with complete responsibility for spreading His Word about salvation, based on the Law of God.
>
> The Bishops of the Church of Norway, guided by their conscience and spurred by the lack of clarity which surrounds them, see it as their clear duty to appeal to the authorities which today govern the life of the Church and State.

Having received no satisfactory answer from either Quisling or Skancke (the Minister for Church and Educational Affairs), the bishops, on January 15, 1942, addressed a subsequent communication to the Department of Church and Education:

All Christians acknowledge Jesus Christ as their Sovereign and Lord. The importance of this solemn declaration exceeds everything else within our Church. The governmental, political and administrative functions do not concern us per se. We are involved only when such functions touch our allegiance to Christ. Luther said, "The secular regime has laws which do not extend beyond life and property and all concrete things in the world. God will not grant to anyone but Himself the right to govern souls".

The Acts of God comprise justice, truth and compassion, as conceived by the Church within the structure of the State. The framework of the national community is no concern of the Church. But when it comes to divine commandments, which are fundamental to all community life, then the Church is duty-bound to take a stand. It is useless to wave the Church aside by stating that it is meddling in politics. Luther said in plain words, "The church does not become involved in worldly matters when it beseeches the authorities to be obedient to the highest authority, which is God".

When authorities permit such acts of violence and injustice and exert pressure on our souls, then the Church becomes the defender of the people's conscience. One single human soul is worth more than the entire world. The Bishops of the Church have therefore placed on the table of the acting head certain facts and official commiuniques concerning governmental administration which, during the last few months, in view of the Church, are against the law of God. They give the impression that revolutionary conditions are abroad in our land and that we are not living under the rules of foreign occupation, whereby all laws shall be enforced as far as compatible with the occupation forces. The Church is not the State, and the State is not the Church. In worldly matters the State may endeavor to use force against the Church, but the Church is a spiritual and sovereign entity, built on the Word of God and a unity of belief.

Despite all its human shortcomings the Church has been given a divine authority to spread His Law and Gospel among all the peoples. The Church, therefore can never be silenced. Whenever God's commandments are deposed by sin the Church stands unshaken and cannot be directed by any authority of the State. From this Rock of Faith we beseech the authorities to strike out all that is against God's Holy Writ concerning justice, truth and freedom of conscience, and to build only on the foundation of the divine laws of life … In an internal struggle all individuals and groups must be guided by moral law. He who promotes hatred of encourages evil will be judged by God … Above all of us stands the One who is Lord of our souls. In our congregation we now perceive a ferment of conscience and we feel it our duty to let the authorities hear clear and loud, the voice of the Church.

Also among those who resigned in protest was the Chief Supreme Court Justice, Paal Berg. He later became a leader in the Underground movement. Quisling and the Germans retaliated harshly to these protests in a number of ways.

One of America's most distinguished war correspondents, Otto Tolischus of *The New York Times*, who won the Pulitzer Prize in 1940, was in Stockholm at the time and reported on the diabolical strategy of the Nazis. They cleverly used the qualities for which Norwegians are most admired—their peacefulness, their democracy, and their high civilization—against them. In the words of another *New York Times* correspondent, Harold Callender, "The outstanding mistake of Scandinavia was that it imagined it lived in a world as civilized as itself."

Sönner av Norge (Sons of Norway), a prominent group of Norwegian–Americans, immediately declared there was no legitimate reason for Hitler's invasion of their homeland. In an open letter to the Sons of Norway, the German–American Society made attempts to declare its allegiance to Norway and its people. It sent a letter stating that in no way did it approve of Adolf Hitler's Nazi Germany or of its action in Norway. The German–American Society wanted to maintain its close ties to the Sons of Norway and continue to be good friends. They declared, "We are all Americans." A Norwegian Relief Fund began. However, no monies or supplies would go to Vidkun Quisling, the Norwegian traitor and head of the puppet government. The Sons of Norway would sponsor a visit to America by Dr. Halvdan Koht, Foreign Minister of the Norwegian Government-in-exile in London. His message was that Norway was fully committed to fight on.

The British had evacuated Dunkirk. "Festung Europa" was in the making.

In the same year, and a month after the invasion of Norway, Professor Einar Haugen delivered an address in Madison, Wisconsin, on Norway's Independence Day, May 17. It described the shock and impact on Norwegian nationals abroad:

> We Americans of Norwegian stock have never gathered to celebrate the 17th of May under such tragic circumstances as in this year of 1940. For over a month our hearts have bled at seeing our ancestral land turned into a flaming battlefield by the great powers of Europe through no fault of her own. We have sat glued to the radio, we have scanned the newspapers, hoping against hope that some effective resistance might be offered to the invaders. We have felt the sharp and cruel pangs of blasted hopes, of the crash of high ideals, and the severance of our dearest ties. Many a quiet tear has been dropped. We have not been moved to hold mass demonstrations; we have not voiced our indignation in loud and inflammatory words. But I cannot recall that I have seen so many sorrowful and distressed faces as I have this last month.
>
> Why, may I ask, has Norway deserved to be "restored"? What have these three million people done to show that they are able to bear the burdens of a free nation? They live amid lakes and glaciers and mountains that are among the most picturesque in the world. But less than three percent of their soil is cultivated. Yet, in the course of the past centuries Norway had built up a civilization equal to that of other west Europeans countries and in some respects, superior. She had done this by hard work and careful management. By utilizing all the openings left by the great powers, Norway had been able to sustain a population three-and-a-half times as big as the one she had in 1800.

The German occupation had disturbed the balance on which all human life in Norway was based. Yet, this was not the first time Norway had lost its sovereignty. It was wiped out from the number of nations for four centuries and still survived. It passed through nearly ten years of hunger and suffering during the Napoleonic Wars and came out of it a free nation for the first time on modern history. Norway had always had to fight for its existence and its people had had always been ready to dig in and work for the future. In 1940, the new enemy was the Third Reich.

Of course, Norway and all the Scandinavian countries, with their limited military resources, were no match for the powerful German war machine. Close ties to other countries and dependence upon their Allied forces was the focus of an address given by Henrik de Kauffmann, Minister of Denmark to the United States, at the seventh annual Scandinavian–American Day in Des Moines, Iowa, on July 28, 1940. He spoke on behalf of other Scandinavian representatives, namely Wolmar Boström, Minister of Sweden, Wilhelm Morgenstierne, Minister of Norway, Hjalmar Procopé, Minister of Finland, and Vilhjalmur Thor, Consul General for Iceland, in New York:

In the World War [World War I], a quarter of a century ago, the Scandinavian countries were fortunate in preserving their neutrality. This time Scandinavia, in spite of our most sincere efforts, has not been so lucky. Today all the five northern countries suffer from the present world catastrophe. The outlook for our future is grave and ominous.

Many of you were born on the other side and many of you have been over to visit the old countries. All of you have a sort of soft spot in your hearts for the old homeland. I know that many thoughts wander over there, now probably more than ever, when our Scandinavian countries are facing great hardships and when their whole future is filled with uncertainties. In moments like the present it is hard to be far away from those we love.

I know these thoughts travel not only eastward, but also westward. I know how many thoughts in Scandinavia today go out to this country, and I know that now again, as in days gone by, millions of Scandinavians and other Europeans look upon the United States as the land of promise, the land of hope.

One European country after another has had to bow to the ruthless force of the Nazi regime during these last months. The liberty that was hard won in Europe by previous generations, a liberty perhaps not sufficiently appreciated, has been thrust aside and darkness has descended over Europe.

But the love of freedom is still burning in the minds and hearts of millions of Europeans. Liberty-loving people the world over, turn their hopes to this country, now one of the last champions for the defense of all the ideals they cherish.

The threat of war clouds that have been gathering in Europe these last three years threw their shadows over the whole of Scandinavia. The common danger brought our peoples even closer. Never has Scandinavian cooperation been better than during these last years. But in spite of that, not close enough.

We never attained a defensive alliance, and I, for one, am sorry that we did not. I think it would have strengthened us. In fact, it might have changed our fate. We did not have the courage and moral strength to take the decisive steps. We hoped, sometimes almost against hope, that peace in Europe would be preserved, and that in case of war, each of our countries would find its traditional neutrality a sufficient safeguard. We thought it was enough to be neutral.

And now the catastrophe has come. Finland, our youngest sister, was first attacked and after one of the most heroic fights the world has known, had to accept a peace which imposed terrible sanctions on her. Denmark was invaded on April 9th, and Norway was attacked on the same day. The Danish Government yielded to the German ultimatum and today Denmark is under German military occupation. Since Copenhagen, situated only one hundred miles from Germany, would have been entirely at the mercy of German bombers, and since Denmark is without any natural means of defense, there was little freedom of choice for our country.

We have followed closely the events in Norway this Spring. Knowing Norway from Kristiansand to the North Cape, most of the places we have been reading about have a familiar sound to me and recall some of the happiest moments of my life. It has been heart-breaking to hear about the destruction and suffering going on in Norway and to see that even the courage of the Norwegians could not prevent the whole of that vast and beautiful country from being occupied, even though their sacrifices did prevent the courageous King Haakon and his Government from becoming German hostages. For all of Scandinavia the future is shrouded in uncertainty and darkness.

CHAPTER 6

Norwegian–American Roots of the Bolland Family

As the saying goes, blood is thicker than water. This is especially true when it comes to my love for the beloved homeland of my ancestors. Even though my own upbringing was across the ocean in the United States, my Norwegian roots and heritage run deep.

I grew up in the small, mid-western farming town of Madison, Minnesota, located about 15 miles east of the South Dakota border. Pretty much an agrarian community, the folks there lived off the land. Their existence depending primarily on what they could grow and raise.

On my father's side, my grandfather, Gulbrand Anders Bolland, was born in Norway in Guldalen, near Trondheim, on March 20, 1837. When he was 30 years old, on May 13, 1867, he sailed from Norway to Liverpool, England, and then on to Quebec, Canada, on the steamship *Victor*. He was accompanied by his wife, Marit Johnsdatter Bolland, who was 38 years old at the time. She was from Flå, which is on the Gaula River, about 35 kilometers south of Trondheim. After she passed away, Gulbrand married Lisbet Henningsgaard and they had two children, Ben Olai (my father) and Sophia Ingeborg. Both were born in Winneshick County in Iowa. Ben was born on October 3, 1871, and was baptized and confirmed by the pioneer pastor, Reverend H. A. Stub, in Hesper, Iowa. Sophia was born on September 20, 1876. In the early 1890s, Gulbrand moved his family to Mabel, Minnesota, where he was engaged in the furniture business. He also had a funeral parlor in connection with the furniture store. In the fall of 1899, he sold the furniture store and bought a farm in Mehurin Township. Marietta is also located in that township in Lac qui Parle County, Minnesota. Gulbrand passed away on June 29, 1926.

On my mother's side, my grandfather, Knute Sandmoen, was born in Våler i Solør, Norway, on December 15, 1842. Later on, his family moved to Hamar. He came to America in 1880 and lived for two years near Northfield, Minnesota, before coming to Lac qui Parle County and settling on a farm in Garfield, which became the main family farm. My grandmother, Johnina Olsen, was also born in

Våler i Solør on December 4, 1846, and was one of six sisters. Knute and Johnina were married on January 14, 1873, and had five children—two sons, Martin and Arne, and three daughters. One of the daughters died in infancy. The two others were Mrs. Ole Sjolie, who passed away in 1897, and my mother, Ida, who passed away on November 27, 1974.

I was actually born in the farmhouse my parents owned on July 11, 1909. Today, it is a wildlife conservation preserve owned by the State of Minnesota. The original farmland contains a slough, which still exists today and is a valuable environmental asset for thriving waterfowl.

Some of my most vivid memories go back to my youth on the old family farmstead in Minnesota. In this small town, on the eastern edge of the Great Plains, nothing stops the cold Arctic winds on their way south in winter. Ironically, running trap lines on my grandfather's farm during the weekends and Christmas holidays was real practical experience for what the future had in store for me with the harsh Norwegian climate.

Another of my fondest recollections was a story my grandfather Knute told me. This was a feat on skis during the early pioneer days of western Minnesota. His family was running low on provisions. It was necessary to venture forth to obtain

Gerhard Leroy Bolland and his mother Ida Catherine (Sandmoen) Bolland Madison, Minnesota, February 1910.

Gerhard Bolland, Ness Lutheran Church Confirmation photo, 1923.

food. Of course, there was a blinding snowstorm at the time and the railhead in Watson, Minnesota, was almost 40 miles away. So off he went, on skis he had made himself, across unmarked wilderness to Watson. He purchased the necessities, including a sack of flour, sugar and coffee (yes, coffee by all means), for his Norwegian family. After a brief respite, he set out to return home. "Home" in those days was really no more than a dugout on the extreme western part of the homestead acres. Nothing but lonely prairie grass and Sioux Indians were to the west of his plot. Fatigue and the blinding snow forced him to plant the flour sack on a hill. He made a mental note of the location and surmised it was a few miles directly south of his dugout, which proved to be correct. With the remaining provisions, he returned to his humble abode where he rested for the night. The next morning, with the storm having abated, there was the flour sack sitting atop the hill waiting for him. Not bad when you take into account he had a stiff knee he had broken in a lumber camp accident on his father's forestland in Norway. This was something to measure up to. Later on, when I found myself engaged in the later phases of the Norway operation, I used his name on my false passport for these clandestine operations. It only seemed fitting that I should pay respect to my rugged pioneer ancestor in this manner. I became Gerhard Leroy Sandmoen from Hamar, Norway. He was Knute Sandmoen from Hamar.

My father, Ben, was well known in the Madison area. He attended the Valder School of Business in Decorah, Iowa, after which he was associated with his father's furniture business in Mabel, Minnesota. After the family moved to the farm on the outskirts of town, he was united in marriage to my mother, Ida Catherine Sandmoen. He owned and operated the local Ford garage store for 15 years. On occasion, my

Pencil sketch portrait by Ben Bolland of Gerhard Bolland as a child. (Author's collection)

Gerhard Bolland with his parents Ida and Ben, 1934.

father later admitted to me that, whenever business seemed a little slow, he would venture out of town a few miles and scatter a few nails on the road. After all, flat tires were a "regular" occurrence back in those days. Of course, he always kept a lot of tire repair supplies on hand for just such emergencies.

He was also known throughout the state as an artist, especially as an oil painter of large church altar paintings. Some of his paintings were exhibited at the Walker Art Gallery in Minneapolis, Minnesota, and at the Minnesota State Fair. The local city council in Madison gave him a room on the north side of City Hall to use as an art studio. He preferred the dispersed lighting the north side of the building offered to create his works of art.

Sadly, my father passed away at the age of 73 on January 27, 1945, while I was fully engaged overseas in the Office of Strategic Services' (OSS) Operation *Rype*. He is buried next to my mother and his parents, Gulbrand and Lisbet, in the First Lutheran Church cemetery in Madison.

Yes, my Norwegian roots run deep. When Germany invaded Norway, it is hard to describe the level of grief that remained not only in my heart but, I'm sure, in the hearts of every Norwegian in the homeland or abroad; a pain that would endure until Norway once again tasted freedom from the tyranny of the Third Reich.

Even in the town in which I currently reside, Stoughton, Wisconsin (1966 at the time of writing), there is a strong sense of Norwegian pride in the population. The town celebrates Syttende Mai every year, which stands for the 17th of May, Norway's official Constitution Day. The town comes alive with a three-day weekend celebration full of festivities and parades. In one particular year, I displayed some OSS artifacts from Operation *Rype* in a local jeweler's window.

CHAPTER 7

German Subterfuge

Norwegian pride and love for their homeland became a strong driving force behind the resistance movement when World War II reached the Scandinavian countries. Norwegian patriots in significant numbers rose against the much stronger and more powerful invading German forces.

Hitler and his generals desired to take Denmark and Norway early in the war. In October 1939, Generaladmiral Erich Raeder, chief of the German *Kriegsmarine* (navy) met with Hitler to discuss seizing bases in Norway before the British could make full use of them, since this would pose a danger to the Third Reich. The British could potentially use those bases to launch bomber raids into Germany. Stopping this "Norwegian Wall" was also somewhat motivated by Hitler's obsession with having a northern flank of which Norway would be a part. Keeping it out of Allied hands became a priority.

From the war in Poland to the invasion of Norway, the German Government and High Command had repeatedly declared that they carried on war according to international rules and did not attack anything but military objectives. There were innumerable instances to show this was not true. On the contrary, the Germans carried on their war at sea, in the air and on land in open defiance of the most binding and definite international rules, rules which Germany herself had promised to respect.

The Germans, without any justification, had torpedoed a number of neutral ships resulting in the loss of many lives. They had even shot at individual fishermen working from their small boats in the fjords. Not only that but they bombed hospital ships with Red Cross markings, hospital buildings, and even funeral processions, with horrific results.

One such incident happened on April 29 when the hospital ship *Brand IV* was attacked with bombs and machine guns near Ålesund. The ship was plainly marked with the Red Cross on the deck and on the sides, so it was impossible to mistake. Several non-combatants were killed: a surgeon, a nurse, a Lotta (Lottas were an organization of women volunteers), a laborer with the sanitary service, and a member of the ship's crew. The ship was on its way to Åndalsnes to take away sick and wounded soldiers from the fighting in Gudbrandsdalen. Two German bombers circled the ship and flew directly over it three times dropping bombs and firing machine guns.

An account of this outrage was immediately sent to the world press, but from Berlin came the instant denial: "German aviators follow their instructions which are in close accord with international law. They never attack hospitals or hospital ships which are protected by the Red Cross provided they carry the Red Cross mark."

The incident of the *Brand IV* did not stand alone. On May 1, the mail boat *Queen Maud*, which had been taken in to use as a hospital ship, was bombed at Gratangen by two German aircraft. The ship was plainly marked with Red Cross symbols and anchored in shallow water. The aircraft circled over it so long that they could not help but see it was a hospital ship. Several bombs fell near the ship and, finally, one incendiary set it on fire. Twenty people were killed, eleven wounded soldiers and nine crew members. Moreover, an additional 33 people were wounded, 13 of them severely. Some of the people on board had jumped ship in an attempt to reach shore but, according to one eyewitness, the Germans shot at them with machine guns, killing several.

At Molde, German planes shot at the civilian population while they were trying to escape. Reknes, a sanatorium for tuberculosis patients near Molde, was bombed and set on fire. Fortunately, the patients had already been evacuated; otherwise there would have been a great loss of life.

Eyewitnesses recounted that, in Valdres, German bombers attacked a funeral procession on its way to church. It was a mass funeral, most of the bodies being those of German soldiers whom the people wanted to give a Christian burial, together with a few fallen Norwegians. The planes shot at the procession with machine guns.

It is well known that Germany put a great emphasis on Hermann Göring's *Luftwaffe*. However, what may not be so well known are the interests Hitler and the Nazi regime had in the ancient sport of falconry. In fact, a main symbol of the Third Reich depicted an eagle. It was called the *Reichsadler* or "Imperial Eagle" and was prominent throughout the war.

This symbol actually had its roots in ancient Rome. It was used by the holy Roman emperors where it was called the heraldic eagle. It found its way into the coats of arms of Germany. After Otto von Bismarck, the founder and first chancellor of the German Empire, was removed from power in 1890, the symbol first showed up in the second German Empire from

The *Reichsadler* or "Imperial Eagle" was prominent throughout the war.

1871 to 1918. It continued on into the Weimar Republic from 1919 to 1933 and finally into the Third Reich from 1933 to 1945.

As early as the summer of 1938, Germany sent a two-man expedition to western Greenland to capture and secure gyrfalcons. Five birds were captured and sent back to Germany. These consisted of four juveniles out of a nest near Godhaven and an adult taken near Uummannaq. This appears to be the first account of Hitler and his leaders becoming involved in falconry.

Apparently, during Hitler's reign, five official government operated falconry centers were controlled by the SS and the Gestapo. Göring was head of these centers and was later joined by Heinrich Himmler, the most senior police officer and a ruthless murderer. As is well known, Himmler and the Gestapo were responsible for the removal of all "undesirables" including Jews, gypsies, clergy and anyone else considered traitors that opposed the Nazi system.

According to an article by Monica Cromarty, where she cites from Document 31/98 of the Buchenwald archives in Weimar, Buchenwald, after the liberation of the concentration camp by the Allies on April 25, 1945, one survivor, Leopold Reitter (prisoner number 4227), gave this statement to a U.S. Army representative regarding one of the falconry centers:

> The falkenhof was built on the orders of Reich's leader SS Heinrich Himmler for the pleasure and enjoyment of the new Nazi aristocracy. It was a group of houses in which eagles, falcons, goshawks and other raptorial birds were kept. The structures were built with superior material, luxuries, and in Gothic style. The Nazi bandits could afford this since the craftsmanship was provided by concentration camp inmates (mostly Jews) without paying and it did not make any difference when daily some returned dead to camp. The comrades had to perform daily, hard labor from early morning until late at night with empty stomachs, under the whip of the SS. Only a few survived. After the Falkenhof was completed, a regular work group of six to eight concentration camp inmates were employed to feed and care for the birds. The SS did not spare any kicks and hits …

Today, the World Center for Birds of Prey located in Boise, Idaho, has one of the mounted goshawks that was once owned by Hermann Göring. This particular goshawk was presented to Göring by then Captain R. L. Meredith, the notable leader of the American Falconry Association, at a meeting of the International Falconry Exhibition sponsored by the Deutscher Falkenorden in Berlin in 1937.

Two excellent books exist on the subject of Germany and falconry. The first is *German Eagle* by Martin Hollinshead. The first edition was limited to 400 numbered copies. The second is *The Last Wolf Hawker, The Eagle Falconry of Friedrich Remmler* also by the same author. This first edition was limited to 600 numbered copies.

In order to keep military communications secret, the Germans developed a device called an Enigma machine. Arthur Scherbius, the German engineer, is credited with inventing the machines that were essentially cipher machines that used an electro-mechanical rotor mechanism to scramble the letters used in a message. As the machines advanced, a plugboard was added to make them more complex. The coding by these machines had the ability to change every day. Thus, breaking the code on day one could be useless by day two.

With the impending likelihood of German invasion, the Enigma code pattern was first broken in 1939 by the Poles under the leadership of the brilliant mathematician Marian Rejewski. This information was turned over to the British. Mathematician Alan Turing then set up a secret code-breaking organization, called *Ultra*, in the United Kingdom. Turing himself spent some time in the United States. Later, he returned to England and joined the Government Code and Cypher School. When the war broke out in September 1939, the headquarters was moved to Bletchley Park, Buckinghamshire, about 50 miles northwest of London.

Because the Germans shared their encryption device with the Japanese, *Ultra* also contributed to Allied victories in the Pacific. It is estimated this code-breaking operation may have shortened the war by about two years.

CHAPTER 8

Norwegian Resistance

On April 14, 1940, five days after Germany occupied Norway, President Franklin D. Roosevelt issued the following statement:

> Force and military aggression are once more on the march against small nations, in this instance through the invasion of Denmark and Norway. If civilization is to survive, the rights of the smaller nations to independence, to their territorial integrity, and to the unimpeded opportunity for self-government must be respected by their more powerful neighbors.

While the Resistance itself was not necessarily what you would normally think of, that is militarily, it was more-or-less a civilized resistance. The Norwegians did not have the military strength to beat the Germans. The civilian population did, however, win many battles proving resistance was successful against the German Army and its rule over Norway.

Immediately after the invasion, the first signs of public, civil, disobedience began to appear at Oslo University in the autumn of 1940. Students wore paper clips, a seemingly innocuous item, on their lapels to demonstrate their resistance to the German occupiers. It was a symbol of solidarity and unity. "We are bound together," implying resistance. The wearing of these paper clips, and the popular H7 monogram, the King's monogram, as well as red garments, especially the bobble hat (a knitted cap that has a "bobble" or pom-pom on its top), was outlawed and could lead to arrest and punishment.

Early on, people in secret resistance organizations had to develop their skills from scratch. They were in danger of Quisling's followers and German spying operations, informers, and infiltrators working within the country. The threat of torture, being assassinated or executed was always a real possibility. They had many serious setbacks and suffered heavy losses, especially during the first two years of the occupation. After a while, these groups became well organized and coordinated with each other and, on the whole, worked very effectively.

Immediately after the invasion, saving the national stores of gold became a high priority. They would be essential for any future restoration of Norway's economic system. With its police escort, a convoy carrying several tons of Norwegian gold set off to Lillehammer on the instructions of the finance minister. The last van had been loaded and locked a mere 30 minutes before Germans troops arrived in Oslo via the airport. The German soldiers said they were sent to "safeguard" the gold. Fifty-five million dollars' worth was slipped out of Norway under the noses of the Germans. It was shipped via trucks, lorries, railroad cars and several ferries which had to make fjord or river crossings. After several weeks of playing hide and seek, the gold was finally sent in four separate shipments on four different days from Norway to England. However, the movement did not stop there. Norwegian officials were afraid that if Germany conquered England their gold would be lost. The decision was made to ship it to Canada and the United States. Eleven shipments later, before the end of July 1940, 34 tons of the gold were safely in the vaults of the Bank of Canada and almost 15 tons in those of the Federal Reserve Bank in New York. About a ton was left in the gold rooms of the Bank of England to meet emergencies that might arise. It is worth noting that, during the entire operation, only 888 equivalent U.S. dollars were lost to a drunken sailor and his night on the town. When one considers the pressures and the dangers involved, it was indeed an insignificant amount. Otherwise, neither a ship was sunk, nor a cask or box lost, not a life sacrificed, nor was a single participant in the saving of the gold apprehended and sent to a concentration camp. It turned out to be a matter of luck that over eleven million Kroner in Norwegian bank notes were overlooked in the rush to save the gold. This money was put into five potato sacks and smuggled out of the Bank of Norway in Oslo under the noses of Germans guards. After being handed over to Anders Frihagen, Norway's minister of commerce, it found its way to General Ruge who badly needed money to pay recruits and purchase food and other supplies.

Later on, Gunnar Sonsteby, who joined the Resistance, became part of what was known as the "Oslo Gang." In his book *Report From #24*, he describes how, in August 1942, he was involved in smuggling out the printing plates that made Krone notes for the 5, 10, 50 and 100 denominations. Working through the printer for the Bank of Norway, this was a high-risk operation. If the operation was discovered by the Germans, it meant certain death. The printer insisted on proof that London was indeed responsible for this plan before turning over the plates to a young 20-something. This came in the form of a letter from Torlay Oksnevad. He was the radio announcer out of London that all of Norway knew about. Sonsteby smuggled the plates out in the bottom of a sack full of charcoal, commonly used for gas generators. All was going well until, on the other side of Kløfta, they had car trouble. Some German soldiers came along and, in the interest of instilling goodwill with the Norwegians, actually helped them get the car working again. They then continued on to Kongsvinger and arranged for transfer to Stockholm before returning to Oslo. London only needed casts of the original plates. Two sets were made in Stockholm before the original plates were returned to Oslo via courier.

The German Minister to Norway, Dr. Kurt Bräuer, was the only official Third Reich representative in Oslo since Hitler assumed Norway would capitulate quickly. Bräuer had no instructions telling him what to do if the Norwegian Government refused to cooperate, which is exactly what happened. He approached the Ministry of Foreign Affairs Office to arrange for Norway's surrender and was rebuffed. To aid Bräuer, Quisling made a broadcast on Radio Oslo the evening of April 9. He announced he had taken over the reins of government and declared resistance to German troops a crime. The broadcast backfired. This was treason. It became the rallying point to begin the Norwegian resistance. Bräuer had no instructions concerning Quisling and the Germans were confused.

From the onset, the Norwegian home forces began to galvanize. Scattered beginnings at first, the force grew to include some 32,000 men. By 1942, the civil resistance defeated attempts by Vidkun Quisling to nazify the Norwegian population. He did, however, make one more attempt to bring the Norwegian population into submission. On February 22, 1943, he proclaimed all able-bodied Norwegians were to register to be a part of a labor reserve. This, in reality, was to be a labor reserve to be used on German military installations. Ration cards would be provided to the labor force. Any Norwegians not registered would not eat. A woman in the Ministry of Justice intercepted Quisling's order and sent a copy to the Resistance, who, in turn, sent it to London. The BBC then broadcast into Norway the message, "No one to report for labor service." Quisling tried again in May 1944. This time the intelligence networks jumped on it quickly and spread the word throughout Norway. The whole effort was foiled when the Labor Card Offices were blown up and the ration cards scattered.

Milorg (the military organization of the Norwegian Underground Army) was gradually established in Norway. They had a few extra problems getting started as the severe reprisals for military operations affected not only the resistance movement, but innocent civilians as well. It finally became formally recognized by the exiled Government on November 20, 1941, and was placed under the Norwegian High Command. Once recognized, its basic mission changed to prepare for action to be taken during the liberation of Norway. The British Special Operations Executive (SOE) worked closely with Milorg, providing them with weapons and other equipment.

Milorg and the SOE soon became a major cause of concern for the *Gestapo* and *Abwehr*. Thousands of Norwegians had fled to the hills to join the Underground. In fact, by the end of the war Milorg had 40,000 recruits as the civilian resistance came to stand beside military resistance and the two groups came into closer cooperation with the exiled Norwegian Government in London. Among the Underground intelligence organizations, one, named XU, became a nationwide network of agents.

It was decided sabotage was perhaps the best, most effective, and cheapest means of ravaging the Germans rather than massive air raids. Milorg was instructed to keep a low profile, carrying out calculated attacks. The vaunted German Army was stymied at almost every turn. After the Norwegians recovered from the initial shock of the invasion and scattered into the mountains, many moved in small groups northward. Colonel Holterman, the Underground Trondheim District Commander of the Norwegian Army, held Akershus, a county in Norway bordering Hedmark, Oppland and Buskerud with Oslo as its main city, against the invading hoards for a while. Even before that, though, other efforts periodically stopped the Germans on their march north. This prolonged the invasion into the months of April, May, June, July and August before the eventual capitulation of the Norwegian forces. The Germans had been previously successful here, there and everywhere on their march toward the domination of Europe, so, to be frustrated by a small nation with a population about the size of my home state of Minnesota was incomprehensible. Understandably, the 17,000 men in the Norwegian armed forces were no match for the weight of the surprise attack and were eventually overcome. Eighty-four thousand Norwegians escaped from the country during the war, 40,000 were arrested by the Germans, 658 died in Norwegian prisons. Another 1,433 died in concentration camps in Germany.

While under German occupation, the Norwegian people continually despised German arrogance since it was ever present as they attempted to assert their ideology. Several efforts were made to win over the Norwegian people. Parades were staged in the cities to impress the populace, but, as they marched by, the Norwegians would busy themselves looking into window displays and so forth, turning their backs to the master race.

Norwegian girls shunned the attention of the German troops, avoiding all social contacts. An attempt was made to prime the fraternization between Norwegian girls and German soldiers by importing about 2,000 blonde German women. They were auspiciously promenaded around in public with the German soldiery, hopefully expecting the Norwegians would now see that their blonde women had accepted their conquerors as friends—a *fait accompli*. The ruse failed. However, I imagine the 2,000 imported women were quite popular among the German soldiers, since there were an estimated 200,000 on occupation duty in the main part of Norway, not counting the crack divisions confronting the Russians in Finland and up in the North Cape.

German officers were ordered to be most circumspect in their contacts with the people, even with youngsters. I was told a story about a cocky little tow-headed Norwegian boy who was down at the Oslo Park where replicas of the old Viking ships were on display. A German officer engaged the youngster in a conversation. "Your forefathers must have certainly been excellent seamen to sail these flimsy little ships on the open sea, even to England." The little fellow drew himself up with an air of righteous indignation and replied, "That's nothing. They used them to invade England every spring!" Keep in mind the Germans had tried but were unsuccessful in invading England themselves. A little salt intentionally poured into a sore spot of the Third Reich.

A clandestine seaborne operation materialized between Norway and the Shetland Islands. This became known as the "Shetland Bus." It was run by seamen who, a thousand years after the Vikings, were sailing the same seas with the same sized boats. Slipping under the hand of the Germans, they ran rescue operations to get refugees out of, and cargo into, Norway. Since there was too much light in the summer, the journeys were mostly made in the winter. They would also transport both British and Norwegian radio operators and saboteurs. Approximately 40 Norwegian civilian seamen made the 180-mile trip to and from Bergen and Lunna in the Shetlands. Lunna was ideal since it was a rather remote location. The main office, however, was in Lerwick where communications were set up. Since German aircraft constantly patrolled the skies and German patrols heavily guarded the shores out to a 50-mile limit, the Shetland Bus had to sail during the worst time of the year in terrible weather.

Perhaps Norway's most noteworthy contribution to the Allied cause came from its merchant ship fleet, the nation's greatest asset. To this end, it deserves special recognition, for, without it, the war's outcome would have been much different. Keeping the sea lanes open across the Atlantic was due in large part to the ships and splendid seamanship of the Scandinavians. While Denmark and Sweden did their part, Norway's contribution was the largest. Of the Norwegian fleet, the British magazine *The Motor Ship* said, "It is probably an understatement to say that, at the present time, this fleet is worth more to us than a million soldiers." The ships flew the Norwegian flag and were controlled by the Norwegian Government-in-exile in England.

Without the Atlantic sea lanes, Great Britain, along with North America and the rest of the world, had no hope of carrying on to victory. Few people realized the gigantic task that confronted the merchant sailors. The British Isles themselves needed, every year, between 60 and 70 million tons of food, raw materials and finished products, all of which needed to be transported across the Atlantic. If an average ship carried about 6,000 tons, that meant, in the course of a year, ten thousand ships would dock in Great Britain, or 28 ships each and every day.

The Norwegian merchant fleet was second only to Great Britain in playing a part in this endeavor. Very impressive considering this was a small country of only three-and-a-half million citizens. Overall, Norway's fleet was the fourth largest in the world.

After the invasion, getting the ships moving again was an enormous problem. In Oslo and Bergen, the offices of the big shipping concerns had been taken over by the Nazis the very first day. The German-controlled radios sent out orders to all captains of Norwegian ships that they should proceed to Norwegian or neutral ports. A dramatic fight ensued between the Germans and the Allies over the radio.

At the same time, a proclamation was radioed from London that Norwegian ships should go to the nearest British or Allied port. The Norwegian captains had another problem. War insurance ceased automatically with the invasion and, since the ships now had no official connection with Norway, many were without means to pay wages or buy provisions or bunker coal. Nevertheless, the Nazis did not succeed in paralyzing Norwegian shipping. Not one single ship failed to obey instructions from the Allies.

A few days after the invasion, the Shipping Committee was formed in London with the Norwegian Minister as chairman. The Government decided on April 22 to requisition all Norwegian ships of more than 500 tons. Afterwards, this was superseded by a Royal decree on May 18, 1940. It was not the ships themselves that were requisitioned by the Government, but merely the right to use them. The ships were to be returned after the war to the owners who would be reimbursed for their use.

On April 25, Öyvind Lorentzen, head of the shipping directorate in Oslo, arrived in London and, with the authority of the Government, instantly began to organize the Norwegian Shipping and Trade Mission, popularly called "Nortraship." One of his greatest difficulties was to find people who knew the business. Practically all the executives and staff members were still in Norway, unable to get out after the invasion. A few did manage to get out. These formed the nucleus of the group. Other Norwegian shipping experts were gathered from other parts of the world.

The first problem, of course, was to get the ships sailing again. New war insurance had to be written and arrangements had to be made to meet running expenses of the ships and take care of their earnings. In order to do this, it was necessary to have information regarding the vessels. To begin with, Nortraship did not have any information to build on. The statistics were in Norway. Nobody even knew how many ships were sailing the seven seas, where they were, by whom they were chartered, or what their conditions were.

In May 1940, a Shipping Committee branch was established in New York and in the course of a year the Norwegian Shipping and Trade Mission had grown from nothing to becoming the world's largest shipping organization.

There were a few misunderstandings regarding the activities of Nortraship that need clarification. First of all, rumors were prevalent that Norwegian ships had been requisitioned by England or that they were sailing under the British flag. This was officially denied over and over again by the Norwegian authorities, but it kept cropping up in the American press. The truth is that, apart from a few ships sold to foreign owners before the invasion, every single Norwegian ship continued to sail under the Norwegian flag. There were also various misunderstandings with regard to Norwegian ships lying in American ports. It had been rumored these ships ought to be taken over in the same manner as Danish, Italian and German ships had been taken over by the American Government. These rumors also derived from a lack of information regarding the Norwegian fleet. True, there were always a few Norwegian ships in American shipyards being repaired, but there was not a single one lying idle. Every Norwegian ship that was seaworthy was working. Many, since they obviously could not go home, came to the United States for periodic overhauling, as well as for more extensive repairs.

The strain on the men of the Norwegian fleet was immense, being forever in the danger zone. Often there were so few men that they were practically never relieved. Even though they were thoroughly seasoned and splendid seamen, it became almost physically impossible to carry on month after month under this terrific strain and constant danger. It was also a great strain on their morale to be separated from their home. For instance, British seamen had a chance to visit their families every time they came home to England. The Norwegians had no hope of seeing their families before the war ended. In many instances, they could not even send or receive letters since a mail service was essentially non-existent. Twenty-five thousand seamen had not heard a word from their families, except possibly through a message from the Red Cross, since the war began. In most cases, they did not know whether their families had anything to live on.

Yet these brave men knew what their battle meant to Norway and the rest of the world. The battle to keep the Atlantic open, the lifeline of the Allied forces, must be won at all costs to get the necessary millions of tons of food and war material delivered. If the Germans won, Norway would lose its freedom and independence. On the other hand, if the Allies won, but Norway lost most of its fleet, the country would suffer from the loss of one of its chief resources and means of livelihood. Not only would the towns and harbors where shipping was carried out be affected, but so would the entire Norwegian economy that was dependent on the shipping industry's income. It was this balance of trade that affected the standard of living in Norway more than any other country. Not only was Norway's freedom at stake, but its whole basis of existence.

In 1941, the most critical year for Britain, Norwegian merchant ships brought in 40 percent of all supplies that came from abroad to England. The seaman's work during the war was more dangerous than the work, on average, by people in the armed forces. There were mines and the ships were subject to German and Japanese bombing, and to attacks from submarines and surface warships. In addition, the Norwegian fleet, along with Norway's navy, participated in all the Allied landings, including Normandy.

In their fight against the Nazi regime, nearly half of the original Norwegian merchant fleet was lost. By war's end, Norway only had the ability to conduct one-million, two hundred thousand tons of shipping. Furthermore, a great part of these ships were old tramp steamers or sailing vessels that ended up being scrapped after the war. A thousand brave seamen lost their lives. The war indeed took its toll on this great nation.

Of course, during the occupation, the Germans took full advantage of the resources available to them. Norway came very close to mass starvation during this time. The German war machine gorged itself on Norwegian food. Norwegians obtained no meats or eggs. Even potatoes and fish were taken in mass confiscations. The Germans closed the very best restaurants to Norwegians. Inside, they ate as many as 10 eggs at one sitting. After the German assault on Russia in June 1941, no vegetables, milk, berries, or fruit reached Norwegian homes. Even fish, one of the last sources of protein, was rationed. For the most part, the fishing industry workers, along with other food producers, tried to continue working their normal jobs. It was an extremely difficult decision as many Norwegians felt they were betraying their country as the Germans were taking the food as fast as the producers could provide it. Large numbers of Norwegians began to lack necessary food in their diets, resulting in poor health. With the riches of the sea close by, the coastal towns were optimistic about always having food. Unfortunately, the Germans demanded so many fish from Norway that months would go by with no fish for sale in the marketplace. The Germans emptied the ample stocks of food and cut the rations for the Norwegians. In 1941, they actually threatened to starve those who did not collaborate with them. The only people who were less deprived were the farmers. Rather than selling their milk and butter, they consumed it and were able to maintain their health relatively well in comparison to the less fortunate city dwellers.

A lack of other basic items, such as clothing, also became the first order of business for many Norwegians. The Germans took everything they desired from the citizens. Even blankets were confiscated. Yes, things were rationed or "on the card" as the Norwegians referred to it, but those meager offerings fell short of what was needed. Being the resourceful people they were, just about everything, from shoes made out of paper to clothing from parachutes they found, was fabricated.

To make up for the confiscated radios, Norwegian men would venture out whenever they heard of a downed German plane. It would quickly be scavenged for anything useful. To be caught meant certain death. The men and young boys also grew their hair out long to purposely taunt the Germans and their "crew-cuts." Any Norwegian citizen travelling by train had to sit on their suitcases in the corridors since the compartments were for German soldiers and always full. With the German occupation now decimating Norway and its resources, acts of individual resistance and support of the Underground began to grow stronger every day.

Norway, being a country which is geographically challenging, is also a country whose people are subjected to the challenges of day-to-day living and survival. These characteristics, or lifestyles, are centuries old and created the will with which to survive the new challenge of German occupation. Most were able to withstand the stress and strain of resistance. Norway's hard everyday life prepared its citizens for the hard times which came with the war. Their love of country and their king also went far in resisting the German nazification tactics. On the other hand, the

German soldiers had to try adapting to a rugged country they knew little about and had to get used to the bitter winters. It was often the Norwegian knowledge of their home which kept them one step ahead of the Germans.

After the Germans requisitioned Norwegian radios, many of which had short wave frequencies on which one could get news directly from abroad, another branch of the Underground developed a network of free, secret newspapers. The official newspapers and magazines and the Norwegian radio broadcasts were, of course, under Nazi control. These underground newspapers were small and usually stenciled. Flyers were distributed to tens of thousands of people, who in turn passed them on to others, and they again to others, and so on. Through these newspapers, Norwegians got all the real news about such matters as the resistance by the King, the teachers, the Supreme Court justices, the bishops, the labor unions, the sports organizations, professional organizations, and important information from the exiled Government, and Underground leadership.

It became clear to both the Norwegians and the British that Norway was to be in the shadow of the main war effort. The British were insistent upon making Norway a "thorn in the German side." Attempts were made to make this the case. A plan was developed called Operation *Jupiter*. The idea was to cut Norway in half. Unfortunately, it led to the tragedy at Majavatn in 1942. The civilian population also suffered as a result of other failed operations, such as in Telaväg, which could not be pushed through to successful conclusions. In the fall of 1942, the SOE changed its outlook to a certain extent.

Kompani Linge, organized by Captain Martin Linge, was a British SOE group originally formed for the purpose of performing commando raids. The members of the unit were trained at various locations in the United Kingdom, including at Drumintoul Lodge in Scotland. Their initial raids took place in 1941 in Lofoten (Operation *Claymore*) and Måløy (Operation *Archery*), where Martin Linge was killed. However, the best known raid was probably the Norwegian heavy water sabotage on the facility in Vemork. Other raids included the Thamshavnbanen sabotage. In the capital area, the *Oslogjengen* also carried out several sabotage missions.

Secret radio stations sprang up in Norway to get messages to England. Broadcasting and messages were received on a hit and miss basis since the Germans were good at detecting regular broadcasting by triangulation. One of the main objectives of the underground radio stations was to provide the outside world with real news of events taking place within the country.

By the summer of 1944, the home forces, in compliance with a directive from the Supreme Headquarters Allied Expeditionary Force, were able to muster some 40,000 men, most of whom were well equipped and well trained.

In fact, near the end of the war in Europe, a February 28, 1945, memorandum to the director, entitled, "Report of OSS Activities during December 1944" by W. B. Kantack, Captain A.C., stated some of the successes by the Resistance:

Sabotage in Norway continued on a growing scale with particular emphasis on attacks against railroad objectives. Local groups also sank five ships in Oslo harbor and destroyed a large amount of stored oil and petrol in the Oslo area. Activities in support of the resistance increased with 76 air sorties attempted, 19 of which were successful (compared to November's 18); air-dropped deliveries totaled 29 tons. Six successful trips were made by the three SC boats operating at OSS [Office of Strategic Services] direction; 11 tons of stores and two persons were delivered and 17 refugees brough back to the UK.

The importance of the Norwegian resistance movement cannot be underestimated. It assisted in aiding thousands of persons to flee the country (Norway's long border with Sweden facilitated escape). It warned those about to be arrested. It carried out national humanitarian work. It helped keep young people from being taken in by Nazi ideology. At the end of the war it could be given credit for part of the German capitulation and the smooth transition back to the legal government, in stark contrast to difficulties experienced in other occupied lands.

CHAPTER 9

OSS Beginnings, Background and History

Before World War II, the U.S. Government traditionally left intelligence to the principal executors of American foreign policy, the Department of War and the Armed Services. Attachés and diplomats collected the bulk of America's foreign intelligence, mostly in the course of official business but occasionally in clandestine meetings with secret contacts. In Washington, desk officers scrutinized their reports in the regional bureaus and at the military intelligence services, the Office of Naval Intelligence (ONI) and the War Department's Military Intelligence Division, better known as the G-2. Important and timely information went up the chain of command, perhaps even to the president, and might be shared across departmental lines, but no one short of the White House tried to collate and assess all the vital information acquired by the U.S. Government.

The State and the military developed their own security and counterintelligence procedures and the Army and Navy created separate offices to decipher and read foreign communications. Senior diplomat Robert Murphy later reflected, "It must be confessed that our intelligence organizations in 1940s were primitive and inadequate. It was timid, parochial, and operating strictly in the tradition of the Spanish–American War."

As another European war loomed in the late 1930s, fears of fascist and communist "Fifth Columns" in America prompted President Franklin D. Roosevelt (FDR) to ask for greater coordination by the departmental intelligence arms. When little seemed to happen in response to his wish, he tried again in the spring of 1941, expressing his desire to make the traditional intelligence services take a strategic approach to the nation's challenges, and to cooperate so he did not have to arbitrate their squabbles. A few weeks later, Roosevelt, in frustration, resorted to a characteristic stratagem. With some subtle prompting from a pair of British officials, Admiral John H. Godfrey and William Stephenson (later Sir William), under the blessing of FDR, a new organization was created to duplicate some of the functions of the existing agencies. The president, on 11 July, appointed William J. Donovan of New York as head. He was responsible for sorting out the mess of the newly created civilian office attached to the White House, now known as the Coordination of Information (COI).

Roosevelt's official declaration read as follows:

DESIGNATING A COORDINATOR OF INFORMATION

By virtue of the authority vested in me as President of the United States and as Commander in Chief of the Army and Navy of the United States, it is ordered as follows:

There is hereby established the position of Coordinator of Information, with authority to collect and analyze all information and data, which may bear upon national security; to correlate such information and data, and to make such information and data available to the President and to such departments and officials of the Government as the President may determine; and to carry out, when requested by the President, such supplementary activities as may facilitate the securing of information important for national security not now available to the Government.

The several departments and agencies of the government shall make available to the Coordinator of Information all and any such information and data relating to national security as the Coordinator, with the approval of the President, may from time-to-time request.

The Coordinator of Information may appoint such committees, consisting of appropriate representatives of the various departments and agencies of the Government, as he may deem necessary to assist him in the performance of his functions.

Nothing in the duties and responsibilities of the Coordinator of Information shall not in any way interfere with or impair the duties and responsibilities of the regular military and naval advisors of the President as Commander in Chief of the Army and Navy.

Within the limits of such funds as may be allocated to the Coordinator of Information by the President, the Coordinator may employ necessary personnel and make provision for the necessary supplies, facilities, and services.

William J. Donovan is hereby designated as Coordinator of Information.

(signed) Franklin D. Roosevelt
THE WHITE HOUSE
July 11, 1941

Thus, the COI was a precursor to the Office of Strategic Services (OSS). It constituted the nation's first peacetime, non-departmental intelligence organization. President Roosevelt authorized it to collect and analyze all information and data which may bear upon national security, to correlate such information and data, and to make such information and data available to the president and to such departments and officials of the Government. As the president may determine, it was to carry out supplementary activities that would facilitate securing information, important for national security, not already available to the Government.

At the time, many embassies throughout the world were little more than postal drops for attachés. Both "information" and "intelligence" were submitted and passed along to the appropriate military agency for interpretation. Copious amounts of data were then determined to be one or the other. For example, the number of ships reported in a foreign harbor could be classified as information. Why those ships were there would be considered intelligence.

In selecting Donovan as his Coordinator of Information, President Roosevelt chose an energetic civilian who shared his desire to do whatever it took to resist

Nazism and the danger it posed to America. Donovan owned a sterling résumé, with distinguished military service, executive and legal experience, an abiding interest in foreign affairs, and a vision of the importance of strategic intelligence colleagues found inspiring.

His military career began in 1916 while many of his future OSS colleagues were still in elementary school. His first brush with unconventional warfare came when he commanded the New York National Guard on the Mexican border hunting down the notorious revolutionary Pancho Villa. As an unrelenting commander, he whipped his elite New York Guard into shape with grueling 10-mile forced marches carrying full field equipment under a scorching Texas sky. They were nicknamed the "Silk Stocking Brigade." Some of the basis tactics he learned would later be applied when his OSS commandos slipped behind enemy lines in World War II.

Donovan was a Buffalo, New York, native who had earned his law degree at Columbia. He joined the 69th Infantry Regiment (also called the "Fighting 69th" from its Civil War days) and earned a Medal of Honor as a battalion commander charging German lines in World War I. After the war he visited Europe, Siberia and Japan. He served as assistant attorney general in the Coolidge administration where he briefly supervised a young J. Edgar Hoover and his new Federal Bureau of Investigation (FBI). Later, he practiced anti-trust law in New York City and lost the 1932 election as the Republican candidate for Governor of New York. His interest in world affairs never diminished, nor did his zest for being where the action was. He even toured the Italian battle lines in Ethiopia in 1935. Donovan also made wide contacts in government, and among public-spirited financial and legal figures in New York City, with men such as Frank Knox, David Bruce, the Dulles brothers, and Allen and John Foster.

When Frank Knox became FDR's new Secretary of the Navy in 1940, he brought William Donovan to the president's attention. FDR and Donovan had actually been classmates, although not companions, at Columbia Law School. That summer, Roosevelt confidentially asked Donovan to visit Britain and report on London's resolve and its staying power against Hitler. Donovan's British hosts understood his mission. Prime Minister Winston Churchill, hoping to win American support for Britain's desperate war effort, ensured Donovan saw everything he wanted to, granting him extraordinary access to defense and intelligence secrets. Donovan also toured the Balkans and British outposts in the Mediterranean in early 1941. Roosevelt was impressed with his reports and his ideas on intelligence and its place in modern war. When the president decided to force the military and civilian services to cooperate on intelligence matters in the summer of 1941, Donovan was the man he tapped to perform this mission.

Donovan happily accepted the challenge and set to work with typical charisma and zeal. When the war came to America at Pearl Harbor, however, Donovan wanted to command troops on the battlefield again and hoped to gain a commission in the U.S. Army. His hopes were soon dashed. An automobile accident in the spring of 1942 aggravated an old war wound and Donovan realized he would never again hold a field command. Nevertheless, he eventually wore a general's star. As the director of OSS, and a representative of the Joint Chiefs of Staff, Donovan commanded thousands of service personnel and it was deemed helpful to recommission him for the duration of the war. He was placed on active duty and promoted to brigadier general in March 1943 and won promotion to major general in November 1944.

According to historian Thomas F. Troy, COI was: "… a novel attempt in American history to organize research, intelligence, propaganda, subversion, and commando operations as a unified and essential feature of modern warfare; a 'Fourth Arm' of the military services."

The office grew quickly in the autumn before Pearl Harbor, with Donovan cheerfully accumulating various offices and staff orphaned in their home departments.

One of Donovan's hand-me-down units brought to COI a mission unforeseen even by himself—espionage. Donovan had intended the clandestine intelligence gathering of his office to serve as its analytical and propaganda branches. He had not originally sought to duplicate the foreign intelligence missions of the armed services. Nevertheless, it was the armed services that were uncomfortable with the peacetime espionage mission that persuaded COI in September 1941 to accept the small undercover intelligence branches of ONI and the G-2. Along with this acquisition, COI won authority to utilize unvouchered funds from the president's emergency fund. Unvouchered funds were the lifeblood of clandestine operations. They were granted by Congress to be spent at the personal responsibility of the president, or one of his officers, and were not audited in detail. Donovan's signature on a note attesting to their proper use sufficed for accounting purposes. These funds, combined with the espionage authority granted to COI by the military, planted the seed for the modern Central Intelligence Agency's (CIA's) Directorate of Operations.

Donovan recruited Americans who traveled abroad or studied world affairs and, in that age, such people often represented the best and the brightest at East Coast universities, businesses, and law firms. As war against Hitler loomed, not a few of America's leading citizens looked for opportunities to join the struggle against Nazism. COI's successor, the OSS, eventually drew such a high proportion of socially prominent men and women that Washington wits dubbed it the "Oh So Social" organization.[1]

Since Donovan himself had traveled widely during his army service in World War I, he had been a careful observer of social, political, and military conditions.

---

1 The author's mother, Eileen K. Bolland had her own variation, referring to it as the "Oh So Secret" organization.

Similarly, his legal briefs on behalf of corporate clients were patiently and volumi-nously documented. As Coordinator of Information, he saw an opportunity to make research a cornerstone of his new information agency.

Donovan quickly realized the volume of documents coming in from various branches of government were too numerous for him to read. Furthermore, specific information on a certain problem needed to be analyzed and condensed in a timely manner. Throughout his various travels, Donovan was always looking to recruit aides, whether that be at cocktail parties, out of his law office on Wall Street, at his Beekman Place apartment in Washington, or at military bases. Since time was crucial, exhaustive security checks were not conducted. Rather, he relied on the people he knew best. One of his first assistants was Jim Murphy. Murphy's main task was to protect Donovan from political backlash. That is, to "keep the knives out of his back" as Murphy was once quoted as saying.

Donovan won cooperation from the Librarian of Congress, poet Archibald MacLeish, for his plan to analyze Axis strengths and vulnerabilities. At roughly the same time, COI established its own Research and Analysis (R&A) branch to test Donovan's hypothesis that answers to many intelligence problems could be found in libraries, newspapers, and the filing cabinets of government and industry. The prevailing thought was, scattered throughout various departments, there were documents and memoranda concerning military and economic potentials of the Axis powers which, if gathered together and studied in detail by carefully selected trained minds with a knowledge both of the related languages and techniques, would yield valuable and often decisive results.

By autumn 1941, Donovan was proudly submitting the first meticulously prepared studies to President Roosevelt. The Branch was still small and focused on Europe at the time of Pearl Harbor. However, it had no role in the operational and intelligence failures surrounding that disaster.

Donovan's diaries are now stored with many of his papers at the U.S. Military History Institute in Carlisle, Pennsylvania. There is no doubt he left an indelible mark on the OSS. Stewart Alsop and Thomas Braden, in their 1946 *Sub Rosa: The OSS and American Espionage*, wrote:

> OSS was a direct reflection of Donovan's character. He was its spark plug, the moving force behind it. In a sense it can be said that Donovan was OSS.

America's entry into the war in December 1941 provoked new thinking about the place and role of the COI. Donovan and his new office, with its $10 million budget, 600 staffers and its charismatic director, had provoked hostility from the FBI, the G-2, and various war agencies. The new Joint Chiefs of Staff (JCS) initially shared this distrust. They regarded Donovan as a civilian and an interloper. The JCS thought, however, they might be able to control and utilize COI if it was placed under their authority. Surprisingly, Donovan himself at this point was inclined to agree. Working with the Secretary of the JCS, Donovan devised a plan to bring COI under their jurisdiction in a way that would preserve the office's autonomy while winning it access to military support and resources.

President Roosevelt endorsed the idea of moving COI to the Joint Chiefs. He did, however, want to keep COI's Foreign Information Service (FIS, which conducted radio broadcasting) out of military hands. Thus, he split the "black" and "white" propaganda missions, giving FIS the officially attributable side of the business, plus half of COI's permanent staff, and sent it to the new Office of War Information.

The remainder of COI then became the Office of Strategic Services on 13 June, 1942. The change of name to OSS marked the loss of the white propaganda mission, but it also fulfilled Donovan's wish for a title that reflected his sense of the strategic importance of intelligence and clandestine operations in modern war. Thus, overnight, Roosevelt's civilian organization was being transformed into a military agency to act as a supporting unit for the Army and Navy. The OSS was to collect and analyze strategic information and plan and operate special services including sabotage, black warfare and similar clandestine operations that did not normally fall within the jurisdiction of the regular armed forces.

New methods of warfare required new concepts and new weapons. Roosevelt said, "The United States was about to embark on activities that had never been indulged in by this nation before." It was a staggering order. For the first time, Uncle Sam was going into the international cloak-and-dagger business and the business was virtually starting from scratch. The prospect would have floored any man, but General Donovan was not just "any man." He had earned the Medal of Honor and the nickname "Wild Bill" for his bravery. He had a unique combination of unbounded curiosity, a flexible imagination that leapt at new ideas, an affinity for danger, and a way of getting what he wanted.

A month later, OSS's institutional rivals delivered a blow to Donovan's aspirations for the new outfit. The Department of State and the armed services arranged a presidential decree that effectively banned OSS and several other agencies from acquiring and decoding the war's most important intelligence source, intercepted Axis communications. Donovan protested, but his complaints fell on deaf ears. The result was that the OSS had no access to intercepts on Japan (code-named *Magic*) and could read only certain types of German intercepts (*Ultra*). Other edicts also limited OSS's scope and effectiveness. The FBI, G-2 and ONI, for instance, stood together to protect their monopoly on domestic counterintelligence work. The OSS eventually developed a capable counterintelligence apparatus of its own overseas, the X-2 Branch, but it had no authority to operate in the Western Hemisphere which was reserved for the FBI and Nelson Rockefeller's office of the Coordinator of Inter-American Affairs.

OSS expanded into fully fledged operations abroad in 1942. Donovan sent units to every theater of war that would have them. His can-do approach had already impressed the War Department, which in 1941 had desperately needed men to serve as intelligence officers in French North Africa. Donovan's COI sent a dozen officers to work as vice-consuls in several North African ports where they established networks and acquired information to guide the Allied landings during Operation *Torch* in November 1942. The success of *Torch* won OSS much needed praise and support in Washington. Unfortunately, General Douglas MacArthur in the South Pacific, and Admiral Chester Nimitz in the Central Pacific, saw little use for the OSS and the office was thus kept from contributing to the main American campaigns against Imperial Japan. Nonetheless, Donovan forged ahead and hoped for the best. Utilizing military cover for the most part, but with some officers under diplomatic and non-official cover, OSS began to build a worldwide clandestine capability.

This global reach benefited from close OSS contacts with British intelligence services. The British had much to teach their American pupils when COI opened its London office in November 1941. Both sides gained from the partnership. OSS needed information, training, and experience, all of which the British organizations could provide. The British good-naturedly envied the relative wealth of resources seemingly at the command of OSS and other American agencies and hoped to share in that bounty to expand their own operations against the Axis. Despite a mutual desire to cooperate, however, relative harmony between the OSS and its British counterparts took time to achieve.

The British in their own right actually had a head start over the Americans when it came to using small paratrooper units to conduct sabotage. David Stirling, who pioneered the British Special Air Service (SAS), would take the best of the best and parachute them behind enemy lines to become marauding forces, hindering the enemy wherever they could. This was a new tactic in combat, unlike anything before it. At the time, the concept was unpopular with most of the traditional military officers in the British forces. Many considered it experimental at best. It ran contrary to conventional warfare thinking where large battlefields and definite lines of demarcation determined success or failure of military battles. The SAS conducted their first raid, Operation *Squatter*, on November 16–17, 1941, in North Africa. After that, approximately a hundred or so operations were carried out by SAS teams in North Africa, Italy, Sicily and France, as well as other locations, during the war with good results. Due to the successes in World War II, small sabotage units of this nature have since found a place in modern-warfare strategy.

The slow maturing of inter-Allied cooperation had several causes. British intelligence services had their own operations, and plans to protect, and feared working too closely with the inexperienced Americans would jeopardize the safety of their operatives in occupied Europe. This British caution kept the Americans in the awkward status of junior partners for much of the war, particularly during the planning for covert action in support of the D-Day landings in Normandy in 1944. For their part, OSS officers worried about making their new agency dependent on even a friendly foreign intelligence service. Conflicting policy goals occasionally hampered liaison with the British services in Asia. American diplomacy quietly frowned on British imperialism and some OSS officers informally opposed British moves they viewed as efforts to expand the empire. Despite these obstacles, however, the liaison relationship gradually grew closer as shared sacrifices and common goals forced officers in the field and in their respective headquarters to resolve their differences.

The goal of the OSS was total intelligence: to know more about the enemy that he knew about himself; to learn every detail of his economic, political and military situation. General Donovan recruited prominent bankers and industrialists for his key personnel. Names such a Vanderbilt, DuPont, Morgan (who knew European finance and had an intimate knowledge of strategic areas), Hugh Wilson (the last ambassador to Germany), and Allen Dulles, whose subsequent dealings in Switzerland with General Wolfe of the SS provided one of the most fantastic episodes in the history of the OSS. Others, from all walks of life included James P. Baxter, President of Williams College, Brigadier General John T. Magruder, ace Hollywood director Captain John Ford (USNR), Garson Kanin, Sterling Hayden, George Skouras of Twentieth Century Fox, Navy Lieutenant Henry Ringling North of Ringling Brothers' Circus fame, and athletes Lieutenant Mike Burke, a Penn State All-American, and Joe Savoldi ("Jumpin' Joe"), a noted professional wrestler from Notre Dame. These were the bluebloods from the top drawer of the social register.

There were nameless thousands of other Americans who never made the headlines; doctors, editors, interior decorators, ornithologists, soda-jerkers, cowboys and clerks. Some were even of Italian, German or Japanese descent, newly made citizens with a burning desire to pay off their obligation to their adopted land as well as drive dictators from their ancestral homes.

William Donovan also had the insight to realize the importance women could serve in the OSS, not just as clerks, secretaries or administrative assistants but actual operatives in the field. The Research and Analysis Branch was considered the heartbeat of the organization and it was here where many women served. This branch studied the economic, social, political and military climates where OSS and Allied military operations were conducted. While many women served their wartime careers in Washington, about 900 were sent overseas as well, with a few rising to relatively high positions. Doctor Cora DuBois became head of the R&A in Ceylon while Agnes Greene, who grew up in China and spoke the language, established the important Reports Section in Chungking. Patricia Barnett, a Vassar graduate, was assigned to the OSS branch in Southeast Asia after serving a short stint with the Institute of Pacific Relations in New York City. By November 1944, R&A outposts had been established in London, Algiers, Cairo, Caserta, Paris, Stockholm, New Delhi, Bari, Honolulu, Chunking, Bucharest, Istanbul, Rome, Lisbon, Kandy and Bern.

The R&A Branch in London employed the greatest number of professional women. Of the 66 Americans, nine were analysts and five were assistant analysts. Necessary to their positions, they were researchers, economists, geographers, political scientists and historians. Many were fluent in several languages. Examples include Julia Phelps, a graduate of Radcliffe and Harvard and a professor of fine arts who had traveled extensively and spoke four languages (German, French, Italian and Spanish). Jaqueline Hare was a Wellesley graduate who spoke fluent French, Italian, Spanish and a fair amount of Russian. Emmy Lou Williamson of Mary Baldwin College in Staunton, Virginia, was a French major.

While Britain was being pounded incessantly, the work at the London office continued with fervor. The British Government reported in July 1944 there were 12,441 civilian bomb casualties, either killed or missing. Of these, 3,876 were women and 485 were children. At war's end, the OSS gave a citation to all the women in the London office who had worked throughout these attacks.

Probably one of the most extraordinary of the female operatives in the field was Virginia Hall. In her book, W*olves at the Door,* Judith Pearson details the life of one of America's greatest female spies:

> She was born to a wealthy family in Baltimore, Maryland, attended Radcliffe and Barnard Colleges, and completed part of her education in Europe. Being fluent in French and German, she worked at several American embassies. Her goal in life was to get a job with the U.S. State Department since she wanted to work in a foreign service. However, a tragedy occurred on December 8, 1933 when a hunting accident in Turkey left her with an artificial leg.
>
> Hall eventually made her way to London and volunteered for Britain's newly formed Special Operations Executive (SOE), which sent her to Vichy, France in August, 1941. She spent the next fifteen months there, helping to coordinate the activities of the French Underground in Vichy and the occupied zone of France. She worked efficiently to create safe drop zones for the Allies. That way, new agents, supplies, money, and weapons could all be brought in. At the time, she had the cover of a correspondent for the *New York Post.* According to Dr. Dennis Casey of the U.S. Air Force Intelligence Agency, the French nicknamed her *"la dame qui boite"* and the Germans referred to her as *La Dame Qui Boite,* "the limping lady". Wanted posters began to appear throughout France, offering a reward for the capture of, whom the Gestapo referred to as, "the most dangerous of all Allied spies."
>
> When the Germans suddenly seized all of France in November 1942, Hall had no choice but to flee France by the only route possible, a grueling thirty mile trek on foot through the Pyrénées Mountains into neutral Spain. Rather whimsically, her artificial leg had its own codename "Cuthbert". Before making her escape, she signaled to SOE that she hoped Cuthbert would not give her trouble on the way. The SOE, not understanding the reference, replied, "If Cuthbert becomes troublesome, eliminate him". After working for a time for the SOE in Madrid, she eventually made her way back to London in July 1943.
>
> Hall joined the OSS Special Operations Branch in March 1944 and asked to return to occupied France. She hardly needed training in clandestine work behind enemy lines, and OSS promptly granted her request and landed her from a British MTB [motor torpedo boat] in Brittany since her artificial leg prevented her from parachuting in. Although many believed, having been given the chance, she probably would have attempted it! With a forged French identification certificate for Marcelle Montagne, and the code name "Diane," she eluded the Gestapo and contacted the French Resistance in central France. Her disguise this time was

as an old farm woman. The heavy clothing she wore, coupled with her masquerading as being elderly, gave better cover to hide her awkward gait. She lived with a farmer's family and tended to the cows. She also traveled to the nearby market to sell the farmer's milk and cheese. There, she often overheard German officers in conversation. As soon as she got back to the farm, she pulled out her radio and would wire in any information she obtained. During this time, she mapped drop zones for supplies and commandos from England, found safe houses, and linked up with a Jedburgh team after the Allied forces landed at Normandy. Hall helped train three battalions of Resistance forces to wage guerrilla warfare against the Germans and kept up a stream of valuable reporting until liberating Allied troops overtook her small band in September.

After the war, President Truman wanted to make public the award she was to be given, but Hall refused. She wanted to remain in her line of work and did not want her identity revealed. Instead, a private ceremony was held at the OSS office on September 27, 1945. Virginia Hall was given the Distinguished Service Cross, making her the only American woman, and the first civilian, to be awarded this honor during World War II.

With the defeat of the Japanese, the OSS disbanded and its operations were folded into a new agency, the CIA. In 1950, Hall married former OSS agent Paul Goillot. In 1951, she joined the CIA, working as an intelligence analyst on French parliamentary affairs. She worked alongside her husband as part of the Special Activities Division until mandatory retirement at age 60. She then retired in 1966 to a farm in Barnesville, Maryland, until her death at age of 82.

It is without question that Donovan's influence carried over into the newly created CIA later in life. In particular, four men who served under Donovan in the OSS went on to become directors of the CIA, namely Allen Dulles, Richard Helms, William Casey and William Colby.

Allen Welsh Dulles was the longest serving director from February 1953 to November 1961. To many, this was considered the "golden age" of the CIA. He was the younger brother of U.S. Secretary of State John Foster Dulles. Dulles received an M.A. from Princeton in 1916 and then served in various diplomatic posts until 1922, when he was named chief of the State Department's Near Eastern Division. After receiving a law degree in 1926, he served briefly as counselor to the U.S. delegation in Beijing and then joined the New York law firm of which his brother was a member.

When the United States entered World War II, Dulles was recruited by Donovan. From October 1942 to May 1945, he served as chief of the OSS office in Bern, playing, in particular, a notable role in the events that led to the surrender of German troops in northern Italy. He is credited with running OSS's most successful spy operation against the Axis. After the war, Dulles was put in charge of a three-man committee responsible for surveying the U.S. intelligence system. He later served as deputy director under General Walter Bedell Smith, and in 1953 he was appointed director by President Eisenhower. The agency was effective in a number of major operations, most notably the overthrow of the governments of Mohammad Mosaddeq in Iran in 1953 and Jacobo Arbenz in Guatemala in 1954. It also succeeded in obtaining a copy of Nikita Khrushchev's secret 1956 speech denouncing Joseph Stalin.

While Dulles was director, however, the CIA suffered embarrassment when a U-2 spy plane flown by Francis Gary Powers was shot down by an S-75 Dvina surface-to-air missile over Sverdlovsk in the Soviet Union. This happened on the eve of a scheduled summit conference in June 1960. Reappointed by President John F. Kennedy, Dulles was also implicated in the failure of the Bay of Pigs invasion of Cuba in April 1961 and resigned that fall.

Richard McGarrah Helms headed the CIA from 1966 to 1973. To his supporters he was a patriot who upheld the security of the country above all else, while to critics he typified the worst faults of the CIA. Helms graduated from Williams College, Williamstown, Massachusetts, in 1935 and worked in journalism for several years. He arrived in Germany around Thanksgiving in 1935 as a correspondent for United Press. At that time, Adolf Hitler was wildly popular and the city of Berlin, with a population of four million, was bustling with nervous energy. Hitler had already put a stop to the city's freewheeling lifestyle, emptying it of its best actors, movie technicians, film producers, writers and directors. Museums were closed, books burned and the 149 newspapers shut down. All forms of entertainment were censored. Jewish composers were banned. Instead, movie houses flourished with propaganda films and grand hotels hosted swanky parties for Nazi Government officials, complete with approved starlets hanging on to them.

Helms's first big story came on March 7, 1936, when he was assigned to cover Hitler's noon address to the Reichstag. This event included 600 deputies, all hand-picked by the Führer of course. Helms noticed Hitler passing a handkerchief back and forth between his hands underneath the open lectern. After starting in a soft-tone, typical of Hitler's speeches, he built up to a roar where he declared, "The German Government has re-established, as from today, the absolute and unrestricted sovereignty of the Reich in the demilitarized zone … At this moment German troops are crossing the Rhine bridges and occupying the Rhineland!" Truly a shocking moment. Helms eventually left Berlin in June 1937 and headed back to the United States.

He got involved with the OSS when Fred Oechsner, his old boss from United Press who had joined the OSS, got back in touch. Donovan asked Oechsner to build a new section known as Morale Operations. This section would be responsible for black propaganda, that is, misinformation; stuff that would deceive and confuse the enemy. Since Helms understood German culture and was fluent in the language, he was a natural fit. Now recruited, Helms was then shipped off to Area E, a secret facility outside Washington, D.C., to begin his training. He eventually moved overseas to the Intelligence Branch's Central European and Scandinavian section where he continued to look for ways to penetrate the Third Reich. He died on October 22, 2002, in Washington, D.C.

William Joseph Casey served from January 1981 to January 1987 during the Reagan Administration. Casey graduated from Fordham University with a Bachelor of Science degree in 1934, and eventually earned a law degree from St. John's University in Jamaica, New York, in 1937. While in the OSS, he organized dangerous missions to penetrate Nazi Germany. He coordinated the deployment of 100 Allied paratrooper teams into Europe during the final year of the war. He also enacted propaganda projects with Donovan's blessing. One was code-named *Harvard* and consisted of publishing a weekly four-page newsletter titled *Handel und Wandel* in German. It contained legitimate world economic news sprinkled throughout with defeatist propaganda. It was circulated in Sweden among visiting German industrialists. Casey also actively recruited Stockholm businessmen travelling to Germany to report back to him on plants they visited so Allied planes could later bomb them.

Casey went on to become Reagan's presidential campaign manager which later led to his appointment to the directorship of the CIA in 1981. Under his leadership, covert action increased in such places as Afghanistan, Central America and Angola, and the agency stepped up its support for various anti-communist insurgent organizations. He was considered a pivotal figure in the CIA's secret involvement in the Iran–Contra Affair, in which American weapons were sold to Iran and then the money from the sale was funneled to Nicaraguan rebels, in possible violation of U.S. law. Just before he was to testify in Congress on the matter in December 1986, he suffered seizures and then underwent brain surgery; he died from nervous system lymphoma without ever testifying.

William Egan Colby, while training to become a parachutist at Fort Benning in Georgia, noticed a sheet on the camp bulletin board with OSS stamped at the top. If you spoke French and were looking for adventure overseas, call this number. Well, by nature Colby was the adventurous type. Being the son of an army officer, he grew up in diverse places such as Georgia, Vermont, Panama and China. This taste for seeing new places and experiencing new things drove his curiosity.

He had no idea what OSS stood for, but it sounded a lot more interesting than his current training, which consisted of collecting and assembling 75-millimeter howitzers that were shoved out of airplanes in nine separate packs. After his time in France, Colby returned to England where he was recruited and heavily involved in Operation *Rype*. His role in leading NORSO I (Norwegian Special Operations) in the field is discussed in greater detail later on in this book.

After President Johnson (1963–1969) signed the House Joint Resolution 1145, otherwise known as the Tonkin Gulf Resolution that expanded the president's authority to increase U.S. involvement in the war between North and South Vietnam, the United States' military presence greatly increased in the war. Both Johnson, and later Nixon, used this resolution as the legal rectification for their military policies.

Later on, as war involvement by the United States increased, CIA activity was suspected. During Colby's tenure as CIA Director, from September 1973 to January 1976, he was called to testify before Congress concerning CIA involvement in the Vietnam War and then later in the Watergate scandal. He died on April 27, 1996, while on a solo canoe trip from his weekend home in Rock Point, Maryland. His canoe was found the following day on a sandbar in the Wicomico River, a tributary to the Potomac, about a quarter mile from his home. His body was located on May 6 in a marshy riverbank, lying face down, not far from where his canoe was found. In the official autopsy report, Maryland's Chief Medical Examiner John E. Smialek ruled his death to be accidental. Smialek noted Colby was predisposed to having a heart attack or stroke due to "severe calcified atherosclerosis" and that Colby likely "suffered a complication of this atherosclerosis which precipitated him into the cold water in a debilitated state and he succumbed to the effects of hypothermia and drowned." Regardless, speculation and conspiracy theories abounded that his death was suspicious and possibly caused by foul play, or even suicide.

At its peak in late 1944, the OSS employed around 13,000 men and women, the latter making up more than a third of the workforce. In relative terms, it was a little smaller than a U.S. Army infantry division or a war agency like the Office of Price Administration, which governed prices for many commodities and products in the civilian economy.

The new agency set up headquarters in Washington in the buildings of the National Health Institute, much to the chagrin of the residents who barely had time to pack up their experimental monkeys, baby chicks and ants before they were tossed out into the street. General Donovan employed thousands of officers and enlisted men selected from the armed services. He also found military slots for many of the people who came to the OSS as civilians. U.S. Army and Army Air Force personnel comprised about two-thirds of its strength, with civilians from all walks of life making up another quarter. The remainder were from the Navy, Marines or Coast Guard. About 7,500 OSS employees served overseas. In Fiscal Year 1945, the office spent $43 million, bringing its total spending over its four-year life to around $135 million (almost $1.3 billion in today's dollars).

Secrecy was the watchword, not the tip-toeing cloak-and-dagger mumbo jumbo of spy fiction films. "The crow flies at midnight" password was replaced with the cautious silence of discreet men and women who realized a careless word might endanger lives and jeopardize the entire prospect.

Individuals tapped for this hush-hush society did not mention the fact even to their families. Your husband or son would have told you simply he had been sent on some special army work, probably a brief training period before heading overseas, and no, he wouldn't have an address for a while. In fact, according to OSS protocol, if he was selected for a top-secret operation, he would not even have a name. He would become a number. Along with a group of other numbers, all in the anonymity of army uniforms, he would be driven in a car with curtains drawn to a secret area outside Washington. Under the watchful eye of psychiatrists, he would be put through a grueling three-day screening. If he did not crack, and qualified mentally and emotionally for the task ahead, he would be moved to another, and even more closely guarded, area. This was a super-secret training ground for subversive warfare tactics that operated for three years, more or less. It was no more than an hour's drive from the U.S. Capitol. He would be taught to meet the enemy on the enemy's terms. He would abandon all ideas of clean sportsmanship and learn to fight barehanded, gutter style, with all the associated dirty tactics; a knee in the groin, a savage slash with the side of the hand across the Adam's apple, a jab in the eye with fingers stiffly hooked in a tiger's claw.

With a masked instructor at his elbow, he would move with drawn revolver through a cleverly designed "scare house" that made any Coney Island chamber of horrors amusement attraction look like a toddler's daycare center. Boards would teeter realistically underfoot as he felt his way along a dark hall. Footsteps would echo mysteriously ahead of him. A concealed phonograph would grind out the rumble of guttural German voices around a poker table. The clinking of glasses and slap of cards could be heard. A turn of the corridor would reveal a suddenly lighted dummy dressed in the uniform of a German soldier confronting him. Whirl, fire, but there's someone else in the room just ahead! Quickly reload, safety off, hammer cocked. Burst open the door, fire and fire again.

He would also be taught other black arts: how to blow open a safe, photograph secret documents in an office at night, to set a demolition charge, or remove a fuse from a time bomb. Even transportation-related sabotage was covered, such as the proper way to get abrasives into a truck's motor or a lethal instrument planted into an aircraft that would explode automatically when it reached a certain altitude. This last tactic was actually used to ground much of the *Luftwaffe* at a critical moment during Rommel's advance on Egypt. Many times, the ingenuity of the OSS fighter was needed to improvise on the spot. For example, secret documents were smuggled across an enemy border by an innocent-looking peasant leading a cow whose teats had been dilated and stuffed with rolls of microfilm.

He would also practice short-wave radio, codes, and sending spot weather reports. He would learn to be alert, resourceful and, above all, inconspicuous and silent.

The Special Operations Branch (SO) of OSS first ran guerrilla campaigns in Europe and Asia. As with many other facets of OSS's work, the organization and doctrine of the Branch was guided by British experiences in the growing field of "psychological warfare." British strategists in the year between the fall of France in 1940 and Germany's invasion of the Soviet Union in 1941 had wondered how Britain, which then lacked the strength to force a landing on the European continent, could weaken the Reich and ultimately defeat Hitler. London chose a three-part strategy to utilize the only means at hand: 1) a naval blockade; 2) sustained aerial

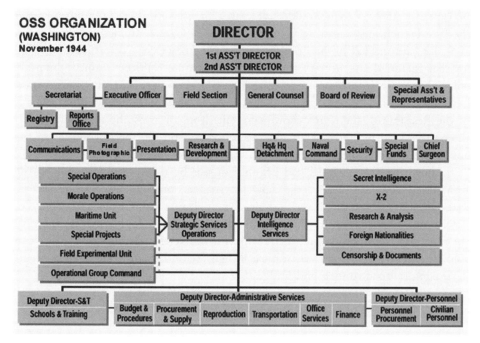

The official organizational chart for Donovan's OSS. However, the OSS was constantly changing organizationally due to a continual state of adaptation to the needs of the war. Later charts were modified to reflect different scopes of activity peculiar to conditions in the various theaters of operation.

bombing, and; 3) subversion of Nazi rule in the occupied nations. A civilian body, the Special Operations Executive (SOE), took command of the latter mission and began planning to set Europe ablaze.

This emphasis on guerrilla warfare and sabotage fit with William Donovan's vision of an offensive endeavor in which saboteurs, guerrillas, commandos, and agents behind enemy lines would support the army's advance. OSS thus seemed the natural point of contact and cooperation with SOE in combined planning and operations when the Anglo–American Combined Chiefs of Staff decided in 1942 that America would join Britain in the business of subversion.

The *Jedburgh* teams parachuted into France in the summer of 1944 to support the Normandy landings. Their motto was "Surprise, kill and vanish." The teams of personnel were from the SO Branch, and the SOE and the French *Bureau Central de Renseignements et d'Action*. Eighty-three American, 90 British, 103 French, five Belgians, and five Dutch personnel were extensively trained in paramilitary techniques for *Jedburgh* missions. Ninety-three Jedburgh teams in all, each of them with two officers and an enlisted radio operator, parachuted into France, and eight went into The Netherlands, where they joined the resistance forces already at work in those countries.

Typically, an OSS man would serve with a British officer and a radioman from the Free French forces loyal to General Charles de Gaulle. Trained as commandos at SOE's Milton Hall in the English countryside, they were a colorful and capable lot that included adventurers and soldiers of fortune. Officers trained alongside enlisted men in informal camaraderie because, once inside France, rank would have to be secondary to courage and ability. After landing (hopefully into the arms of the Resistance), the teams coordinated air drops of arms and supplies, guided the partisans on hit-and-run attacks and sabotage, and did their best to assist the advancing Allied armies.

So now, the shadow wars had begun, but not by those who appeared on the front lines, and headlines of the daily newspapers, but by spies stealing secrets, mathematicians breaking codes, academics analyzing the German economy to determine which crucial industries should be targeted by Allied bombers to cripple the war effort, radio propagandists transmitting messages to demoralize the German soldiers and civilians, operatives trained to fight behind enemy lines, and saboteurs destroying railroad tunnels and bridges.

CHAPTER 10

Prelude to a Mission

Early November 1944 found Lieutenant Colonel Gerhard L. Bolland in Andover, England, in the 507th Parachute Infantry Officers Mess Hall engaged in a conversation with one Captain George Roper.

Bolland: "How's your weekend pass in London, George?"

Roper: "Oh, kind of quiet. Adolf didn't even work his V-2 rocket pile down as far as I could tell. Didn't hear a single boom."

Bolland: "Did you steal any Red Cross girls away from the fly boys?"

Roper: "Naw, not even that, just a few beers, a fairly good meal, slept in late. Oh, I almost forgot. Scuttlebutt has it that there are 50 Norskies pulled from the 10th Mountain Division. Some were on Jedburgh teams that were in France. They have been re-assigned to the OSS and are now being sent to Scotland for training on a potential mission in Norway."

Bolland: "Oh no! Not now! I guessed wrong on the initial assault. I thought it would be in Norway instead of Africa. But now it sounds like Norway will be low profile operations"

Roper: "I noticed on your file card you're bilingual, Norwegian fluent."

Bolland: "Even back in '42, while training in Georgia, got a bunch of books, dictionaries, etc, to bone up. George, you're a skier, aren't you? Do you jump?"

Roper: "Yes, I have a Class B rating."

Bolland: "You ought to join the Norskie boys. I'll bet there's plenty of snow where they're going!"

Roper: "Skiing would be okay, but I can't speak their lingo. Don't reckon the ol' man would let me go anyway."

Bolland: "You know I've been saving my weekend pass for something. I think I'll go over to London town and find out what's cooking with those 50 Norskies. They are still in the OSS, aren't they?"

Roper: "Oh yes, they're getting more parachute training, too."

Bolland: "Most interesting, most interesting."

As the London weekend materialized further, I made, with some dispatch, for the plush environs of the OSS headquarters tucked neatly away in the better part of the city. After proper security checks and a polite wait in the hall, a guard ushered me into a nicely appointed office and an introduction to G. Unger Vetlesen ensued. He was dressed in a naval commander's uniform of the U.S. Navy, a genteel, perspective, gray-haired gentleman of the old school. His manner was quiet and disarming, yet determined. This war was definitely of his own choosing. A guess would put him in the mid-sixties, age-wise. A large map of Norway covered a wall of the room; we were soon to discuss it at great length.

I had learned, or gleaned would probably be a better word, a meager bit of information about the commander. He had been an emigrant from Norway as a young man, settled in Canada and later moved to the U.S. During this period, he had truthfully found his fortune in this new land, and was purportedly a man of considerable financial stature. "Multimillionaire" was the noun used. He was a personal friend of King Haakon VII and Prince Olav. His insight into the power, politics and intrigues of the everyday world were quite a revelation to say the least. He had been commissioned directly from civilian life for his self-appointed task as Chief of the Scandinavian Section of the OSS, directly under General Donovan, OSS's big boss. Any interpolated commands between the two bothered neither, I can assure you, and this worked to some advantage both ways. Commander Vetlesen was a happy choice in this slot and dually appreciated by all his subordinates. We all felt a deep loss later in life at the news of his death.

By the way, regarding King Haakon's time while he was exiled in London, a humorous story made the rounds. One day, when he came into a vestibule-like hall in the British Broadcasting Corporation's (BBC) headquarters, he went up to a young woman who was sitting behind the counter and said, "Good afternoon. I am the King of Norway and I have an appointment with mister so-and-so." She looked up at the lanky fellow with a large mustache in front of her, who was wearing an old raincoat and holding a gray felt hat in his hand and said, "Pleased to meet you, King. And I am the Queen of Sheba!" The King bowed to her and said, "I have always wanted to meet the Queen of Sheba. I can't tell your majesty how delighted I am to make your majesty's acquaintance." And they kept on joshing back and forth like that until a door opened to an office quite some distance away and one of the top officials of the BBC came out. He bowed and said, "Your Majesty, please come in." The King walked toward him and, when he came to the door of that office, he turned around and waved with a smile to the young woman.

After an exchange of pleasantries about places in Norway, my grandparents' birthplaces, etc., the conversation gradually took a more serious turn. Even at the start there were searching, leading questions prying about things which were irrelevant; or were they? It was time to the take the "bull by the horns" so to speak, and the following conversation did just that.

Bolland: "I'm interested in an operation in Norway. I hear you have OGP's[1] now back, from Underground assignments in France, here in the UK, getting ready for a job in Norway."

Vetlesen: "Well, that's partially correct. We anticipate increased action there shortly. Right now, some are busy training at the British Parachute School prior to movement. The best terrain and conditions available here and most closely resembling those found in Norway.

My morale sank. Yet was there a "joker in the deck?" to be found in that third-degree dialogue I had just experienced? I didn't have long to wait.

Vetlesen: "I have just recently set up an operation for northern Norway called *Husky*. It's a solo job. We haven't settled on anyone to take it yet. Would you take it?"

Bolland: "Well, that depends. What is it?"

Vetlesen: "The King is worried. Rumor has it that a foreign power is busy at this moment surveying a proposed railroad from Finland to Narvik in search of an all-year, ice-free harbor. We feel it is more than rumor. This *Husky* operation is an intelligence probe to be conducted on the ground as soon as possible. We both know the candidate cannot be detected by any person, friendly or enemy, and needs to bring back the message to Garcia. There's about six feet of snow up there now and below zero temperatures this time of year. It's a rough one! What do you say?"

A strange silence crept over the proceedings. This was a shocker to say the least. Frankly, at that moment I was damn badly bewildered while trying desperately to maintain some sort of an outward appearance of composure. The seconds seemed to become longer. This was becoming an embarrassing delay.

The commander never let his gaze wander from mine. So, what happened next? I opened my big mouth and said, "I'll accept on one condition. That if I survive, you'll give me operational troops in Norway."

Vetlesen: "That's fine with me."

We shook hands. The commander, having General Donovan's ear and he in turn President Roosevelt's, had my orders issued and routed back to me in around three days.

---

1 Operational Group Personnel or "bodies" as the OSS called them.

CHAPTER 11

The Scandinavian Section, OSS London

I reported to Commander Vetlesen for duty shortly after Thanksgiving Day, 1944. The Scandinavian section was hidden in an old brown building about six blocks from Marble Arch. It housed the OSS and its English counterpart as well as the Norwegian Underground section, which was being continuously built up as Norwegians escaped from the Quisling Nazi regime and reported to the chief, a Lieutenant Colonel Oien of the Royal Norwegian Air Force. When France fell, Winston Churchill, in June 1940, set up the Special Operations Executive to train exiles from German-occupied nations to conduct sabotage so they could return to their homelands and have an effect on the war.

All unit identification markings were dispensed with. Parachute badges, combat infantry badges, battle stars, etc., met the same fate. Ostensibly, I was part of the quieter rear echelon of the Supreme Headquarters Allied Expeditionary Force. Even walking to and from our working quarters was done as casually and inconspicuously as possible. No conversation regarding our tasks outside the building was permitted. We used a scrambled telephone line and the voices heard on them bore not the slightest resemblance to the person talking. Security clearances were secured with power to classify orders as Top Secret. With very little initial briefing, I was tucked in a small desk over in the corner with the instructions to study all available maps and information relative to Operation *Husky*. I was told a final briefing would be given at the appropriate time. Incidentally, an opportunity to secure whatever type gear necessary or desired, plus special funds to buy things commercially that were not generally available in either the U.S. or British military supply facilities, were provided prodigiously. OSS was definitely not cost conscious.

I began to embark immediately on the task at hand of securing the proper equipment. Of course, there were the inevitable suicide pills. In addition, an escape kit was developed. It was small, flat and could be readily concealed in personal equipment or clothing, fitting into a five-inch-by-five-inch pouch. It consisted of a small compass, nine-sixteenths of an inch in diameter, a four-inch by half-inch escape saw, a silk escape map that was both waterproof and noiseless when unfolded, and three document-sized one-and-three-quarter inch by one-and-a-half inch photographs that were prepared while wearing civilian clothes. These photographs were to be carried in the escape kits and used in the preparation of forged escape documents. Of course, everything was impervious to a dunking in water.

All of a sudden I was becoming increasingly aware of the fine balance between the necessary weight to be carried and my mobility under a sustained chase. These equipment procurements for what I thought would be a solo endeavor for *Husky* ended up becoming a precursor to the future needs for Operation *Rype*.

CHAPTER 12

The Inception and Importance of Operation *Rype*

Early on, it became obvious Norway figured into the German war plans. Admiral Erich Raeder and Reichsmarschall Hermann Göring saw the advantages of seizing Scandinavian naval and air bases. The admiral took the lead in convincing Adolf Hitler that force must be used to insure Germany's continued access to 11 million tons of iron ore from Swedish mines. The Third Reich depended on this consumption for its military hardware. It was transported by rail to Narvik and other Norwegian warm-water ports and then delivered through the Norwegian territorial waters to the Baltic.

By 1942, Norway's military resistance organization, Milorg, was virtually shut down by the Germans. The harsh reprisals by the *Gestapo* on Milorg members convinced many Norwegians to become more passive. Allied forces were concerned whether Norwegians could keep secret any covert operations carried out by commando teams.

The Allies developed a plan, called *Jupiter*, which proposed an attack on northern Norway. It was changed to a carefully orchestrated scenario of deception called *Fortitude North* in August 1942 at the insistence of Winston Churchill. He wanted Hitler to remain convinced the Allies would launch a flank attack on Norway at any time, even up to the time of the demise of the Third Reich in May 1945. This deception forced Hitler to transfer practically all of his remaining German naval units to Norway. He also gave high priority to the task of turning the Norwegian coast into an impregnable fortress.

In 1944 and 1945, the Germans had the notion that, should the Fatherland fall to the Allies, the 350,000 German troops would make a last stand in "Festung Norwegen." After D-Day, Supreme Headquarters Allied Expeditionary Force wanted to sabotage the railroads in northern Norway to prevent massive German troop movements to the south. The Germans were retreating from the Russian Army through the northern province of Finnmark. The Allies held back on this action because the expected collapse of German lines on the Continent itself had not taken place.

Initially, Allied air force officers were convinced their ever-strengthening armadas could bomb Germany into submission regardless of location. This meant targets of occupied countries were not exempt. There were heated discussions at our London office. A major split developed between the British and American air force officers and the Norwegians. Under no circumstances would the Norwegians approve an air campaign against Norwegian targets. Such a campaign would threaten destruction of plants and port facilities, collapsing the industrial base on which the country's post-war recovery depended.

Allied policy changed in November 1944. German reinforcements from northern Norway would only prolong the war if they could reach the continental fronts. Since Milorg was virtually non-existent in northern Norway by this time, the primary mission of any covert operation was to disrupt the Nordland rail line as a means of transportation for German troops. Its secondary objective, given the Allied policy of unconditional surrender, was to disarm overwhelmingly superior German forces in an orderly manner should such a surrender occur.

I was still officially involved with Operation *Husky* when, in January 1945, Lieutenant Colonel Hans Skabo approached me and ordered me to write up the formal operational orders, and work up the equipment and supplies for a new operation to be carried out by the Norwegian Special Operations (NORSO) Group. The codename given for this new operation was *Rype* (pronounced "Ree-pah"). It is the Norse word for Ptarmigan, a game bird that was plentiful in our operational area and changes colors in the winter. They are, incidentally, also found in larger numbers in Alaska. Thus, Operation *Rype* was officially born.

If there was one word to describe the major objective of Operation *Rype*, it would be sabotage. In fact, *Rype* was one of many successful sabotage actions carried out by Allied teams against the Axis powers during World War II. Rather than an isolated operation, *Rype* was part of a larger Allied scheme of unconventional warfare against the Germans with all such actions being carefully orchestrated by Allied Joint Commanders from London and Washington to strategic locations across the globe.

The *Rype* team first formulated and began its training in 1943 at Camp Hale, Colorado. Almost 1,000 Norwegians, mostly exiles and merchant seamen, and Americans of Scandinavian descent, gathered at Camp Hale to train in mountain warfare. Their unit, the 99th Infantry Battalion (Separate), was earmarked for Norway's liberation from German occupation. They were to become experts in skiing. The U.S. Government assumed everyone of Scandinavian descent was an excellent skier, but that was not always the case.

Originally the formation of the 99th Infantry Battalion took place on July 10, 1942, when the War Department activated it at Camp Ripley in Minnesota. From the outset, it was intended this unit would only consist of Norwegian nationals, that is aliens, or aliens with first papers. The authorized strength was to be 931 enlisted men. The infantry battalion would consist of 884 enlisted men, with 36 in the medical detachment, 11 in the transportation platoon, and officers of Norwegian extraction who could speak Norwegian. These officers would eventually be replaced by Norwegian nationals once they graduated from officer candidate schools.

Louise Borden, in her book *Ski Soldier, A World War II Biography*, gives an excellent account of Pete Seibert. He was one of the men who trained at Camp Hale with the 10th Mountain Division and later saw action on Riva Ridge, a seemingly impossible assault on a string of peaks in the Apennines of northern Italy.

Leif Oistad, an excellent skier, taught many officers how to ski well. "If you can't out-ski the Germans, you will not return." Training began in earnest in mountain climbing, fording rivers and canyons, and the arduous task of hauling supplies and weapons.

Two high-ranking Norwegian officers, Oberstløytnant Munthe-Kass and Oberstløytnant A. H. Dahl, visited Camp Hale, as did representatives of the Office of Strategic Services (OSS). They were there to recruit and select candidates out of the ranks of the 99th Infantry Battalion. Since the 99th was mostly Norwegians, with a few Finns and Swedes thrown in, it was logical to look to them for possible recruits.

The interviews began with a team statement that the OSS "was looking for men to volunteer for extra hazardous duty behind enemy lines in Norway." The men were interviewed in Norwegian. These interviews were also the first to assess the psychological profiles of the candidates to go on suicide missions. They were told they would have to take parachute training if chosen.

Out of one thousand men of the U.S. Army's 99th Infantry Battalion (Separate), 84 volunteers were initially chosen for the NORSO Groups. Forty percent of this unit consisted of Norwegian merchant sailors stranded in North America without a home port after the German occupation. The rest were American volunteers of Scandinavian descent. While in training at Camp Hale, the OSS conducted extensive interviews and continued to ask 99th members if they would volunteer for very hazardous missions behind enemy lines in Norway. Once these men were selected, vigorous training would begin in commando tactics at both American and British military facilities.

Final selections were narrowed down and the OSS sent the following men to Washington, D.C., for additional training:

Rank/Name/Serial Number (ASN)
Captain Harold Larson 0-408800
1st Lt. William F. Larsen 01292011
1st Lt. Harry L. Solberg 01294032
2nd Lt. Erik J. Andersen 01295649
2nd Lt. Birger Berg 01317260
2nd Lt. Ralph N. Elsmo 01552483
2nd Lt. Reider J. Grunseth 01308635

2nd Lt. Melvin J. Hjeltness 01291641
2nd Lt. Adolf Lieum 01310732
2nd Lt. Tom Sather 01305655
S/Sgt. Einar A. Eliassen 6871912
S/Sgt. Alvin Toso 37081378
Sgt. Alf G. Amesen 20285570
Sgt. Kenneth R. Johnson 37271917
Sgt. Edward E. Kjelness 39230883
T/ 4th Sigurd T. Gilbertson 32109847
T/4th Einar Kristiansen 13143869
T/4th Curtis Olson 17011137
Cp1. Sigurd M. Baro 32424096
Cpl. Trygve Berge 39031393
Cpl. John I. Halvorsen 32172154
Cpl. Kai O. C. Johansen 32624833
Cpl. Karl Larsen 31157147
Cpl. Lars Motland 32312707
Cpl. Erling Olsen 32597128
Cpl. Olav S. Reinholdtsen 32423629
Cpl. John Sunde 32497497
T/5th Marinus D. Myrland 32708477
T/5th Johannes S. Rorvick 37311880
T/5th Morris A. Syrstad 17017008
T/5th Otto Twingley 37272189
T/5th Arthur J. Westgard 37168513
Pfc. Olaf H. Aanonsen 3244967 7
Pfc. Sverre Aanonsen 32502869
Pfc. Siewert Dymbe 36261072
Pfc. Leif Eide 37096441
Pfc. Olaf J. Eide 36628943
Pfc. Knut J. Falck 32421335
Pfc. Hans H. Flater 32429065
Pfc. Asmund Gravdal 32498841
Pfc. Olaf Hall 32260389
Pfc. Harry A. Hansen 32804609
Pfc. Arne I. Herstad 39193561
Pfc. Berger I. Hjelvik 37543019
Pfc. Arne M. Hoff 36711189
Pfc. Finn E. Hoff 32408508
Pfc. Adolf I. Hogfoss 39378559

Pfc. Nels Huus 39389700
Pfc. Knute Joa 39826167
Pfc. Rudolf Johannesen 32616086
Pfc. Torleif B. Johansen 32108856
Pfc. Lars S. Larsen 32259479
Pfc. Arne N. Listeid 32423677
Pfc. Harold E. Ness 36381243
Pfc. Halvor H. Nipe 32423623
Pfc. Gjerulf Ottersland 32624142
Pfc. Lars N. Rottinger 32497632
Pfc. Tosten Rusdal 39614529
Pfc. Hakon A. Skgolsvik 32428443
Pfc. Eddie O. Sondeno 39614907
Pfc. Oddberg Stiansen 32721719
Pfc. Bernhard W. Tallaksen 32248895
Pfc. Christopher Torper 32541582
Pfc. Hartwick E. Weberg 36626931
Pvt. Harold Anderson 32880527
Pvt. Mike Baarsvik 32624289
Pvt. Randolph Kristiansen 33737566
Pvt. Borge Langeland 32876287
Pvt. Rolf Lilleby 32721635
Pvt. Leif E. Meland 32869494
Pvt. Leif Oistad 32502646
Pvt. Sverre B. Rogne 32497506
Pvt. Erling K. Salvesen 32797393
Pvt. Paul P. Thomle 36802727

At the time, the OSS had several training facilities, mostly around the Washington, D.C., area. They were simply referred to by a letter designation:

Area A was located in Quantico, Virginia, and used primarily for Special Operations training.

Area B was used for paramilitary training and is now the Camp David presidential retreat.

Area C was also located in Quantico, Virginia, and used for communications training.

Area D was also located in Quantico, Virginia, and used for maritime training.

Area E was located north of Baltimore and used for OSS basic training.

Area F was actually the Congressional Country Club and used for Operational Group training.

Station S was located in Fairfax, Virginia, and used for assessment.

Station W was located near Georgetown and also used for assessment of clerical and service personnel.

There was also a Camp X located in Canada above Lake Ontario, between the towns of Oshawa and Whitby, in the province of Ontario. This was actually the first combined British and OSS operational training facility while the others around Washington, D.C., were being constructed. Camp X played such an important role in the war that the head of the British Security Coordination, Sir William Stephenson, referred to it as the "clenched fist" of all Allied secret operations in World War II. It is rumored that Ian Fleming, the English author, journalist and naval intelligence officer, drew from his underwater frogman experiences at Camp X to come up with his James Bond character.

Once in Washington, D.C., the 99th Battalion recruits were taken to Area F, the grounds of the Congressional Country Club. Major W. E. Fairbairn, Major Joe Alderdyce and Captain Al Cox taught the candidates hand-to-hand combat there. Detachments of Greeks, French and Italians also arrived in late 1943 to undergo commando training. Alf Paulsen, a farmer from Crosby, North Dakota, was also interviewed by the OSS. He was stationed in Louisiana and was never a member of the 99th Infantry Battalion but was proficient in Norwegian. Paulsen was asked by his interviewers if he was a volunteer for hazardous duty. Paulsen replied, "The whole U.S. Army was hazardous duty." He was put down as a volunteer and sent directly to the Congressional Country Club for commando training by the OSS. Paulsen had never seen a country club and was curious how the elite lived. "Some country club!," he exclaimed. Tents were pitched around the clubhouse and the fairways of the golf course were used as commando training courses. The thickets on the sides were denser than many jungles. It was difficult to sneak up on opponents without being detected. Booby traps were everywhere. The men were trained in the art of Oriental warfare including hand-to-hand combat, weapons use and night patrols. Cadres of young officers were recruited from Fort Benning, Georgia, with the aid of General Donovan since parachuting was a key to the success of OSS operations. These officers, in turn, were to train others.

When the Norwegian detachment arrived, they were taken out at seven in the morning for training and they did not return until midnight. A small Marine raider unit acted as the Germans. NORSO continued training at Area B, or "Shangri-La" as it was nicknamed, then on to Popponesset Beach and Martha's Vineyard to train for more night patrols, compass reading and boat attacks. They also made amphibious assaults on a "secret" radar installation. Demolitions and calisthenics continued to be the norm.

One of the men on these training exercises gave this account:

> One last exercise, [was] a real problem before we went overseas. The site was a radar station called Gay Head, located on Martha's Vineyard. Most of the boys were transported by LST

[landing ship, tank] boats and used assault boats on landing. Einar Christianson and his men camouflaged these boats to await our return. Radar was new and secret. This installation was guarded by a high electrical fence with guards walking in pairs. The personnel were highly trained Marines! The Marines were [made] aware of this simulated attack sometime during the week. We landed and alerted no one. At one time it was suggested getting Manners and throwing him over the fence to mark with chalk the ammunition dumps, the shops and equipment.

After several days of watching, it was decided we would go thru the main gate, where one can get in, one can get out. Instead of a thorough search we found that the guards let in vehicles by certain flicks of their lights at different times of day. It was rumored that James Cagney had a summer home on Martha's Vineyard and reported some large, rough, foreign speaking men had invaded the island. It happened fast. Captain Saether took over. The observation post reported three trucks, with personnel for an evening of fun had come thru the gates. Before they had advanced a mile, they were high-jacked by our Norwegian OGs who were black faced and camouflaged. The Marines were unloaded, sent into the woods and tied up Fairbairn style. Saether spoke Norwegian and worked fast. He told me I was in charge to guard them and I made a mistake. "Yes, Sir!" The top Sergeant immediately asked me, "What the hell was going on?" Out comes Saether's knife and a gesture across the "prisoner's" throat and saying, "If he makes a move, slit his throat". Again, "Yes, Sir!" I'm sure I could see all these men turning white even though it was dusk. Two trucks, now with our men made a perfect execution. They chalked up everything, abandoned the trucks, threw away the distributor caps and all climbed aboard the third truck, heading for our escape boats. We ran out of gas and walked the last mile where Christianson and his men were ready for us. Three things happened. The LST of the Army went afoul, they called the Navy who ran aground, so the Coast Guard came to our rescue. Officers all the way to Washington got into lots of trouble over this raid. Although tired, dirty, bearded and smelly, the EM looked very innocent. Come to think of it, I wonder if that Marine Sergeant and his men are still tied to the trees![1]

NORSO left in December 1943 for more training in Wales. Of the men that made up the final allotment, twelve were officers. Later, in April 1944, Director Donovan would put out an Operational Groups (OG) Field Manual stating OGs would ideally consist of four officers and 30 men each, but, for now, NORSO consisted of two groups and a station complement. Each group had two sections. A section was 16 men. The section was further broken down into two squads. Each squad had a leader with either a medic or a radio operator and six more men. Each section also had an officer. Once in Wales they proceeded to Northland Lodge near Inverness, Scotland. The majority of training was skiing exercises. It was here NORSO spent its first Christmas overseas and experienced a slight case of food poisoning. Then on to Stronelairg Castle near Loch Ness for over six months more of ski and demolition training. NORSO then went to Weedon, England, and Brock Hall which served as the base of operations for over a year. From there on to Ringway for additional parachute and balloon jump training. NORSO finally ended up at Dalnaglar Castle, Perthshire, Scotland, in the Grampians area for extensive training, the area being quite similar to Norway's rugged terrain.

---

1 30th Reunion of the OSS held October 10–12 in Minneapolis, Minnesota; Newsletter produced October 25, 1975.

Dalnaglar Castle.

Norwegian and Greek OGs training at Dalnaglar Castle, 1945. (Courtesy Linda Hall)

Lt. Roger Hall and Cpl. Leif Eide parachute training off the roof at Dalnaglar Castle, 1945. (Courtesy Linda Hall)

Lt. Roger Hall jumping off the roof at Dalnaglar Castle, 1945. (Courtesy Linda Hall)

Earlier on in the war, on March 28, 1940, Winston Churchill proposed the Royal Navy mine the passage through Norwegian coastal waters to deny their use to Germany. If Germany could be cut off from all Swedish ore supplies, it would be a severe blow to its war-making capacity. On April 8, England announced this had been accomplished.

Now, during the latter stages of the war, because the Royal Navy had successfully mined Norway's coastal waters, it became more apparent the Nordland rail line was viewed as the only viable way for the Germans to move their troops south to the Continent where they would be needed during the final battles. Thus, Operation *Rype*'s primary mission was to cut the rail line at two points in the North Trøndelag area and destroy bridges, making it impossible for the Germans to move their estimated half a million troops to reinforce their armies after the D-Day invasion. These included over 150,000 crack German ski and mountain troops the Red Army had pushed out of Finland towards the end of 1944. Later studies, conducted by historians some 70 years later, put German troop strength in all of Norway at just over 600,000 for the month of November 1944. For this reason, Operation *Rype* was considered to be of high strategic importance.

The secondary objective also remained in place. That was, if needed and given the Allied policy of unconditional surrender, to disarm the overwhelmingly superior German forces in an orderly manner.

CHAPTER 13

Meeting the NORSO Group Personnel

Back to our brown brick building hideaway in London. This is where I first met the aforementioned Lieutenant Colonel Hans H. Skabo, Office of Strategic Services' (OSS) Norwegian Special Operations (NORSO) Group Operation, the Chief of the Scandinavian Section. He was from Indianapolis, Indiana. A member of the U.S. Army Engineer Corps and a native-born Norwegian, Hans was the original instigator of the NORSO Group. He had gathered about 50-odd Norskies together for the job, including those from the 99th Mountain Battalion that had trained at Camp Hale. Some had already been bloodied on multi-national *Jedburgh* team operations for the OSS in France. They conducted sabotage and guerrilla warfare in occupied France, the Netherlands and Belgium and led local resistance forces in actions against the Germans. They were excellent personnel indeed!

As a young man during World War I, Hans joined the U.S. Army in France and fought as a sergeant in the American Expeditionary Forces. After the war he became a naturalized citizen, settled in the Midwest, Indiana to be specific, and became a highway engineer in civilian life. He retained his military interests by joining the Indiana National Guard and had, by World War II, attained the rank of lieutenant colonel.

Hans had been an adventurous person all his life. He took on the challenges of jumping the largest ski jump in Oslo, the Holmenkollen. Even as a young man he drove race cars in the Indianapolis 500. He had served in the Norwegian merchant fleet during winter maneuvers no less, eking out a frugal existence on the barren rock peninsulas, considerable forests and miles and miles of coastlines. Many Norwegian boys "ventured forth in the world" in such a way. The ultimate challenge was to serve on a Norwegian whaling ship operating in Arctic waters in the dead of winter. That became the "mark of a man." Fortunately, some of my people on NORSO I and II had that experience. It proved to be invaluable.

So now World War II found Hans right back where he started, after Germans. He and I became the best of friends. We spoke the same language. He was liked by everyone and a terrific leader under the hardships and stress of combat. Hans had gotten the NORSO Group together and it moved to the northern area. Area P as we called it in the OSS. He was desperately trying to get a waiver on age to qualify as a parachutist to lead his NORSO Group into action and a chance to go back to the land of his birth. However, due to his advanced years, higher headquarters kept frowning upon it. He kept firing request after request for parachute training but the answer "no" kept coming back. He finally gave up and settled down to the task of getting an operation into the field.

Some of the men from Area P would come to London on weekends and naturally report to the Scandinavian section of OSS Headquarters. There I met First Lieutenant Tom Sather, a Norwegian-born American citizen. He was raised in Tromsø and infantry commissioned as a doughboy, always a correct title for a fighting man. He was probably fitted with skis the same time he obtained his first walking shoes; Tom was an excellent skier to say the least. He was one of the few who could handle the ski jelka, a type of ski trailer, with great skill. Give Tom some rope and a few boards and he'd rig up most anything you needed; a great improviser. Tom had also been a Norwegian merchant sailor. On April 9, 1940, he was stranded on a Norwegian vessel in the harbor of Long Beach, California, with the same ambition to enlist. The immigration authorities were reluctant to give him a green card so he could not even find work in the United States, let alone gain permission to enlist. In late 1942, the Army eventually allowed Sather to enlist, commissioning him as a second lieutenant in early 1943. He mastered English and chose to serve in a Norwegian unit, a bilingual battalion of the 10th Mountain Division which trained at Camp Carson, Colorado, before going overseas. He stood about six feet, two inches, 190 lbs, rawboned, mean and intent upon doing something about the Nazi occupation of his dearly beloved homeland. NORSO gave him his chance.

While up in northern Scotland, Tom told the story of some of the other men in the NORSO group. They decided to augment their diet with some fresh fish. One of them made the announcement he was going out to catch a mess of fish for the group's larder so they might enjoy fresh fish for their next meal. The question was raised whether he had the proper equipment. He stated he really didn't need any. He could get enough fish in his own manner. Tom watched the man go down to the mountain stream and crouch beside it. When a desirable fish came by, with one swipe of the hand the fish was landlocked and in his power. This procedure continued until enough fish were secured for the evening meal.

Tom's father, Carl Sather Sr., operated the British Counsel for British interests in the Tromso North Cape area of Norway. He had extensive interests in the shipping industry, especially whaling in the Spitsbergen region. He had even helped equip, and saw to the safety and wellbeing of, many world Arctic explorers so they didn't freeze to death on their safari type ventures into the Arctic regions. That is, if you could call a trip into the Arctic region a "safari." Incidentally, Carl Sather Sr. owned the icebreaker *North Star* which he later sold to Bernt Balchen for Admiral Byrd's expedition to the South Pole. A colorful person if ever there was one.

On one of the weekends, I was privileged to meet, not necessarily a giant, but a large, powerful man by the name of Edward E. Kjelness, a staff sergeant in the NORSO Group. He would be assigned various tasks because of his tremendous feats of strength. One of them would be to always accompany the jeep along the slushy, snowy roads. In the event it became bogged down, Kjelness would disembark, go to the stuck wheel side and physically lift it out of the rut. Later on, during training, I learned of a humorous account of his physical powers. Kjelness was visiting a pub, which he did occasionally in the evening or on weekends, and met with some of his friends. Among them was a Scotsman who he had become quite friendly with, an acquaintance from previous social gatherings. In the exchange of greetings, Kjelness was so happy to see him that he took his large hand and clamped it down on his friend's shoulder. Upon removing his hand, he forgot to release his grip. Lo and behold, the Scotsman's sleeve ended up in the air and fell to the floor. Kjelness instantly belted out a profuse apology and offered remuneration to soothe the Scotsman's miffed feelings. They ended up becoming even closer as friends before the evening ended.

In another story, Kjelness was stationed up at Dalnaglar Castle. His room was quite small and he suffered from a temporary bout of claustrophobia. He decided he needed more space and air. As a result, he went right through the plywood wall into the next room. That was Kjelness.

Next, I learned of a man called Borge O. Langeland, a technical sergeant. I was very impressed by the twinkle in his eye and knew he was a sharp man. Delving into his history, I learned he was born in Flekkefjord, Norway. Before the war broke out, he served in the Norwegian merchant fleet. While serving as second mate and radio operator on board the Norwegian vessel *Grenanger*, they were attacked, on May 2, 1943, and sunk by the German U-boat *U-120*. After surviving seven days in a lifeboat, he was rescued by the United States Coast Guard and taken to the Virgin Islands. He then volunteered for service in the U.S. Army, joined the 99th Infantry Battalion and proceeded to join the 10th Mountain Division bilingual battalion for service on the Scandinavian peninsula as the war developed. Because of his excellent radio skills, he was selected to join the OSS. His reputation already preceded our meeting.

I heard of quite an unusual incident on his trip to Britain from the U.S. He was en route in a convoy that became fogbound off Newfoundland and came to a grinding halt. There it floundered, daring not to move, fearing collision, and yet, at the same time, becoming splendid targets for U-boat attacks. Langeland's brow furrowed. He'd already had one harrowing experience with a U-boat. Everyone was naturally uneasy. Somehow, he got word to the convoy commander that there was a young tow-headed Norski ex-sailor popping off with information on how he could get the convoy moving pronto. What an astounding statement coming from a young man speaking English with a Scandinavian accent, and one who recently joined the army at Camp Hale after escaping the grips of German occupation in Norway! The idea that he could make it possible to move this convoy through fog without collision must have been met with a lot of skepticism. Grasping at straws, I imagine, the convoy commander gave him an ear. Langeland simply said, "I can move it. All I need is lots of rope and a couple of logs." Those were furnished. Langland tied the logs in such a manner as to create a lot of foam and splashing. The logs were then swung out to the sides of the lead ship from the furthest protruding mast or available place of fastening. The result was a frothy wake that was clearly visible. The men steering the ships to the right and left behind the lead were then ordered to keep the logs in constant vision and stay just outside them. That was the model for the remaining ships, copied as needed. Thus, Langeland's contraption resulted in "full speed ahead" and the convoy was once more in motion, slicing through the fog to England.

As a footnote to Langeland's military career, after World War II he returned to military sea transport services where he initially worked in the Panama Canal area. He would later go on to receive a battlefield commission and be awarded both the Purple Heart and Bronze Star for valor in combat civilian duty with the Department of the Navy as captain of the USNS *Card* (T-AKV-40). During one of these voyages, after finishing delivering shipments of helicopters and fighter-bombers to Manila in the Philippines, the *Card* sailed to Saigon Harbor in Vietnam to await a load of old helicopters to be returned to the United States. The loading itself was done by civilian Vietnamese stevedores. One of them, by the name of Lam Son Nao, planned to sabotage the *Card* when he learned it would be arriving in Saigon on April 30, 1964. In Nao's words:

> I was educated by the revolution, given a mission by my superiors and protected by the city inhabitants. My job when I was a docker was to gather information on all the American areas, on all their boats and all their military storage facilities. When I found out that the USS *Card* was coming up the river—this was a ship which was carrying all kinds of airplanes to the country in order to kill the Vietnamese people—I got extremely mad. But I was able to turn my anger into action when I was given the job of trying to blow the ship up in order to give support to the political struggles of the city population.

Nao was able to bribe the port police, crawl through the narrow sewer system across the entire dockyard, then swim into the water undetected, plant two mines on the hull of the ship and set them to go off at 3am. Nao's sabotage was successful. Captain Langeland recalled the attack:

> The explosion hammered through the ship, jarring the engine room attendants. The ship began to take on water immediately, forcing several crewmen to hurriedly evacuate their quarters. The crew immediately closed off the lower compartments.

Miraculously, no one was killed. Sections of the ship's steel railings and planks from the pier ended up across the wharf and the superstructure was bent by the blast. Captain Langeland saw his ship sink in Saigon Harbor. Ironically, his old friend William Colby served as CIA Station Chief in Saigon two years before the attack, from 1959 to 1962.

Langeland ended up becoming my radio operator and came in on the first NORSO schedule, four hours after the parachute drop into about six feet of snow near the Arctic Circle. That night he sent an understandable message back to Net Control in London 700 miles away. Quite a trick because the radio was no bigger than a portable suitcase set. Inside was a British Type B, Mark 2 radio powered by a 6-volt battery. The radio itself had crystals that could transmit six different frequencies. These frequencies were assigned and altered for each scheduled transmission. We also had concerns about the operators receiving and sending messages from England. They were mostly young women and members of the exclusive British women's organization, the First Aid Nursing Yeomanry of the Princess Royal's Volunteer Corps. They had been hurriedly trained as radio operators and, in Langeland's opinion, graduated too soon. Despite these circumstances, communication was maintained with England on a regular basis. Incidentally, I tried to talk Langeland into accepting a commission in the regular army after hostilities, but without luck.

A Norwegian by the name of Torsten Rusdal comes into focus. He was a tree topper on the west coast before the war. To the NORSO Group he became just plain "Tom." His rank was Technician 5 which had the chevrons with a "T" in the design. A guy you'd think twice about mixing with in a bar room brawl, he was hard as nails and built just like Jim Taylor, the 1960s fullback for the Green Bay Packers football team. It seems he had violated some rule back in Area P at Dalnaglar Castle. The major then commanding the NORSO Group decided to bust him down to a private. That was done, but the next day Torsten appeared, minus his stripes but still with the "T" on his sleeve. The major asked him why he hadn't also removed the "T," to which Tom replies, "Ya'll can have my stripes but ya'll can't have the "T" 'cause that stands for Tom, and that's me." The major didn't have guts enough to carry out his order. At the time, that eventually became a problem. Lack of discipline and toughness created morale chaos in the group. Upon consideration, the decision was made to secure a new commanding officer.

Enter the familiar Major William E. Colby. He had just returned from France where he was involved with *Jedburgh* team *Bruce*. They helped protect Patton's vulnerable right flank as his tanks roared across France. Free from his work there and back at OSS Headquarters, he was now looking for another job. Colby was a graduate of Princeton. Sharp, gutsy, with plenty of savvy, and he already had experience in the field; he was looking for a small operational group. The feeling was, "Let's grab him quick." He was ordered to Area P in command of the entire detachment, quickly earning the respect of the unit who soon gave him the title of "Skin and Guts," a deviation of "Blood and Guts," General Patton's nickname. "Skin" because he probably weighed all of 130 pounds soaking wet. Soon after Colby took charge, morale was up and training took a serious turn in preparation for the pending mission to Norway. Incidentally, William Colby, Sr., Bill Colby's dad, was a regular army infantry colonel, so Bill was raised right, despite the field artillery branch he was commissioned in.

One of Colby's recruits was Glenn Farnsworth who was born in Chicago and grew up in Baltimore. He had attended officer's training school, but his specialty was demolitions; a perfect fit for the intended sabotage operations to be carried out in Norway. Besides, he had already been involved in *Jedburgh* operations, having parachuted into France in 1944.

One day in came a harried young Norseman by the name of Hans Hoel. That was his Underground name. His real name was Herbert Helgesen, a meat-packing plant owner from Trondheim, Norway. He had quite a story. When Norway was attacked, he joined the infantry in Nord Trøndelag and saw action near Steinkjer. The German advances, however, overwhelmed the Norwegian forces and they were forced to retreat to the northern reaches. Helgesen was active in the resistance work around Trondheim and later had to flee to Sweden with his wife Anna. Due to the harsh conditions, and the fact that Anna was pregnant, she died on the journey while they were attempting an escape by skiing to the Swedish border. She was killed by a German border patrol. Helgesen later made it into Sweden and joined up with Norwegian counterparts there responsible for deciphering information coming in from the Trøndelag area. Later, he made his way to England and joined us as a liaison to the NORSO Group. He became an invaluable asset and carried about him an attitude the Germans had taken from him so dearly, so now he had only one reason to live: to eradicate the Nazi scourge, especially from his beloved homeland. He reported to Lieutenant Colonel Oien, the Norwegian section boss. Oien let us have him. He was sent up to Colby, given a quick parachute training program, and became invaluable on our entry into the field in northern Norway. He had contacts within the now quite highly organized Norwegian Underground.

Another story of heroics from one of our NORSO team members is worth mentioning. His name was Harold (Hans) Larsen whom Herbert Helgesen picked up for our operation shorty after Colby got in. Larsen had been incarcerated in Grini prison camp, Norway, and treated harshly for his non-cooperative behavior towards the German occupation. He did not even receive a proper diet. This same man would join our efforts in the field. What a gem he was! The champion long-distance skier of Norway, Larsen broke out, skied to Sweden and purchased all the dynamite he could carry back to Norway. He planted the charges on a railroad trestle bridge across a deep gorge and waited for the arrival of a German troop train evacuating troops to Oslo. At the opportune moment, he blew the bridge. This was in late October 1943. Results were 250 German soldiers and 50 German officers dead. The line was inoperative for almost two weeks. These figures are hearsay but probably essentially correct. Anyway, as a result, German High Command decided to put guards on all sensitive points like tunnels, bridges, etc., along the railroads. This immobilized another 2,000 German troops. Thus, future *Rype* operations had to plan for the elimination of all guards that could deter our missions. We knew their approximate strength and routine operations.

After his blast, Larsen took to the mountains and, through the splendid Norwegian Underground, we were able to help him. He was our trail blazer and did this while still bleeding internally, the result of the "starve or submission" sojourn in prison.

More people came, reporting in almost every day after escaping from Norway. One was Knut Haugland. He would not tell me a darned thing about his escape but kept it all quiet. Quite a man. He was later involved doing the radio and photography work on the *Kon-Tiki* film. This was a documentary of the 1947 expedition where a raft was floated from South America to the Polynesian Islands to prove the theory that the South Sea islanders came from east to west. This was Thor Heyerdahl's theory and he and four others, including Haugland, set out to prove it.

Knut helped me with my communications problem. First, he set up a code the Germans never cracked. It was so simple yet one that, if broken, would be so ancient as to be of little or no value to anyone. Next, he came up with a light radio set encased in a regular men's suitcase of British manufacture. I looked at it. What I had in mind was a more substantial set encased in a rugged olive drab metal case, something to stand the gaff, but he swore by it. He had tested it, or so he said, and guaranteed it to reach my target in London some 700 miles away.

To further befuddle the issue, his explanation was that the radio beams would take off toward Norway at a slightly skyward angle, hitting the ionosphere once, bounce back to earth, hit the ionosphere a second time and then bounce right down to the target. He'd vouch for it. Funny, nobody at Fort Benning, Georgia, had ever touched on this point while I was in school. There it was, take it or leave it. The set was light and highly portable, very essential to our needs. I slept on that one for a while, but in the end he sold me on it without me fully understanding his secret shenanigans. You know, it really did work! He completed the set by furnishing and installing the proper crystals to do the job. This contraption was used extensively by our radio operator Borge Langeland to send messages between *Rype* and London. The transmitter on the ground was code-named *Eureka*, the same codename used by the Pathfinders for the D-Day invasion, and *Rebecca* was the name of the receiver in the plane which was also equipped with a small directional finding device. The transmission from *Eureka* could be picked up by the plane within a 50-mile radius. The BBC assisted with covert messages during the war. They broadcast news both in English and the native language to all of the occupied countries. At the end of the broadcasts, certain messages were read that seemed gibberish, except to the

Underground agents operating within that particular country. For example, "The finch has laid three eggs" meant that the code-named *Finch* reception party was to expect three drops that night from Colonel Bernt Balchen's group of specially converted B-24 Liberator bombers.

Speaking of Bernt Balchen, he was an interesting character in himself. Here was the man who was well known for flying then Commander Byrd to the South Pole. He also piloted the first multi-engine aircraft, a tri-motor, across the Atlantic shortly after Lindberg's *Spirit of St. Louis* solo flight and had something to do with getting Amelia Earhart prepared for her trans-Atlantic venture and national fame.

Early in his career he rescued Nobile, the Italian nobleman when his dirigible airship went down on his attempt to explore the North Pole. On that excursion, Balchen, then a junior officer, flew one of the flimsy old crates operated by the Norwegian Government. Armed only with a navigational aid and a magnetic compass that, as he said, "goes berserk up there most of the time anyway," Balchen finally found Nobile and made it back to base, gas tank empty. Balchen said, "You know, that *&%$# didn't even thank me!"[1]

Well, a first-class war was going on, which I imagine was a little slow for him. Oh, in addition he had fought in World War I in the first valiant stand of Finland against Russia. Being stabbed once, he lay bleeding on the ground. Along comes another Russian and stabs him again. That did it! He was mad as hell at Russians for the rest of his life.

Balchen relayed a story to me that had a humorous touch. It seemed that while he was up in northern Sweden, a German Messerschmitt Me 109 fighter fell into his hands. In addition, he just so happened to have a *Luftwaffe* colonel's uniform as part of his unofficial wardrobe. Suddenly, he had an idea. What did he do but put on the uniform, climb into the plane and took off for a visit with an old friend up in northern Norway, fairly close to the Bodø area. He spent the evening visiting with his friend. The next day he decided to go back to his base in northern Sweden. Well, Messerschmitts use a particular type of fuel, which was plentiful, but only at German bases in Norway. So Balchen flew to a German airfield and issued instructions to a ground crew flunkee to gas it up and that he'd be ready to go shortly. After all, he spoke German fluently. German is a language taught in all Norwegian schools as well as English. Getting ready to depart, while sitting in the cockpit he scribbled a little note, folded it and beckoned a fellow flyer over. He handed it to him with instructions to deliver the note promptly to his commanding officer. He then sent the crewman off with a sharp salute and a snappy "Jawohl!" After all, a "German colonel" from Luftwaffe headquarters on an inspection tour commands respect. They go in diverse directions. Balchen got off the taxi strip and onto the runway, then,

---

1 As noted in Balchen's autobiography. His widow would note the same in a 1998 interview. Byrd would thank Balchen later on in life.

once into the air, he turned towards the direction of his base in Sweden. The air crewman dutifully delivered the message to the commanding officer. It was promptly opened and read: "Thanks for your hospitality. Bernt Balchen."

Balchen first got involved in OSS operations after meeting with General Donovan in Washington, D.C. Donovan told Balchen the Norwegian Government-in-exile in London needed Norwegians in the war. Many had fled to neighboring Sweden. Norway had purchased two Lockheed Lodestars, but the trickle of flights between Stockholm and London provided very few Norwegian escapees.

Initially, Sweden collaborated with Germany by shipping them high grade ore. It also allowed German troops to cross its borders to attack the Soviet Union. But, by 1942, although officially neutral, Sweden was becoming more sympathetic to the Allies because of the atrocities by the *Gestapo* in occupied countries. They also suspected Germany might lose the war. However, Stockholm was still a favorite "listening post" for both Allied intelligence and Axis agents alike. By early 1943, Donovan said Sweden was willing to defy Berlin and he had 75 officers in Stockholm collecting intelligence on the Nazis. Further orders by Donovan were to set up an adequate air transport service to bring 2,000 Norwegians from Stockholm to London.

Thus, with Balchen on board the American program, Operation *Sonnie* was born. Balchen did encounter some red tape at first. The British denied him use of RAF Leuchars in Scotland. Their excuse was Americans had no business in that area. Balchen explained the problem to Trygve Lie, Norwegian foreign minister, at Kingston House where the exiled Norwegian Government was conducting business. Lie told Balchen he would address the issue at lunch the next day with King Haakon VII, Crown Prince Olav, Anthony Eden and Winston Churchill. At this lunch, the King asked Churchill why the British had turned down American requests to use Leuchars as a staging base to fly men out of Sweden to help with the war effort. Churchill said he had no idea why it was turned down, but he would take care of the issue. This was settled by mid-March 1944 and, two days later, Balchen deployed four Liberators to Leuchars. Operation *Sonnie* officially began on March 27. Balchen flew the first B-24, on March 31, from Leuchars to Bromma Airport near Stockholm. The flight took him over Kristiansand, Balchen's hometown and enemy air space. Night fog over the town prevented German flak from disrupting the Liberator's flight and tailwinds helped an early morning landing at Bromma. Once on the ground, the dark green B-24, with no insignia, was parked by the Swedish ground crew next to a camouflageed DC-3. Balchen looked closer and saw a small swastika painted on the tail. Obviously, it was a German courier from Berlin that must have arrived earlier. The German crew was wearing civilian clothing, as was Balchen's crew, and took quite an interest in the B-24. Both crews were transported to the Grand Hotel. After a hot bath, Balchen went to the dining room for some breakfast. It was full of foreign agents. After breakfast, Balchen and his crew were en route to the American Embassy when they discovered they were being followed.

It turned out to be Dr. Gressman of German Intelligence, who Balchen knew as a press attaché in Oslo. Balchen thought he would turn the tables, so he approached him and greeted him pleasantly. Gressman was stunned when Balchen saw right through his false whiskers. He said a nervous goodbye and disappeared into a store.

While at the embassy, Minister Hershel Johnson was briefed on the evacuation of 2,000 Norwegians to Britain. Doctor Harry Soederman, Chief of the Criminal Institute in Sweden and a great friend of Norway, reported that 12,500 Norwegian youths were being trained as "police soldiers." He also said 40,000 young men had fled to the mountains in Norway to escape German recruitment and asked if the United States could resupply them. Balchen contacted General Carl Spaatz in London, saying "Ve can do its." Spaatz's response to Balchen was "You're the 'Ve can do its.'"[2]

Later on, in a memorandum dated October 18, 1944, Commander Lester Armour of the United States Naval Reserve, Office of Strategic Services, European Theater of Operations, requested Major General F. Anderson of American Transportation Command increase Balchen's fleet of Liberators in Scotland from four to ten. Armour pointed out that Balchen's aircraft were used exclusively for operations over Norway. Between July 17 and September 28, sixty-three sorties were attempted; 33 were successful, which resulted in 52 tons of material dropped to 27 operational groups. Approximately sixty percent of these flights were made during the long daylight hours experienced at these latitudes.

After the British ceased dropping supplies in May 1944 because they were concerned the bright summer nights were a high risk to their aircraft, Balchen obtained permission from the Swedes to secretly use Kallax airfield at Luleå in order to continually supply arms, food and medical supplies to the resistance forces. He also used that base to transport Norwegian police forces into Finnmark, the extreme northeastern part of Norway.

All in all, Balchen made 166 flights into Norway, dropping agents and more than 700 tons of sabotage material. This, along with his other endeavors, such as Operation *Sonnie* where 270 trips were made between his base at Prestwyck, Scotland, and the neutral airfields of Sweden, evacuating about 6,000 who had crossed the border, including 1,000 Americans, earned him a Congressional Medal and a Distinguished Service Medal. He eventually retired from the U.S. Air Force in October 1956.

---

2   Balchen used this term quite often and so this response was a friendly rib by Spaatz. Sven Heglund's book *Høk over Høk* notes that Balder was sometimes known as "Ve do it" as a friendly rib of Balchen's English pronounciation.

CHAPTER 14

NORSO Beginnings

Now Norway, which was so dastardly attacked and occupied by hundreds of thousands of German troops to handle the "recalcitrant" Norwegians, suddenly became, as mentioned, just plain sticky flypaper. This northern flank turned out to be costly to the Nazi regime. In all, it tied up an estimated 300,000 to 400,000 German military personnel. Besides *Panzer* and artillery units, and even one *Fallschirmjäger* (paratrooper) battalion, many of the *Kriegsmarine*'s (navy) major units were also deployed. The *Luftwaffe*'s 10th Air Corps was sent to Norway. It consisted of 1,000 aircraft including 500 transports and 186 Heinkel He 111 bombers. Of course, the Allies made sure to try to maintain a credible threat of invasion to take back Norway through elaborate ruse measures. This all ramped up in late '43 and early '44.

When Colonel Bernt Balchen was stationed in England with Air Transport Command (ATC), he was busy dropping supplies to the Norwegian Underground by parachute at night. He dropped more supplies in four and one-half months than the United States Army Air Force (USAAF) was able to deliver in a year and a half.

The Norwegian Special Operations (NORSO) Group arrived in England in December 1943. We had an airfield near London where Office of Strategic Services' (OSS) supplies were stocked. Various items the Underground needed, such as carbines, communication equipment, ammunition and the like, were kept there. We also had a little testing program. We tested the weights of the canisters and practiced dropping them in various nearby fields to see how things survived delivery.

The Underground radio nets were quite active at this time. Various stations would report to London on the success of the drops. Times and locations were set up so the reception parties could go out into the fields and mountains and send out proper light signals for the aircraft to identify the drop zone. These drops would occur at favorable times of the moon since this was critical in all our sorties. Too much moonlight and the parachutes could be observed, resulting in an immediate response from the Germans. On the opposite extreme, complete darkness with no moonlight was not desirable either. A "favorable moon," as it was called, was one where there was just enough light so lakes and rivers could be seen for navigation. Therefore, most drops were done while the moon was not at full strength. The Underground used red lights to communicate with the respective plane.

For his drops, Balchen used unarmed C-47s since the legality of an ATC mission involved in arming the Underground was frowned upon. At the time I did not know why he had not continued. It was only later that I learned he had been assigned to the base in northern Sweden to conduct Operation *Sonnie*.

We tried to get him to fly us into our delivery operational base. The request was denied by the USAAF. Later on, I did get Commander Vetlesen to lay out an alternate supply plan with Balchen where he could buy food and supplies commercially in Sweden and drop them to me later on when I entered as a spy through Sweden. From there, we were relatively close compared to the 700 miles from our operational base in England. This was never used, however, since action ground to a halt in May 1945.

Radios had been dropped to clandestine groups in the mountains and they joined the Net Control of the British radio net. I remember one particular message coming to us in OSS Headquarters. It simply stated that an irate Norwegian farmer with his Krag–Jørgenson rifle determined the German Army should not pass through his lands. He set up his own private roadblock in a mountain pass in front of the German march to the north. He alone was able to stop the might of the Reich for half a day.

Feats like this spread like wildfire and soon this was the norm. Small units and people were giving the German Army a very difficult mission. The officers of the Norwegian Army escaped to neutral countries and found themselves in various other parts of the world devising ways to enhance their opportunities of reclaiming their dearly beloved country.

Of course, with every major conflict there are always problems within the "sphere of influence" arena as I called it. The weight of those three little words and their true meaning were soon to become increasingly important with each passing day. It seemed the mere winning of the war was to be relegated to an almost secondary role. Of utmost concern was the way it was won and the position the victors held after hostilities ceased. Thus, even before victory, definite spheres of influence were drawn. An eye opener indeed to the simple soldier who is basically taught to apply all possible force available to destroy the enemy's will to fight. Now it became apparent that you may or may not use all available means to accomplish the end result. You must temper your effort and tailor it to satisfy all interested parties.

Higher headquarters decided to amalgamate the OSS with the British SOE and the new force was henceforth called Special Forces Headquarters (SFHQ). This was an organization composed of the personnel of the Special Operations Branch, Office of Strategic Services, Special Operations Executive, and the Norwegian High

Command. SFHQ was charged by a directive of the Supreme Commander of the Allied Expeditionary Force to coordinate guerrilla warfare and acts of sabotage in Norway. This opened the avenue for a joint British and American effort.

A group of British commandos under Major Andrew Croft had returned from the Mediterranean area and were now available for new missions. Commander Vetlesen sought their services to augment the strength of his Underground for a mission in Norway. Major Croft was a holder of the Polar Medal of the British Empire. He was given this for extensive peacetime explorations in the Arctic regions. His experience was felt to be of particular value to the mission in Norway. He had many valuable and useful survival tricks which were to be used in our operation later on. The end result was that Major Croft and I were joined together with the British commandos and sent to northern Scotland to prepare and train for a mission in Norway. It was felt the commandos were somewhat short on ski training, which proved to be accurate. This brings to mind the abortive effort of the U.S. Army to start a ski-parachute unit early in World War II. The approach was to make ski troops out of parachutists. It takes a few months to train a qualified parachutist. It takes quite a few years to train a good cross-country skier and that is only if you are lucky and work like the devil at it. Anyway, off to the mountains of Scotland we went.

I had the good fortune of having worked personally with Viljalmar Steffanson, the Arctic explorer, the first week after graduation from West Point in June 1934. He gave me his autographed book, *The Northward Course of the Empire*, which is one of my most prized possessions. His productive years were spent in elaborate work with Eskimos in the Arctic regions. My first contact with him was when he lectured the Corps of Cadets at the U.S. Military Academy in 1933. The time spent with him in Greenwich Village, New York, was most memorable. A great man. He wrote the *Arctic Survival Manual* for the USAAF during World War II. His college days were spent at the University of North Dakota in Grand Forks.

The training period with the British commandos in the mountains of northern Scotland lasted a brief two weeks. In that short amount of time we were supposed to produce, by some weird alchemy, a polished group of ski troopers. The results were less than acceptable for the intended mission. We returned to London. A fortnight later, I was told there would be no joint American–British group for that job. Commander Vetlesen informed me the mission would be 100 percent American, even the airlift. I queried about using Norwegian RAF fliers to fly us in. The answer was no. There went the opportunity of having personnel who knew the terrain well to be able to deliver us to the target. How about using Colonel Balchen? He could find it if anyone could. Another resounding "No." Everyone in the Scandinavian section from Commander Vetlesen on down was fuming even more vociferously than I. So, I then put the question to Vetlesen. How about infiltrating through Sweden? No. The Swedes were not ready for this type of cooperation yet. I had visions of our rugged parachute delivery during the D-Day drop into Normandy. Well, at least a dunking, like the one I had when I landed in the Merderet River in France, would be absent. Even if I hit a body of water, it should be well frozen over. But these decisions did sort of shatter my confidence somewhat in our delivery system. Everything was either ice or snow in the target area now.

CHAPTER 15

Operation *Rype* Preparation

In September 1944, there was a peace accord struck between Finland and the Soviet Union. German troops were now retreating from Finland through Norway. Since the battle on the Continent continued to rage on, it was now thought those troops, along with the occupying forces in Norway, would be sent back to defend the Fatherland. Now the goal was to prevent that from happening. A main objective was to disrupt the Nordland rail line that ran down through the interior of Norway. There were actually four special forces organized by the Allies to do this. They were code-named *Coton*, *Waxwing*, *Woodlark* and *Rype*. The latter of course, was an operational group of the Office of Strategic Services (OSS).

Even before *Rype* became official, about a year earlier on October 18, 1944, Commander Lester Armour, United States Navy Reserve, wrote a memo to Major General F. Anderson, Director of Operations, United States Strategic Air Forces, regarding the requirements for air drops into Scandinavia:

1. We have rather informally discussed the subject of aircraft requirements for Scandinavia. After consultation with the representatives of S.F. HQ [Special Forces Headquarters], who are in daily touch with the situation in Norway and Denmark, we have come to the conclusion that it would be wise and desirable to specifically request ten American Liberators for operational use over Norway and Denmark. At the present time the Resistance Groups in both countries are serviced by the R.A.F. flying from Tempsford. These aircraft have, in the past, confined their operational commitments to sorties flown exclusively in the moon periods. We have adequate aircraft for such continued operations.

2. Prior to 28 September 1944 this HQ enjoyed the operational support of Colonel Balchen's Detachment, comprising of six American Liberators with crews, flying from Leuchers [sic], Scotland. The planes were employed exclusively for operations in Norway. Between 17 July 1944 (the inception date of such operations for this Detachment) and 28 September 1944, 63 sorties were attempted and 35 were successful, resulting in an aggregate of 52 tons of material dropped to 27 organizations. Approximately 60% of these flights were made during daylight or non-moon period. Aircraft were not available from any other source because of the Air Ministry's restriction of flights by R.A.F. craft during such periods.

3. We feel that the strength previously enjoyed and recently withdrawn should be reinstated on the same basis as before, with Colonel Balchen responsible for the Command, but to include as well prospective drops to Denmark. If this strength is added to that which is currently available

from the R.A.F., we do not anticipate encountering any difficulty in keeping the aircraft fully occupied as before for the following reason:

a. Facilities will always be available for non-moon period drops, and for certain targets north of latitude 62° which Sterlings [sic, the Short Stirling] cannot attempt and which [the RAF's] 38 Group may not particularly care to undertake.

b. We are planning for 100 successful sorties between now and 31 December 1944 for Norway, and 400 successful sorties for the same period in Denmark. This forecast presumes no change meanwhile in the internal situation of those countries. We feel that any of these, because of weather interference during the moon period must and can be carried out during the non-moon period.

c. If the internal situation in Norway should alter so as to call into action the S.F. HQ Groups and the Norwegian Military Organizations now situated there, the requirements for that country during the aforementioned period would increase to 400 or more successful sorties. Such an occurrence would re-emphasize the reason stated under b. above.

d. If a general uprising should take place in Norway, we anticipate a need for approximately 2,400 successful sorties in order to supply not only the S.F. HQ Groups and Norwegian Military Organizations, but the civilian population (Maquis) [French term for guerilla groups] as well. Such an occurrence in all likelihood would call for the use of more aircraft than is now available, including those requested. It is only in the event of this happening that we would welcome support from the 492nd Group [a special operations unit flying B-24s and C-47s]. Whether or not this Group should be kept in reserve for such a call or contingency we feel is a matter which should rest entirely with your discretion.

e. Since integration between British and American services is the established policy for S.F. HQ, we feel that participation of American aircraft, together with the British, for combined operations on a reasonable share basis, is entirely proper and advisable.

f. According to our past dropping experience, only about 60% of attempted sorties have been successful. Therefore a proportionally greater number of sorties will have to be flown in order to provide us with the required number of successful drops.

4. There are 27 SOE/SO Groups organized in the field at this time. Of this number, 11 are operating north of 62° latitude. Estimated strength of the Norwegian Military Organization ranges between 15-25,000. Also at present there are 59 separate requests from the field organizations waiting to be flown.

5. We trust the above will serve as an adequate justification for reinstating the American Liberator strength up to ten aircraft under Colonel Balchen's Command, for use on behalf of this HQ, and that our request for these facilities will meet with your approval.

Prior to our pending missions, extensive surveillance work was done earlier, in particular by two Norwegian nationals, Gunnar Steen and Alf Bromstad. Both had local knowledge and Bromstad had been a fireman on the railroad in the area, enabling them to offer useful recommendations for potential attacks against railroads, tunnels and bridges. In early October 1944 they traveled by bicycle, train and car to survey possibilities. They recommended the 335-foot-long Grana bridge as an excellent target because its repair would cause a significant delay in troop movements. This bridge, south of Agle, was the original objective for *Woodlark*—the British sponsored operational group which comprised British personnel and members of Norwegian Independent Company No. 1 (*Kompani Linge*), but the bridge proved too well guarded for the small party.

Steen and Bromstad went onto survey a 150-meter-long bridge and two short tunnels north of Bunes Bridge; then railroad points between Lurudal and Formofoss along with a stone bridge and tunnel south of Formofoss. This tunnel seemed desirable for an attack as the terrain was suitable for both approach and retreat routes. A curved railroad tunnel south of Hurmofoss station also seemed promising. They continued on to survey Formofoss station; Grong Station; the Tommeraas Tunnel; Bunes Bridge; a 350-meter-long tunnel north of Snåsa; and the 100-meter-long, 20-meter-high railroad bridge over the Grana 4 kilometers south of Snåsa station. The Grana bridge was surrounded by barbed wire, with German patrols and an installation nearby. After the completion of their mission, Steen and Bromstad's information was couriered by ski to Milorg in Stockholm, Sweden and then flown to SFHQ in London.[1]

With this knowledge and other gathered intelligence in hand, feasibility and planning began in earnest. Major H. P. Larson of Force 134, a Special Forces Detachment located in Scotland, submitted a list of railroads, bridges and tunnels north of Trondheim as potential targets for sabotage to Commander Vetlesen. Larson told Vetlesen a successful OSS operation in this area would please Supreme Headquarters Allied Expeditionary Force (SHAEF) because it would force the Germans to use the sea routes in their evacuation from north to south. Larson included an appendix of vulnerable railway sites between Agle and Formofoss. He also included weather and climate considerations consisting of visibility for aircraft drops, average temperatures and snowfall, topography and hours of daylight.

The German High Command was engaged in transferring 150,000 mountain troops, driven out of Finland, from the Narvik–Tromasø area of northern Norway for use in the defense of Germany. On January 15, 1945, Major J. E. Nordlie wrote a memo to General Hansteen of the Norwegian High Command in London to brief him about the proposed use of the OSS Norwegian Special Operations (NORSO) Group to hinder the enemy's overland evacuation from northern Norway. In the memo he discussed the use of parachute troops. He stated that the Allied authorities had approved the Norwegian–American installment be prepared as soon as possible to go against the railroad between Grong and Snåsa. In summing up the situation, he pointed out that Milorg and some Nordic groups under the direction of SHAEF were positioned to interrupt the north–south railroad without exposing themselves too much.

Rail transport from Trondheim south had been substantially disturbed by this ongoing work and he expected the same would soon happen to the north of Trondheim.

---

1 Bruce Heimark, *O.S.S. Operation RYPE: Cutting the Nordland Rail Line in Occupied Norway at Two Points in the North Tröndelag Area*, thesis presented to the University of Nebraska at Omaha.

He further went on to explain that the means were available to completely stop German evacuation from northern Norway. These would include:

1. Installment of paratroopers from the United Kingdom.
2. Installment of a police force from Sweden. In his opinion, several places between Steinkjer and Vefsn would be ideal for this. A single, well-trained battalion would be enough to stop the Germans from using its railroad for the rest of the winter. However, getting the Swedish Government to cooperate might prove difficult. To get around this, a bridgehead, a corridor, could be established near the operation's domain. This informal "occupation" could be done with a small force by the Norwegians and the territory considered "liberated" by the Norwegian Government.
3. The evacuation lines should be bombed. Of course, this would have to be approved by Special Forces Headquarters (SFHQ) and should be done in addition to the above-named alternatives.

He concluded the best would be a combination of the above, although he was quite uncertain about the use of a police force. It might hinder the operation in ways unknown.

After examining the map area along the railroad from Mosjøan to Hell, he saw another opportunity. Several stretches seemed tactically feasible for destruction by a "single troop," as Nordlie described them. This troop would consist of two parts. The first would be the leader, a party of ten men and a radio operator. The remaining main force would consist of 24 men to be parachuted in later. The first party would take on the following tasks:

1. Establish connections with London.
2. Reconnoiter a base for the troop and a place for receiving the main party.
3. Reconnoiter and lay plans for the attack.
4. Effect acts of sabotage against the railroad during the waiting period before the main party arrived.

In particular, the stretch between Snåsa and Formofoss, and the stretch between Grong and Majavatn, seemed the most advantageous. Conditions in these vicinities contained comparatively safe districts where the troop could retreat after the attack and would be effective for escape as long as suitable snow remained for skiing. He proposed putting at least one troop in place to attack the line between Grong and Majavatn. This troop would be placed under "operational control" of SFHQ but actually sent in as an integral part of a regular division of the Norwegian Army. The timing for the attack needed to be implemented right away because the German evacuation was ramping up quickly and the snow conditions would soon put a stop to the operation. A favorable moon period of January 20 to February 4 was coming up and a Norwegian party was already in the area. The Norwegian parachute troop could be dropped at the same time as the Americans or, at the latest, a month later. Ideally, the first troop would go in during January and the remainder in February. The advantage, however, of waiting to drop in later, would be the Norwegian troop would have the added benefit of learning from the experiences of the American attack beforehand. Since the American Operational Groups would be delivered by Liberators, they could also be used to transport both parts of the Norwegian troop. If, for some reason, the troop could no longer retain themselves on Norwegian territory (supply problems, etc), they would go to Sweden and register in small groups as refugees. Necessary civilian clothing would have to be available in a depot on the Swedish side of the border. Major Nordlie brought this idea up in a meeting with Brigadier General Mockler-Ferdman and Colonel Alms from SHAEF. The general was interested in the plan and expressed his support.

The Special Operations Branch, Scandinavian Section, estimated that enemy units were passing from north to south along a single railway line. Enemy troops were believed to be garrisoned along the route. A field order was received on January 29, 1945, detailing the approximate rates of German evacuation to the south:

Namsos	700 men
Grong	150 men
Ekker	Few men
Formo	Few men
Formofos	Ammunition dump and guards
Nordli	Patrols, 23 men (Intelligence annex details)
Agle	Hutments
Krogsgard (Snåsa)	Camp and ammunition dump, –500 men
Maelester Tunnel	VB with railway guard. Bicycle patrols twice daily along the railway line.

This amounted to about one battalion (500 men) per day. Since the Nordland line in the North Trøndelag area was the only means of transport, it was carefully guarded the entire length by a line of mobile and permanent guards.

The same report also raised several questions. What does the German guard system look like on this rail line? Which are the most favorable points of attack, taking into consideration the character of the masonry and steel, the character of the soil and location of weak points in construction? Where are points from which reconnaissance can be made and can photos be taken? What are the most favorable routes of approach?

Furthermore, if the situation required the *Rype* group to abandon the mission, then they were to retreat to Sweden and contact *Woodlark* to obtain civilian clothes. All uniform, equipment, identification cards and money were to be discarded, reason being, it was of utmost importance to avoid any action whatsoever which might let the Swedes suppose the *Rype* party came from the U.K. Upon entering the border, they were to state plainly they were ordinary Norwegian refugees escaping because of the intolerable German restrictions. *Rype* personnel would then be sent to Kjeseter, where they needed to use the greatest caution since the camp was under Swedish authority and may contain Quisling refugees that could double as informants. Once inside Kjeseter, contact could be made by asking to see the head of the *Rettskontoret* without specifying the name of any official. The password, "*Holmenkollrennet er avlyst i aar*" (The Holmenkollen ski race is cancelled this year) would be given, to which the reply was, "*Ja det var det ifjor ogsaa*" (Yes, that was the case last year too).

Further directives were formalized for *Rype* as follows. If successful to this point, you would be sent to the Norwegian Legation in Stockholm. Ask to see Major Baumen or his assistant and give him the password, "*Vi er globetrottre*" (We are world travelers). This phrase would be communicated to Vetlesen, who would know it could only be given by a member of the *Rype* party.

If all else failed, you were to move to the nearest Swedish authority and surrender as American paratroop soldiers who escaped from operations in Norway. In this case you were to retain your uniform, identity card, dog tags, money, etc and would be interned for the duration of the war.

Finally, in the event that Headquarters suspected you were under duress, it would ask you which types of skis you took into the field that worked out best. If you were free and not under enemy control, you would answer the flat ones which you received when you were with the unit. If you are under duress, you would answer the ribbed ones you had just received.

Code letters, names and BBC messages were also determined for landing parties and resupply drops. The signal letter for *Eureka* transmission was "P" for Peter and the "C" system of lighting would be used for bonfires at the reception point. Twelve locations were assigned as follows:

1.	Area	:	B	*Sterk som gress* (strong as grass)
2.	Mars	:	C	*Full av sol* (full of sun)
3.	Jupiter	:	R	*Mere stillhet* (more silence)
4.	Zeus	:	F	*Taus som telefonen* (silent like the telephone)
5.	Diana	:	G	*Solem fikk en sonn* (Solem got a son)
6.	Astarte	:	J	*Rev bak oiet* (tongue in cheek)
7.	Hermes	:	K	*Hallomannen var stum* (the radio announcer was mute)
8.	Merkur	:	L	*Blekkhuset blev* (the inkwell remained)
9.	Athene	:	W	*Monster uten kant* (monster without form)
10.	Vesta	:	X	*Hold ilden vedlike* (keep the fire going)
11.	Hygea	:	Y	*Gaa til legen* (go to the doctor)
12.	Juno	:	Q	*Mannen med to ansikter* (the man with two faces)

On January 30, 1945, when the NORSO Group was kicking into high gear, Skabo sent a memorandum to Commander Vetlesen in Stockholm about the immediate laying out of Operation *Rype*. SHAEF was contacted about OSS plans and not only endorsed them but urged Vetlesen to do everything possible to get the operation through. Skabo knew *Woodlark* had a mission to perform in the same area, but *Woodlark* was small and the OSS believed the American Operational Group, augmented by *Woodlark*, would provide more personnel for *Rype* and thus accomplish more damage to the railways. Skabo stated the advance party would consist of one officer, Lieutenant Tom Sather, and two sergeants, Listed and Langeland. The Swedes had been uneasy with *Woodlark* on their border and it was not possible to expect those men to be a reception committee. Skabo recommended that, in spite of the recommendation to "lay low for the present time," it was critical to get the advance party in during the favorable moon period. He also mentioned the three men were asked if they had any objection to being dropped in blind. They had no objections and wanted the chance to go in, even if it meant there was no reception committee.

Prior to a technical planning meeting that took place at 88 Chiltern Court on February 2, 1945, I was given a chance to pick my own targets for destruction. With *Rype* now an official OSS operation, I secured detailed engineering data on the Nordland railroad that Norwegians escaping to London had brought with them. Being quite technical in nature, it was still a challenge to my linguistic abilities. It was all in Norwegian, of course. I poured over the data for two weeks and eventually chose a railway tunnel for destruction. The reason being that the German High Command had ordered an orderly disengagement of their troops opposing the Russians in Finland and northern Norway in the Nirkeness area. They were hurting for troops on the Western Front. Since Sweden refused the Germans permission to travel through their country, the only way to move troops south was via rail. They could then get to Oslo, then to Bornholm and Denmark where they were re-equipped and fighting within 48 hours after disembarking.

The tunnel I picked had two drainpipes, one on each side, which drained all collecting moisture in the tunnel and funneled it out the end at both entrances. These drains were necessary to keep the tunnel dry. Railroad tunnels through the mountains have a three-degree climb to the middle and a three-degree drop to the other end, but once you crack the roof really well, the water pitter patters down beautifully, hits the rails and freezes. A passing engine has no traction on the ice. No engine, no railroad transportation.

In the meeting, a stretch of railway with numerous tunnels in northern Norway was discussed along with a Z-span steel bridge. Lieutenant Thorn of the Norwegian Army, who was present, had worked on this stretch of railway as a civil engineer. He produced additional drawings of typical tunnel construction. The masonry arches with corresponding drainage channels were discussed at length. It was decided that round or square charges with primers threaded onto cordtex would be adequate. The ends of the charges would be fitted with wooden fairings to allow for insertion into the drainage channels, pushed into place by drainage rods. Charges in units of four or five pounds would be adequate. These charges would also be adequate

for the steel bridge. Other charges included single French rail cutting charges fitted
with either a Bickford two-minute timing device or time pencils. The operational
charges were to be ready for packing by February 15 along with dummy charges for
operators to practice with. In total, about eight thousand pounds were intended to
be dropped into Norway for sabotage operations.

On February 3, 1945, Hans Skabo sent a memo to Captain A. W. Brogger,
acting Chief of the Scandinavian Section, providing highlights of Operation *Rype*.
In it, he stated the intended drop of the advance party would be at Gauptjernet.
Stockholm was notified that, if a reception committee could be arranged, they
would flash a dot-dot-dash-dot, the Morse Code letter "F," for Fred. The BBC
would broadcast the message *"Kaal rabien er lekker"* which meant a plane was
coming that night. The password of the reception party would be *"Hvordan staar
det til paa den andre siden av Dammen?"* (How are you at the other side of the
pond?). The advance party would reply, *"Vi ser lyst paa frentiden"* (The future
looks bright). The supplies dropped with the advance party would include the
following:

1 container of gasoline
1 container of K rations
9 containers of British Mountain rations (40 rations per container)
1 container of miscellaneous equipment for base camp (shotgun, axe, saw, hand
grenades, lathe, etc.)
2 packages containing *Eureka* radio sets
1 package of a B-2 radio set
1 package with a gasoline generator
3 packages of ruck sacks
2 packages of skis (3 pairs per package)

On February 2, 1945, Skabo wrote a memo to Lieutenant Colonel Charles Brewer,
Executive Officer, SO Branch, summarizing the meeting:

1. Everyone present agreed that the target area now laid on of No. 1 NORSO Group, that
is, the stretch of line between Lurudal and Formofoss, is the most vital and logical target for
this group. The writer suggested that an alternate target be assigned to NORSO Group on the
stretch of railroad north of Grong. It was pointed out, however, by both Major Nordlie and
Major Douglas that a Norwegian paratrooper group consisting of 36 men have been laid on for
operations on the stretch of line from Grong to Majavatn. It was not believed that reinforcements
by American NORSO men to this group would be advisable, however, that additional targets
were available south of Agle Station.
2. The original WOODLARK party had as its objective the bridge spanning the Grana River
which is located a few kilometers south of Agle. After reconnaissance of the target, however, this
group found the bridge too well guarded for a small party of 7 or 8 to attempt the destruction
of the bridge. They, therefore, selected a target further south which was the bridge south of
Joerestad. This bridge was blown by the WOODLARK party and traffic was stopped for better

than two weeks, however, repairs have now been completed. The WOODLARK party is now lying quiet on the Swedish side of the border and no action is contemplated for this group.
3. It was believed that the original WOODLARK target, namely the Grana Bridge, would be an excellent target for a group as large as the first NORSO Group (approx 3 officers and 32 EM). It was pointed out, however, that the terrain is very difficult and whoever attempted an approach and get away from the target would have to be a first-class skier. If, upon reconnaissance, it should be determined that even this target was so well guarded that the first NORSO Group would be unable to cope with it they could, as an alternate target, demolish the rail lines between Snaasa [sic] and Agle. In discussing this later with Colonel Bolland he agreed and we have, therefore, set up as alternate for the first NORSO Group the following:
    a. The Grana River Bridge
    b. Destruction of rail lines between Agle and Snaasa [sic].
4. In discussing possible targets for the second NORSO Group (approximately 2 officers and 20 EM), Major Douglas and Captain Fraser-Campbell both suggested that no definite targets be assigned at this time for the reason that no targets are as yet available south of Trondheim for American NORSO Groups and second, that the men in the second NORSO Group are not first-class skiers. Major Douglas suggested that this group continue their training in Scotland and be held in readiness with supplies laid on so that if opportunity presented itself a little later in the Spring they could be dispatched to the field on short notice presumably in areas where skiing would not be required at that time. Everyone present agreed that this would be the best procedure and Colonel Bolland and I also agree.

While waiting for the weather to break, Vetlesen sent a reply from Stockholm to Skabo in London about the anticipated difficulties in connecting *Woodlark* with *Rype*. The former had been set up in Sweden without Swedish permission. Sooner or later, the Swedish authorities were bound to discover its true purpose. Its official cover story was that it was a weather station when, in fact, it was an outlet to get men, supplies, and explosives meant for sabotage operations into Norway. Sweden was irritated by the high-handed British proceedings. However, through recently completed negotiations, *Woodlark* was eventually recognized by Sweden with Swedish protection. This would be important as a precedent for establishing other bases in the future. *Woodlark* would not be available to *Rype* until such time as the British thought it possible to release *Woodlark* from its inactivity. Until then, once in the field, supplies and couriers would come directly to *Rype* from Stockholm.

    Therefore, I found myself heavily involved in drawing up finalized plans at SFHQ in London for the continual cutting of this railway. Volunteers from Special Forces Groups (operational teams of the SFHQ) were selected, given training and prepared for delivery by parachute drop into the North Trøndelag area. *Rype* was charged with the responsibility of paralyzing the north–south Norwegian rail service for the maximum time possible.

    The Scandinavian section was really humming during this period. There were about 50 radio sets for active underground reception parties all over Norway. They all took on the code names of birds like *Blackbird*, *Sparrow*, etc., and were assigned a Morse code letter on their radios, "P" (dot-dash-dash-dot) for Peter and so forth, which was also flashed by a light to locate the drop zone for the aircraft delivering the hardware. All had radio contact with the Net Control station in London.

By this time, my original mission, *Husky*, after several postponements, was finally scratched when the goal of the mission was learned in a bizarre manner. It seemed that someone had managed to get a high-ranking Russian leader in charge of forces in Finland and the North Cape rather inebriated and loose lipped one night. Well into his cups of liquid courage he blurted out that he had two divisions ready to seize Narvik in Norway when given the green light. This astounding news hit the fan! Our supposed ally was ostensibly crossing us up! An educated guess would be that political pressures from several directions were applied to that "big friendly bear" and it was decided not to hug this hapless country in its typical death grip at this time. However, future darker motives were suspected to be on the horizon.

For this reason, the surveying efforts for the railroad roadbed to Narvik ceased. Not exactly trusting the playful bear, our OSS Scandinavian Section in London instead set up a watch dog cell in the area east of Narvik, where the three countries of Norway, Sweden and Finland joined. Indigenous personnel were used to avoid arousing suspicion. The leader, Odd Sörlie, was none other than the older brother Kjell Sörlie, who would join *Rype* by recruitment from the Norwegian Underground while in the field.

As related to *Rype*, at a reunion of OSS members, that took place later in October 1975, Kjell recounted his involvement and contributed the following to a newsletter for the group:

I had been a military courier in the landing area (North Trondelag) about half a year). My brother, Odd, who was chief of the military resistance movement in Trondheim, asked me if I could take the job of reception chief for RYPE and go to a place called Gauptjønna in Snåsa. The boys from OSS should "work" on the railway. I was, at that time twenty-one years old and said, "Yes" but asked to take with me Erik Gaundal, who also was a courier and was well acquainted with the dropping area. That was December, 1944. We left Stockholm with a lot of USA equipment, white overclothes and two Colt pistols. We had only one radio receiver for taking the special message from BBC Norway News, "*Kalrabien Er Lekker*" that I can translate into "The Swedish Turnips are Delicious".

The following night you should arrive and we should put up a fire at Gauptjønna. Ten miles after we crossed the border and we were into Norway, we discovered a man who had discovered us. We didn't have any choice but went up to the man and, lucky we were. It was Hans Leimo, a real mountain hunter. Erik knew him very well and said he was a good Norwegian. We didn't have any time to tell him our job but asked what condition that small hill farm cottage was in Gauptjønna. He told us the place had not been used in fifty years and there was no possibility of staying there. But nearby at Deisjøen (Coalfish Lake) there was a cottage. We went to Seisjøfjellet and from there we had a reconnaissance in the area to find a suitable place to receive you. One night at two o'clock in the morning we were awakened by Hans who told us that twenty Germans were coming to pay us a visit. He had heard it from his friend in Snåsa. What now? I decided to break up at once and try to send a message back to Stockholm.

That night we went some fifteen miles on skis to the nearest Swedish telephone and lucky again, I found my brother Odd in the apartment in Stockholm. I couldn't say so much on the Swedish phone but since I knew Odd knew the signal from BBC I just said, "Don't send those Swedish turnips. They are not delicate!" And further, I said, "We would come down to Stockholm". Odd immediately telephoned our contact in the American Embassy in Stockholm and operation RYPE was stopped (for the time being).

Back in Stockholm I suggested Jaevsjo (Lake) as a safer and bigger place for dropping and that was accepted. Then in January a new group went over the border and that was Thoralf Lian, John Moan, Ludvik Kruksve and me. With much better equipment we could send a signal with the Eureka (radio) so the pilot could find us. I think it was in February you tried but on Jaevsjo it was a full snowstorm. We could only hear you but do nothing. So, on the 24th of March… the rest you know.

Being winter, there were no open roads, just snow and more snow. To supply this cell, after considerably cajoling and dickering, it was decided that a Lapp Reindeer pack train would work best. One was to be hired to haul in the necessities. It was quite surprising to find out reindeer could pack about half as much as any good old army quartermaster pack mule. Their hoofs do not break through the top crust of snow very readily. They sort of "pussy foot" on top without sinking in.

Dealing with equipment needs and coping with cold weather was no small task. As a young boy setting trap lines in Madison, Minnesota, I had my first taste of cold weather challenges. In addition, Major Andrew Croft had been on an expedition studying the Sami people (commonly known as the Lapps) that live in a very wide territory stretching from the coasts of Norway to the Kola Peninsula in Russia. They are nomadic shepherds, depending on reindeer rearing for their survival. They follow the herds as they move in search of new food sources. Lapps live in reindeer skin tents and their food is mainly reindeer meat and fish. All of these combined experiences and knowledge helped us prepare the NORSO groups for survival near the Arctic Circle.

Equipping a special operations unit for covert Arctic warfare requires attention down to the smallest detail. I am reminded of a quote by General Patton, "The Germans didn't beat us. The weather did." As field commander of *Rype*, I was not about to let the weather dictate the success of our mission.

The personal effort in searching out specialized clothing and gear for the now cancelled *Husky* operation gave me a head start when Colonel Skabo asked me to work up the equipment details for *Rype*. My simplistic thinking at the time was it was simply a matter of multiplying by 70 for *Rype* and it would all fit beautifully into place for this portion of the equipment needs. Of course, it turned out much more complex than that.

Part of the process involved borrowing many ideas from Norwegian whalers since they were experts in Arctic weather living. From this I was able to assemble effective cold weather clothing and devise ways of wearing it. Special whaler's vests were made in London. These were insulating vests made from fishing net cords to Norse specifications; a modified version of what would be a thermal cold weather undershirt as sold today. Our whaler's vests were much more effective than conventional long underwear. They were a necessity in the Arctic whaling industry of the Norwegians. The main advantage was a layer of air pockets to provide adiabatic insulation. It was also made to be loose-fitting so as to not to cut off circulation. When worn, we looked like ragamuffins. These vests proved invaluable for staying dry while being pursued by German patrols.

Many of the Germans, on the other hand, wore heavy fur coats, causing them to sweat profusely. The NORSO men were directed to stay cool by allowing a measure of air to flow into the clothing while on the trail. During the chase, one must stay dry. When stopping to rest, the collar was closed and the men buttoned up to retain static, dry heat. In those harsh conditions, sweat will kill you since water steals heat from the body. If not removed it will chill the body down in a hurry when it freezes. Even with temperatures down to -35 °F it is possible with exertion to perspire.

Colby wanted Eskimo muklus. My response? "No." Those can get your feet wet, especially during the spring thaw. Boots with insulated rubber bottoms, leather straps and interchangeable felt insoles were ideal. This turned out to be the right decision.

A parka with hood and fur lining was supplied to each man. We quickly discovered in the field that our breath on the fur formed hoar frost. Army visored wool caps were issued as well as snow goggles. Socks consisted of two sets with three pairs in each set—one lightweight pair of army socks, one pair of size ten heavy wool socks and one pair of size twelves. Additional equipment included one lightweight silk undershirt, one 100 percent wool undershirt, one long-sleeve wool army shirt with a flare out collar, and one long-sleeve light wool army sweater.

Unlined windbreakers with rabbit fur lining around the face were ordered. The windbreaker was reversible, white on one side and army drab, olive green on the other. Of course, we had no way of knowing if Norway was to be a last-ditch stand or not. My plans were all made for that contingency. It was not known how long the war would go on and fighting could last well into the summer.

A quick note on the effectiveness of white garments against a winter backdrop. They helped, but complete camouflage was impossible. There was no way to hide your shadow against a snowy backdrop. When out in the open, the men were trained to stop and lay down in various curled up positions whenever engine noise from aircraft was heard overhead. Furthermore, they would randomly disperse quickly so as not to appear, for example, like a straight-line row of rocks that might seem out of the ordinary and catch the eye of a vigilant observer. After a while they became quite adept at distinguishing the sounds of different German aircraft. Colby never told me whether or not he had to use that tactic in the field.

As the weather warmed to around 30 to 40 °F, only a light brown army shirt and the windbreaker were to be worn during chases. I even had requisitions made out for mosquito bars, netting, repellant and summer uniforms, etc., before leaving for the field myself. You may say, "Mosquito bars near the Arctic Circle?" You have no idea. In the summer up there, there are so darned many of them, they'll eat you alive! When the snow melts, those mountain streams become raging torrents throughout the vast landscape and form numerous still water ponds; ideal conditions for breeding mosquitoes.

At various times, due to the intensity of the chase, there would be no time to set up a formal camp and the men would be forced to bed down in the snow. If understood properly, snow can also act as an insulator and you can use that to your advantage. Since three pairs of socks were worn at a time, dry socks were put on immediately before crawling into your sleeping bag. The sweaty socks were then laid on top of your chest. Due to sublimation, that is solid ice crystals evaporating directly into the air, these frozen socks would be dry by morning.

I also ordered ski jelkas which were sleds made to NORSO specifications. The jelkas were a cross between a wide ski and a narrow toboggan pulled behind oneself. The jelkas were handled by torsion bars which would meet in a semi-circle apparatus attached to an individual at the hips. This setup made it possible to control the jelka and keep it behind you. All fine and dandy. Just try to keep it from running you over while going down a precipitous descent with a load on it; it had no brakes.

Skis and ski poles were issued. The skis were black tipped so you could see them skimming under the snow. During the operation, the ski poles were stuck in the snow in pyramid fashion to mark supplies and keep skis from being blown over with snow.

The rucksacks came with harnesses so they could attach to the tubular, aluminum torsion bars of the ski jelkas.

Little stoves, the size of a grapefruit with three folding legs and one quart of kerosene, were carried into the field. These came in handy for filling a thermos with hot chocolate, soup or coffee which was usually made in the morning and carried throughout the day. Fires were started with dry alcohol tablets the size of a silver dollar. The moisture that formed while cooking in the tent was a problem. British mess kits with covers were used. They collected all the moisture from cooking that otherwise would rise to the ceiling, getting the tent wet. A wet tent meant a heavy tent, too heavy for carrying. The mess kits also had collapsing utensils.

Of course, every member of an OSS team carried the infamous "L" tablets to be taken should he be captured by the enemy. He thus could kill himself in seconds to avoid the brutal torture by Nazi interrogators and potentially divulge information on OSS operations.

You have no idea of the supply problems this operation entailed. Even on the initial winter parachute drop, we ended up adding snowshoes on the jumper's chest so he could put them on and move around to find the ski bundles and get at them. We had to plan on six feet of loose snow in the drop zone. I had arranged for a 50 percent overload of skis alone to allow for breakage during the drop. This, of course, had been tested in practice drops back in England. We had to operate in sub-zero temperatures most of the time. Every piece of equipment was worried over, discussed, tested, evaluated and reevaluated. It was down to ounces for the individual's personal equipment. Weight meant work and work was perspiration. That could result in extreme exhaustion, meaning almost certain death to the isolated soldier. If he fell asleep alone he would very probably never wake up.

The men were paired up to watch for frozen areas or white spots (frost bite) on each other and to render first aid if needed. Each team carried a two-man mountain tent with a waterproof floor and tunnel entrance to be pointed away from the wind when set up. These two-man teams also divided up duties. One would set up the tent and prepare supper while the other performed outside camp duties. One fact remains that can be pointed out with pride. Operation *Rype* never had a single case of frostbite.

As far as rations were concerned, much needed energy to set up camp was a priority. Small chocolate candy bars, hard wheat crackers, sugar lumps and dried apricots were carried in our pockets, plus whatever was in the thermos at the time to meet those needs. Regular bread was not carried since it took up too much space.

One learns quickly that a harsh environment changes your taste. The canned cylinders of bacon we carried were the tastiest. Our bodies needed more fat content for the cold weather. For extremely cold weather we consumed Pemiccan. It consisted of 40 percent lean beef and 60 percent yellow fat and looked like a "cake" of soup. For warmer weather, the Pemiccan ratio was changed to 60 percent lean beef and 40 percent yellow fat.

Melted snow and ice were used to make hot chocolate or coffee if time permitted at the end of the day. Ice was preferable because you didn't have to collect nearly as much and it turned to liquid faster than snow. Both were plentiful since the NORSO teams continuously operated in four to six feet of snow during *Rype*.

Yes, we were definitely living on our wits and skiing ability. As re-supply caches were dropped, it was understood by everyone that capture by the Germans while trying to retrieve them meant certain death. That was a good deterrent when dealing with cold and hunger.

During preparations, Colonel Skabo and I went out to Hargrove to visit a secret English demolition factory north of London. As far as the overall operation was concerned, the Americans provided the personnel trained by the OSS in the United States and later in Great Britain, as well as the supplies and the long-range B-24 Liberators to deliver the *Rype* mission. The British provided the explosives since they had the ability to make all kinds of devilish devices for the Underground. They developed a special RDX plastic explosive for our operation. RDX is the base for a number of common military explosives. At the time, RDX also conveniently served as an acronym for Research Department eXplosive or Royal Demolition eXplosive. The formal chemical name for the one the British developed for us is cyclotrimeth-ylenetrinitramine. It is also called cyclonite hexogen, or T4, a derivative of the powerful explosive discovered by German Georg Friedrich Henning and patented in 1898. It was not used extensively until World War II. The RDX was placed in 20-pound cylinders and fused so that each cylinder could detonate in a series and thus create a simultaneous explosion of the entire chain. The idea was to ram a bunch in both drains of the tunnel I selected in an elongated fashion one after the other, as many as we could carry to blow them to smithereens. Those lovely cylinders could do the job to perfection and that railroad would have been in one sad shape. The Germans wouldn't be able to use that tunnel for the rest of the war. Twenty-pound cylinders were also chosen as a satisfactory weight for an individual skier to carry to the target since it was quite a haul from the clandestine base to the railroad. Personal arms, ammunition, food, fuel, liquids, sleeping bags, etc., must also be carried individually.

Meanwhile, Hargrove also developed a little half-pound RDX plastic explosive device with a time pencil attached which could be planted on the track. Then, by pulling the time pencil, they would explode a few minutes later, cutting the narrow-gauge rail clean as a whistle. We ordered and received a bunch of them. They proved invaluable later on.

In addition, Hargrove also developed an explosive device called a limpet. These came in various forms, depending on their particular use. The larger limpets were used to blow a hole about 25 square feet in the steel plate of a ship below the waterline. They attached to the vessel with magnets powerful enough to withstand the flowing water force caused by the vessel in motion. The main waterproof plastic case was about eight-and-three-quarter inches long and weighed eight pounds when loaded. A keeper plate protected the magnets of two limpets packed face to face. Each end of the plastic case was threaded to receive a waterproof time delay detonator with a safety pin and thumb screw. An accompanying place holding rod fitted onto a bracket on the case to aid in underwater installation. Certain types of these limpets were fitted with a set of time pencils which were preselected by color based on water temperature. They could be used to sink a ship in deep water if the correct sailing hour was known.

Another limpet, without magnets but instead with a pinning device, was also developed to sabotage ships. This was called the "Pin-Up Girl" and was attached to the plates or planks of an enemy vessel's hull by a cartridge-driven pinning device. The cartridge fitted into the metal bracket on the case. The size of the pinning device was only five-and-a-quarter inches long with a diameter of one inch and weighed only eight ounces. The corresponding plastic case containing the explosive charge was eight-and-three-quarter inches long and weighed five-and-a-half pounds fully loaded. It had extending brackets or arms to help in holding the unit flush to the surface of the hull while firing the cartridge. It was fired by removing the safety pin and pulling a string to displace the firing yoke, releasing the firing pin. The noise and percussion of the pinning device were surprisingly unnoticeable to the crew inside the hull. The pin penetrated the thick steel plating, making the unit practically irremovable, even if detected. Like the magnetic limpet, it would blow a hole about 25 square feet in the hull. The best target on a ship was near the boilers, which are usually amidships.

The cartridge used on wooden hulls was different. It had a special pin and was marked with a green band around the cartridge body to distinguish it from those used on steel hulls. This pinning device was factory loaded and also sealed for underwater use.

Hargrove also developed an aerometer limpet designed to be concealed in an enemy aircraft while on the ground. It consisted of three parts: the triggering mechanism, the booster and the flexible container for the high explosive charge. The assembled unit was one-and-a-half inches in diameter and 17 inches long. It was armed by removing an arming strip and safety pin. The strip served as a screwdriver for tightening a screw which sealed the pressure chamber. The aerometer limpet was designed to explode when the aircraft reached an altitude of approximately 1,500 feet above take-off level. It could destroy the wing or tail assembly of a large aircraft or cause anything smaller to disintegrate completely. Numerous locations would work for this limpet such as the weight-lightening holes in the wall of the wheel wells, which are accessible when the wheels are down. These holes opened directly under the wing fuel tanks and cannon ammunition drums, ensuring total destruction. The weapon could also be placed in the tail assembly where the lifting bar is inserted. Installed between the engines of a larger aircraft, it could tear off the wing and outer engine. If the plane had only one wing engine per side, it could be placed between the engine and fuselage and the weight of the engine would tear the wing off. The front fuselage-heavy German aircraft were particularly vulnerable either in the front where much of the crew sat, or in the long narrow fuselage and tail structure which could easily break away. Many of these suggested locations were in places not usually checked by pre-flight inspections.

One of the more interesting, shall we say, explosive devices developed by Hargrove was the "Tire Buster." It resembled horse droppings. If run over, it would explode enough to burst the tire of the vehicle. A rather humorous thing in my opinion, but it was another attempt at sabotage. Not sure if they would have shortened the war by five seconds or five minutes.

On a serious note, in an ideal world there is no place for weapons of secrecy. However, in a world of undeclared hostilities, these weapons become necessary to counter the onslaught of an invading and occupying force. It may seem unnecessary to stress such an obvious point, but these weapons of secrecy by their very nature must remain shrouded in secrecy. Otherwise they are rendered ineffective. This runs counter to a free democracy where one of the conditions is freedom of information. It would be preferable to know how intelligence agencies function and the details behind their operations, but this information, once made available in the public domain, disarms us.

The limpets now found their way into the hands of the Norwegian Underground. A touching story reached the OSS Headquarters' Scandinavian Section one day. I recall hearing about a young Norwegian who attempted to sink a German ship. This is a sad tale. As a patriot, late in 1944 he found out the sailing date and hour a certain German ship was to leave the harbor. It was several days hence. He snuck through the German sentries, went under the wharf and lived there until the sailing date, surviving in the cold with rats for company. At the opportune moment, he time-fused a limpet, submerged, planted it under the water line and got out of there. The ship left port and headed out into deep water. Time for the limpet to do its work. No … no … it didn't explode! Here comes a most heart-rending report of the malfunction. "I failed! I failed my King! I failed my country! My one big chance to do something for the cause and it came to naught!" That one malfunction had dire consequences for this patriot. His name I cannot recollect.

During this time, formal attack orders and intelligence annexes were drawn up and trips were made to see how the weaponry, demolition and associated training were progressing. We had dry runs in northern Scotland up at Dalnaglar Castle. A simulated attack was mounted and promptly carried out on a similar tunnel. We found out we could hit it and allow for the elimination of the German guards at both entrances at the same time. We figured we could demolish the tunnel in less than a minute. Now it was just a matter of getting into the field and await clearance.

To my dismay, somewhere topside the decision was made to scratch the potential tunnel job I selected. The answer came back. "No soap!" It was decided the Allies may need the railway later on and the Norwegian Government wasn't too anxious to be rebuilding tunnels after hostilities ended either. Did we intend to use those tunnels on an invasion northward ourselves? They had been built by a terrific effort on the part of the Norwegian Government and quite recently too. Our group, being small, was gathered together in a large room at the castle and briefed about the tunnel project being put on hold. After issuing the order, the usual "any questions" was brought to the floor. One of the Norwegians who had escaped Norway and became part of the *Rype* group exclaimed with much relief, "I helped build those tunnels north of Trondheim."

My orders were to choose another target. So back to the scratch pads we go. This time I had a precedent to use. Two targets in particular looked most desirable, the bridge in the Tangen area and railroad lines at Lurdal, especially around the Flutten Tunnel. The Tangen Bridge itself was not very long. It consisted of four, 36-foot steel I-beams that crossed a 13-foot creek. It was unguarded and destruction would disrupt troop movements at least for the short term. The Lurdal lines were a vital link to the railway as proven by the fact the Germans had approximately 250 guards for a distance of approximately five kilometers.

The limpets were delivered at night in canisters under parachute to Norwegian Underground reception parties. We kept filling requests from the various reception

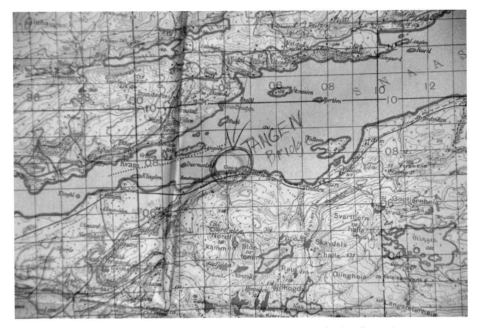

Map markings by Lt. Colonel Gerhard Bolland. (Author's collection)

teams on pre-determined nights when favorable light and weather conditions allowed and also subject to aircraft availability for the missions.

The next target selected was a similar high bridge across a gorge at Granauel. We had detailed data on this one. Major Colby had the *Rype* personnel construct a replica in Scotland with no outside help whatsoever. The self-reliance of the group was superior. Lieutenants Glenn J. Farnsworth and Blaine E. Jones, both demolition men, were busy. Farnsworth was aptly nicknamed "Rocky." He had been busy rocking northern Scotland with his numerous explosions.

First Sergeant Einar A. Eliassen had a background of acrobatic performers in his family and it dovetailed well. He drilled the men on how to close in quickly on the "ersatz" bridge back in Scotland. He had them climbing and crawling all over it to practice fusing it properly. The men perfected this so well that very little reaction time was left for the Germans after the elimination of their sentries on both ends. The final drill was a real blowing up of the structure.

Parallel to this, I busied myself with final special equipment procurement for the missions. We added British automatic rifles, U.S. folding-stock carbines, Swedish primus stoves, and Swedish skis procured in the field. Money seemed to be no barrier to our equipment. As Serge Obolensky said, in effect, "Money is one of our best weapons. Use it." Previously, he had headed up many of the groups on their initial war effort on *Jedburgh* teams, parachuting into France to bolster the

French Underground prior to the invasion. How fortunate we were to get him for our nefarious business. We started our operation with tremendously heavy U.S. ski-mountain boots. I jokingly told Colby, "In case of enemy contact, all you have to do is build up speed ahead of time and the momentum of those boots will carry you right on into them. The rest is up to you."

In the group also was T/5 Delphis L. Bonin, already wearing a Silver Star for gallantry. He had been decorated with a Purple Heart in North Africa with the Big Red One, 1st Division, and, upon recovery, was transferred to us. Men like this had been "bloodied." They were pros. In the heat of the battle, you could count on them. When, if ever, would a group like this ever be assembled again? A commander's dream!

I insisted on each plane unit complement being loaded to operate quite self-sufficiently for 40 days without contact with the others or the outside world. Ideally, each aircraft was to fly zig-zag flight patterns and at one point would pass over the target area for the drop. Once on the ground, even if the initial target was missed, each unit had several alternate missions before moving to the rendezvous area. In a last-minute change, the emergency snowshoes were added. Although I had originally planned for them, others were not so convinced at the onset, but now that the operation was in its final preparations, they relented. They were placed across the outer garment, across the chest and under the parachute harness. You could imagine the energy they would conserve as opposed to efforts floundering in the snow four to six feet deep in search of skis and other equipment dropped by separate chutes in the darkness.

I never forgot a lecture by the sea wolf Count Von Luckner at West Point in 1933. The count had disguised his German ship as a Norwegian merchant ship and had captured unsuspecting ships on the open seas by boarding without firing a shot. He spoke Norwegian fluently. The flamboyance and acidity of it! In that very element was the ingredient of success.

Who, in our entire group in the Scandinavian Section, upon counseling, weighing and careful consideration, would decide to go into Arctic regions, into six feet of snow and sub-zero temperatures for a mission? Yet, therein was our advantage! Colonel Skabo, Commander Vetlesen and myself were also finally of one mind. I said, "Why not stick? If we solve the re-supply issue, recruitment from the field Norse Underground would be very easy." A Castro type of operation in the snowy forests and mountains of Norway (as contrasted to the Cuban jungle terrain). I got the green light from them. Even authority to legally recruit the Norwegians into the U.S. Armed Forces was requested. We were going all the way. The commander said that if the Germans indeed plan a last ditch stand in Norway, we'll get *carte blanche*. That is, to write out our own ticket. In that long-range view, everything was planned for, even plans for brief leaves to Sweden for the men. The border was practically open for all intents and purposes anyway.

The British did not stand idly by on the side lines during this period either. My queries brought about curt brush-offs and coolness. I didn't have long to find out why. One day the commander alerted me by saying, "Bolland, I think the British are cooking up something. I believe they call it Operation *Ibrox*. Find out what you can. They're secretive about it." Now there happened to be frequent afternoon absences of the British from our jointly occupied brownstone building. Two majors would march up to the British Foreign Office for orders and were usually gone several hours at a time. We kept the British informed of our every move, but it was definitely not reciprocated. One fine day, when I found out they were off again to the Foreign Office for fresh signals, and only a young female stenographer held down the fort, I sauntered in and said to her, "By the way, we're all set with *Rype*. How are your people coming along with *Ibrox*?" She replied, "I really don't know, they don't tell me much about it." There was a nice big fat file behind her desk against the wall. "I was wondering about a couple of minor details I'd like to check on. Possibly avoid unnecessary duplication. Do you mind if I check it?" "No, go right ahead" she said, "Just put it back where you found it."

Out goes the file. I climbed all over it in ten minutes, gave it to the commander and had it back in their files in about 20 minutes. *Ibrox* turned out to be a mission to be commanded by a brigadier (our corresponding rank is a full colonel) promoted just for that single mission; a British Special Forces operation for 11 men of the 2nd Special Air Service and two Norwegians to destroy the Snåsamoen railway bridge near Trondheim in the northern part of Trøndelag. This was to take place on or about March 26 to April 7, 1945. The mission location was just 30 kilometers from our operational area on the Nordland rail line. Explosives, especially 20 pounds of RDX plastic, were hardly considered a nuisance raid! I could just imagine the brigadier marching into my command post with his party of six and, being the senior, assuming command of *Rype* as a joint British–American operation. After all, we were ostensibly integrated into a single SFHQ unit and thus our efforts would be trumped. Here comes that ugly phrase "sphere of influence" once again. This wasn't the last time it was to annoy us either.

Continuous drops to Norwegian Underground reception parties at night were being mounted by us concurrently. One morning a message on my desk was from one of their cells. It stated, "You don't need to drop us any more rocks. There's plenty here already." Apparently, the loading crew at the departure airfield had loaded the plane from the pile of test canisters loaded with rocks instead of the ones with carbines adjacent to them. Here were pilots and reception parties risking their lives, only to receive bundles of rocks. This was snafu number one that I experienced. I was to experience more as the operation progressed.

About this time, into our old brownstone building of American, British and Norwegian "shenanigan boys" (we were all together room-to-room on the second floor), Herbert Helgesen reported for duty. We had the good fortune of having him assigned to our operation. He was immediately sent to join *Rype* at Area P in northern Scotland. Herbert was invaluable to us for our field recruiting from the Norse Underground after getting back into Norway with *Rype*. After his parachute training, he immediately joined Major Colby and stayed with him for the duration.

In the British office of our SFHQ there was a middle-aged woman of intense resolve. Her very existence and life were dedicated to doing everything humanly possible to defeat the Nazis. Why, you may ask? Yes indeed, she told this story of her life. Married to a British naval officer, they reared a son who also became an ensign in the Admiralty. The war took them to sea and there they were both killed. She was now beyond her childbearing years. Her future happiness questionable, but her dedication to the task at hand? Never!

Knut Haugland, my communications officer, who officially reported to Lieutenant Colonel Oien, who was now head of the Norwegian section of SFHQ, was made a lieutenant in the Norwegian Army and busied himself around London in his quiet, serious way. I queried Commander Vetlesen and Lieutenant Colonel Skabo about formally adding him to our operation. The answers were evasive and, finally, a flat no. However, as mentioned, he was loaned to me for a short period to help get my radio communication plans readied.

The only thing Knut had brought with him upon his escape from Norway was a formula for deuterium oxide, D_2O, or "heavy water" as it is commonly called. A professor from Oslo University accompanied him to explain the monkey business going on at the Norsk Rjukan Hydro-Electric plant at Vemork. Research into nuclear fission was a relatively new field. The German physicist, Otto Hahn, had discovered that atomic fission could cause a super explosion. The Germans were pursuing heavy water, necessary to control the fission process since they thought this was the pathway to a nuclear bomb. Heavy water is water composed of oxygen plus deuterium, the hydrogen isotope with a mass double that of ordinary hydrogen. The physical properties differ from that of ordinary water as well. It weighs approximately 11 percent more and freezes and boils at higher temperatures. A nuclear reaction must be controlled in a laboratory for research and development purposes. Thus, heavy water was sought as a moderator or braking agent for a nuclear reactor built around a uranium pile. At the time, it was a logical step towards the development of an atomic bomb. The Germans were pushing an accelerated program to produce lots of heavy water. Norway began producing heavy water in 1934, above Lake Tinn at the eight-story hydrogen plant at Vemork. After Hitler invaded Norway in 1940, he ordered his troops to move straight for the nuclear plant in Vemork. Britain feared Hitler would use this substance against his enemies.

Knut disappeared for quite a while and did not appear back in London until near the end of the war, a man of mystery. I found out he went back into Norway, but why was he so insistent on getting back there? I learned later that Knut was actually the radio operator for the SOE team, led by mastermind Leif Tronstad, that blew up the heavy water hydro-electric plant at Vemork!

The initial plan to take out the plant by the British met with tragedy. Personnel assigned to the task were killed in a bad glider landing. However, once the British were able to successfully get more personnel in, Knut recruited Norwegians and together they carried out the sabotage successfully.

This came about because Roosevelt and Churchill met on June 17, 1942, and realized there was an urgency in sabotaging the Nazi nuclear bomb threat. On American soil, the Manhattan Project was already underway. If Germany built the bomb first, it would turn the tide of the war in a hurry. The Allies had to have it first. Therefore, the only heavy water plant in south central Norway in Vemork had to be sabotaged at all costs.

The time was October 1942. The target was the heavily guarded and a virtually impregnable, strategic material plant. Attempts had been made earlier to bomb it but, due to its location and the steep terrain, only one bomb managed to hit the roof several stories up, causing minimal damage. Thus, any hope of success had to be an operation on the ground. The assault force Knut was part of consisted of four Norwegians from Great Britain and six other locals from the area who were vigorously trained by British Intelligence in Scotland. These landed by parachute on desolate, forbidding terrain. Colonel Leif Tronstad of the Norwegian Army said that if this mission was successful, it would live in Norway's memory for a hundred years. The target was the high concentration room in which the heavy explosive charges would be secured around the conic cells of heavy water production. When it actually happened, the explosion sounded astonishingly feeble and innocent. When the raiding party was no more than 300 feet away, the Germans still did not know what was taking place. The explosion was, in fact, significant and tremendous. The concrete building was strong enough to muffle the sounds. Bjarne Nilssen, Director of Norsk Hydro, called it perfect sabotage. The Reich scientists suffered a delay of many months, a delay they could not afford. General Niklaus von Falkenhorst called the sabotage, "Britain's finest coup." The adventuresome Viking on that raid, Knut Haugland, as mentioned earlier, was the man responsible for *Rype* radio communications. I had full confidence in him to say the least.

Upon rebuilding the plant, the Germans produced considerable amounts of heavy water which Knut got once more by sinking a ferry boat while it was en route to a larger ship for transport to Germany. Despite blowing up the plant at Vemork and sinking the ferry, the Norwegians did not destroy all the German supply of heavy water. The Nazis began to move what was left the following year by train and ferry. An excellent book, *Assault in Norway: Sabotaging the Nazi Nuclear Program* by Thomas Gallagher, gives an excellent account of these sabotage efforts. The English also made a film called *Heroes of Telemark*. However, in the film, Knut Haugland's character was called Knut Strom. By the way, the movie has him in the air and on the ground on the first try. I guess it saved the film makers some time. He was actually in the air four times, hunting for the drop zone with three aborts, getting skinnier and more hollow-cheeked each time.

Failed attempts at airborne missions are not at all pleasant trails. I can personally attest to this. During the invasion of the Netherlands, my battalion in the 507th Parachute Infantry was prepared to go, locked and loaded, departure assignments and all. Then, at the last minute, we were scratched. That's the time to let down with a bottle of scotch.

Several years later, the 170-foot "hydro ferry" was discovered by scientists and naval historians in Norway. It was dragged up from the 460-foot-deep Norwegian lake. It contained 40 barrels of heavy water. The quantity would have been more than enough to catapult Germany on her way to becoming a nuclear power. It is believed Hitler was intent on destroying London had Germany been successful in developing a nuclear bomb. After the war, those involved in the German nuclear program said the loss of that heavy water was absolutely decisive. It stopped the reactor program in its tracks. This sabotage operation has been called the most important sabotage operation of World War II.

During this time, Colonel Oien made a trip from England to Norway by devious routes, skied in, and inspected the Norwegian Underground. He gave them training directives and goals to achieve for contemplating action when opportune moments arrived. The Underground were undergoing extensive maneuvers out in the woods on skis at the time. These were purposeful and well disciplined.

Back in London, SFHQ ran a command post exercise. Canned messages were passed back and forth from the Underground cells to London Net Control radio. Each message carried specific requests or orders, assuming a real invasion was taking place. This tested the entire communication network and helped improve or correct any deficiencies that showed up. I'm willing to bet the Germans were down on the beaches "google eyed" the nights we ran those tests!

Meanwhile, Colby was busy putting *Rype* through extensive training up at the castle. "Rocky" (Lieutenant Glenn Farnsworth) was busy rocking the area with his explosives. Farnsworth was amazed at Colby's stamina while skiing since Colby was only five-foot, eight inches tall and only weighed 130 pounds. He definitely did not stand out among the burly, six-foot tall Nordic skiers. "How can that little @*#! take it?" Yes, the nickname "Skin and Guts" fit him perfectly.

A lot of stumps were blown up at the castle. The training area also had a fine soccer field constructed for the men's use during some down time. Some of the blasting noise met with adverse results from an old Scottish herdsman one day. With staff in hand, he made an angry verbal attack upon the *Rype* personnel. They beat a hasty retreat to the castle to the tune of the Scotsman's blandishments. His sheep were lambing and not to be disturbed. When Colby learned of this he retorted,

"And I'm supposed to send you intrepid men into Norway against the Nazis? You can't even stand up to one lone herdsman!"

At this time Colonel Oien decided to begin setting up a parallel type of operation, although smaller with exclusively Norwegian personnel, in the Lierne area, a little way north of our area but just close enough to contact each other by skiing when both groups were in the field. Lierne is a municipality in Trøndelag County. It is part of the Namdalen Region and is the largest municipality by area in Trøndelag. Major Baungstead of the Norwegian Army was given command. Well, why couldn't the two units get to know each other? We sent him up to Dalnaglar Castle to spend some time with *Rype*. This was a sensitive move. The feeling we had was that the British were not too desirous of the close ties between the Yanks and the Norwegians. Here comes that ugly "sphere of influence" again. Fortunately, at the time, in London, a lieutenant colonel of the British Army, a regular, was on a short leave of absence. A lost, fresh major had replaced him. I popped in to his room one day and said, "Since Colby and Baungstead will be within mutually supporting distances of each other, why not have them on the same radio frequencies? We must give them the proper crystals and test them before they leave, of course." The major said, "Sounds reasonable to me. Go ahead." We could now stagger our blows against the Nordland railroad. Mutual confidence was developing. A chance to come to each other's aide in case of attack was more of a reality.

"Bang and boom" sabotage raids on Norwegian railroads were not new since other Norwegian groups were already operating in Norway. Between 1941 and 1942, refugees were trained in Great Britain and later quietly returned to Norway to begin their operations. The groups had code names such as *Archer*, *Heron* and *Falcon*. They arrived in January and February 1944. In addition, between October 1943 and March 1944, SFHQ sent more groups to Norway to wreak havoc on the railroads. This time they targeted lines between Trondheim and Oslo. Their code names were *Grebe*, *Lapwing* and *Woodpecker*. They consisted of three to six men each. These groups were closely controlled by the Norwegian High Command, in exile in London, through its station in Stockholm. Messages had to be brief for fear of detection by the Germans which would enable them to pinpoint locations of the operating groups. The quality of radio reception varied with the atmospheric conditions. For detailed reports, the groups depended on couriers from Stockholm. SHAEF in London closely coordinated these groups, much to the chagrin of Milorg, who wanted more overall sabotages. SHAEF only wanted selective operations to preserve assets necessary to reestablish the Norwegian economy after its liberation.

Major Baungstead's small *Woodlark* group was delivered to a target near Lierne by the RAF. If recollection is accurate, this occurred shortly after the partial *Rype* group was delivered. *Rype* had been ready to go since January 29, 1945, but the U.S. Army Air Force reported repeatedly that flying conditions were not suitable. It was delayed until March 24.

The *Rype* plan was, briefly, to have two groups of approximately 35 men each, both commanded by a major, overall command conducted by the lieutenant colonel for both groups and the operational and supply bases. A view to finally sending in our spores and setting up more cells was always uppermost in our minds.

The initial mission was to retard the movement south of German troops located in northern Norway by repeated cuts in the Nordland rail line in accordance with SHAEF directives. The operation was planned to be flexible enough to accommodate changes in mission from one of sabotage to other endeavors like arming, organizing and training the Underground in northern Trøndelag. The Underground was running an avenue of escape from there to Sweden for Norwegian nationals in trouble with the Germans. Some of these had fought on initial Underground penetrations by the Norwegian police force. These forces later became the new Norwegian Army. It had been organized in Sweden from escapees. By the way, *Rype* and *Woodlark* were to become the extreme left flank of the Allied effort. These objectives, of course, had to be within the limitations imposed by SHAEF and within the characteristics of operations for the OSS.

It wasn't the easiest undertaking to be sure. Besides a potential rugged delivery scenario, the supply problem itself was an extremely difficult one. That is why I designed each plane load to be a self-contained unit capable of independent operation in the field, on skis, at sub-zero temperatures for 40 days without outside help. If dropped at the wrong place, they would still be able to perform sabotage missions and proceed to the designated operational base. This base was Jaevsjo Lake, east of Snåsa in Nord-Trøndelag.

Several additional targets for the first and second NORSO Groups were discussed in a meeting. Lieutenant Colonel Skabo wrote a memorandum to Lieutenant Colonel Charles E. Brogger, Executive Officer, Special Operations Branch, detailing these additional targets for the first NORSO Group and potential targets for the second. All in attendance agreed the stretch of railway near Formofoss was another vital and logical target for the first group. The group was to be released in the course of two moon periods. The leader, a party of ten, and one radio operator, would be sent in the January period, the remainder of the group, 24 men, would come in the February period. The tasks for the first party were to establish communications with the United Kingdom, reconnoiter a base for the full troop, identify an area to receive the second party, and reconnoiter and lay plans for sabotage against the railroads.

Skabo suggested an alternate target for this group, the stretch of line north of Grong to Majavatn. However, Major Nordlie of the Norwegian Army, and Major Douglas of the SOE, pointed out that a Norwegian paratroop unit of 36 men had been relied on for operations on that stretch and did not believe that NORSO augmentation was necessary. They said additional targets were available south of the Agle Station. The destruction of Grana Bridge, south of Agle, was the original mission of the *Woodlark* party. After reconnaissance of the bridge, this group had found it too well-guarded for a small party of eight to attempt sabotage. The party had then chosen a target farther south, the bridge south of Jørstad. It had destroyed the bridge on January 13, stopping rail traffic for over two weeks. By now, the Germans had completed repairs on the bridge. Meanwhile, the *Woodlark* party was lying quietly on the Swedish side of the border with no immediate operations pending. The Grana Bridge would be an excellent target for the first NORSO Group, but the terrain was very difficult. In order to escape after blowing up the bridge, the men would have to be excellent skiers. If reconnaissance proved Grana to be better guarded by German troops than what *Woodlark* encountered, alternate targets were the rail lines between Snåsa and Agle.

Final details for the first NORSO Group were planned by the field order for February 22, 1945, or any night thereafter. The Nordland rail line was to be the prime target. The British Broadcasting Corporation (BBC) message to indicate the reception for that night would be "*Foxtrot i mastetopp*" (Foxtrot on the top of the mast). BBC times for these messages would be 2pm and 5pm Greenwich Mean Time. The advance party was to operate in uniforms only. If captured, the men would give only their name, rank, and serial number. The Geneva Convention entitled the men to be treated as prisoners of war. If in uniform and forced by the enemy to flee into Sweden, the men should expect detention. They were to tell Swedish authorities they had escaped enemy capture and they were to request internment in neutral Sweden. When the men went into Sweden to resupply, they were to wear civilian clothing obtained by *Woodlark*. They were to appear unimportant.

CHAPTER 16

Carpetbaggers

Special Operations units in enemy occupied territories were dependent upon delivery of personnel and supplies by air. During the war, this undertaking was dubbed Operation *Carpetbagger* and those involved adopted the nickname, "Carpetbaggers." There were only about 600 Carpetbaggers in all. This included not only flight crews but ground maintenance, equipment, and office personnel as well. The enlisted men lived in tents and the officers lived in quonset huts.

The first Carpetbagger missions began in early 1944, even before the D-Day invasion, under control of Donovan's OSS. In fact, after training with the Royal Air Force, who had been flying these missions for several months, the first all-American Carpetbagger mission (code-named *Wheelwright 57*) took off on the night of January 4, 1944. It was flown by pilot Lieutenant Colonel Clifford Hefrin. The original pilot of the crew, Wilmer Stapel, actually sat in the co-pilot's seat for this initial mission. Other crew members included Tressemer (navigator), Nesbit (bombardier), Millan (flight mechanic), Goodman (radio operator), Elliott (engineer), and Wezmak (gunner). During operations from mid-September 1944 to the end of the year, the Carpetbaggers also ferried fuel to depots on the Continent to supply advancing Allied armies. Taking off around dusk they flew missions no higher than 7,000 feet and plotted routes to avoid enemy gunfire before dropping to between 400 and 600 feet to make their drops. The Carpetbaggers flew more than 3,000 missions and were successful in dropping 536 agents and 4,511 tonnes (metric ton) of arms, supplies and equipment into France, Belgium, Holland, Denmark and Norway. In addition, some of the Group's squadrons went into training for night bombing operations. At its peak, RAF Harrington was home to about 3,000 personnel, including the Carpetbaggers, sixty-four B-24 Liberators plus several C-47s. All in all, Operation *Carpetbagger* itself lasted approximately one year. It was one of the best kept secrets of the war. Upon discharge, all Carpetbaggers were sworn to secrecy for 50 years with the threat of life imprisonment in Leavenworth. There is not one recorded incident of any Carpetbagger breaking that oath. It was not until after the operation was declassified in the mid-1980s that their stories began to come out.

The Office of Strategic Services (OSS) depended upon one particular Carpetbagger unit, the 801st/492nd Bombardment Group stationed at RAF Harrington, which was located about ten miles west of Kettering in Northamptonshire. This group was used exclusively to drop personnel and supplies into Norway for the *Rype* operation. Harrington airfield was simply known as Station 179 and was designated for secret missions only. In fact, it was so top secret no politician or newsreel person was ever allowed anywhere near it. The locals obviously knew there was an airfield nearby with aircraft taking off and landing, but even the administrative officers and crew members were kept in the dark. The Carpetbaggers flew B-24 Liberators as the air arm for the operation. These B-24s were more advanced aircraft than the older B-17 Flying Fortresses. More than 18,000 were built, making it the most-produced American military aircraft in history. The Liberators were powered by four Pratt & Whitney, fourteen-cylinder engines rated at 1,200 horsepower each. Top speed was about 300 mph at 25,000 feet and the aircraft had a service ceiling of 28,000 feet. They had a maximum range of 3,700 miles empty or 2,300 miles with 5,000 pounds bombs or other cargo. Their fuel capacity was more than 3,600 gallons if long-range tanks were fitted in the bomb bay. During the course of the war, there were actually 31 variations of the B-24 built at six different factories in the United States. After the basic design and prototypes were finalized, production variants were designated by a letter such as B-24C, B-24D, etc.

One of these variants, the B-24H, was modified for the pending *Rype* operation. Nose guns, waist guns and any other equipment unnecessary for the mission were removed in order to lighten the load (as was standard for Carpetbagger aircraft). These included the bombardier's heater on the right side of fuselage and plug lines in the nose wheel well. These were deemed not needed at low altitudes, provided better egress for the crew member, and reduced the possibility of fogging on the plexiglass. The fuel transfer pump and hose from the bomb bay were removed since the pump was not used to transfer fuel from an auxiliary tank. The D-12 compass, which navigators considered excessive, was also removed. It could not be read at night, especially when the Liberator was flying a zig-zag course. Instead, a B-16 mount compass was installed in the nose compartment. This was used as a tracking compass so the bombardier could tell if the pilot was drifting off course. It also acted as a check compass for the navigator. Also removed were: the VHF radio sets; all transmitter tuning units; the oil-slick release used by daylight crews if ditching into water; oxygen bottles, brackets, regulators and flow meters for high altitude flights; the astrograph and mount useful only on long ocean flights; all armor plate in the rear to reduce tail heaviness; unused radio antennas to reduce airframe drag; and the bombsight since supply drops were made visually. This all allowed for more cargo space and allowed the B-24 to travel at a greater speed. The rear guns and top turret guns were kept as protection in case night fighters were encountered. In reality, these guns were retained for crew morale more than anything else; a psychological element that they could defend themselves should the need arise.

What was installed, however, was a clandestine VHF radio system known as *Joan-Eleanor*. One transceiver was named after the wife of one of the developers and the other after his colleague's girlfriend. The signal from the agent/s on the ground had only a three-foot radius detection zone which did not allow the Germans to triangulate their position. Their radio was called *Redstocking*. They would first send up intel information (troop movements, etc). Then they would transmit requests for supplies/personnel for the next drops. Once received by the Liberators, these transmissions were then passed to specially-equipped British-built Mosquito aircraft flying at a much higher altitude. The Mosquito was mostly built from wood, allowing them to be much lighter and able to fly at a higher altitude, around 40,000 feet. This meant they were mostly out of reach, not only from German ground fire, but most interceptors as well. These Mosquitos had a 60-mile radius for picking up the signal from the Liberators. They would then take that information back to England to prepare for the next sorties.

For the *Rype* operation, the belly gun turret on the Liberators was replaced with a "Joe Hole" for paratroopers to jump out of. Two sets of static lines with two strong points each were added. They were set flush to the floor approximately 75 degrees apart and each strong point could accommodate eight straps, allowing a "jump string" of eight "Joes" at one time. In practice, this allowed two men to sit in front of the Joe Hole and six men to sit behind it. All projections near the Joe Hole that could entangle the paratrooper were either removed, ground down or covered up.

Due to the extreme secrecy of *Rype*, the flight crew never saw supplies or personnel being loaded. All was done after the crew was already on board. At the last minute, a dark vehicle would drive up and whoever was going to get in would load from the back of the plane. The flight crew did not know what the mission was, or who or what they were dropping. Thus, all passengers were commonly referred to as "Joes." That way, if the flight crew ever had to bale out and was captured, during their inevitable interrogation, if they were asked, "Who did you drop?," the answer would always be "Joe." Supplies were crated so as to be dropped through either the Joe Hole or loaded into containers designed to fit inside the bomb bay and released by existing equipment. The Liberators were painted black to elude detection at night. Curtains were installed over windows to ensure light from the equipment would not escape the interior. Some of the Harrington airmen questioned this and were simply told it was for night pathfinding operations. The exhaust pipes were fitted with dampeners to conceal their red glow. Flame arrestors were also installed on the machine gun muzzles.

None of the flight crew knew where they were going, not even the pilot; only the navigator knew. Information was strictly kept on a need-to-know only basis. The

801st/492nd Bombardment Group's mission also included dropping containers of supplies and explosives to Underground teams in the mountains of Norway. The *Rype* operation was at the extreme range of the Liberators. To make matters worse they would be flying at extremely low altitudes of only 400 to 600 feet. In the end, 208 American aircrew men gave their lives flying missions out of Harrington.

CHAPTER 17

Operation *Rype*

As the situation in Norway progressed, it became clearer that sabotage operations were pending. The Norwegian Special Operations (NORSO) Group was in Scotland undergoing skiing and mountain training in December 1944. This was in addition to the mountain training they had already received at Camp Hale in Colorado with the 99th Battalion. By January 1945, the unit received further screening procedures. As a result, about half of the men from the original group of 100 were returned to the United States. They eventually ended up on operations in the Far East. Fifteen men stayed on in Scotland to undergo even more training under the command of Major John Olmsted. These men could be used later for reinforcements, or for a separate mission altogether. The remaining 35 for the NORSO Group relocated to new quarters near the city of Peterborough, England, and the headquarters of Allied heavy bombardment. Our group, under the direction of Colonel Skabo, finalized plans and equipment to get them into Norway.

The first NORSO Group, called NORSO I, consisted of Major Colby, three other officers, 31 men and the attached Norwegian officer, Lieutenant Hoel. First Lieutenant Tom Sather with two enlisted men and radio reception equipment were selected to form the advance party and were standing by at Area H from January 29. However, the weather prevented any drops during this period. The February moon period was also met with snowstorms over the target, so we scrubbed those drops as well.

Again, on March 2, this advance party left Harrington airfield for Leuchars in Scotland. From there they would proceed to the target. However, an error was made in the briefing back at Harrington in that the time over the target should have been between 10pm and 2am, whereas the crew was briefed to be over the target between 1am to 5am. Actual time over the target was at about 2:30 am. The target was not visible, and the *Eureka* transmission was not heard over the *Rebecca* radio. The navigator was uncertain as to their location so Sather decided not to drop. Fuel consumption was high due to strong headwinds. The pilot decided to jettison the entire load including everything that was not bolted down—parachutes, personal equipment, machine guns and the *Eureka* and *Rebecca* radios. Sather and his party landed back at base practically in their birthday suits. The plane returned to Leuchars with approximately 50 gallons of fuel remaining, just over one percent of its 3,600-gallon capacity.

In fact, it was fortunate this advance party had not dropped. Heavy German troop activity was reported in the target area by Norwegian-in-exile newspapers. Apparently, the Germans got wind of Operation *Rype* and a large ski party had been dispatched from Steinkjer to Gauptjernet that night. Lieutenant Harold Larsen of the Norwegian Underground had observed the patrol. Since he was a superb skier, he quickly arrived at Gauptjernet in time to warn the reception party to disperse. That ended that favorable moon period. Besides, new radio equipment had to be procured and checked out since Sather had been forced to jettison his while limping back to Scotland.

Finally, on March 23, 1945, NORSO I once again moved to the departure aerodrome. Weather reports looked favorable. Aircraft were loaded with equipment, 'chutes and bundles. The adrenalin fluids were building up pressure. Fitful catnaps during the night in an attempt at calm nerves were not too successful. The feeling had much the same elements as a criminal awaiting his execution day, I should imagine. Breathing is heavier and faster. Pulse is up and all you can feel is "Let's get this damned thing over with and see if we make it or not."

Early in the morning of the 24th, Commander Hans Skabo, Sievert Dymbie and I were off to the departure airfield. We arrived two hours before take-off. The supplies were already on board and included 40 ten-pound drainage channel charges, 700 one-pound rail charges, 100 ten-pound Cramlingon blocks (standard charges), and 1,500 pounds of bulk explosives and ancillaries (special explosive containers containing plastic explosives). In addition, there were 16 extra sets of skis, four extra rucksacks, and one Nichols radio set as well as miscellaneous equipment for the base. Uniforms and personal equipment were also loaded. The individual escape kits included silk maps, a button compass, and 100 Swedish Kroner. A separate unit kit contained fifty thousand Norwegian Kroner and 400 Swedish Kroner.

With the supplies already loaded, last minute instructions were issued. With all our hopes, feelings and a final handshake, the personnel were loaded quickly. Doors closed, engines already warmed and off to meet their destiny.

The trip back to London was quite pensive. My personal feelings were of deep concern, yet I had a slight tinge of envy from watching the men take off, rather than participating in the action. A bottle of whiskey was passed around the car by the commander but barely touched. The only words I can recollect saying, were, "The men are riding the road to high adventure tonight." The collective answer was a quiet "Yes."

Now we all felt like mother hens with the brood lost or scattered and imminent danger lurking everywhere. The night that ensued turned out to be a long one indeed. Colby wouldn't be able to come up with a report by radio from the field until after daybreak at the very earliest. Would that little suitcase radio, that Knut conned me into using, deliver? Was the drop seen by the enemy? A dozen unanswered questions kept popping up.

If all went well, the rendezvous procedures would work according to plan. Reception committees for the B-24s would be using the visual aid "C" system consisting of three torches, usually red, in a row, with a white signal-flashing light set up at the downwind end of the line. The B-24s would come in upwind for drops. The signal lights would not come on until the first plane was heard. Sometimes the B-24s were asked to give an identifying signal if the reception committee thought there was danger of discovery by the enemy. The containers and packages were then dropped in train over a target at 400 feet absolute altitude, which is the altitude above the terrain, using an indicated airspeed of 135 mph and a flap setting of half. Although this was near stall speed, this procedure allowed the men to exit the aircraft with less wind resistance. It also reduced the scattering of equipment and gave the container 'chutes a better chance of opening so the equipment would not be destroyed. Of particular concern was the terrain. It was mountainous and changed abruptly between the hills and valleys. Up and down drafts could cause a fatal encounter with the terrain. Also, to add to the difficulty, pretty much all of Norway's remote terrain looked the same in winter because of the snow cover. This could make the location of the drop zones difficult.

I was down to headquarters at the crack of dawn to get the news, good or bad. No early reports were forthcoming, and the morning dragged on slowly. *Woodlark* was in and had reported to Net Control. Their radio was fine. They had the ability to call *Rype* on the mutual channel we had prearranged. "Any word from Colby yet?" was being bandied about. An officer in the overall Office of Strategic Services (OSS) headquarters impatiently suggested, "Why not have Major Baungstead see if he can't raise Colby?" He said this in the presence of the British officer, no less. Up to that point, the British had been in the dark as to our previous preparations. Quite obviously, some lack of cross-information flow had broken down. *Ibrox* and *Rype* both ended up being uninformed.

About noon time, flash! London received a message from *Rype*. The message arrived about four hours after the drop. How about that, Langeland came through! … or at least so I thought. We found out later that one of the radios was lost and the other damaged. The reception party gave NORSO I a replacement and, despite low battery power, their message got through. As soon as it was decoded, I had the message on my desk:

ONE OF TWO FIVE STOP PLANES BILL, SAETHER, GLENN, EINER ARRIVED STOP OTHERS NOT REPORTED STOP EQUIPMENT BADLY SCATTERED AND MUCH WILL BE LOST STOP DETAILS LATER STOP CORRECT RECEPTION WITH EURICA STOP MUST HAVE AT LEAST TWO MORE PLANE LOADS BEFORE

ATTACKING OBJECTIVE STOP CONDITIONS FAVORABLE FOR RECEPTION TONIGHT.

It is to be underscored that, at this moment and time, an important, historical event in World War II had just taken place. The very first American soldiers had landed on Norwegian soil to begin the liberation from Nazi occupation. The reception committee had done their part. They had come from Stockholm to wait at this particular spot on the Norwegian side of Lake Jaevsjo. The signal consisted of three large stacks of dry wood laid out in a straight line. A fourth stack was placed at a right angle to create an inverted "L". At the sound of four-engine planes, the kerosene-soaked stacks were lit and a single man stood with a flashlight pointed directly at the plane to give the correct identification signal.

We learned later that those initial transmissions were made by NORSO I out in the open during the day and from a pup tent at night using a flashlight in order to be able to see the radio instrumentation. Antenna wires were suspended into the trees for a better signal. In effect, this first transmission stated that although scattered over the whole of Lake Jaevsjo and into the woods to the northeast, Colby was collecting and assembling equipment and supplies and had made contact with the Norwegian reception party. We now knew he only had four plane loads at this time.

We later learned more details as to the outcome of these drops. The four planes that made successful drops on Jaevsjo were code-named *Glenn, Einar, Tryge* (Sather's advance party) and *Bill*. Slow dispatch of equipment from the aircraft caused difficulties. *Glenn* had one container go through the ice. *Einar* had one H-1 container come apart in the air and its contents scattered. *Tryge* was actually changed at Kinolos Airport since the original had no *Rebecca* radio. Consequently, it contained personnel plus their packages but it was not known whether a radio, batteries and a generator were changed or not. It also had *Ed's* containers. *Bill* had one package of skis, two rucksacks for Colby and F. Johansen, plus one package of stemming rods. Among the losses were three packages with four rucksacks and two packages of skis. Also presumably lost (if they were taken) were one radio, batteries and a generator. One container of Bren guns fell through the ice. Additionally, not all of the contents of the H-1 container that broke apart in mid-air were retrieved. In all, the drop zone was over a radius of about 10 miles, with some packages falling into the surrounding woods. Many had no static cords attached and plummeted to the earth without 'chutes, burying themselves into the snow. It took over eight hours before the NORSO I men were able to assemble in one spot. The snow over which they traversed was five feet deep.

We responded with the following radio transmissions:

26 March: We hear you. Three planes returned, one dropped Sweden near border. Report your condition.
27 March: Nothing tonight. Continue area weather reports. Sending four planes soonest.

28 March: our one cancelled. Ref. your two. Skis bags, medical kits, food from Sweden. Ari's generator by air with men. Send detailed weather report barometer, etc. Nothing tonight.

The men later described their experience of parachuting in that night. Inside the Liberator it was drafty. The outside temperature was 50 degrees below zero. The men put on face masks prior to the drop. This was to protect them from the sub-zero prop blast. The bottom hatch Joe Hole was removed. Static lines were checked by the jumpmaster. Without these attached to the aircraft, the parachutes would not open. Four OSS personnel then sat on the edge of the hatch. When the jump light came on, the jumpmaster shouted "Go" and gave a kick in rapid succession to each man in turn. The men literally jumped on each other's shoulders. The canopies opened 30 feet below the aircraft and provided for a very short trip to the lake.

By the time Kai Johansen hit the ground, where the temperature was 20 below, he felt like he had encountered a heat wave. Karl Hoffman (Matti Raivio) jumped late from his aircraft. He saw Major Colby land next to one of the fires. Hoffman landed softly and rolled down in the snow. He stood up, collapsed his 'chute and gathered in his canopy. He was soon aware he was not near the drop zone. Hoffman then took bearings off the terrain with his button compass. He discovered he was just across the border. Three-quarters of the lake was in Sweden and only one-quarter in Norway. He sped to the reception fires in the distance. He was determined not to be captured by a Swedish patrol and face internment. He wanted nothing more than to be on the winning side in this war for once!

Later in life, Colby wrote about that night drop in a CIA memo entitled *OSS Operations in Norway: Skis and Daggers*:

> The eight planes continued north, across the North Sea, over the stark fjords and the white mountains, then up the Norway-Sweden coast past Trondheim, Namos—almost to the Arctic Circle. By now, night had fallen and the moon was coming up. Below, a faint mist was spreading, taking the sharpness off the rocks, but meaning trouble later.
>
> Then it was midnight, and the pilot called to say that we were twenty-five miles off course over neutral Sweden. I told the men and they began to buckle on their white equipment. The pilot veered left and angled earthward.
>
> Now I could see the swath of shaved forest demarcating the two countries. "This is it," I told the pilot. Paulsen and Aanonsen pulled up the trap door, and I went through into the awful quiet that closes in when the engines recede. Then there was the cold and the wonder if there are friends below… and above. Dimly I counted the others slipping into the air- one, two, three- formation perfect, five seconds apart. At five hundred feet, the underground's landing fires pierced the haze, and with them came the sure knowledge we were at the rendezvous point.

A predetermined question and answer password was agreed upon by Milorg through Stockholm for the final recognition between *Rype* and the reception party. *Rype* would ask, "*Er fiskeriet godt her?*" ("Is the fishing good here?"). The answer from the reception party would be, "*Ja, saerlig i vinter*," which meant "Yes, especially in the winter." Hans Liermo of the reception party was either too excited to see *Rype* or completely forgot at that moment what the correct response was. Instead he replied, *"Nei, Fan! Det er daarlig fiskeriet her!"* ("No, it's no damned good at all!"). A stunned First Lieutenant Glenn Farnsworth, who was the only member of *Rype* who could not speak Norwegian to any degree, drew his .45 pistol, then asked, "Hans?" Liermo responded, "Me Hans." Farnsworth knew that the leader of the reception party's first name would be Hans. Liermo immediately recognized his mistake and gave the proper response. Amazing how a .45 pistol prodding into one's belly can generate a spontaneous and correct identification. The reception committee provided a horse and a sled to help *Rype* gather its equipment. Langeland later described the setup:

> The paratroopers quickly set about gathering their equipment. They were assisted by a local farmer who had brought his horse and sled. To the great amusement of the troopers, the horse was equipped with snowshoes. They had never seen a horse on snowshoes. It really was a treat to watch the horse maneuver through the high snow drifts with relative ease.

The NORSO I personnel dropped onto Lake Jaevsjo were:

T/5 Sverre Aanonsen, 325028869
T/3 Odd A. Anderson, 36610621
Maj. William E. Colby, 0-403761
Pvt. Einar A. Eliassen, 6871912
1st Lt. Glenn J. Farnsworth, 0-1293523
T/5 Asmund Gravdal, 32490841
T/5 Matti Raivio, 32905009
Cpl. Kai O. C. Johansen, 32624833
T/3 Fred J. Johnanson, 32932314
2nd Lt. Borge Langeland, 0-2025735
S/Sgt. Arne N. Leisteid, 32523677
T/3 Marinius D. Myrland, 32708477
T/5 Halvor H. Nipe, 32423623
S/Sgt. Alf H. Paulsen, 17157296
Lt. Tom Sather, 0-1305655
T/5 Oddberg P. Stiansen, 32721719

Norwegian patriots that made up a part of NORSO I, as well as some of those in the Underground, included Paulsen, Johansen, Iversen, Eliassen and Oistad. True heroes they were, for the bulk of them had been stranded on Norwegian ships in the early days of the war and one way or another found their way into the U.S. Army.

Lieutenant Langeland had been a ship's radio man. Sergeant Leisteid had been a seaman. Raivio, a Lapp, had fought the Russians in Finland and escaped to America as a ship's crew member. Corporal Andreasen had been a first mate and talked of nothing but the sea. Myrland was a former ship's engineer. All were mature men, competent, born skiers, violently anti-German, yet lovers of a country, fighting for the liberation of Scandinavia and Europe, whose uniform they wore.

Just to get an idea of their dedication, Lieutenant Tom Sather had injured four vertebrae in his back on a previous parachute jump. He kept silent about this because he did not want to miss the drop into his beloved Norway. Fortunately, the snow covering the hard, frozen lake cushioned his landing. The forged papers he carried with him identified him as "Ole Olsen." Thus, if a German patrol captured him, the *Gestapo* would not take out reprisals on his family back in Tromsö. His father was prominent in Tromsö and had represented the British Consulate before the war broke out.

Colby described the team as, "Men who could do anything from butchering a cow to fixing a motor with a piece of wire or operating on a casualty with a jackknife."

Clean up and establishing radio communications was first and foremost. The group had landed just before the Easter holidays. In Norway, there are four Easter holidays: Holy Thursday, Good Friday, Easter Sunday and Monday. The city people would be descending upon the wilderness for holiday outings. They must not stumble onto Operation *Rype*. Nobody was to get any sleep on Palm Sunday. The scattered equipment dropped from the Liberators had to be retrieved and concealed from any German spotter plane that may have been curious about the night's noisy activities. Parachutes, which were white, helped conceal the base camp on shore from the planes. The radio transmitter and battery had been dropped without their parachutes fully opening but were found only slightly damaged in a deep snowdrift that softened the impact.

Colby described their first night as follows:

> That first night was spent in bitter cold, twenty below zero and one thousand, nine-hundred fifty miles from the Arctic Circle, gathering up the packages with their colored chutes and hiding them under the trees and under snow. This was vital for the arrival of eight four-motored planes in a normally inactive sector and, even without dropping any explosive, they were certain to bring out German observation planes, followed by lots of security—or worse. The men worked silently and efficiently. I heard only one comment that night. It was by Lieutenant Farnsworth, and he was needling Lieutenant Saether [sic]. He was always needling Saether [sic], a Norwegian seaman soon to become an Army Captain.
>
> "There are two ways to do things lootenant," Farnsworth drawled as they tugged on a massive rucksack. "The wrong way and the Army way."
>
> "Yah," came Saether's [sic] thick reply. He never could understand American humor despite his years in Brooklyn and North Hollywood.

Communication with England was not easy due to atmospheric conditions. As mentioned, *Rype's* radio operations began on the frozen lake before being moved to a pup tent in the woods, where a fir tree housed the antenna.

Next came a report in from the departure airfield in England. Three aircraft returned after failing to find the target. All three were intact and safe. No word from the eighth plane. Since they had no radio to reach us, if indeed they were safe, they could do a job commensurate with their size since they had the where-with-all and were adequately equipped. They could eventually rendezvous with Colby. We were, of course, concerned because no news can be bad news.

We found out later what happened to that eighth plane. Those five men were actually dropped into Sweden by one of Colonel Clifford Heflin's Carpetbagger B-24s because of a navigational error. Those five men were:

T/Sgt. Leif Oistad
Cpl. Knut Andreasen
T5 Tom Rusdal
T5 Sivert Windh
T5 Eddie Hovland

They dropped in on the night of March 25, 1945, around 2am onto the frozen Lake Landosjoen in Sweden. There was no reception party to greet them and their equipment was scattered all over the area. Seeing lights on the far side of the lake, they concluded they would join up with the reception party by morning. Morning came and the only one to show up on the frozen lake was a man on a bicycle. Sivert Windh greeted him as he approached and asked where in Norway they were. The man chuckled and told them they were in Sweden. Norway was 60 kilometers west! Shortly thereafter, a company of Swedish ski troopers arrived to investigate. The noise of low-flying aircraft over the lake during the night drew their attention. They were more than curious about why American paratroopers were so deep in Sweden. Interrogations began immediately. Was this drop the beginning of a large-scale invasion? The men responded with only their name, rank, and serial number, as was common practice for any captured soldier. Well, Stockholm was immediately notified since Sweden did not want to be drawn into the war and, with U.S. soldiers now on its terrain, that could become a possibility. Rumors about the bizarre incident of five American paratroopers being found spread quickly. OSS Special Operations in Stockholm picked up on the rumors and knew it had to act swiftly. Later, in 1975, at a reunion in Minneapolis, Minnesota, Leif Oistad recounts those events as follows:

Those who were in Operation RYPE will remember this well. Those who went to China missed a good one. We were accidentally dropped in Sweden instead of Norway. We then said a few appropriate words to the pilot's ancestor that went mildly something like this: "May a thousand small devils dance sharp shod on your grave." Anyway it was just a matter of hours before the whole Swedish Army located us. We found out that they're darn good skiers too!

They gave us routine interrogation—name, rank, serial number, where are you from? what were you going to do?, etc. They took all our belongings. My .45 caliber and binoculars went first. Then our clothes! It was delousing time. We were led into a hot brick building. Inside there were five large tubs full of steaming water, and behind each tub was a smiling young girl! They were from the Royal Swedish Woman's Voluntary Army Corps (same as WACS to us) and they had brushes in hand. Tom Rusdal loudly hoisted the flag in protest. NO mere woman was going to give <u>him</u> a bath! If Roosevelt found out about this, it would cause an international incident. Tom was a bright cherry red from head to foot with embarrassment and the girls were delighted with amusement.

Since 1945, I have met veterans from U-Boat Commanders from Hitler's Kriegs Marine [sic] to the famous French Foreign Legionnaires, but I have never seen a soldier who fought so bravely, yet surrender so gracefully as Tom did as he slowly slid into the tub. Tom Rusdal, Sivert Windh, Knut Andreasen, Eddy Hovland and I were dropped inside Sweden. I have since become an aviator and can understand how the pilot made that mistake. Finding Jaevsjo in the middle of the night was like trying to find a needle in a haystack. And besides, he was running out of gas. He must have thought better Sweden than dumping us in the North Sea. It is one of the phenomena of flying without gas. You don't get very far!

After that hard scrubbing, they were given clothing and transported to Falun, 35 miles northwest of Stockholm, where a permanent internment camp was located. They were treated decently by the Swedish officials. They were given money to buy clothing and also began receiving $5.00 per diem. The men were happy about this, but not too happy about sitting out the rest of the war. The only thing they could be thankful for was being captured by Swedish troops and not German ones.

Now, back in London, how do you suppose we found out about this eighth plane? The Fourth Estate no less! It hit the newsprint in Sweden and England and extensive coverage was even on the radio news media. Just buy the latest London newspaper.

A strange by-product from this missed drop came spinning off. The grapevine circuit in Norway became alive. Now, at last, we have the Yanks actively on our side, a shot in the arm to the Norwegian people!

On March 28, we received a message from Lieutenant Colonel George S. Brewer (codename *Apollo*, code number 444). He was the Special Operations Chief of the Scandinavian and German desks at the Westfield Mission in Stockholm.[1]

Brewer's official cover was press attaché for the U.S. Legation in Stockholm. The following message came into our London office:

A. Have just interviewed member RYPE reception committee.
B. Four planes made successful drop between 0130 and 0200 hours on the 25th.
C. COLBY, SAETHER [sic], FARNSWORTH AND ELIASSEN and men are safe at rendezvous JÄVESJÖ.
D. Party believes they recovered most of the containers but cannot be sure as they did not know exact contents owing to changing planes before start. All supplies now safely stored.
E. No radio contact made because one set was lost and the other damaged. However, spare set was given them by the reception committee but battery too low to give proper signal. The battery should properly be charged by now. Damaged set being repaired and will be sent tomorrow of Friday. All supplies requested SKABO's cable will be sent same time.

---

1 The Westfield Mission also used various code words for purposes. Examples: *Norbiton* = Norway; *Norbiton Capital* = Oslo; *Shadwell* = Sweden; *Shadwelian Capital* = Stockholm; *Twickenham* = Denmark; *Twickenham Capital* = Copenhagen; *Eton* = Germany; *Eton Capital* = Berlin; *Club* = Legation; *Cowards* = Gestapo.

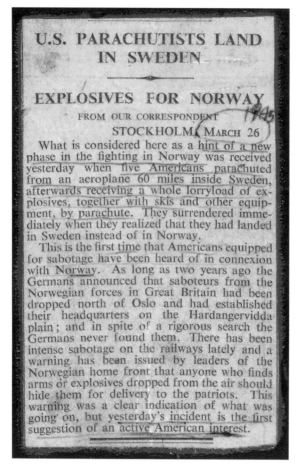

U.S. PARACHUTISTS LAND IN SWEDEN

EXPLOSIVES FOR NORWAY

FROM OUR CORRESPONDENT
STOCKHOLM, MARCH 26

What is considered here as a hint of a new phase in the fighting in Norway was received yesterday when five Americans parachuted from an aeroplane 60 miles inside Sweden, afterwards receiving a whole lorryload of explosives, together with skis and other equipment, by parachute. They surrendered immediately when they realized that they had landed in Sweden instead of in Norway.

This is the first time that Americans equipped for sabotage have been heard of in connexion with Norway. As long as two years ago the Germans announced that saboteurs from the Norwegian forces in Great Britain had been dropped north of Oslo and had established their headquarters on the Hardangervidda plain; and in spite of a rigorous search the Germans never found them. There has been intense sabotage on the railways lately and a warning has been issued by leaders of the Norwegian home front that anyone who finds arms or explosives dropped from the air should hide them for delivery to the patriots. This warning was a clear indication of what was going on, but yesterday's incident is the first suggestion of an active American interest.

Newspaper article reporting the fighting in Norway. (Author's collection)

F. Party does not repeat not know that the fifth plane landed in Sweden. You should send them signal this effect and warn them that Germans may realize other planes dropped in Norway and may send patrol to investigate although this is pure surmise on our part.

G. Reception party will scout area for possible German patrols.

H. COLBY requests rest of party be dropped soonest. Please include one extra radio set and batteries when drop is made.

I. Apparently two planes did not rpt not have REBECCAS and consequently their drops were not rpt not as efficient as the others as there was ground mist to the height of 100 meters.

J. Please notify me immediately when radio contact is established.

K. VAUDEVILLE[2] returning today after interrogating interned members.

L. Will send complete written report soonest.

---

2 *Vaudeville* was the code name for Hans Ericksen, code number 598, chief of the Norwegian Special Operations desk. He was located in Stockholm under the cover of Clerk, Naval Attaché Office.

Vetleson also messaged back to London from Stockholm on the same day:

1. Ken interned at FALUN. All well and unhappy.
2. High degree of security maintained and men have deported themselves excellently. In our opinion no blame can be attached to them.
3. Drop took place at LANDEGESJOEN or LANGSJOEN rpt LANGSJOEN about sixty kilometers southwest of target.
4. Pilot ordered jump after stating that EUREKA contact showed plane over target and that signal letter F rpt F received.
5. Pilot's decision unquestioned since men could not see ground from stations in fuselage.
6. All equipment in Swedish hands except plans codes crystals for RYPE to WAXWING and RYPE to HOME radio contacts. This not seen by Swedes and brought to Stockholm by me.
7. Courier to base may not be available until Tuesday. Can duplicates of para six material be sent RYPE with drop of remaining men.
8. Men at JAEVSJOEN base require also our emergency WT set powered direct from hand generator. Set of this type dropped but damaged and sent to Stockholm for repair. It was returned from Stockholm to field Wednesday. One spare set desirable however should be dropped if available.
9. Written report soonest.

We sent the following radio transmission NORSO I:

29 March: Leif's plane dropped five men in Sweden now interned. Extensive publicity, Germans may send patrols. Knut's codes and crystals safe will be delivered to you first courier. Ordering petrol generator for you in Sweden. Requesting Stockholm to maintain two weeks food level. Nothing tonight.

After setting up their early base using white parachutes as shelter, Colby's group surveyed the area and discovered a not-too-distant farm. The owner, Alfred Andersson, was persuaded to turn over his place for their use, aided and abetted by Swedish money, and convinced it would be in his best interest to go to Stockholm for the winter. This was followed by a little threat of duress and warning to keep his mouth shut or a follow up would be set in motion wherever he was. The day we moved in, Andersson, his wife, two children, his 70-year-old mother and 75-year-old father strapped on their lightweight Norwegian skis and sped off on their 40-mile hike. In Norway, everybody skis. Even the horses wear winter gear, such as the aforementioned snowshoes in Langeland's description.

After Andersson evacuated his family to Sweden, he eventually returned and joined the *Rype* group. He was useful because of his hunting abilities.

Incidentally, the farm still exists to this day. It is run by Nils Christian Gjefsjø who took it over in 1983. The main source of income is tourism and farming.

Now that the Jaevsjo farmhouse was acquired, radio operations were moved there.

At the farm there was, fortunately, a fresh cow and a horse in the adjoining barn. The horse was used to lug the scattered equipment bundles into the now newly acquired base. Colby did what was expected of him, promptly organizing the perimeter defense of the base, setting up final protective lines and the whole bit.

NORSO I was somewhat like a football team in a huddle, except that, in breaking out, it could go in any direction in response to an attack at any moment.

A guard post, consisting of two men in a mountain tent, was established. From this point the probable routes of approaching German patrols could be easily surveyed. A system of signaling was devised and the guard at the camp watched for signals.

On March 30, a young group posing as eleven "vacationers" arrived at the Jaevsjo farm during the holiday period. Lieutenant Hoel interviewed them while wearing his Norwegian officer's battle uniform. They were sent the next day to Sweden as escapees from the Germans. Kjell Sörlie accompanied them as a guard to ensure their security. At no time did they see or hear of the Americans and were told that they blundered into a Norwegian Underground security base. From his conversations, Hoel decided they were good Norwegians and the clandestine location of the farm remained intact.

Colby sent a progress report to our London office updating on more packages that had been found. The container from plane *Tryge* was found along with one other container, two packages, all the rucksacks and the generator. Still missing were two ski packages, and one or two H-1 containers most likely scattered in mid-air.

With NORSO now in the field with less men than anticipated, Lieutenant Herbert Helgesen got busy recruiting almost immediately. He picked up Harold Larson, the superb long-distance skier, and many others. We could afford to be selective. The

Aerial view of Jaevsjo Farm. (Author's collection)

supply of recruits was practically limitless, contingent only upon what we could handle with our available hardware and supplies.

Meanwhile, back in London, Skabo and this commander were also able to have OSS Headquarters pull 20 Greeks from the Mediterranean Theater to reinforce the NORSO group. They were all seasoned veterans of Operational Group missions in the mountains of Greece. Not skiers, but the snow would soon go away. At first there was some hesitation about how the Greeks and Norwegians would get along, but those fears soon abated. They got along tremendously. They were Americans you understand, although their personal grooming had been sorely neglected to the point where they bore a striking resemblance to a gang of Sicilian bandits. To meld them into a homogenous unit, the decision was made to send them and the rest of NORSO II through a quick refresher course at the British parachute school. Since Colby had our "barber" in the field with him, their locks up at the castle had become quite straggly. This unit began to resemble a band of Viking raiders and, to the surprise of nobody, unofficially named themselves the "Norgreek Group." I understand when the commanding officer, Captain Peter Leghorn, of the school first saw them he gasped, "Deliver us from the scourge of God and his vandals!" Some initial reservations as to the integration of the two groups were quickly dispelled. Soon Theophanes Strimenos and Knute Jog were sealed together like a Mafia for intended ventures. The morale of the unit picked up remarkably. It had suffered its first blow by being screened initially on the criteria of skiing ability and then the recent loss of members by air. Many had been together for over three years.

It is worth noting here our codename *Rype* had a material significance. The men, when time was available, would set up traps to catch actual Rype (grouse) birds to augment their rations. The trap was very simple, unique and very effective. It capitalized upon the habits of the bird. It seems that Rype birds will almost unfailingly follow a set pattern. The bird walks along fixed trails a good deal of the time. Where the trail passes by a bush, the bush is bent down and locked by a simple trip device to which is attached a small wire noose at head high level. The bird is evidently snow blind or far sighted because it will bob along, hit the noose, trip the trap and hang itself. In Norwegian winters the bird is preserved beautifully in a perpetual deep freeze. The traps can then be unloaded at will.

The reports fed to us from Sweden about enemy troop movements, especially those en route to future targets, were essentially meaningless. Colby encountered no trouble on the way in. Meager intelligence was fed to him from London but, strangely enough, new recruits picked up in the field supplied the operation with much more current and pertinent information.

You could never guess what type of an informer accidentally fell into *Rype's* hands one day. The area was used by nomadic Lapps who moved into our latitudes during the winter with their reindeer herds. The deer could easily get through the snow and fed on lichen during the cold months. The Lapps eventually moved all the way up to the North Cape as the weather warmed, some 300 to 400 statute air miles to the north. These people were self-sufficient, if left to their own devices. Their lives were centered almost entirely around their reindeer herds. They would do everything with them. They ate the meat and cured the skins which were then used for clothing, straps, laces, etc. The Lapps even rode the reindeer and used them as pack carriers. Their surplus was sold in the market. Not even the bones were wasted.

Well, into the *Rype* base one day comes a Lapp herdsman. The men got busy working on him and would win him over to our cause. He swore secrecy to our presence there. I'm sure the Swedish Krone he was given also helped. Soon he loosened up and started talking about the German troop deployments and strength. This war was of no concern to him, German or Allied. He plied his trade as usual, going and coming as he and his forefathers had done for centuries. Thus, Colby now had a floating S-2 Intelligence Officer, whether he knew it or not. This relationship continued smoothly for quite some time up to a point where an incident almost broke it up for good. It seems that the men were becoming just a wee bit tired of pemmican, that hard cake of lean beef tallow developed for Arctic explorers and quite old from storage. It is not too palatable to put it nicely. During the maneuvers in the Scottish mountains, it was the meat product ration used by myself. I found the best way to get it by the tongue was by super saturating it with curry powder that came straight from India. To make a long story short, one day the men killed one of the reindeer for the larder. He discovered it and, by golly, he was ready to join the German cause right then and there! Take one of my reindeer? Alliance or not, to a Lapp herdsman that was utterly despicable. Out comes plenty of Swedish Krone, apologies and down-to-earth diplomacy. He was finally placated, but for a while it was touch and go.

Speaking of surviving the Arctic, there is another skill used by the locals that is worth mentioning. If you want to see something startling, you should see how the old timers ski. The approach is entirely different from ours. They use only one long ski. The other foot has a shorter ski which gives propulsion. Instead of two poles they use only one long pole, somewhat in the fashion of a tight rope walker uses it for balance. They also have fur skins attached to the bottom of the skis. The fur bristles would dig into the snow going uphill but allow the skier to slide downhill reasonably well. At one point I seriously considered equipping our men with similar gear. In the end, we finally settled on more conventional skis and a choice of three waxes: one for climbing, one for downhill, and an in-between compromise wax. By teaming up in pairs, each man could in turn kick up his ski and have the other apply the wax for the task at hand. This worked quite satisfactorily. Actually, the only difference between waxes was simply changing the amounts of beeswax and tar, thus getting more slide or more drag. Ours was not the problem of the recreational skier since this was a back-breaking job of many ups and downs, carrying heavy loads. The rucksack becomes invaluable as it allows for a lower center of gravity for the loaded skier. Herringbone and side-step motions became the order of the day weaving through the mountainous terrain. No matter how well Larson ferreted out the best trail, it was still rough. One would surmise that the men, if seeing a mirage, would well have imagined a splendid cable ski tow whisking merrily upward and onward.

While waiting for directive from England, and with idle time on his hands, Colby was becoming more agitated. He was tempted to scrap the original plans and fight their own war. After all, the men were looking to him and Helgesen to supply an answer. He recorded the event as follows:

> The report I sent back that day said simply something had to be done. Actually, the few Americans in the bunch felt, and each day with growing intensity, that the entire reputation of America and its future in the Baltic area depended on pulling this thing out of the ice. Like Jesse James might have.
>
> Our plan was lifted boldly from the history of the West. We would seize a train, board it, throw her into reverse and blow up every tunnel and bridge we could until ammunition had run out; then drive the train into a ditch. We hope to succeed by sheer bravado. Farnsworth, the demolition expert, was in seventh heaven. The others smiled again. This was the kind of direct American action they'd heard about, read about, and knew went on all the time.

Except *Rype* consisted of only 16 men instead of 36. There were not enough to blow the Grana Bridge as Colby had dreamed up. *Rype* would just have to wait. They sent a condition report to London on March 27. Langeland had to decode and encode messages by hand since he had no machine to do it for him:

> Staying at Jaevsjo repeat Jaevsjo farm STOP establishing dumps around lake STOP request food be sent to Swedish side of lake as arranged in Stockholm STOP many packages lost STOP drop was scattered over eight kilometers STOP send two containers Brens, one container Garand Mane rifles, one container Springfield Rifles, gasoline generator Baker Mark two radio and battery, medical kit, twelve pair skis and sleeping bags, spare clothing STOP send Sgt. Kyllo, Sgt. Ausen and Harold Andersen to operate base STOP Rpt. Kyllo, Ausen, Andersen STOP need more men for bridge job STOP will receive other planes on northeast corner of Jaevsjo Rpt Jaevsjo Lake STOP wonderful weather STOP no alarm by Germans yet but are moving to woods to avoid vacationists until Monday STOP hope to leave for bridge then STOP send salt, pepper, and condensed milk.

The *Woodlark* party visited *Rype* to give some tips on how *Woodlark* had been so successful in blowing up the bridge at Jørstad in February.

Hans Liermo reconnoitered the Grana bridge and Colby began to devise an alternate plan to destroy it with personnel on hand. There were 20 German guards, three on duty, one at each end and one at the bottom. The main guardhouse was on the south and a smaller one to the north. Andreas Andersen had been an engineer on this very line a year earlier. As Colby had envisioned it, *Rype*'s plan was to capture an empty train approaching from the south and, while in the target area, drop and plant explosives. Then they would climb back on the train while Andersen began to back it up slowly. The *Rype* party would drop from the train as Andersen began to move it forward. He would jump from the train, the explosion would occur, and the train would plummet into the Grana River. This would provide a better escape for *Rype* since it could rapidly distance itself from the explosions and the German guards.

Colby also sent a letter with his report addressed to Vetlesen. He stated the melting snows in the days to come would make travel difficult for resupply. He reported that *Rype* had befriended the Lapp herdsman named Jama who would provide one reindeer per week to supplement the party's food supply and would also report on German troop movements. Colby also desired a weekly mail service from Stockholm to keep *Rype's* morale high and that Langeland had kept his messages brief and sent them as quickly as possible. He had heard interference, which indicated that German signal intelligence was trying to pinpoint *Rype's* location. Colby also reported that Lieutenant Farnsworth had planned so the charges would maximize damage to the Grana Bridge. *Rype* planned to blow the bridge with or without additional men. Another 15 Norwegian locals could be absorbed by *Rype* because they had demolition training in England. Colby's ideal

Woodlark party. (Author's collection)

plan was, upon destruction of the Grana Bridge, he would then conduct rail sabotage using small groups.

It is worth pointing out that the War Office maps Colby was using were incorrect. The actual bridge was located some 750 meters northeast from where it appeared on his maps:

We sent word to Colby ordering him to await the delivery of the remainder of NORSO and to remain inactive except for cautious reconnaissance of routes to the target railroad and to avoid detection by all means. We would mount a new air drop as soon as possible. The second NORSO Group should be better armed than the first group had been when it was dropped. Each man should have an M1 rifle, with every third rifle having a grenade launcher. Mortars and cannons should also follow in resupply.

On following drops, I had included paperback books, crossword puzzles, playing cards, etc., which became increasingly important as time went on to overcome boredom while NORSO I waited out orders for the impending strikes.

On March 30, 1945, we sent a series of messages from our London headquarters to *Rype* that four planes were coming from Scotland that night to resupply the operation with men and equipment:

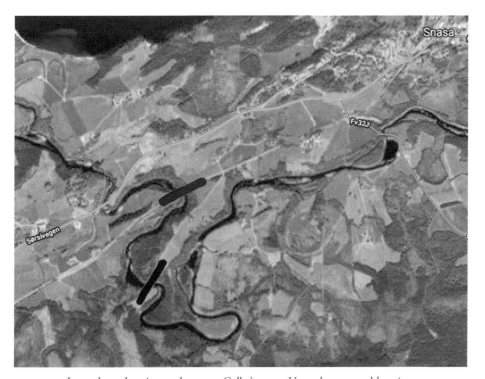

Lower bar = location as shown on Colby's maps. Upper bar = actual location.

30 March: Four planes coming tonight. NE corner of lake P for Peter. Listen for BBC.
30 March: We have been informed from SL rpt SL switches and crossings are bottlenecks for the enemy owing to repair difficulties.
30 March: To X 38. Message received. Action taken. If equipment not dropped this period will send soonest via Sweden. Greetings.

Exactly a week after Colby got in with his four planes, the remaining four were sent winging northward on March 31. However, the weather did not cooperate, as clouds and snow moved into the reception area. The reception committee was frustrated to hear the Liberators overhead and not be able to see them. *Rype* was not given the means to have two-way radio contact with the Liberators. Had the pilots known their planes were directly above *Rype*, they could have dropped their men and equipment. They loitered overhead for as long as their fuel window would allow, but the clouds would not lift. They were heard droning away and *Rype* knew the planes were returning to Scotland:

> 31 March: To M 20. Hope X 38 has cleared misunderstanding. Considered useful that you take care of Swedish connections but always bear in mind you must not be caught by enemy. Best greetings.

The next day we reported to them the unsuccessful attempt:

> 1 April: Planes returned unsuccessful. Two accumulators and baker mark two radio ordered sent to you from Sweden. Twinkle stores available to you now are carbines, BARs, stens, pistols, marlins, one bren. Sending Springfields to TWINKLE[3] soonest also badges requested.

On April 2, Borge Langeland sent a message to London advising us at Special Force Headquarters that the lake was too soft for future drops of men and equipment. Lillefjell (Little Mountain) was to be used instead. Headquarters planned to conduct dawn drops after the moon period. We responded:

> 3 April: Air will try dawn drops after moon period. Stand by time dawn drops later. Lillefjell confirmed. Swedish supplies on way to you now.

Meanwhile, Colby wanted to go ahead with sabotage using the resources *Rype* had on hand. One day, he decided to take a personal look at one of the targets. He skied westward toward civilization and the railroad. At about the extreme range of his probe he suddenly saw a lady coming down the mountain on skis "hell bent for election" and coming right towards him. She snorted to a stop right in front of him and promptly started to dress him down in angered tones. Now Colby wasn't too fluent in Norwegian, but she got her message across in no uncertain terms. The context was essentially "Well, it's about time you people got back here. You've been

---

3 The codename *Twinkle* was given to the operation to transport supplies from the United Kingdom to Sweden by diplomatic baggage for the purpose of establishing a stockpile at Stockholm for eventual transport to Norwegian and Danish supply dumps. This was carried out by Norwegian and American Special Operations Personnel.

overdue long enough!" She had mistaken Colby for a Britisher she had in mind when the raid on Narvik took place earlier in the war, which the Norwegians mistook for a real invasion. But what astounded Colby most was her rapid descent on skis. The lady was in her late seventies.

On April 4, Langeland sent the following message to our headquarters in London:

> Dawn drop agreed STOP but bridge must be blown soon to be effective STOP rumors that Germans to guard for three more weeks only as traffic from north cease STOP if remainder of party not here wish to do bridge with present group plus Norwegian friends STOP could not receive at same time STOP have found sufficient weapons and explosives STOP full report has left via Stockholm, send crystals and communication plan with Norwegian group STOP

That same day London radioed *Rype* that a second NORSO Group would be dropped in the next moon period. *Rype* was to assess its present and future needs of food and equipment. The aircraft code-named *Jones* and seven men were standing by for a dawn drop:

> 4 April: Plan sending second group in to you next moon. Is this advisable. For each 12 containers how many should be demolitions, Springfields, Brens, food. Consider your shortage and total future requirements. Jones and seven men still standing by for dawn drop. Lillefjall. Weather reports very important.
> 4 April: Your 15 of 4. Weather improving. Hold up mission until Saturday. Send weather reports. More information tomorrow.

After some initial transmissions, on April 5, we notified the bridge job would be pending with what *Rype* had on hand:

> 5 April: To X 38. Give names of men dispatched to Namdal and Steinkjer. Who are their contacts? Give also their addresses and possible passwords.
> 5 April: To X 38. Stockholm informed of your 15 and 17.
> 5 April: If not reinforced by Saturday plan of bridge with what you have. Definite orders then. Courier will explain number standing by.

On April 6, we sent word to *Rype* that four planes would arrive for a dawn drop on the 7th:

> 6 April: Four planes coming tonight. Two with personnel and Rebeccas, two with supplies but no Rebeccas. Dawn drop about zero three three zero GWT Lillefjall. P for Peter BBC message, FOXTROT I MATSETOPP.
> 6 April: Planes left for advance base one six zero GMT. All information I have. Hope daylight finds them there.

Three planes were heard, but not seen by *Rype*. These returned intact, unable to locate the target. Again, the cloud cover prevented a drop. The fourth plane drew the black card. It crashed in the mountains. *Rype* reported a possible plane crash 15 miles west of its base. A young Sami reindeer herder named Bengt Jåma later confirmed to *Rype* that *Jones* had crashed, immediately killing everybody on board, or so he thought. Colby told me later they were waiting as directed, but to no avail. It was a "no show." A distant explosion pierced the night, however. NORSO I instituted a search the next day.

Later, on April 30, Colby sent his official report to Skabo describing the details of the crash and burial of personnel:

1. On the morning of 7 April 1945 in the course of a reception it was believed that one plane was heard to crash. A compass bearing of West was taken on the sound, and a patrol was sent to investigate. From the distance the sound seemed away and the direction the crash was believed to be on IMSDALFJELD (4400). The patrol went to RAUFJELD (5597) and searched the country believed affected but saw nothing. On the morning of the crash, a strong Northwest wind was blowing and there were heavy snow squalls. Plane JONES was reported not to have returned to base after this mission.

2. On 26 April, on returning from the LURDAL rail attacks, we were informed by a local reindeer herder of the location of the plane on the West side of PLUKKETJERNFJELD [Plukkutjørnfjellet] at (574039). As the men were extremely tired, they rested the next day and the following day a severe storm prevented a patrol. On Sunday, 29 April, a patrol visited the plane.

3. From the position of the plane and its equipment, it is believed that the plane hit the top of PLUKKETJERNFJELD travelling West, and bounced down the slope. It is also believed from the positions and conditions of the bodies that all were killed instantly. The plane was broken into hundreds of pieces, scattered over a large area, the containers were all broken open and equally scattered, and the men were badly battered about and half-burned. Identification was possible by identification tags on those who had them and only by close personal acquaintance with the four OSS men involved.

4. The bodies were removed from the wreck and wrapped in parachutes found in the area. They were buried in a rock cavern on a slight knoll overlooking the site and the whole of LANG LAKE. An American flag was placed on the grave and a short ceremony held. Three volleys were fired over the grave and pictures were taken which will be made available to families concerned. The men are in the grave in the following order, from South to North:

    1st Lt. Blaine E. Jones
    Cpl. Knut J. Falck 32421335
    T/5 Bernard N. Iverson 36289300
    T/3 Robert N. Anderson 3250618
    Sgt. Jack H. Spyker 36453523
    2nd Lt. Richard A. Bosch 0-783238
    Unidentified air crewman[4]
    Unidentified Bombardier
    Unidentified Air Crewman
    Unidentified Officer
    Sgt. Angelo Santini 42003373
    1st Lt. William H. Hudson 0-829029

These were all bodies recovered and it is believed that they may include the full complement of the plane.

---

4 These unidentified air crewmen later identified as: 1st Lt. Lean G. Dibble Jr. 0-467431; F/O Arthur H. Barbknecht T-131697; Sgt. Gilbert L. Magruder 37615907; and Sgt. Fayette Shelledy 39144844.

5. There was practically no useable equipment in the area. A few odds and ends were picked up and brought back to camp. The Rebecca was discovered to be thoroughly smashed up. Lt. Jones' field bag was found with mail for members of this unit. Snow had fallen since the crash, so much is probably still hidden. Another visit will be made to the spot after the snow is gone.
6. Those identification tags found, F/O Bosch's badge of rank, the bombardier's wings, and two medallions belonging to Santini are enclosed.

The Liberator wreckage near the top of Plukkutjørnfjellet Mountain was just 10 kilometers northwest of Jaevsjo Lake from where NORSO I was located. The irony of it all was, if it had been just 20 feet higher, it would have cleared the mountain top. It will never be known, but one probable cause could have been the altimeter setting was wrong. For high-risk missions there are so many things that must go right. It would only take a single error and the results can be catastrophic. As it was, much of the crash was strewn over the top on the reverse slope. This Liberator was piloted by First Lieutenant William Hudson. There were twelve men on board and no survivors. NORSO lost three men:

Cpl. Knut Falck 32421335
T5 Bernard Iverson 36289300
T3 Robert Anderson 32580618

Here, in subzero temperatures Colby's men gave the dead an improvised military funeral on the spot even, as noted in his report, firing three volleys.[5] One casualty's home address read Luck, Wisconsin. The mailbag found nearby was intact and contained mail to *Rype* from loved ones. Usually it was a joyful occasion to receive mail in the Norwegian wilderness, but not in this instance.

As far as Colby was concerned, it was time to do something. On April 8, Langeland sent the following message to London:

> Will you drop in next six days? STOP If so will leave four man reception. STOP Answer today STOP Grana Bridge too much for present force STOP planning to attack bridge Jørstad to Valøy STOP

Major Colby was getting impatient and wanted to strike at least alternate targets. If London was to resupply *Rype* soon, he would provide the reception committee. What he was not aware of was that Skabo and myself were fervently trying to work out the details of aerial support, which was becoming more difficult day by day. On the same day, we gave the orders to begin sabotage operations and let *Rype* know that *Jones* never returned:

---

5   A memorial now stands at the crash site on Plukkutjørnfjellet Mountain and one of the recovered engines is now a monument in Trondheim, Norway.

8 April: Attack bridges Jørstad to Valøy. No drops until next moon our last chance then. Plane Jones failed to return to base may explain crash heard. Want Olmsted mobile, are skis necessary in fortnight. Advise us on ration demolition weapons, food containers immediately. Consider yourself, Olmsted and friends. Will station close during attack.

As if that tragedy wasn't bad enough, we lost more men when another aircraft crashed in the Orkney Islands in the early hours of March 25th. The all-black B-24H Liberator was also part of the Carpetbagger top secret operations squadron, the 492nd Bombardment Group, out of Harrington. It was returning from a scrubbed mission over Norway because of heavy cloud cover when it crashed at Walliwall. Due to icing of the carburetors, which caused engine failure, the doomed aircraft lost height and came down in a field near a Wivenhoe cottage and burst into flames. Only two men baled out, but one died when his 'chute failed to open at low altitude. The other, co-pilot Lieutenant Peter Pulrang, survived with minor injuries. The fourteen on board were:

Aircrew
Pilot: 2nd Lt. Henry L. Polansky
Co-Pilot: 1st Lt. Peter C. Pulrang
Bombardier: 2nd Lt. Fred W. Smickle
Navigator: 2nd Lt. Charles J. Allessio
Radio Operator: S/Sgt. William E. Lewis
Engineer: Sgt. William K. Stevens
W/Gun: Sgt. Edward W. Kussman
Tail Gun: Sgt. Eugene J. Graf

NORSO men
T/5 Gjerulf Ottersland 32624142
S/Sgt. Edward E. Kjelness 39230883
T/5 Eddie O. Sondeno 39614907
T/5 Johannes S. Rørvick 37311880
T/5 Leif E. Meland 32869494
T/Sgt. Trgve Berge 39031393

Colby radioed us to inquire about the remaining men but I decided not to notify him by radio, partially for fear of detection. Our military attaché in Stockholm, Lieutenant Colonel George Brewer, Jr. was notified instead. He relayed the message to the field by courier several days later.

NORSO and the *Rype* operation, being such a small and tightly-knit group, try as one might, it was difficult to keep things on an impersonal basis. I found it difficult, if not almost impossible, to relate this story until this late date. Memory has a wonderful quality of screening out the misery with the passage of time and retaining some of the more favorable events.

Chalk pastel portrait of Ida Catherine Sandmoen, Gerhard's mother, by his father Ben Bolland. (Author's collection)

Oil painting of Gerhard as a West Point cadet by Ben Bolland. (Author's collection)

This piece was painted for Little Sauk Lutheran (Long Bridge) Church, Osakis, Minnesota, and completed in 1926. Many members of the Henningsgaard family, relatives of Elisabeth "Lisbet," mother of Ben Bolland, are buried in the church cemetery. (Author's collection)

Ben Bolland was a renowned artist. This piece was originally located at Agusta Lutheran Church, Marietta, Minnesota, and completed in 1909. It is now on display at the Lac qui Parle County Historical Society, Madison, Minnesota. Anders A. and Beret Henningsgaard are buried in the cemetery at Agusta Lutheran. Anders is believed to be Ben Bolland's uncle. (Author's collection)

West Point Rifle Team, 1932. Cadet Bolland.

The Minnesota National Guard was allowed to select one candidate per year to attend West Point. This newspaper article, dated May 10, 1929, describes how Gerhard was the candidate selected for 1929.

Gerhard L. Bolland (right), West Point Cadet.

West Point First Indoor Team, 1932. Cadet Bolland 2nd row, far left.

West Point athletes, Bolland is listed as a "Wearer of the Minor 'A'" for rifle shooting. He is on the back row, far right.

GERHARD LEROY BOLLAND
Madison, Minnesota   *Minnesota National Guard*
"BOLEY"

WHEN you first meet him you are impressed with his air of detachment—you decide that he is strange and perhaps aloof. These impressions are, however, but outward signs of the innate reserve and quiet dignity which characterize Boley so completely.

While ever the most loyal and generous of friends, he seeks no confidences and grants few. Under no circumstances will he brook any intrusion on his private reveries. Having realized that true happiness comes only with peace of mind, he has earnestly sought answers to his questions—questions which most of us are too busy or too lazy to investigate.

His arch enemy is Father Time. Slow, deliberate in his every undertaking, he makes few mistakes the second time. His unwavering devotion to duty and his determination to succeed have carried him over many obstacles. Fortified with a steadfast faith in himself he has justified this faith in others.

Sergeant (1); Indoor Rifle (3, 2); Minor "A" (3); Outdoor Rifle (3, 2); Minor "A" (3, 2); Chapel Choir (4, 3, 2, 1); Rifle Expert; Pistol Marksman.

West Point yearbook entry.

1935, B Company, 21st Infantry. Captain Bolland bottom row, second from right.

21st Infantry Pack Train, July 6, 1936. Lieutenant Bolland commanding.

Obstacle Course. Lieutenant Bolland.

7-1/4" Presto M2 switchblade knife that Lt. Colonel Bolland carried with him during the D-Day parachute drop into Normandy. A small portion of the red attachment band still intact. (Author's collection)

Front and back of the shoulder patch worn by Lt. Colonel Gerhard L. Bolland during the Normandy campaign. (Author's collection)

The OSS maps used by Bolland for *Husky* and *Rype* operations. (Author's collection)

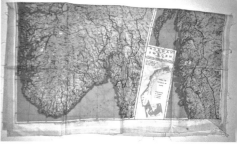

Some of the contents of the escape kit issued to Gerhard Bolland for Operation *Rype*, including a silk map, button compass (actual size = 9/16" diameter) and pouch. (Author's collection)

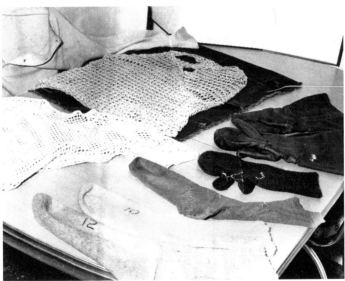

Some of the Arctic gear worn by *Rype* including whaler's vest, socks and mittens, as displayed for a newspaper article in 1966.

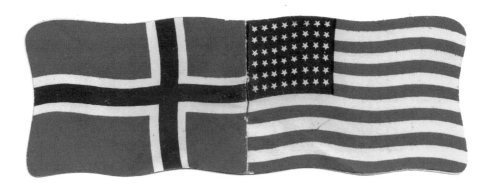

Extract from address by Hon. Calvin Coolidge when as President of the United States, he spoke at the Norse American Centennial Celebration at Minneapolis, Minn, June 8, 1925.

«When I look upon you and realize what you are and what you have done, I know that in your hands our country is secure. You have laid up your treasure in what America represents, and there will what your heart be also. You have given your pledge to the land of the free. The pledge of the Norwegian people has never yet gone unredeemed.»

JA VI ELSKER
(Bjørnson)

Ja, vi elsker dette landet,
som det stiger frem.
Furet, værbitt over vannet
med de tusen hjem.
Elsker, elsker det og tenker
på vår far og mor,
og den saganatt som senker
drømme på vår jord.

Norske mann i hus og hytte
takk din store Gud,
landet vilde han beskytte,
skjønt det mørkt så ut.
Alt, hvad fedrene har kjempet
mødrene har grædt,
har den Herre stille lempet
så vi vant vår rett.

Ja, vi elsker dette landet
som det stiger frem
furet, værbitt over vannet
med de tusen hjem.
Og som fedres kamp har hevet
det av nød til seir,
også vi, når det blir krevet
for dets fred slår leir.

GUD SIGNE NORIGS LAND
(Garborg)

Gud signe Norigs land
kvar heim, kvar dal og strand,
kvar lund og lid,
han lat' det aldrig døy
han verje bygd og øy
han verje mann og møy
til ævleg tid.

Her stig det stort og blått,
vårt fagre heimlands slott
med tind og tårn
og som det ervdest ned
alt fagrar' led for led,
det bygjast skal i fred
åt våre born.

KAN DU GLEMME GAMLE NORGE
(Ukjent forfatter)

Kan du glemme gamle Norge?
Aldri jeg dig glemme kan,
med de stolte klippeborge,
du er mine fedres land.

Kan du glemme Norges skove,
glemme furu, bjørk og gran?
Vannets klare blanke vove
aldri du forglemme kan.

Svever dog ei titt din tanke
hjemad hvor din vugge stod?
Føler du ei hjertet banke
for det landet du forlot?

NÅR FJORDENE BLÅNER
(Paulsen)

Når fjordene blåner som markens fiol;
og breene glitrer i spillende sol,
når liljekonvallen ved foten av hegg
står duftende skjønn langs med klippenes vegg
mens elven bak orkrattet danser sig vill
og trosten fra granlien synger dertil,
da røres mitt bryst, da blott hviske jeg kan,
Gud signe dig Norge, mitt deilige land.

Å EG VEIT MEG EIT LAND
(Blix)

Å eg veit meg eit land langt deruppe mot nord
med ei lysande strand millom høgfjell og fjord.
Der eg gjerne er gjest, der mitt hjarta er fest
med dei finaste band.
Å eg minnest, eg minnest so vel dette land.

Og eg lengtar så titt dette landet å sjå,
og det dreg meg so blidt, når eg langt er ifrå.
Med den vaknande vår vert min saknad so sår,
so mest gråta eg kann.
Å eg minnest, eg minnest so vel dette land.

Pamphlet printed and given out for victory celebrations in Norway at war's conclusion.

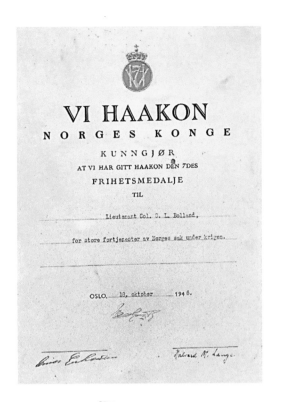

Norwegian Haakon VII Liberation Citation and Medal awarded to Lt. Colonel Gerhard Bolland. Signed by the King and Minister of Defense. At the war's conclusion, King Haakon VII of Norway, who was exiled in England at the time, made his triumphal return. As a result of Bolland's involvement with OSS Operation *Rype*, the King awarded him a signed citation and liberation medal. The citation states, "Haakon, King of Norway hereby declares that we have given H. VII liberation medal to Lieutenant Col. G. L. Bolland for great services to the Norwegian cause during the war." (Author's collection)

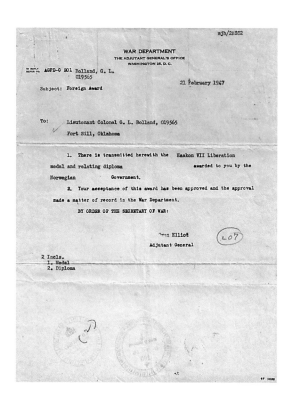

Photo that appeared in a local paper in 1965. Gerhard Bolland holding the King Haakon VII citation and wearing the medal.

Bolland's War Department I.D. Card.

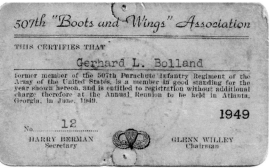

507th PIR Boots and Wings Association, 1948–49.

Lieutenant-Colonel Gerhard Bolland, Camp Gordon, Georgia, October, 1946.

Lieutenant-Colonel Gerhard Bolland, Head of Provost Marshal (Military Police), Sapporo, Japan, 1950.

Reunited with his family, Madison, Minnesota, 1950.

NA - Not Applicable

CHARACTER OF SEPARATION	REPORT OF SEPARATION FROM THE ARMED FORCES OF THE UNITED STATES	DEPARTMENT
HONORABLE		ARMY

1. LAST NAME—FIRST NAME—MIDDLE NAME	2. SERVICE NUMBER	3. GRADE—RATE—RANK	COMPONENT AND BRANCH OR CLASS
Bolland Gerhard Leroy	019 565	Lt Col 17 May 43 RA Inf	

6. EFFECTIVE DATE OF SEPARATION			7. TYPE OF SEPARATION
DAY	MONTH	YEAR	
31	May	51	Release Retirement

5. QUALIFICATIONS
SPECIALTY NUMBER OR SYMBOL 1510 RELATED CIVILIAN OCCUPATION AND D.O.T. NUMBER None

8. REASON AND AUTHORITY FOR SEPARATION	9. PLACE OF SEPARATION
Retired Par 37 SO 96 Dept of the Army dtd 15 May 1951	Denver Colorado

10. DATE OF BIRTH	11. PLACE OF BIRTH (City and State)	12. DESCRIPTION
DAY 11 MONTH July YEAR 09	Madison Minnesota	SEX M RACE W COLOR HAIR Light Brown COLOR EYES Blue HEIGHT 6'1" WEIGHT 172

13. REGISTERED YES NO	SELECTIVE SERVICE NUMBER NA	14. SELECTIVE SERVICE LOCAL BOARD NUMBER (City, County, State) NA	15. INDUCTED DAY MONTH YEAR NA

16. ENLISTED IN OR TRANSFERRED TO A RESERVE COMPONENT YES NO	COMPONENT AND BRANCH OR CLASS NA	COGNIZANT DISTRICT OR AREA COMMAND NA

17. MEANS OF ENTRY OTHER THAN BY INDUCTION	18. GRADE—RATE OR RANK AT TIME OF ENTRY INTO ACTIVE SERVICE
ENLISTED REENLISTED X COMMISSIONED CALLED FROM INACTIVE DUTY	2d Lt

19. DATE AND PLACE OF ENTRY INTO ACTIVE SERVICE	20. HOME ADDRESS AT TIME OF ENTRY INTO ACTIVE SERVICE (St., R.F.D., County, City and State)
DAY 12 MONTH June YEAR 34 PLACE (City and State) West Point New York	111 3rd Avenue Madison Minnesota

STATEMENT OF SERVICE FOR PAY PURPOSES

	A. YEARS	B. MONTHS	C. DAYS	25. ENLISTMENT ALLOWANCE PAID ON EXTENSION OF ENLISTMENT, IF ANY
21. NET (NA) SERVICE COMPLETED FOR PAY PURPOSES EXCLUDING THIS PERIOD				DAY MONTH YEAR AMOUNT NA
22. NET SERVICE COMPLETED FOR PAY PURPOSES THIS PERIOD	16	11	19	26. FOREIGN AND/OR SEA SERVICE
23. OTHER SERVICE (Act of 16 June 1942 as amended) COMPLETED FOR PAY PURPOSES	2	11	15	YEARS 5 MONTHS 6 DAYS 17
24. TOTAL NET SERVICE COMPLETED FOR PAY PURPOSES	19	11	4	

27. DECORATIONS, MEDALS, BADGES, COMMENDATIONS, CITATIONS AND CAMPAIGN RIBBONS AWARDED OR AUTHORIZED
World War II Victory Medal American Defense Service Medal American Campaign Medal Bronze Star Medal European-African-Middle Eastern Campaign Medal w/2 Battle Stars & Bronze Arrow Head*

28. MOST SIGNIFICANT DUTY ASSIGNMENT	29. WOUNDS RECEIVED AS A RESULT OF ACTION WITH ENEMY FORCES (Place and date, if known)
Parachute Infantry Unit Commander	None

30. SERVICE SCHOOLS OR COLLEGES, COLLEGE TRAINING COURSES AND/OR POST GRAD. COURSES SUCCESSFULLY COMPLETED	DATES (From-To)	MAJOR COURSE	31. SERVICE TRAINING COURSES SUCCESSFULLY COMPLETED
Infantry School	1938	Regular	Map & Aerial Photo Reading
Command & General Staff School	1943		
Parachute School	1942		
Air Force School Command	1947	Liaison Pilot	

GOVERNMENT INSURANCE INFORMATION: IF PREMIUM IS NOT PAID WHEN DUE OR WITHIN THIRTY-ONE DAYS THEREAFTER, INSURANCE WILL LAPSE. MAKE CHECKS OR MONEY ORDERS PAYABLE TO THE TREASURER OF THE UNITED STATES, FORWARD PAYMENTS FOR N.S.L.I. TO THE COLLECTIONS UNIT, V.A BRANCH OFFICE HAVING JURISDICTION OF AREA IN WHICH YOU MAINTAIN PERMANENT RESIDENCE. FORWARD PAYMENTS FOR U.S.G.L.I. TO COLLECTIONS DIVISION, VETERANS ADMINISTRATION, WASHINGTON 25, D.C. WHEN MAKING INSURANCE PAYMENTS BE SURE TO GIVE FULL NAME AND PERMANENT ADDRESS FOR MAILING PURPOSES. SERVICE SERIAL NUMBER AND POLICY NUMBER(S) IF KNOWN.

32. KIND OF INSURANCE (amount and premium due each month)	33. MONTH ALLOTMENT DISCONTINUED	34. MONTH NEXT PREMIUM DUE
(U.S.G.I.) (N.S.L.I.) $10,000 $12.80		July 1951

35. TOTAL PAYMENT UPON SEPARATION	36. TRAVEL OR MILEAGE ALLOWANCE INCLUDED IN TOTAL PAYMENT	37. DISBURSING OFFICER'S NAME AND SYMBOL NUMBER
NA	NA	NA

38. REMARKS (Continue on reverse)	39. SIGNATURE OF OFFICER AUTHORIZED TO SIGN
*Combat Infantryman Badge Norwegian - Haakon VII Liberation Medal France-Fouregerre of Croix de Guerre Croix de Guerre w/Palm (2) Presidential Unit Citation Army of Occupation Medal w/ Japan Clasp Cadet USMA 1 July 1929 to 12 June 1934 Retired for Physical Disability Certificate of Retirement Issued See reverse side	[signature] NAME, GRADE AND TITLE (Typed) PETER CALZA LtCol AGC Adjutant General

40. V.A. BENEFITS PREVIOUSLY APPLIED FOR (Specify type) COMPENSATION, PENSION, INSURANCE BENEFITS, ETC. None	CLAIM NUMBER None

41. DATES OF LAST CIVILIAN EMPLOYMENT FROM None TO	42. MAIN CIVILIAN OCCUPATION Student	43. NAME AND ADDRESS OF LAST EMPLOYER None

44. UNITED STATES CITIZEN X YES NO	45. MARITAL STATUS Married	46. NON-SERVICE EDUCATION (Years successfully completed) GRAM-MAR 8 HIGH SCHOOL 4 COL-LEGE 4 DEGREE(S) BS	MAJOR COURSE OR FIELD Academic

48. SIGNATURE OF PERSON BEING SEPARATED Gerhard L Bolland

47. PERMANENT ADDRESS FOR MAILING PURPOSES AFTER SEPARATION (St., R.F.D., County, City and State)
111 3rd Avenue Madison Minnesota

DD FORM 214 1 JAN 50

INDIVIDUAL'S COPY (TO BE DELIVERED TO THE INDIVIDUAL BEING SEPARATED)

1

Par 27 Continued
Parachutist Badge
Glider Badge
Liaison Pilot Badges

Lieutenant-Colonel Bolland ended his military career as quite the decorated soldier.

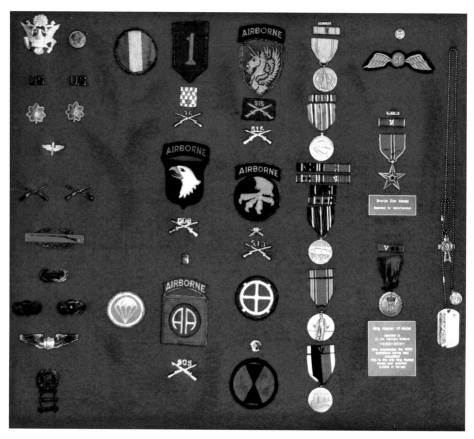

Display includes: World War II Victory Medal; American Defense Service medal; American campaign medal; European-African-Middle Eastern campaign medal with two Battle Stars and Bronze Arrowhead (arrowhead denotes participation in a combat parachute jump, helicopter assault landing, combat glider landing, or amphibious assault landing, while assigned); Bronze Star (with bronze "V" device worn to denote valor/heroism); Presidential Unit Citation medal; Army of Occupation medal with Japan clasp; Army Airborne Glider badge (this badge is one of the rarest medals obtained by a soldier since gliders were used only for a short time during World War II and are now obsolete); Army Combat Parachutist badge (star in center signifies jumping into battle behind enemy lines. Service Stars are also affixed to the Parachutist Badge to denote participation in a combat parachute jump, retroactive to 07 Dec 1941); Liaison Pilot Wings (Qualified to fly light, single-engine liaison aircraft). Missing is the French Fouragere of Croix de Guerre with Palms medal, unfortunately lost by family members. Also included in the display are Lt. Colonel Bolland's dog tags.

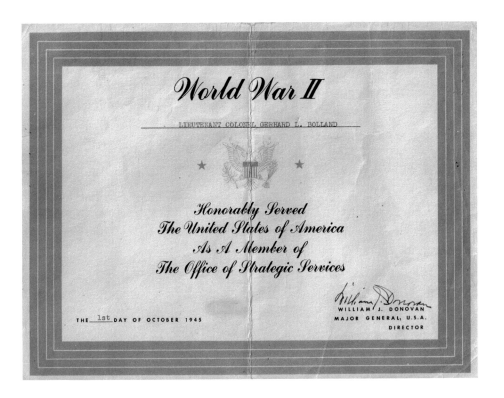

OSS Discharge Pendant and Pin. (Author's collection)

Medals revive war memories

By John Newhouse
Written for The State Journal

For a mild-mannered man, Col. Gerhard Bolland has seen quite a bit of violence.

During World War II, he was an OSS spy in Norway, heading an underground unit of 196 men intent upon blowing up railroad tracks.

And, before that, he parachuted into Normandy one dark night a few hours before the D-Day invasion, his mission to knock out German gun emplacements before the Allied troops hit the beaches.

Of his days in Norway, he says: "The Germans desperately needed more men on the Western front in the closing days of the war, and there were a lot of German soldiers in Norway. They began shipping men, by train, to southern Norway, and in 48 hours they were on the front lines.

"The trains carried about 500 men a day and it was our job to keep the trains from moving.

Bolland shows war medals.

Half-pound explosives

"We carried half-pound plastic explosives, which we attached to the tracks. A few minutes later, BOOM! and no train would be moving over those tracks."

And the colonel and his 196 or so men would disappear in the Norwegian wilds, a step ahead of the Germans looking for them.

They had planned to enter Norway by plane, but . . .

"There was only 15 minutes turn-around time over the target," Bolland said, "for the planes were heavily loaded with men and explosives.

"We lost two planes, and nine men, and decided to fly to Sweden instead, and come into Norway by train, disguised as Norwegian farmers."

The language was no problem for Bolland. Born of Norwegian parents in Minnesota in 1909, he had spoken the language as a child.

Captured airport

Near the end of the war, he and his men liberated the Vaernes airport, near Trondheim, a bomber base from which the Germans attacked the North Atlantic sea lanes.

"We took the airport, disarmed the men, and drove them to the sea, where their ships picked them up," he recalls.

The night before D-Day, he recalls, was brisk.

As a battalion commander, in charge of about 1,000 men of the 82nd Airborne division, he parachuted into France in the dark of night.

"We could see the flares of the

guns firing," he said, "and tried to drop close to them. I didn't do so well, in the dark, I dropped into a nearby river, and almost drowned."

He tried to get out of his chute in the water, and that was a mistake, for he was being dragged underwater.

"Then I had a few quick words with the Lord, and He said, 'Roll over on your back' and I did, and the chute, blowing on the surface of the water, pulled me up to the top."

He arrived on a spit of sand, but his troubles were not over. It was cold. His hands cramped so he could not unbuckle the chute until he had blown on them and rubbed the cramps away.

Was it an unhealthy place to be?

"They had their chance at us on the way down," he said, "but, when and if we made it, it was our chance. We were pretty aggressive."

His group fought for 35 days, without letup or reinforcements, knocking out two German divisions, but losing two-thirds of their manpower.

"There were about 3,200 when we went in," he said, "and only 733 the day we went out.

"When the guy to the left of you is gone and the guy to the right of you is gone, it's a little lonesome."

He now lives in Oakwood Village, and on the wall of his room is a citation from Norway's King Haakon which reads, "For store fortjenester av Norge's sak under krigen," which translates to: "For great acts for Norway's sake in wartime."

And he has a medal from Norway's king, also, which came a year or so after the war.

"The Norwegians are a little slow about awarding medals," he said.

"But when you do get it, it really means something."

Local newspaper article, November 6, 1984.

Final salute. Lieutenant-Colonel Gerhard L. Bolland, one of many of that "Greatest Generation," that the world may never see again, was laid to rest on November 12, 1999. Photograph from a local newspaper shortly before his death.

Bench dedicated to Gerhard L. Bolland at the Veterans Memorial Park in Stoughton, Wisconsin.

Although half of *Rype* was not in the field yet, persuasive efforts were made by me to get into the field myself, especially after the crash on Plukkutjørnfjellet Mountain. Concern for my men was paramount. Skabo could push the remaining elements in without my assistance. Therefore, I proposed the help of an RAF Mosquito to take me to the crash site. I felt that if the pilot pulled it straight up into a near stall, it would be feasible for me to bale out at the top of the climb and thus avoid collision with the tail surfaces. External winds would have little effect on one's body at stall speeds. A single 'chute could be brought down very quickly by voluntarily collapsing it until a couple of hundred feet from the ground. This is a standard maneuver practiced in the U.S. Parachute School and I had already proved it worked during my night drop into France on D-Day. Detection at 30 miles in the dusky light would have been negligible, so that would work in my favor as well. After I presented this plan, quizzical looks came my way. Despite my efforts and arguments to the contrary, the request was denied. But I still think it would have worked.

After our orders to attack the bridge between Jørstad to Valøy were sent, Langeland encoded Colby's reply but atmospheric conditions prevented *Rype*'s transmission of it that night. Pretty much, at this point, the Grana Bridge was out. The message would not be transmitted until *Rype* returned from its mission. In the message, *Rype* said the station would be closed, that skis would be necessary until the first week of May, that there were no Germans within 20 miles and that *Rype* wanted its containers as requested by Colby's letter to Vetlesen. In addition, Odd Stiansen would go to Stockholm posing as a Norwegian refugee, but *Rype* wanted to be sure he could be sent back.

Colby also planned on cutting rail lines in a future attack by small parties east of Lurdal and southeast of Snåsa Lake, which would occur after the bridge attack. He requested container drops in the next moon period closer to the targets. Jeeps should also be dropped after the spring thaw to replace skiing as a mode of transportation.

In the progress report of April 5, Colby really pushed for the Lierne plan. He stated they talked with natives in the region and said it would be easily defendable by a force the size of NORSO I and a Norwegian parachute company, especially during the winter and spring months when the road entrance is blocked by snow. Transport other than by this road was prohibitive because of the mountains. Once the road opened, however, a larger force would be needed. Colby summarized his plan. At the beginning of May, NORSO I plus the Norwegians would seize the area and provide a base for the formation, training and arming of Norwegian patriots from the Trøndelag area. Additional Norwegian forces would then move in from Sweden. Large resupply missions would come from Sweden, by one or two large Flying Fortress daylight missions. This was similar to what Colby saw in France. Once enough men were armed to defend the area, it could serve as a large-scale base of operations to clear the Germans from central Norway. Colby ended by proposing to meet with Major Bangstad in the near future and to have detailed reconnaissance done by local citizens.

Looking ahead to possible non-snow operations, Colby really pushed to have jeeps dropped. He stated this would be the most effective way of harassing German road communications. He claimed maximum damage to the Germans could be done by speedier communication other than by walking. I had grave concerns about this. My fear was that Colby, who saw what was used in France, thought it would work just as equally well in Norway once the snow left. The weather and latitude above the Arctic Circle, even in warmer months, may have had something to say about that.

He also had a special request for canned pineapple. The locals had not enjoyed eating any for many years. Colby perceived the availability of pineapple would be a tremendous morale booster for the Norwegians.

He finished his report with a complaint. Apparently, the dropped rations were missing items such as cigarettes, candy, and soap. He suspected there was theft going on when the rations were being assembled back in England and he wanted it stopped. He called it, "… a particularly rotten bit of theft."

Finally, Colby wanted on the record the unit's appreciation of Lieutenant Hans Hoel. In Colby's words, "He handled all liaison with Norwegian citizens of the area, has organized the transport of supplies to the unit from Sweden, and has given much valuable advice on routes and areas in the surrounding territory."

Vetlesen radioed London from Stockholm summarizing Colby's April 5 letter to him:

April 9:
1. Following paras summarize Colby letter of 5 April to Skabo.
2. Plans for bridge action complete and attack will take place with present force if necessary.
3. Anxious for reinforcements. Expecting one officer and seven EM soon and wants second NORSO group dropped to him next moon.
4. Suggests addition of eight AEHLBY trained men to present force and fifteen more to join second NORSO group upon arrival. If you agree please cable 8654 asking that first eight be selected and sent and other fifteen earmarked.
5. COLBY feels LIERNE rpt LIERNE PLAN feasible. Road entrance blocked by snow until spring thaws and area easily defended by present RYPE force plus WAXWING. Thereafter more men would be needed. COLBY's plan as follows. RYPE and WAXWING seize area about May 1 and form a base for training and formation of Norwegian patriots. Enough men armed to defend area after opening of roads by means of resupply from HARRINGTON, by daylight Fortress ops, and by transportation from Sweden. Large scale base would then exist for operations intended to clear Germans from central Norway.
6. In re para 5 COLBY has asked for opening of communication to WAXWING and plans visit to Major BANGSTAD while simultaneously making distant reconnaissance of LIERNE area. Detailed reconnaissance to be made by natives.
7. Since all or part of para five and six plans are in violation of para three x of field order two as presently written, COLBY asks for your concurrence.
8. Rail cutting by small parties from base planned after bridge operation. Container dumps wanted at following points to facilitate this work:
    East of LURDAL rpt LURDAL
    Southeast of SNASSA rpt SNASSA LAKE

Pinpoints will be radioed direct form RYPE. EUREKA reception available both pinpoints on same night.

9. Each dump to get two planes each carrying two rail-charges, eight SNF rpt SNF, and two K rpt K ration containers.

10. Arrangements should be made to drop JEEPS to RYPE as part of plans for non-snow operations and when suitable has been secured. Contact HQSAS liaison officer on this.

11. Second Group should be equipped as follows:
One M. 1 rifle per man.
One TSMG per three men.
One M 1903A4 rifle per squad.
One BREN per squad.
Every third rifle equipped for firing rifle grenades.
Two 60 mm. mortars per unit.

12. Second group should also have one container of each of the following calibers ammo:
Three hundred three
Thirty
Forty-five.

12. Wants resupply of clothing for men including OD uniforms etcetera. We have all necessary items except for shirts and insignias. Can these be sent. Also please send complete list of sizes for all men. Sgt KYLLO rpt KYLLO should have these.

13. Letter pouch next bag.

By this time the favorable moon period for that month had ended. The ever-lengthening evenings were gradually working towards the midnight sun phenomenon at those latitudes. Chances of visual detection were becoming ever more acute. Someone proposed the idea that if the drop was made an hour before sunrise, the German garrisons would then be at their sleepiest and at their lowest ebb of activity. Chance of detection, therefore, would be the least. The nearest German soldiers were about 30 miles away. The Scandinavian section bought into the idea. Another drop was made on April 9. The Army Air Force promised their best pilots. The field was notified to provide reception.

The Scandinavian section in London, along with the blessing of Hans Skabo and myself, had now made the decision to unleash NORSO I full force. *Rype* was now completely underway to disrupt German troop movements as much as possible. The die was cast. From now on there could be no lack of resolve. Information copies were sent to all interested agencies, including our embassy staff in Stockholm. The British representative in Stockholm was also notified. Afterwards, I started receiving reports, from Sweden via Stockholm, of suspected German patrol activity at various points in the areas adjacent to or on our route of march from base to target. This struck a sour note. Could the ugly head of the "sphere of influence" be rearing its ugly head once more? Was this "voluntary sharing" of intelligence a hint at political considerations of who would operate in what zones? A radio message was sent back to Stockholm, cleared by the Scandinavian section as follows:

RYPE PREPARED TO FIGHT WAY TO TARGETS AND ACCOMPLISH
MISSIONS. WILL BE RUN FROM THIS END. BOLLAND

No rebuttal was forthcoming. We decided to not inform Colby of this exchange. A calculated risk? Maybe, but we felt most prudent at the time. A radio message was then sent to NORSO 1:

ATTACK THE NORDLAND RAILROAD

This was the one Colby had been anxiously awaiting. The time had come! At long last, Colby and NORSO I could move in on the targets. Jelkas were loaded with explosives and essential personal gear decided upon that each individual could manage. Every man carried on his back a heavy rucksack, weighing 60 pounds and containing explosives and provisions. One man in particular, Lieutenant Tom Sather, was responsible for the jelkas. Our Norwegian recruit, Harold Larson, came through beautifully. He was our trailblazer and had the dubious pleasure of tramping down the trail in advance of the group. His cross-country experience paid off. A poor trailblazer could have just about killed the men with needless climbs, descents and extra distance. Navigation in the snowy mountains was a huge problem but Larson accomplished it magnificently while still bleeding internally from his harsh treatment as a German prisoner. What a man!

On April 9, the unit departed the Jaevsjo farm to trek to the target area between Tangen and Jørstad. The Norwegian liaison officer in the group, Herbert Helgesen, recruited four members of the local military resistance to participate in the mission. Three men were left behind to guard the farm. The unit set out on a 100-mile, six-day cross-country ski trip. These are the true names of the men that trekked to the target:

> Angar Andersen
> Robert Andersen
> Odd Anderson
> William Colby
> Einar Eliassen
> Glenn Farnsworth
> Asmund Gravdal
> Jörgen Havik
> Herbert Helgesen
> Kai Johansen
> Borge Langeland
> Harold Larson
> Toralf Lian
> Hans Liermo
> Arne Listeid
> Jon Moan
> Marinus Myrland

Halvor Nipe
Alf Paulsen
Matti Raivio
Tom Sather
Kjell Sörlie

Leif Öistad and his four men were still in Sweden and Odd Stiansen was on his way to Stockholm.

The first day of the trek started in the afternoon and was kept purposely short in order to get within one day's march of the next convenient stopping place. Still, it was rough with rain and a strong wind. The unit halted for the night at a vacant Nazi sympathizer-owned summer hut. The men took turns pulling a toboggan carrying 60 pounds of explosives, three men to a toboggan. The provisions were very small, only six days of rations were carried and sleeping bags, not tents, were carried to minimize weight. Pulling toboggans was not difficult on level land or downhill, but when climbing the mountains on skis, pulling the toboggans uphill was exhausting. Daytime skiing in sticky snow was dangerous. Nighttime was much better. A big concern of Colby's was that if one of his men, or even himself, should break a leg, medical attention was not close by. He told his men to sit on their skis should they lose control. Nobody received even a sprain using this undignified tactic. In the two days following, a wet and sticky snowstorm with a strong westerly wind hindered progress. On April 12, the storm abated, but the wind did not. The unit climbed past Imsdalsfjeldet Mountain, went south of Flatfjeldet Mountain, to avoid a German observation post, and onto Bronstad Seter where they camped for the night at about 7pm. The next day they moved down the Roktdalen Valley, then up an extremely long slope and stopped for lunch at Rodben Seter. They crossed over Pass 572 then traversed the extremely broken terrain to Olingen Lake where they stopped for the night at about 11pm. Colby, Hoel and three men went around Bjornhifjeldet Mountain along the tree line to the north to observe the Jørstad Bridge from a distance. They made note that three or four Germans were on guard duty at the bridge at all times and the remainder lived close by. They also observed a train as it passed by, slowing down to a near stop and then going on. Since a train was intended to be used in the planning, it was observed to be mainly freight with some empty box cars. There was a caboose in the middle. It gave no whistle signals when approaching the bridge. The bridge itself was a straight plate girder span from abutment to abutment. Later, the group retreated, went over to Korsmaeren, and slept in a cleft in the rocks on the south side.

Two more reconnaissance parties struck out the next day to reconnoiter Valor Station and the Tangen Bridge. However, due to the extremely broken up nature of the terrain, which did not show on the map, the party was forced to return before reaching the bridge. NORSO I then had to rely on a locally acquainted Norwegian's report that the Tangen Bridge was a replica of the original Jørstad Bridge.

The second reconnaissance party moved to a hill overlooking Valoy Station, approximately 300 meters from the station. The German guards had apparently observed Sather, Larson and Langeland while they were reconnoitering the station at Valoy. The German guards rushed out of their quarters to put on their equipment and hurried to get into a position to fight. The party counted about 10 Germans and then skied away in great haste to avoid damaging security any further. The Germans did not go very far, as they were observed by Sather, Larson, and Langeland before they encountered some Norwegian woodcutters during their chase.

One additional reconnaissance mission was made by the party that looked at the Jørstad Bridge. This was the Strindmoen Bridge. The morning was used up again traversing broken terrain leading down to it. Lieutenant Helgesen and Jens Leksvik[6] were left to complete reconnaissance of enemy positions and met the evening northbound train south of Strindmoen, identifying it by a white flag waving from the right side of the cab. They met the train but no signal was given so they remained hidden and noticed the train on that particular day contained three passenger cars full of people. They were not sure whether they were Germans or Norwegians. The rest were cargo cars of coal and coke material.

When Colby arrived back at Oiigen, he was informed of the results of the reconnaissance. He was told the hour and a half he allowed for the trip from Oiigen to Valoy Station was insufficient due to the broken terrain. Because of this and the alert at Valoy Station, Colby and Sather decided to attack the Tangen Bridge.

So now plans had to be changed to carry this out. With every unprecedented operation there came a level of anxiety, and this was no exception. They chose to attack considerably south of the nearest point to the railroad. It was felt this would confuse any pursuers. The bridge was approximately 17 kilometers from *Rype* headquarters at the Jaevsjo farm. Reconnaissance of other bridges proved they were too heavily guarded and *Rype* did not have enough men to attack those targets with any prospect of success. If the German engineers were worth their salt, they would have the Tangen Bridge reconstructed within a matter of days. Therefore, rail damage would also have to be done.

The unit moved out at 9pm on April 13, leaving their rucksacks in the nearby woods. They went from Oiingen to Rausjoen–Kvern Lake and then north to the village of Tangen. As the maps indicated, this would be the best route. It was not. Skis had to be frequently removed and boulders climbed over in the wooded areas. Even cliffs had to be descended. The men did not arrive on the cliffs overlooking Tangen until 4:30 am on April 14.

Colby gave this account of the approach to the Tangen Bridge:

---

6 Jens Leksvik may be an undercover name for one of the OSS men or one of the four local resistance fighters that Helgesen recruited, it's not specified in Bolland's notes.

Finally, we got to the peaks overlooking the Tangen Bridge, somewhere north to Tangen, where the railroad skirts Oiingen Lake. The terrain was the most difficult I had ever seen.

Picture the Hudson River, visualizing the Palisades three times their true height. Place a railroad snug against the foot of the cliffs, and then crust the whole thing with four feet of snow and six inches of ice. Now place twenty-three skiers atop that mountain, and they are carrying revolvers, tommy guns, Garandes, Brens and one-hundred-eighty pounds of explosives plus other equipment on a massive sled.

Helgesen said it would be impossible to get down. Men would break their legs, their skis. But I was a novice at skiing and knew motion is possible in positions other than upright. One patrol found an ice-logged waterfall that descended in fairly easy stages in a deep, rock-lined gorge. It ended in the lake. Perfect, I thought. Mad, thought Helgesen. We would sleep on it- and did, in a crevice in the rock. Next morning, we started, the men having been instructed to sit whenever they felt themselves losing control. Our only casualty was one of Helgesen's skis. He did not think much of the sitting idea. He was re-rigged and sent into the foothills beyond.

Helgesen was a national hero, known to everyone, even in this bleak area. He headed for a hunter's cabin, where every move of the Germans was recorded. From these, he could learn what the enemy was doing, then pick up later by flagging a train. [7]

Meanwhile, Colby and Langeland went out on reconnaissance with the rest of their unit close behind. They stumbled upon a house. There was no evidence of ski tracks there. They entered the house and found a family that had been evacuated from Finnmark. The man said frequent German patrols passed through Tangen but the bridge itself was not guarded, except for fairly frequent patrols and that the nearest guard stations were at Valoy and at Strindhem, about three kilometers to the south. While Langeland visited with the family, Colby inspected the bridge. The rest of the unit then moved into the house and duties were assigned:

Covering North:	1st Sgt. Eliassen (M-1)
	S/Sgt. Listeid (B. Gren)
	T/5 Raivio (BAR)
	Alhus (TSMG)[8]
	Sörlie (Carb)
Covering South:	S/Sgt Paulsen (R Gren)
	T/3 Myrland (BAR)
	Sverre (Bren)
	T/5 Aaronsen[9]
Demolitions:	Lt. Farnsworth
	T/3 Odd Anderson
	Cpl. Kai O. C. Johansen
	T/5 Nipe

---

7 *OSS Operation RYPE/NORSO*, https://www.99battalion.org/index_files/rype.htm
8 Not in trek list, possibly another undercover name, not specified in notes.
9 Sverre and Aaronsen not on trek list, possibly undercover names.

T/5 Gravdal

Reserve and possible assault party:
Lt. Sather
Harold Larson
Hans Liermo
Lian
Andersen

Left at base at Jaevsjo:
T/3 Fred Johansen (twisted ankle)
T/5 Oddberg Stiansen (being sent to Stockholm for medical care)
Gaer

Hq:
Major Colby
T/Sgt Langeland

The time had come. Tom and his group moved out quickly to the north with four men entering homes in the surrounding area. After crashing in and interrupting sleep, he announced his intent to the residents as politely as he could, all the time ripping telephones from the walls and snipping wires. The area was three percent Quisling followers, the infamous Norwegian traitor who sold out to the Germans. You can imagine what the local residents were like. Malcontents that would not hold a decent job in open competition in peacetime. Willing to do the Nazi bidding and being stupid enough to think the occupation was not of a temporary nature. The reason this area was three times as strongly German oriented was because of the fine hunting and commerce enjoyed in peacetime. Incidentally, Colby toyed with the idea of using Krup Von Essen's hunting lodge nearer the rail line. The major drawback was that certain privileged Quislings were permitted to keep it and use rifles for hunting. We could well imagine what a donnybrook that would be when they came wandering in. Thus, Colby chose to be deep in the wilderness, accepting the extra effort for added security. By contrast to this area of three percent Quisling followers, the average Quisling ratio for the rest of Norway was less than one percent.

Reconnaissance and the laying of charges at Tangen was about to begin. Four teams converged on the bridge. At the bridge, they carefully cased the joint, knowing exactly what each man would do. There were those infernal guards to take care of. That was done speedily and in a coordinated effort. Lieutenant Farnsworth led the demolition team. Three other teams approached from different directions. It was daylight and the snow was glossy enough to alert the community to ski and foot movements. Once everybody was in position, Farnsworth and his team set their

80-pound plastic explosive demolition charges on the bridge. The bridge was 12 meters long and had four one-inch-thick I-beam metal stringers. The men then redeployed on the heights overlooking the bridge to await a train. The ultimate goal was to destroy the bridge just as a train was crossing. Two birds with one stone, if you will. However, this bravado was not going to take place at Tangen. Major Colby posted lookouts with walkie-talkies and binoculars to ensure a southbound train heard in the distance did not carry Norwegian civilians. The group wanted to catch a German troop train right on top of the bridge so both could be blown up at the same time. An hour passed and no train came towards Tangen. Colby got nervous and gave the order to blow the bridge at 6:30 am on April 14.

It is difficult to blow up steel. Most of the time it simply bends out of shape, but the second Farnsworth touched the wires together and the explosives went off, the structure vanished. The noise was tremendous, rocking back and forth between the hills. Even the nearby lake gave off a cracking sound like distant thunder. The happy men stood around with smiles on their grimy, weary faces. At last, they had done something and the Nordland line was stopped!

A milestone had been reached. Sabotage attacks by Operation *Rype* were now playing no small part preventing German movements southward. In fact, after *Rype*, that railroad didn't work worth a tinker's damn. American shoulder patches were left behind so the Germans would not take revenge on the people of Tangen.

Once the bridge was blown, because of the tired condition of the men, they withdrew to Oiingen again for a short rest and some food. During the afternoon a single engine spotter plane was heard overhead, but no visual contact was made. It was fortunate the men stopped for this short rest because that plane could have easily observed a group of skiers making a hasty retreat. But after the short break, the adrenalin now began to pump. All the men knew the Germans would definitely be in hot pursuit.

So now the merry chase began. Training and superb conditioning were about to pay off. *Rype* had to outski German troop-carrying trucks. Some of the inland roads to Sweden had already been cleared of snow. Although they left their toboggans behind and lightened their escape loads, it would be a grueling return. There was little food left. German patrols were sighted but no contact was made. Harold Larson, the champion cross-country skier, set a fast pace.

The Germans were in error by dressing too heavily. Some even wore furs. The perspiration flowed freely and the added weight tired them out a lot sooner. Come nightfall, wet and exhausted, they were practically forced to find a cabin or house to rest in. This was *Rype*'s saving grace. By contrast, *Rype* was light and perspiration free. The Norwegian whaler's undershirt, covering most of a man's upper body, acted as a spacer between his skin and outer clothing and worked beautifully. A warm air layer enfolded the skier's torso while vigorously skiing. He opened his wide flared shirt collar and allowed cold air to filter around and keep his clothing dry from perspiration. At rest periods, the collar was again closed and it warmed the body immediately.

The retreat started at Oiingen at midnight. The route followed was to Langvasheia, then Brandheia, then Flaa Lake where the men stopped to eat breakfast and rest from 9am to midday. From there to Dal Lake, then to Aasvas Lake and Gommelien, arriving at about 10pm on Monday. They intended to stop there to get some substantial rest, but when they contacted Lieutenant Hoel at nearby Aasuas Seter, he reported the presence of a 25-man German patrol at Tjoklien that had been searching the area all day. Colby decided, with the men tired, he did not want them to engage the patrol, so they departed at about 6am for Gronhaugen. It was also named "Benzedrine Hill" because, with the aid of benzedrine sulfate, that contains amphetamines, the unit made it to the top. The men were exhausted, but they pressed on to Fiskelosbkn, then to Nyamocokka to a *Woodlark* base camp which was actually across the border in Burvattnet, Sweden. Here, they rested and were well fed on elk and supplies received from Stockholm. It was here also that the Americans in the NORSO I Group first learned that President Franklin Roosevelt had passed away. The following Wednesday, Colby, Hoel, Langeland and Larson left to get back to the Jaevsjo farm and get the radio back in operation.

If memory serves me correctly, I believe this was the first chase where Larson led *Rype* down a precipitous slope. A German broke his leg and that, for all practical purposes, ended that pursuit. After this initial strike, NORSO I ended up back in camp and rested for a few days before planning the next operation. The attack was successful with no casualties to *Rype* personnel.

Colby cited the courage and stamina of his men in his April 18 progress report:

> Special letters are being written regarding several of the men, but every man of the unit deserves nothing but the highest of praise. Under the most trying conditions possible, wet, cold, tired, not particularly well fed on K and other dried rations, and with nigh impossible terrain, their spirit, discipline and determination were never in the slightest degree impaired. Of a limited skiing ability (due only to a lack of months and years of training) in comparison with the native Norwegians, they have gained the unrestrained admiration of these Norwegians by the spirit of determination which carries them through obstacles which lesser men would declare impossible.

Sabotages and subsequent pursuits were certainly not a gentleman's game by any stretch of the imagination. Consider the pursuers trying to see a white string in white snow strung across a trail. It became particularly bothersome if one end is tied to the pin of a hand grenade.

By this time, the Germans had repaired the Tangen Bridge from the Easter Sunday blast so the time was ripe for another strike. On the Tangen job, Colby attacked while many of the German soldiers were off to church in a nearby village. Now they would be increasingly alert and difficult to deal with.

We were having trouble communicating with *Rype* in the field due to disruptions in the ionosphere, resulting in a loss of signal bounce. Here are some earlier transmissions from our London office during that time:

> 10 April: Do not contact Waxwing now. Their strength only 12 men. Maintain complete security after initial attack. Remain in hiding.
> April 10: Following in Norwegian. EN SA LIC HILSEN I AMLEDNING AV NI APRIL TIL ALLE SOLD T R I HS FRA FORSVARSJEFEN STOP TO EN AV NULL.[10]
> 11 April: Your 19 of 5. Suggest you use emergency channel if frequency B rpt B is difficult. Will make no alternation as frequency should be OK in a few weeks.

Since NORSO I transmissions were not getting through, Kjell Sörlie was most critical as a courier to our communication with *Rype*. He was also a member of Milorg who used Stockholm in neutral Sweden as his home base. He regularly departed on missions from Stockholm by rail to the northwest as far as the train would go. Then he would ski to *Rype*'s camp, avoiding Swedish and German patrols. The approaches to the mountains were desolate. Had he broken a leg or had some other debilitating misfortune, there would be little chance of someone coming to his aid. The sub-zero, ever-changing weather, and the need to carry as little food as possible in order to be mobile, made this a very dangerous run indeed. The courier run was essential to the passing back and forth of detailed reports. *Rype*'s radio transmissions had to be brief and rapid otherwise German signal intelligence might be able to pinpoint the unit's location. *Rype*'s written reports and incoming correspondence were flown back and forth between London and Stockholm. Anxious to hear from NORSO I, we sent the following transmission:

> 17 April: Report progress and requirements. No signal since 8 April.

By this time, the big jobs were forbidden by higher headquarters, so rail cutting jobs were settled on. We had RDX plastic that could be molded into half-pound blocks, fused and combined with a small time pencil, which provided a desired delayed explosion. Many could thus be planted by a single person before they started popping. Don't forget *Rype* had three tons of explosives and five tons of equipment at their disposal. We had the potential of putting the Nordland railroad out of business for the duration and then some. All we needed was the green light to stay green.

With the loss of *Rype* personnel due to the Liberator crashes, Skabo was now looking at different strategies to get the rest of NORSO, myself included, into Norway. He discussed this at length with me. The plan was to get personnel into Sweden as spies with civilian cover and then infiltrate across the border into Norway. He wrote a letter to the Chief of Special Operations Branch of the OSS as follows:

---

10 Translation reads: A SPECIAL GREETING ON 9 APRIL TO ALL THE SOLDIERS IN HS FROM DEFENSE CHIEF (STOP 2. 1. OF ZERO.

16 April 1945
SUBJECT: Infiltration of NORSO Group to target.
TO: Chief;   SO Branch, OSS

THRU: Chief, Scandinavian Section, SO, OSS
and Lt Col L. Gable, Deputy Chief, S.F. Hq

1. The situation of the NORSO Group at present is as follows:
We have three officers and thirteen enlisted men, with Major Colby commanding, now in Norway. Five of Major Colby's original group were, through mishap, dropped in Sweden. Arrangements have been made for infiltration of these men to Major Colby's base in Norway. This is more fully expressed in incoming Stockholm cable No. 873.
2. The following four men of Major Colby's original group are still in the UK:

T/Sgt. Knut Joa	Cpl. Vernon L. Austreng
T/5 Otto Twingley	T/5 Wilton N. Rasmussen

In accordance with the clearance indicated in the aforementioned cable, arrangements are under way to provide these men with passports and clothing for their movement to Sweden for infiltration to the original group.
3. We propose to follow up the movement of the above-mentioned group with four others plus two officers named below:

T/4 Einar M. Kristiansen	Cpl Arne M. Hoff
T/4 Otis L. Ausen	1st Lt John W. Kroona
T/5 Harold Andersen	Lt Col Gerhard L. Bolland

4. In due course, and provided approval can be obtained in Sweden, a matter with which DS/US will deal personally during his visit to Sweden, we hope to move the remainder of the NORSO Group now in the UK to Sweden for infiltration to Norway. This group consists of the following:

T/Sgt Clifford G. Kyllo	T/5 Olav J. Eide
1st Lt Roger W. Hall	T/5 Elmer Kvasager
S/Sgt John T. Halvorsen	T/5 Harold E. Ness
T/5 Morris A. Syrstad	S/Sgt Erling E. Olsen
T/5 Jorgen F. Andersen	T/5 Albert Nordang
T/5 Delphis L. Bohin	T/5 Erling R. Salvesen
T/5 Bernard W. Tallaksen	T/5 Paul N. Frangas
T/5 Torleif S. Johansen	T/5 Gus L. Palans
T/5 Rolf Lilleby	1st Sgt. Theophanes G. Strimenos
Major John M. Olmstad	Cpl. John Sunde
Cpl. Karl Larsen	T/5 Steve P. Marthiakas
S/Sgt Boris Spiroff	Cpl. William Johnson
Sgt. George G. Boosalis	Pvt Bernard F. Brady
Cpl. Otto N. Feher	Pvt Mike Mountouris
T/5 Demetrius Frangis	PFC Nolen R. Cooper

The members of this group will be moved in the order in which they are listed, singly or in small groups, depending upon transportation and reception facilities.
5. While the prospect for this movement is pending, it is proposed to send all of the men listed in para 4, with the exception of Major Olmsted, to an abbreviated radio course for W/T instruction if this can possibly be arranged. It is felt advisable that as many of this group as possible be trained as operators for further inter-communication purposes and for direct contact with the UK.
6. It is intended that Colonel Bolland assume command of the augmented group in the field. This arrangement will complete the plans previously established and known to the present leaders of each of the groups. The commander of the combined forces will be responsible for:

a. Guiding the military operations set out in present operational orders.

b. Dealing militarily and administratively with any expansion of activity that may now or in future be imposed upon or prove feasible for the groups.

7. There is an immediate need to provide specially for the responsibilities suggested in para 6 b above, because each of the present group leaders will be concerned primarily with carrying out their operational missions, leaving the task of overall control and coordination of activities with Norwegian groups and S.F.Hq unattended, unless provided for as stated above.

8. Lt Col Bolland has been assistant to the Chief of NORSO Group, S.F.Hq since its inception. As such he has participated in all planning and operational procedure. His command background as a field officer, as well as his knowledge of S.F.Hq activities and the Norwegian language, makes him the logical choice for position as combined Group Commander for NORSO operations.

9. It is also intended that Lieut. Kroons, after familiarizing himself with our supply procedure, the movement of material to Sweden from the UK, join Captain Dammen's organization in Sweden, as assistant with special responsibility for supplying the NORSO Group in the field. His activities will include all those duties relating to the initial supply, re-supply and procurement of supplies, both from the UK as well as in Sweden, as may be required by the NORSO Group.

(Signature)

HANS H. SKABO

Lt Col CE

Section Chief, NORSO Group

Approved:

(Signature)

Arne W. Brogger,

Major, AUS

Actg. Chief, Scandinavian Section.

cc. Lt Col Wilson

** P.S. Since this paragraph was written we have learned that it will not be possible to properly train all of the men within the time allowed. Two of the group have had previous W/T experience; therefore they will be given requisite refresher training.

Meanwhile, London had also approved a plan for Gunnar Sonestby and the Oslo Gang to blow up the railway administration and office building. This would cause chaos as the Germans tried to coordinate repair of the rail lines and restore service. Sonestby contacted a liaison in Milorg. They calculated it would take four, 50-pound charges to level the place. According to Sonestby, a contact at a fish warehouse opposite the railway building allowed them to store suitcases full of explosives there. They assembled at nine o'clock in the evening where two of them would place the charges and link them with a cordtex fuse. Sonestby and another man would take care of the guards. The operation went rather smoothly with the exception of one guard whom they had handcuffed earlier. Despite being watched over by one of the men with a pistol equipped with a silencer, he began kicking and shouting loudly to alert his comrades. Sonestby went to see if the charges were ready, but they weren't. Since the German guard kept shouting they had no choice but to quiet him with a few rounds from the pistol. It only took another five minutes to finish placing the remaining chargers and link them with cordtex. After escaping the building and making their way back home, the distant roar of the building explosion and collapse indicated their sabotage mission was a success.

After the Tangen Bridge attack, Colby got a letter to Skabo through the courier to Stockholm. In it he summarized their situation. He also requested more personnel, grumbled a bit about the political conditions of combining American and British personnel, made suggestions for getting supplies to them, and outlined plans for future sabotage:

19 April 1945
TO: Lt. Col. H.H. Skabo, Scand. Section, SO Branch
      OSS Detachment (Main), APO 413.

1. Upon arrival at JAEVSJO T/Sgt. Leif Oistad and the four men dropped in Sweden were found. For their arrival here, we are most grateful, and they are high in their praise of the manner in which the Stockholm office took care of them and got them up here. They possess however, only one uniform each, and practically no military equipment, although they do have some beautiful civilian clothes. Please have Sgt. Kyllo fill up a rucksack for each of the men with required articles, as in our list of FO-2, and drop them in with the next group coming.
2. An attack by the Germans against JAEVSJO FARM must be declared as a likely possibility. We are making dispositions to fight should we be here or to avoid its consequences should we be off on a job. It is rumored in SNAASA [sic] that allied paratroopers are in the vicinity—a combination of factors giving rise to the rumors. The main trouble is that the number of planes coming on fruitless drops makes the Germans think a far larger force is here, and they will naturally send a large force to attack.
3. We still need Olmstad's group badly. They can live on the Swedish side and be protected by this unit until the snow goes. The snow seems to be going rapidly this year. By SNAASA [sic] LAKE it is almost possible to attack without skis, and soon the mountains will be clear also. With the reinforcement his group could give us, I feel that we could take GRANA BRIDGE, and I should very much like to do so.
4. The WOODLARK question needs settling. Because of the tremendous shortage of men, I was compelled to borrow some of the WOODLARK men for the TANGEN job. They are extremely fine men, and I should very much like to keep them. There is talk of "conditions" of their working with us, "conditions" I believe, imposed by SOE Headquarters. It seems a strange way for allies to prosecute a war, lending men on "conditions" that they not do too much against the common enemy. My aim is to do the maximum damage to the Germans in this region, and in order to carry out this mission I wish to be able to use the men available as I see fit. The mountains of Norway are no place for the existence of petty political maneuverings. I should like to keep the men and also I should like to have Lt. Hoel with me, as his knowledge of the region and the people in it is vital to the proper fulfillment of my mission.
5. The next job in mind is the destruction of rails in the vicinity of LURUDAL. This unit will move to within striking distance of the RR and then break into small groups for the actual attack. All will attack at the same time and withdraw to the forward rendezvous, returning here as a unit.
6. Knowing that the Air Corp [sic] cannot fly here after this moon period, I think we had best look out for some system of air resupply from Sweden. The old idea of asking Bernt Balchen and his Fortresses to help us out seems the best. Either the complete containers could be shipped to Sweden, loaded up and dropped, or else contact could be made with Troop Carrier Command and arrangements made for the use of American type packages, etc., for

the drop. Then packing could be done in Sweden and the drops made. Transport here in the mountains is the greatest problem. When the ice leaves the lakes, as it will soon, there will be a short spell in which nothing can be done. Then things will depend on a combination of boats and horses. Air resupply is such a simpler and faster system that it should be used if at all possible.

7. Experience on this just past operation indicates the necessity for forward bases for food and demolitions. The exact DZ locations have been sent you and I hope they will be served this moon period.

8. We still need Sgt. Kyllo, Sgt. Ausen and Harold Andersen. Supply is the biggest headache and they can do much toward smoothing out its difficulties.

9. At present we have two supply channels: London and Stockholm. Some things come easiest through Stockholm, other through London. Sometimes we have been asked what we want and have answered our requirements to each, and are running the chance of a double supply and of considerable confusion and exasperation on both ends. I am suggesting in a letter to Stockholm today that I submit all supply needs to them, that they fill the things they can handle, and pass the remainder on to you for air supply from UK. There is no use of having planes filled with things over from UK when they are easily procured in Sweden. Anything specifically wanted by air, such as food and demolitions for advance bases, can be mentioned as such, and quantities enumerated for that particular purpose. I hope that this system will be agreeable to you.

10. My thanks for the way things have been pushed from your end. The five men who came up from Stockholm feel that it was largely yourself who raised enough hell to get them here so soon. I feel the same—and very grateful.

WILLIAM E. COLBY

Major, FA.

The Scandinavian Section congratulated NORSO I for the fine job at Tangen and authorized the attack on Lurdal with the following transmission:

April 20: Congratulations on job well done and safe return. Reinforcement by air of men and supplies impossible. Resupply thru Sweden only. Lierne not feasible at present. SHAEF [Supreme Headquarters Allied Expeditionary Force] approval necessary. Go ahead with Lurudel rail attack. Hoel to remain with you as long as there is work to be done. Written instructions to Stockholm for you today.

On April 22, Vetlesen travelled from Stockholm and met with NORSO I at the farm at Jaevsjo Lake. He and Colby discussed the possibility of infiltrating from the valley and taking Lierne. In order for this plan to succeed, however, there must be caches of weapons just across the border in Sweden for use once the area was captured; otherwise arriving German reinforcements would quickly retake the area. Of course, higher headquarters would have to approve this plan first. Vetlesen left with hopes London would give approval and the attack could happen a few weeks later, around May 8.

In the meantime, on Monday April 23, NORSO I was once again loaded for bear and off for the railroad lines at Lurdal. No doubt, after the Tangen job, the Germans would have beefed up security at other bridges. In addition, three men were too sick to participate in the mission: Kjell Sörli, Harold Larson and Sverre Aanonsen. The route took them by Fisklosa Lake to a hut at Seisjöen Lake. On Tuesday they moved north by way of Andorsjöen Lake and Gaos Lake to Skjorstohaugen where, again, they stayed at a hut. The next morning the reconnaissance party left first, followed by the main party at noon. The remaining trek was at a 90-degree angle to their journey so far. They travelled to Agle Seter, Berg Seter and then to Skartnes Seter (a summer dairy) which was used as the final assembly point. The reconnaissance party included Hans Liermo, a local guide who found approach routes to the rail line at points selected to be blown. The men were divided into eight teams with Liermo joining Sergeant Alf Paulsen's team as its fourth member:

1. Maj. Colby
   T/6 Windh
   Andreas Andersen

2. Lt. Sather
   T/3 Myrland
   T/5 Hovland

3. Lt. Farnsworth
   Cpl. Knut Andreasen
   Gaer

4. Lt. Hoel
   T/5 Gravdal
   Jens Leksvik

5. 1st Sgt. Eliassen
   S/Sgt. Listeid
   T/3 F. Johansen

6. T/Sgt. Langeland
   T/5 Rusdal
   Thoralf Lian

7. T/Sgt. Oistad
   T/3 Odd Anderson
   T/5 Raivio

8. S/Sgt. Paulsen
   Cpl. Kai Johansen
   T/5 Nipe
   Hans Liermo

The teams moved out. Lieutenant Sather and Sergeant Paulsen's teams were led into position by Liermo, via a route discovered in the afternoon. All others, except for Major Colby's team, were led in line to a point used earlier by Sergeant Langeland for reconnaissance. From there, the teams left Skartnes at staggered times to permit simultaneous arrival to their points of attack since the distances were different. Colby's team found their way by familiarity gained during reconnaissance.

Fortunately, the weatherman cooperated and sent in a blinding snowstorm to the target, offering perfect cover and noise abatement over the hard and noisy crust. The loads carried by the men during this operation were much lighter and the distance to the target area was shorter than to Tangen. The objective was to take out as many rails as possible with small charges on isolated portions of the Nordland line. Scouts found a German guardhouse was right in the middle of the mile-and-a-half segment of railroad to be destroyed. There was no moon and that would aid in the escape.

A time of 11pm was set to move to the line and the first charges to be blown at 11:45 pm on a green signal flare from Colby. If no signal was sent, then the charges were to be blown at 11:50. This is exactly what happened since Colby's team was too close to the German guardhouse to light the flare. All teams were equipped with 30 rail charges, to be joined in pairs. The teams were instructed to attach the charges to the rails at alternate fishplates, where the rails were joined together. The charges were prepared in advance. Two men were to attach the charges by wrapping them around the fishplates with an additional man setting the fuse. That would damage the rails up to two feet on each side of the joint. When it came time, all men were to pull the charges to have it done faster. Since the rail sections were 12 meters long, this meant each team had approximately 200 meters of rail assigned to it. Timing was extremely critical. The fuse could be activated by pulling a small wire. Detonation would come 10 seconds later. One could pull one wire, run down the track and pull another until all the charges were activated and exploded. The teams were then to withdraw to Skartness and try to escape as a unit.

At 11:50 pm, a crescendo of explosions followed. The Germans were completely caught by surprise and numerous flares went up. The explosions sounded like a heavy bombardment. One flare went off 50 yards from Colby's position. In the darkness, a German tunnel guard shot several volleys from his rifle towards Colby's group. A bullet kicked up a pebble into Colby's face. He instructed Sergeant Sivert Windh not to return fire with his Browning automatic rifle. He did not want to tell the Germans a regular unit was in the area. German machine-gun fire was also shot in the direction of Sather's group. One-hundred and nine double charges destroyed 218 rails covering a distance of two and a half kilometers. "Achtung, Achtung," the German defense mechanism started in motion. The mission was a complete success.

Rype's escape was next on the agenda. The team retreated and reassembled at a point defiladed to the rail line and readied for the next chase. Wait a minute; is there time for coffee? Okay, if you hurry. So out came the coffee. Someone watched from the rise to appraise German alert procedures. Soon the *Rype* observer informed them that it sounded like they'll soon be ready to start the pursuit. "All right men, gulp it down." Liermo then started the group out. Yes out, but in the direction of camp? No! The movement was at right angles to the azimuth for the base. Instead of striking off northeasterly, Liermo stamped out the trail to the southeast. Thus continued pursued and pursuer, hour after hour. The snow was crisp and the skiing was good. When daybreak came, *Rype* took a break and ate some British field rations. The pemmican inside them was nourishing but, as pemmican is, not very tasty. They spent the rest of the day putting as much distance as possible between them and German ski patrols. Five-minute breaks were the norm. The group was so exhausted at this point that, during one of these breaks, one man actually fell asleep while standing and leaning on his ski poles. To slow down the Germans, live explosives were left behind on the trail. These were not powerful enough to do serious harm in the event they were detonated by a casual Norwegian skier.

Eventually, the Germans started dropping out due to exhaustion. However the Norwegian Quisling followers, now aiding and abetting the Germans, hung on longer. Eventually it became apparent their numbers were declining as well and that, possibly, *Rype* was about to become larger or equal to them. Perish the thought! Liermo now employed a method to lose the rest of the pursuers. As evening developed into nightfall, the dropping temperature formed a solid crust on top of the snow. It soon became strong enough to support a man's weight and leave no tracks. The skis were then removed and carried a half mile or so in the direction of base camp. At that point, the rest of the return back to camp was now more leisurely. All remaining pursuers would now chase a ski trail that vanished into thin air. On April 26, the unit arrived back at Jaevsjo after a roundabout tour through Sweden. Colby radioed our London base that *Rype* had no casualties in the group and that there was only an incidental encounter with the Germans.

So you want to play our game in our own backyard? The outnumbered men of NORSO proved they could take on the Germans and come away successful, although no idea of false security was ever envisioned by *Rype*. Retaliation was always to be expected. *Woodlark* was also making attacks further north. NORSO lay coiled in its lair like a deadly cobra ready to strike in any direction at any time. Final protective lines of fire were laid for automatic weapons, loaded and cocked. Personnel were on them in an instant and ready for the decision to fire. This was a battle of wits from moment to moment. A cache of French champagne and flour had been found; a nice addition to a well-deserved brief celebration, I might add. It had been hidden in the mountain by the Germans, after being lifted from their French campaign no doubt.

One Sunday morning, Tom said he would try to produce some pancakes for the group. So off he went to the cook shack. He fired up and started in on his culinary art.

With the aid of the double-sifted flour, and a perhaps a little "axle grease," he proudly developed an adequate stack of cakes and proceeded with flair out of the cook shack to the main cabin. No sooner had he emerged than … it couldn't be … a German patrol advancing on the cabin! He dropped the stack and went for his gun to get into position. However, Colby saw them first. A field recruit by the name of Karl Berre from Trondheim forgot his good sense and rushed out toward the patrol. A powerful man who was also the subject of maltreatment in prison, he only wanted to get his hands on a German to tear him apart. The patrol fired a grease gun, the common name given to a German sub-machine gun, directly at Berre. It jammed on the second round. The first one went through Berre and he dropped like a stock pig. He had been shot in the intestines. Colby ordered, "Fire!" A rattle of gunfire from *Rype* ended it all. The German patrol was annihilated. When the adrenaline settled, it was back to living again, minus the pancakes. A mass grave was made and the German patrol buried.

Now, after a respectable period of waiting, the question to be answered by the Germans was simply this. What happened to the patrol? *Rype*'s question, however, was how will the Germans react? Colby was told and understood that no prisoners were to be taken. After all, running a clandestine prisoner of war camp was obviously not within NORSO's capability. Tom Sather and another *Rype* man were elected to evacuate Berre. He was doped up, bundled on a ski jelka and dispatched to neutral Sweden. Berre was given the required penicillin and follow-up dosages were administered. It was quite an arduous journey for the escorting team. Into Swedish territory, the party finally stopped. Berre's identification insignias were removed. Tom wrote a note for the potential discoverer, identifying Berre as a Norwegian patriot, with the message: "This man has been treated with penicillin." The team left as a Swede was coming their way. When Berre was finally taken to a Swedish doctor, I should have liked to have seen the expression on that doctor's face upon reading the note. Sweden had no penicillin at that time.

Until its decision on the Lierne Plan was made, *Rype* was to continue harassing the Nordland line. SHAEF now appeared to favor a more passive policy of keeping transportation networks intact for the liberation of Norway, which seemed close at hand. London radioed the following transmission:

> April 28: Congratulations on rail destruction. Decision on Lierne forthcoming next week. Kronophyttan can be used for desired purpose. Taciturnity in office today sends best greeting.

In fact, Vetlesen sent a letter to Colby via courier the day before, rehashing much of the mission to date, letting him know what happened to some of the other personnel and indicating that Germany may surrender soon:

> 25 April 1945
> TO: Major William E. Colby
> FROM: NS/NOR
> THRU: VAUDVILLE, WESTFIELD MISSION

1. Thank you for your written reports, also various signals received, some which were excellent. Langeland is to be complimented on the good work he has done.

2. It was tragic that our air dispatches turned out the way they did. When we received word of Berge's plane having crashed in the Orkneys I flew up there in a C-47 with some Air Corp [sic] officers to investigate and brought the bodies back to Harrington. They were buried at Cambridge Cemetery, Friday April 6. All their personal belongings have been sorted out and listed and will be returned to the next of kin as soon as official notification of the casualty has been made. The funeral was attended by Mr. Miller, Major Brogger, four men from Area "P," six men from Area "H," Sgt. Dymbe, and myself.

3. 6 April was also the date of the dispatch of our last three planes, two of which carried personnel. Two planes, one with T/Sgt Joa and three men and the supply plane returned to Harrington. However the third plane with Lt. Blain E. Jones, Bernard N. Iverson, Knute J. Falck and Robert N. Anderson is still missing. Your signal to the effect that it was believed a plane crashed about 15 miles West of your Base is the only lead we have had so far as to what might have happened. It is our hope that our men and also the crew of the plane were able to jump over Norway, in which case, they are undoubtedly held as prisoners.

4. Due to extremely poor results of dispatch of Norso-Group by air, we decided that we would not jeopardize lives of any more of our men and have, therefore, cancelled all air operations including re-supply by air. We have sent you several signals to that effect and also notified Stockholm that all supply for you must come from there.

5. Upon receipt of information from Stockholm to the effect that our five men, who were dropped in error in Sweden, were released to WESTFIELD, we asked that if possible, they be infiltrated to you. At the same time we also asked that arrangements be made for infiltration of T/Sgt Joa and his three men from here. Stockholm replied to us that this could be done and that our personnel could be sent to Sweden under their regular military status. However, a few days later a cable was received to the effect that none of our men in England could be infiltrated to you through Sweden, except under Norwegian cover names and with Norwegian passports. We received a cable today that on this basis we can send in all Norwegian personnel in groups of six each. We are at the present planning to send in Knute Joa and his three men, plus Austreng and Anderson. These will be followed shortly by six additional men. I cannot send Kyllo at this time because he will have to arrange for the Norso-Group supplies and equipment for Areas "P" and "H". We are planning to ship all excess equipment from Area "P" to area "H" and to also make arrangements to store all personal baggage of Norso officers and men in the main building at Area "H".

6. As you know Major Olmsted proceeded, about two months ago to France where he spent over four weeks attempting to get additional personnel. He succeeded in getting twelve men who originally belonged to the Greek OG's. I haven't seen any of them yet, but I understand that they are pretty good, and they have had field experience in Greece, Yugoslavia and Italy. Incidentally only eleven are now at Area "P" as one man developed malaria in Paris and was sent to hospital. In view of the fact that Major Olmsted and Lt. Hall, also several enlisted men of the original Norso-Group do not speak Norwegian, together with the Greek Contingent, we will probably have to make other arrangements with Stockholm for the infiltration of these men. My plan, however is to send everybody in to you as soon as all red tape has been taken care of.

7. We were very glad indeed to get your signal advising us of your successful demolition of the Bridge at Tangen and particularly the good news that there had been no casualties, and that all men were back safe at base. We were also very much pleased to learn that you had no contact with the Germans. We have not received your written report as yet, but hope it will be forthcoming soon. In this respect we are very much at a loss here to understand how you could move to your target with a total of twenty-four men. The only thing we knew was that you had three officers and thirteen men, one of whom was injured (Stiansen), which would

leave you fifteen men including yourself plus Lt. Hoel, and as we understand, two men from the old WOODLARK Party, which would have made a total of eighteen men. On reports in the future, I want you to give us a clear picture of exactly how many men you have and how many Norwegian volunteers you have accumulated also whether or not they are operating in uniform or as guerrillas. We <u>must</u> abide by the instructions issued by SF Hq which, as you know, are to the effect that we are not to recruit Norwegian personnel nor incite the local population to uprisings. With reference to SHAEF instructions, we have recently received information that sabotage generally should be on a diminishing scale. We are, however authorized to do anything which will tend to force the Germans in Northern Norway to take the sea route to the South. Therefore, continued sabotage of the Nordland Railway, roads and bridges are still in accordance with SHAEF plans.

8. With reference to Lierne, this has been discussed to quite some extent, and we all feel that for the present this must lie dormant. We do not have sufficient personnel to attempt an undertaking of this kind, particularly in view of the fact that Norwegian's group only numbers twelve to sixteen men. Even if successfully accomplished it would only enable you to hold territory like this for a short period of time after which in all probability you would have to withdraw to Sweden. We do not want this to happen because it would simply mean that the Germans would move in with a large force, and the result would be reprisals against the Norwegian population located there. Conditions in Germany are becoming very acute and in view of statements made by General EISENHOWER, we feel it will only be a matter of time until the Germans now occupying Norway will be classified as outlaws, in which case the picture should change from the Swedish standpoint. For the time being, therefore, we do not wish you to undertake any operation which might embarrass the Swedish Government, SHAEF, or others. We feel that there will be plenty of operations for both your group and Olmsted's group to perform in Norway. We visualize the possibility of utilizing the Norso-Group either jointly with MILORG or perhaps separately as Jedburgh Teams. For the present we want you to carry on with your original instructions and whenever you return from any sabotage operations you should go into hiding as much as possible.

9. We have assigned 1st Lt. John Kroona, who will shortly proceed to Stockholm as Assistant to Captain Dammen, who is in charge of all supplies. He is now being put in the supply picture for Norso-Group by Lt. Coon and T/Sgt. Kyllo, and his primary job in Sweden will be to look after resupply for you. This will include equipment and supplies from Swedish stores, also such equipment which may have to be purchased in Sweden and also all such supplies which will have to come from the UK. He and Kyllo are at present working on the movement of the organic equipment for Olmsted and his men plus resupply for all.

10. On 21 April we sent you a signal advising you that it would be satisfactory to have Lt. Hoel remain with your group as long as there was any work to be done. It has been agreed between SO and that all other personnel belonging to WOODLARK should be released from the Norso-Group. The reason for all this is that MILORG has other plans for their use, and we must not interfere, you will have to plan your operations based on your present Norso-Group personnel plus the six Norwegians who reported to you from Stockholm. We will send you additional men from here as soon as feasible.

11. In view of the fact that the Norso-Group has six casualties, I wish you would indicate in an early report who you wish promoted to fill the vacancies created by the casualties of T/Sgt. Berge, S/Sgt Kjelness and Col. Heflin.

12. All of us here extend to you, your officers, Lt. Hoel and your men our congratulations for the good work done, and the best of luck in future operations.

Obviously the Scandinavian Section, through Vetlesen in Stockholm, thought there were three officers and thirteen enlisted men, but Colby reported that, by then, there were 24. He was told to identify how many Norwegian locals had been recruited and whether they were in uniform or not. Milorg had a role for these men. The Scandinavian Section said the locals should not be recruited for *Rype* because of possible German reprisals against these men and their families. Colby should not violate SHAEF policy. The Lierne Plan was to train new recruits for Milorg. *Rype* and *Woodlark* were to remain dormant because they were too small to defend Lierne should the Germans have a notion to take it. Thus, Lierne was not authorized. Sweden was the linchpin for Norway at the moment. Colby was not to embarrass the Swedish Government in front of German officials with blatant operations in Norway that appeared to come from Sweden. The Scandinavian Section ordered First Lieutenant John Kroona to proceed to Stockholm to assist Captain Dammen in the Milorg supply area and to be in charge of resupplying *Rype*.

In a memo to Skabo dated April 27, Vetlesen had just returned from a conference with Colby on the 23rd. He reported the men were in good spirits and the base was well organized. There were 20 OGs with an additional 10 Norwegians. Supplies and future operations were discussed. The Nordland line appeared to be quickly losing importance as a high priority target since it now only served as a link between troops in northern and southern Norway. In addition, SHAEF policy was moving towards a more passive stance in preparation for final liberation. Vetlesen proposed *Rype* orders from SHAEF should be changed since he believed pursuing recruitment and training of Norwegian personnel would be beneficial and the Lierne area had now become suitable for this purpose. In addition, German retaliation to the families in the area was almost a non-existent threat. Together with Lieutenant Hoel, *Rype* had the ability to hand pick Norwegian recruits best suited for this purpose. Vetlesen also proposed *Rype* operate only in the Lierne sector which included the area south to their present base, west to Steinkjer, north to the Namsos coastal area and east to the Swedish border. Also, *Rype* would refrain from offensive guerilla action unless specifically authorized by Special Forces Headquarters.

Woodlark also received orders to proceed on Milorg's original orders. Regarding this, we notified NORSO I:

> April 28: For X 38, Woodlark to begin new work as Milorg and protection party. /T operator Trond to be sent with other Woodlarks except you to Burn at base. Trond to take /T equipment to base. From there he will go to Stockholm soonest for briefing and completion of /T equipment.

Three days later, London radioed and confirmed that *Rype*'s mission was to make small and frequent attacks on the Nordland railroad, but not to tackle the Grana Bridge:

> May 1: In view of tense German situation your mission now changed to make small and frequent attacks on railroad rather than larger scale attacks. Do not attack Grana river bridge or similar larger targets. Avoid contact with Germans. Waxwing operating under similar instructions.

A second message on the same day came with the decision on Lierne:

> May 1: Woodlark party must proceed as per original Milorg orders. Lierne plan cannot be executed now for obvious reasons. Olmsted's arrival date uncertain. Hope to send six men from here this week. Stockholm now insists on fluent Norwegian speaking personnel. This will come first. Trying other arrangements for remainder.

When Colby read, "... the Lierne plan could not be authorized for obvious reasons," he radioed back that he did not understand what was meant by "obvious reasons." On May 2, he pleaded his case to London contending that *Rype* had the wherewithal to organize a guerrilla force. Regardless, Colby was ordered to release the men from *Woodlark*. They were actually sent to Follafoss, a small village on the northern shore of the Beitstadfjorden where a power plant and dam were located. It was feared the Germans may attempt to conduct "grudge sabotage" after their impending defeat. What Colby did not know at the time was that SHAEF was conducting very delicate negotiations with the German High Command over the disposition of its troops in Norway. The Allies, had they given *carte blanche* to Colby, would have reneged on their promise that German troops would be allowed to make an orderly withdrawal from Norway. A flamboyant action in Lierne would be damaging and inappropriate. Colby was in no position to know how policy was being formulated at the highest level of commands during this time.

In anticipation of larger alerted combat patrols by the Germans, NORSO I turned nomadic and broke camp. It removed itself from the vicinity of the proposed routes that had undoubtedly been set up before their departure and subsequent demise. Brief contacts with the outside world, although erratic, indicated things were going quite badly for the Nazi cause, elsewhere at least. Vetlesen wrote that, if there should be a complete German capitulation in Norway, Colby might be instructed to encourage German prisoners to cross the border into Sweden and claim to be deserters. Vetlesen knew *Rype* could not feed them.

Two days later, lengthy transmissions (by radio standards) were sent to *Rype*:

> May 1: Instructional order from F.O. to H.S. In the present situation as the possibility for a general German capitulation exists it is of decisive importance that absolute calm and discipline is preserved. Action of aggression by H.S. or others against German troops, German or Norwegian police or Norwegian Nazis has, at this moment, no military purpose but may only cause the greatest difficulties for an orderly German capitulation. It is now more imperative than ever before that an unbreakable discipline is preserved and that officers and jegere keep their hands clean. Orders according to the above must be issued forthwith to officers and jegere. Furthermore, it must be ascertained that all leaders keep continuous contact with superiors as well as subordinates. If the Germans capitulate we enforce standing orders that RYPE shall respect the armistice and take up tasks mentioned for this alternative.
> May 1: Any break on the part of U.S. might cause inestimable damage. If the Germans, contrary to all reasons, should continue the opposition in Norway after the war is finished in Germany, it is important that the organizations are kept intact and ready for fight so as to be able to support from within the Liberation of the country in cooperation with the arriving Norwegian and Allied forces.

On the following day, May 2, Vetlesen sent a message from Stockholm to Skabo in London. He admitted fault at not giving London a detailed picture of the difficulties in connection with the *Rype* operation, especially how it related to the Swedes. Apparently, the British counterpart, *Woodlark*, was set up without Swedish permission and it was almost a forgone conclusion that trouble would ensue sooner or later because the Swedes were fully aware of its existence. They were irritated by the rather high-handed proceedings *Woodlark* ran under. At the same time, because of *Twinkle* and the necessity to establish other bases with Swedish protection, negotiations were underway to obtain necessary Swedish recognition. At this stage, Vetlesen and others involved in the negotiations desired peace and quiet until they were completed; it was at these talks that *Rype* came up. He felt it best to separate *Woodlark* activities completely from *Rype*. Vetlesen obtained permission for a plan to send couriers directly from Stockholm. He arranged for a third man to follow the first two with additional supplies in order to replace Kjell Sörlie, who was needed in Stockholm to perform other duties. Before this was to happen, Vetlesen suggested *Woodlark* be released from its present position of inactivity.

The next day, a detailed message was sent to Colby updating him of recent events and responding to the various issues Colby brought up:

Stockholm ....3 May 1945
Dear Major Colby,
Before going into all the various matters which are greater interest to you, I wish to thank you for your hospitality and to let you know how much I enjoyed meeting you and all the rest of the boys. I should also like you to accept on behalf of the entire unit my sincere congratulations on the last job which appears to have been very successful. Then down to business.
1. T/5 Windh arrived here yesterday and conveyed the good news that he had not suffered from appendicitis at all and that it had been some kind of frozen intestines which had probably been caused by drinking too much ice water in the mountains. He is returning with the courier tonight in addition to some men who are to serve with you as general assistants and bottle washers.
2. All supplies unobtainable here have been ordered from UK.
3. No supplies are being sent up at this time because Erik Gaundal reports the transport conditions to be impossible. By this time I suppose you have received all of the previous shipment with the possible exception of skis. It won't be too long before these are unnecessary of course.
4. We are working hard to get permission for drops to you on the Swedish side near the base. Have today cabled London to ask you to submit pinpoint on Swedish side where drops could be received. We hope to have this settled within a short time, but at the moment it is as yet undecided by the powers that be.
5. We are daily expecting a number (six) of men from your original and second NORSO group. These are being infiltrated on Norwegian passports, and will be sent to the field as soon as we have equipped them.
6. I have discussed LIERNE with Vetlesen and Apollo and have submitted a request for a change in your Field Orders to London via the US line so that the British would be held out of it for the time being. However, the result was entirely negative. London—our side—was entirely firm on the point that your present field orders were still in effect and that the objectives still held highest priority. You will presumably get specific information on this from London by W/T, if you have not already obtained this information. I am sorry but there seems to be little that can be done about this. Whatever or whoever the obstacle is seems to

be at such a high level that my puny efforts on your behalf seem stranded. Major Bangstad has however arrived in town and I hear he is discussing the same project and it may be that sufficient pressure can be built up over a period of time. I suggest that any info regarding the lack of priority of your present target be sent UK direct as this will of course have some influence on the eventual decision.

7. Have just received a report indicating that your last job was effective for about two days or a little more. Congrats!

8. Regarding the other matters discussed I have varying degrees of success in meeting your desires:

a) Getting Skabo to Stockholm appears impossible at this time. There is too much going on behind the scenes for me to understand all of it and I can merely see that it would be impossible at this point. You probably know enough of this to know why better than myself. I have not asked directly but felt my way with the Commander and judged that it would lead to no results. As regards to an explanation of your field order, it is definitely of greater value for you to have Skabo in London.

b) To Hoel: I assumed that Schneideren would take care of Kjell, Engh and Öyen and have done nothing on this point.

c) To Såter: Balchen has been here but left before I realized and I couldn't greet him. Will do at next opportunity.

d) As regards pay for irregulars--- in the first place London says you cannot recruit any resistance personnel and in the second place if this should be permitted they cannot in any event be paid. Milorg as such will not be paid and it would not be permitted for such a distinction to exist as would be created if you paid any men attached to you.

e) The transport command has been held up because the peace crisis has caused great commotion here as regards manpower and because we are trying to avoid it by minimizing their use by means of the drops which are projected. If you run dangerously short of food, wire London as we shall try to get some rations up to you. I am afraid, however, that there will be no large transports for a month unless we can use air lift.

f) W/T contact to RYPE is being worked on by the radio people but they found initially that it could not be done successfully without material from London. Hope to have more favorable news with next mail. The biggest snag here will probably be that the only station that can be used here is heavily overloaded. Our radio man refuses to stay on the air because of possible difficulties with the Legation [diplomatic minister and staff]. I think the best thing would be if you directly asked London for permission to have radio contact to Stockholm in order to facilitate the movement of supplies, etc. and to coordinate personnel movements. Also ask them if they agree to send me by pouch all the necessary crystals for such a circuit, also codes. We can work up signal plans here.

g) You should lay off the German prisoner deal entirely for the time being. If there is a complete capitulation, it will merely confuse things. If there is to be a last stand, we have plenty of time. At that point I think the best thing to do would be to encourage desertion i.e. permit them to surrender to you and then send them across with instructions to report themselves as deserters. The other scheme is too complicated.

h) We are looking into the horse feed deal but we cannot do anything until we solve the transport end of it.

i) The recce [British word for reconnaissance] of Lierne border area was dropped in view of the thumbs down attitude of London.

j) Packing lists will invariably be sent in the future.

k) All supplies procurable locally are being obtained and held pending solution of the transport problem.

I realize that this will have been a very disappointing letter on the whole and I regret it. The thing that bothers me most is the transport difficulties which must be solved, and there appears

to be only one chance, namely by air. I am concentrating on this point to the exclusion of all others at this point and hope to be able to give you some good news in this respect soon.
My best wishes to all of you,
Vaudeville

Rype twice radioed London. The first message acknowledged that *Rype* would do nothing until further orders and that the party was running out of food. In the second message, Colby complained that *Rype* had been promised answers to many questions to be sent via courier, but none had been received. *Rype* had been completely kept in the dark about the status of the war. At this point, and unbeknownst to Colby, a sort of informal truce had been understood between the Germans and Allied forces. Any disruption could cause severe harm and cause the German troops to revolt. Thus, it was crucial that further resistance efforts in Norway come to a complete halt. The next day's message brought an immediate response. London replied that *Rype* was to stay in place, not make any contact with the Germans and not make contact with Milorg either. Disciplinary action would result if *Rype* did not follow orders:

> May 5: Ref your 38 of 2, your 41 of 4 and your 42 of 5. Your orders are to stay in hiding. Refrain from further sabotage. Stand by for additional orders. Any unauthorized contact by you with enemy or Milorg will be subject to immediate disciplinary action.

In response, *Rype* sent a long message requesting a list of clothing, material and food needs. *Rype* observed tired and hungry Austrian mountain troops walking south. A German grenadier regiment followed them and appeared to be well-disciplined and healthy. *Rype* also sent messages to, and received messages from, *Woodlark*. London was curious about the German activity in the Snåsa area. *Rype* also reported that the *Gestapo* had made a mass arrest of thirty to forty Milorg personnel in Verdal. Eleven had escaped and wanted to join *Rype* rather than go into Sweden. Norwegian Border Policeman Jon Albertsen assisted the *Gestapo* in the whippings of the Milorg members and *Rype* requested the BBC broadcast his name so that would not happen again. Also, the message "*Stormvarsel Paa Kysten*" (storm warnings along the coast) must not be broadcast from the BBC in London as the Milorg group in Verdal was destroyed. Once its true meaning was known, the message might cause Nazi infiltration of other Milorg groups.

On May 7, *Rype* was notified that the Germans would surrender:

> May 7: Enemy will surrender under terms be ordered to concentrate in several places in lower Namdal area at Grong, Ekker, Formo, Snaasa, Steinkjer, Verdal, Pinnleirt, Levanger hutmen camps. Important avoid any contact with enemy. To evade clashes stick to terms. You are not to disarm enemy.

It was becoming more obvious now. Resistance organizations and Allied personnel in Norway would now transition into support roles for the liberation of the country. However, even after the German capital of Berlin collapsed on May 2, there was concern that pockets of die-hard, dedicated Nazis might still fight to the last man. It would take some time to build up the necessary Allied forces to handle the situation.

CHAPTER 18

Spies through Sweden

It must be noted that, during World War II, a whole string of spies operated in Scandinavia. The so-called neutral Stockholm was, during the war, a "Casablanca of the North," with a flow of refugees, traveling businessmen and diplomats. The Swedish capital was a hotbed for exchanges, but also an environment in which warring parties spied on each other and secret agents exchanged classified information. William Donovan, the head of the Office of Strategic Services (OSS), had placed 75 officers in Stockholm to gather information on Nazi activities. Despite their official neutral stance, many Swedes also helped in this effort. Stockholm also served as a launching pad to get agents infiltrated into Germany, Norway and Denmark. The agents in Stockholm were able get a code clerk working in the German Embassy onto the OSS payroll. He provided them with secret diplomatic cables. The Swedish intelligence service also provided the agents with transcripts of phone taps at the Japanese embassy.

Despite preliminary announcements of enemy surrender, until it actually took place and there was no reneging on the part of the German Army, it was "business as usual" in Stockholm. After all, rumors still swirled that Germany would make a last-ditch stand in Norway. The unfolding of Operation *Rype*'s new strategy continued to progress. Remaining objectives still included sabotaging railroads if necessary.

This commander was fussing around, as was Skabo. A few days later, in a meeting, I was approached and asked, "Bolland, will you go in as a spy and take a small group in with you?" I believe it was Skabo who broached the question. "Yes, sir, when can we get going?" The attempt would be made through Sweden, albeit we'd chance the Swedes' reaction if caught. If successful, this method would be used in the future. What weighed heavily on this decision was the repeated failures of air sorties. Seventeen flown and only four successful in getting all Norwegian Special Operations (NORSO) personnel into the field. By now, the short periods of darkness were becoming a detection hazard as well. Consequently, several sabotage opportunities in Norway were discussed once our group infiltrated into Norway through Sweden. We pored over them thoroughly.

The first possibility was an obvious single rail line that ran out of Trondheim as far north as Neverneshagen. The roads in that area were in poor condition, especially in the winter, so movement of troops, supplies, and equipment, without the line would be difficult. If the lines were cut between Mosjøen and Mo I Rana, the Germans would have to make a longer sea haul from the port of Narvik, north of Mosjøen and Mo I Rana. By continually cutting the railway between Trondheim and Mosjøen and south of Grong, the Germans would have to come to Trondheim by sea, well within range of the Royal Navy and Coastal Command. Larson understood that, because the area was in close proximity to Sweden, it could provide field operations and an excellent escape route. The area was also within range of American aircraft for dropping personnel and resupplying them. The terrain was harsh, especially so in winter, a feature that would be more of an advantage than a hindrance to the party undertaking this operation.

Another possibility was to destroy the railroad between Grong and Majavatn. If the full group of NORSO I and NORSO II could be assembled beforehand, the attack could be undertaken with the goal of making at least one large break on the road and railway that would halt traffic for the longest time. The group would remain in the operational area for as long as possible in order to retard repair work and bring about new breaks. The group's base would be resupplied insofar as possible from Sweden. The biggest supply problem, however, would be food for such a large group.

A third possibility was the rail line connecting Narvik to Sweden. War wise, this area had a history of importance, especially to the Germans since Hitler depended upon the 11 million tons of iron ore from the Swedish mines to support his war machine. The ore was shipped by rail via Kiruna from Swedish mines to Narvik and other Norwegian warm-water ports and thence through Norwegian territorial waters to the Baltic. To this end, Germany reinforced Narvik by air. Ten Junkers Ju52 transports landed on a frozen lake nearby and a battery of mountain artillery crossed the Swedish border, 10 miles east of Narvik after having passed through Sweden with Swedish permission.

Early in the war, back on April 24, 1940, the British fleet bombarded German positions around Narvik. Four Norwegian battalions were north of Narvik. Half had been killed in action. British troops, under the command of Major General P. J. Mackesy, landed but were stalled by four feet of snow. In late April, three battalions of French *Chasseurs Alpins* arrived. Then, in early May, two battalions of French Foreign Legionnaires and four battalions of Polish troops arrived. The final Allied attack in the area was May 28, 1940. The exhausted German troops withdrew eastward on the railroad into Sweden. Because the Western Front was in a crisis after the Germans had overrun the low countries and invaded France, all Allied forces withdrew from Norway on June 11, 1940, to go to France.

And now for our infiltration plans. Until official announcements that the war was over, we continued with our preparations to infiltrate into Sweden and conduct further deterrent actions against the Germans. I selected Technical Sergeant Knute Joa, Corporal Vernon Austreng, Tech 5 Harold Anderson, Tech 5 Wilton Austreng, Tech 5 Otto Twingley and Tech 4 Otis L. Ausen to make up my party. These six men had already been involved in three unsuccessful attempts to parachute into Norway, so I felt they were both hungry enough and well prepared to attempt to get in through Sweden.

Messages to NORSO I were sent to inform them of this development and to relay further instructions:

> May 10: Ref your 49 and 50. Bolland and six men arriving in Sweden today. Will proceed to your base immediately. Remain, awaiting their arrival with instructions.
> May 10: Inform us about exact location of transmitter.
> May 10: Stockholm suggested you give Woodlark all your surplus arms. Can you contact Woodlark by messenger? They have not yet come up on air contact expected today. How many days food supply have you?
> May 10: Instruct any group near Todt camp if they meet any prisoners wandering away from camps to tell them to return to their camps which are the only places where they can be fed.
> May 10: M.I. IV has ceased working. All courier and transport traffic cancelled.

Later on, a top-ranking American officer at Special Forces Headquarters (SFHQ) in London was to arrange for the following men to join us upon his visit to Stockholm:

Sgt. Clifford G. Kyllo
1st Lt. Roger W. Hall
S/Sgt. John T. Halvorsen
T/5 Morris A. Syrstad
T/5 Jorgen F. Andersen
T/5 Delphis L. Bonin
T/5 Bernard W. Tallaksen
T/5 Torleif S. Johansen
T/5 Rolf Lilleby
Maj. John M. Olmsted
Cpl. Karl Larsen
S/Sgt. George G. Boosalis
Cpt. Otto N. Feher
T/5 Demetrius Frangis
S/Sgt. Boris Spiroff
T/5 Olav J. Eide
T/5 Elmer Kvasager
T/5 Harold E. Ness
S/Sgt. Erling E. Olsen
T/5 Albert Nordang
T/5 Erling R. Salvesen

T/5 Paul N. Frangas
T/5 Gus L. Palans
1st Sgt. Theophanes G. Strimenos
Cpl. John Sunde
T/5 Steve P. Marthiakas
Cpl. William Johnson
Pvt. Bernard F. Brady
Pvt. Mike Mountouris
PFC Nolan R. Cooper

Non-Norwegians would supplement the group because the primary source of Norwegian volunteers, the 99th Infantry Battalion (Separate), was understrength. The men would be moved in small groups in the order listed. They were to be given refresher training as radio operators so they could be in contact with London.

Since I was commander of the augmented group in the field, and having worked with Hans Skabo, Chief of the NORSO Group, since its inception, I was well qualified to command the combined NORSO operations. Lieutenant John Kroona would familiarize himself with the supply procedure and its movement to Sweden from the United Kingdom. He would then join Captain Dammen's organization in Sweden. Milorg in Stockholm indicated that all men to be infiltrated into Norway must have Norwegian cover names and Norwegian passports. Headquarters could then send in the Norwegian speaking men in teams of six. Other arrangements would have to be made with Milorg in Stockholm to infiltrate non-Norwegian speaking men, such as the Greeks and the Italians.

So off we go to London in haste for a fitting of civilian wardrobes. These were worn immediately to show a used look. The English labels were okay since a great deal of clothing sold in Norway came from England. We battered up the new suitcases a bit too to give them that well-used look. Our pictures were taken, our pseudo-names chosen and false passports quickly forthcoming. Under-the-arm holsters were issued for our personal weapons. I kept my Colt .45 automatic, which was a trusty old friend of years standing, and chose the proper holster to accommodate it. Then came the formal signing away of the Geneva Rules of International Warfare. Now we are officially "bodies." No one would admit to owning us from this point on. I was thenceforth Mr. Gerhard Leroy Sandmoen, taking on the name of my maternal grandfather and posing as a small businessman from Hamar. Lieutenant Colonel Oien, head of the Norwegian section SFHQ, gave me my briefing on linguistic pitfalls. This is what came up. My grandparents on my father's side of the family were from the Trondheim area north and those of my mother's side (Sandmoen) were from the Oslo area south. It became quite apparent that in normal conversation I would give myself away since some words were distinctively northern while others were southern. I was warned to be extremely careful of this. Actually, my fallback plan was to do lots of listening, gestures, plenty of grunting and "yes," "no" and "maybe" variations. Strangely enough, swearing sounded the same in both latitudes. Imagine a person mixing colloquial words from the Boston area and that of Atlanta without arousing suspicion. The problem was, in reality, that acute.

We were all issued neat little waterproof escape kits. The contents were a silk escape map of Norway and Sweden, a diminutive button compass, a steel file to optimistically have with oneself for use as an escape from prison, and some coin of the realm.

A letter was dispatched to home from my normal post office in London. It stated simply that work was normal, except extremely busy at times and, when I had more time, I would write. If not too promptly, I would have someone not so busy drop a note as a favor. I would do the same for him when the shoe was on the other foot. I found out from my mother after the war that the effort was not too convincing.

Next we find the spy "Gerhard Sandmoen" dressed in civilian clothes gawking at the activity in the Stockholm Airport terminal while curiously stealing a furtive glance at incoming diplomatic mail pouches. My, my, the mail for the U.S. Embassy looks heavy and cumbersome these days. Treat gently please! And what about those Swedish airline planes? None other than older refurbished B-17s! Yes, our planes were impounded by Sweden upon landing in neutral territory during hostilities. Mr. Sandmoen goes into the airport café for a snack. Sitting at adjacent tables are German officers and downed American officers making grimaces and gestures at each other; our officers in Class A uniforms, no less.

Upon leaving the airport, strangely enough, five of our young Norwegian men end up in the same taxicab. A Mr. Arne Dammen ends up "bird dogging" all of us. We end up at the U.S. Embassy and meet Lieutenant Colonel George Brewer, our military attaché to Sweden. The briefing is just that, brief. We pick up hotel room assignments for the night, Swedish money for our needs and, yes, Norwegian money as well. After establishing a firm time to report at the station, we all scatter in diverse directions. The evening is ours. Oscar did show me the clandestine warehouse at our disposal, however. Lo and behold, the 60mm mortars did make those pouches a bit unwieldy. The warehouse was set up by a John Erickson, a U.S. citizen and officer whom I had yet to meet.

The evening found me enjoying a live show of superb pantomime. The thespian had a worldwide reputation. The show called for audience participation, much like Olson & Johnson's *Hellzapoppin'* in the late thirties. I understand it antedated this show considerably. Stockholm was a different world. As opposed to blackouts, it glittered with neon signs. Well-fed, well-dressed people were everywhere. A pungent, but not offensive, odor of the by-products from charcoal burner units used on all automobiles was present everywhere. This ingenious device solved the gasoline shortage for the duration. And the women looked like those well-dressed ladies in an Easter Parade on Fifth Avenue. I had to drink it in that night. It wouldn't last.

Round about town were many men wearing trench coats with the wide brown leather belts and massive brass buckles, a type resembling the ones we wore in the National Guard back in the late twenties. I asked a local citizen why they dressed in such a way. This was his explanation. The men were protesters. They were showing the world they wanted to fight but their government, officially neutral, wouldn't let them.

Early the next morning, I had a splendid breakfast, some wine cake rolls and coffee, that for some reason or other, the equal to which I've never since found. A young man and lady at an adjoining table were leisurely dining there too, obviously in love and radiantly happy. This was my last impression of Stockholm in the spring of '45.

Erik Gaundal, a courier, rode with us to Storlien, close to the Norwegian border. He left us there to our own devices. Now our honeymoon was over. The target base was near the Atlantic Ocean north of the 64° latitude. At first, I decided I would try to eventually make it to Trondheim almost due west. Maybe with some luck there would be rail activity going northward, and then I could find some transportation down to Trondheim from there. Colby, don't blast the one we're on! That would be unfortunate … or fortunate, I guess, at least for the Allies. It all depends upon how you look at it, doesn't it?

The German Army handled all rail transport in Norway. Now that the war was winding down an extra car was tacked on for use by Norwegian citizens. It just so happened one was leaving that very evening headed up near our operational area. I bought seven tickets. The evening meal was a bread sandwich with a little butter smeared on it from a grim looking, little hole-in-the-wall restaurant. From the sublime to the ridiculous. Everyone was now pretty haggard, yet unflinching.

One sensed an undercurrent of optimism. The train we boarded was making German troop movements. The station bristled with soldiers in combat packs, rifles slung and loaded, plenty of grease guns, etc. Some soldiers seemed quite young, many with the swagger of the "master race," which they wore with little, if any, grace.

All aboard! In we went, still not acknowledging each other. For the record, the real names of my fellow spies I will repeat here. They were Knute Joa, Vernon Austreng, Harold Anderson, Wilton Rasussen, Otto Twingley and Otis L. Ausen. Their cover names I have since forgotten.

Fortunately, my seat was beside a vivacious young lady just bubbling over with good cheer and expectancy. Her name was Mrs. "Turalf" Lian, as it sounded to me the way she pronounced it. That hit me like a ton of bricks! I almost choked and faked a cough to cover it up. We had a Thoralf Lian, a Norwegian patriot, attached to NORSO I. Colby had already picked him up in the field. Mrs. Lian's eventual destination was Steinkjer, same as mine. My questions were probing and leading. Little did she know that the Lian farm was actually designated as a rendezvous point for both NORSO groups, directly west some 30 miles from our potential operational area for further sabotage. She didn't know exactly what her husband was doing at present, but she had decided to leave Sweden and return to their estate and await developments. Things were grinding to a screeching halt on the Continent and maybe her husband would soon return to the fireside. She was determined to be a welcoming committee. Of course, a last-ditch stand in Norway was the joker. No one really knew what the Germans were up to.

Our bags and suitcases were intact and with us. No inspection was even requested. Our uniforms, ski boots, even an extra set of clothing, including civilian shoes and a second suit, were in them. Gutsy yes, but intelligence informed us early on that precious little, if any, checking was done by German soldiers at these busy stations. My pistol holster, which held my trusty Colt .45 automatic, rested comfortably under my arm. No give-away bulges were present in my clothing. The fully cocked hammer had by this time been checked and rechecked by myself anxiously, if not nervously. I seemed to be getting by with my accent quite well. Confidence grew with every verbal sally. Since this was a nighttime move, the relief stop for the troops was easily handled by stopping and detraining for a reasonable amount of time.

After a few hours, a stop was ordered. Everyone piled out for a break, excluding the ladies of course. Soon, the soldiery was milling around the platform at will. I saw individuals of our party occasionally while walking about, but no contacts were made. Dispersion was the order of the day. The platform was about three feet high along the tracks. A great number of us had wandered to the back of the train and some even onto the loading platform. Blackout conditions prevailed except for moonlight. Norwegians were required to show deference to the *Herren* by politely stepping to the side as the soldiers passed.

A thought raced through my mind. I flashed back to June '44 during the Normandy invasion when I jumped in behind enemy lines with General James Gavin. Those Germans whose lives were spared were all well behaved, subdued and never certain of their fate, even in the prison compounds there. What I saw now at this railroad station was the exact opposite. German soldiers striding along, lords and masters of all they surveyed. Six abreast came sweeping down the platform. I was going in the opposite direction. We met, four to the left of me and the other two to the right, closest to the tracks. All had their grease guns. A sudden impulse overtook me. "I don't think I will!" That is, step politely around this formation as expected. We got abreast. I immediately pierced the group and with a heavy shoulder block and sent the two on my right sprawling out onto the tracks, weapons and all. "Corporal! Corporal!" came loudly from the entanglement down below. Now that was basically stupid. I had reacted emotionally and thoughtlessly, much the same way Berre did on contact with the German patrol. I moved as unobtrusively into the throng as possible. Visibility was on my side. Joa approached me and asked, "Do you need help?" "No, get lost! I don't want anybody to show his hand."

Before the search for the obstreperous Norwegian could be initiated, I had lost identity in the throng. Do you know how quickly it is possible to change one's appearance? Goodbye hat, tousle the hair as "Gerhard Sandmoen" moved around the outer fringes of the platform crowd. I waited to reboard until the last possible moment. Some surprise was evident in Mrs. Lian at the changed appearance. I was also able to make some minor unobtrusive suitcase changes, such as a different necktie for example. I also had a second hat along. Mrs. Lian held her composure and did not reveal my hand.

I decided to play the role of a slap-happy Norskie. Why not? The conversation became animated, especially while observing train guards looking up and down the seats while walking in our direction. With Mrs. Lian and the others next to us, who also fortunately played along, I knew one good surefire laugh-provoking joke. Boy, was this the moment of truth! The timing wasn't bad either. I, at least, was in raucous laughter as the guard passed our seats. Must be just another crazy Norskie with his companions. But much to my relief, it worked.

The train was now in motion once more. You would have thought that after that episode I would have learned my lesson on disrespecting Germans. Well, after a few more stops, yet another one was ordered. Really? Were the Germans still trying to assert their authority in the waning days of their occupation? After disembarking into the bustling crowds and moving about pretty much shoulder to shoulder, a different set of circumstances presented itself. Still, with a similar hatred for the German occupiers, I let my poorer judgement get the better of me once again. Off near the corner of a building, a lone German soldier was harassing a young Norwegian girl. She was very distraught and crying. My blood began to boil. Surveying the area quickly, it appeared there were only Norwegian citizens in the immediate vicinity. Either emboldened from getting away with sending those Germans sprawling onto the tracks or having a fit of sheer rage, or both, I approached the guard from the back and blindsided him with the biggest sucker punch I could muster. One clean shot to the side of the head did the trick. His head ricocheted off the side of the building and he dropped to the ground, knocked out cold.

But now I was in big trouble all over again. Bolting into the throngs of crowds, I used the same tactics to change my appearance as quickly as possible. For sure, the German guards would be alerted soon. I suspected they would be looking for someone trying to leave the area outright, so I made no attempt to do so. No doubt news of the incident of a rogue Norwegian that sent the guards sprawling onto the tracks at a previous stop had made the rounds to guards at other stations as well. Since they never found that culprit on any of the trains, they must have suspected he escaped on foot. At least that was my optimistic thinking at the moment. But if they were shrewd enough, they just might think he was gutsy enough to come by train. In fact, the very one that just so happened to arrive at their station a few minutes ago. How else could this culprit be in their area so soon?

With this in mind, I thought my best chance was to throw away my original ticket and purchase another one. That way, I would appear as an innocent civilian just starting my journey from this station. In the event the Germans demanded to see my ticket, it would be legitimate. After about 20 minutes had passed, I purchased another ticket to Steinkjer. The train would be leaving in about 45 minutes. I waited until about five minutes before departure to board. As luck would have it, I found a seat next to a rather attractive Norwegian girl. She was immersed in a book and just gave me a slight nod as I took my seat. Just before the train departed a German patrol boarded, with the intent, I'm sure, of looking for the culprit who dared to attack one of their own. Realizing they were looking for a solitary passenger, I feared my present appearance might not be enough to escape suspicion. Thinking quickly, I turned to the girl next to me and whispered into her ear in the best Norwegian I could muster, "I'm with the Underground. Those guards coming towards us are looking for a lone passenger. Please help me and go along. My life depends on it." Thank God my Norwegian was good enough that she understood! We began to embrace and kiss. The pretense worked and the patrol unit passed us by. After they disembarked, the train departed and we were on our way. I was overwhelmed with relief and thanked her profusely. I also explained I could not divulge any more about myself, not only for my own protection, but for hers as well. Still, I could not help but wonder for the rest of the trip if she suspected I gave her that line just to steal a smooch. However, I think my relieved demeanor after the incident was enough to convince her that it was for real. I guess the phrase, "A kiss for good luck" really does hold true. After what seemed like an eternity, we finally arrived at Steinkjer where both the girl and I disembarked.

CHAPTER 19

Impending Victory

It became more apparent each day that a complete German defeat was an inevitable conclusion. But even as the end neared, the German High Command was kept in the dark. After Adolf Hitler committed suicide in his Berlin bunker on April 30, the German High Command was more than ready to surrender to the Allies. On May 4, it surrendered all troops in northwest Germany, Denmark, Holland and Norway to Field Marshal Bernard L. Montgomery. Lieutenant General Franz Boehm, who had replaced General Niklaus von Falkenhorst as Commander of the German *Wehrmacht* in Norway, was hesitant. On May 5, he still expected to establish the notion of a "Festung Norwegen," a fortress in Norway where German forces would make a last stand. The Allies had tried to reach Boehm by wireless on May 6 and 7. Even after the unconditional surrender on May 6, General Dwight D. Eisenhower could not get a direct contact by radio to Boehm. The German High Command re-emphasized to Boehm that he was to surrender his forces. Boehm eventually went on Oslo Radio and told his German troops to obey their new superiors.

On May 6, Colby sent a transmission with his observations:

> Germans in valley are two groups. One, walking south are Austrian Mountain Troops badly fed, poor shape. Other garrison are grenadier regiments well fed, good morale and discipline. Only higher officers, few troops and material moving by three of four trains daily. Many Russian prisoners available for repair labor.

Colby had an American flag that was hoisted in full view of the German troops in the town. It remained unchallenged. On May 7, London radioed *Rype* the following message:

> Enemy will under surrender terms be ordered to concentrate in several places in lower Namdal area at Grong, Ekker, Snaasa, Steinkjer, Verdal, Rinnleiret, Levanger Hutment camps STOP important avoid any contact with enemy STOP to avoid clashes if they stick to terms STOP you are not to disarm enemy STOP

On May 8, *Rype* sent the following message to London:

Give precise orders. Can we go to valley? If so, we must contact German commanders for our security. Have we any further mission? Please get us out of hills. The radio broadcasts indicated that the war is over.

On that same day, King Haakon VII broadcast a message from London to all the peoples of Norway to let them know the Germans had officially surrendered. He praised them for their courage, sacrifice and perseverance. Even though German forces remained in their country, he asked everyone to remain calm, act in a dignified manner and refrain from any unforeseen behavior. He stated Norway's difficulties were not over, but as they started the process of becoming a free country again, Norway would stand together to rebuild for themselves and their children. He ended the speech with:

> Compatriots. We all feel the same on this day. Let's hold on to the unity that has brought us to victory. And let's remember at this moment those who sacrificed life in the struggle for Norway. Let's gather in the promise: Everything for Norway.

The men were anxious to participate in the festivities in Steinkjer. The most immediate problem was food as people who had joined the *Rype* party also had to be fed. Livestock on the Jaevsjo farm could be slaughtered to feed the men, but this would hurt the Andersens when they returned to the farm from Sweden. The radio operator tried alternate times of transmissions to London and different frequencies to raise London, but to no avail. Major Colby sent a message to London on May 10:

> We are extremely short of food and reduced rations. We absolutely must move to a food supply. Can we leave contact here to meet Bolland while we go to valley or can we meet him in Norway at Snaasa [sic] or Verdal or Hell wherever you say. Please answer today as food is serious problem. Why can't instructions be sent by radio?

Rype perceived that the people manning the radios in London were partying, as well as the high commanders who could make the decisions. In a message to London on May 11, Colby complained that arriving Allied troops to Norway would win the hearts of Norwegians and those in the hills who worked hard would be overlooked:

> Ref your 40. Does this mean Bolland not coming? Raining here now, snow in patches, lakes and rivers uncrossable. Bolland would need three days from end transport in Sweden to here and two days here to Snassa [sic]. Recommend he cross border by rail and we meet him at Hell. Request that he bring jeeps assigned this unit now in Stockholm full of cigs and coffee. Morale is sinking rapidly as all praise and glory to troops arriving in Norway to take over from a surrendering enemy instead of those who worked and fought for the liberation here. The whole world celebrates, Norway madly greets arriving troops while the first allied uniformed troops in southern and central Norway sit in hiding in the hills on reduced rations without orders of even information with which to plan. Please sign answer so we know who is directing us. Signed Colby.

On May 11, *Rype* received the following message:

Ref your 51, move all RYPE personnel except rear detail to Steinkjer where you should report to Milorg leader. His name is Torberg Johansen. Password to him is quote: "OFTENAASEN BRATT" unquote. Reply quote FRA DEN SE MAN SYV KIRKER unquote. He is living at Nordica close to trunk road to Trondheim. Rear detail to receive Bolland and party to follow. Upon arrival at Steinkjer RYPE is placed under command of district commander Colonel Holterman. SFHQ officer is Major Thompson.

All but the four men who remained at Jaevsjo were elated to go to Steinkjer! May 11, the message ordered *Rype* down from Jaevsjo to the Snåsa Valley. It did not take long to pack for the trip. Four members of the Norwegian Home Forces were left behind by *Rype* to await for my arrival through Sweden. However, getting to Jaevsjo did not materialize. Those four men were told to return to their homes. Instead, the plan now changed to my taking command of the combined Norwegian Special Operations (NORSO) Groups in Steinkjer. The men of the *Rype* party did not get much sleep that night. On May 12, they began their journey. Late in the afternoon, they approached Steinkjer. As they approached the shores of Snåsa Lake, they discarded their skis for the snow was gone.

Thoralf Lian's farm (also known as the Hegge Gård). (Courtesy Claus Lian)

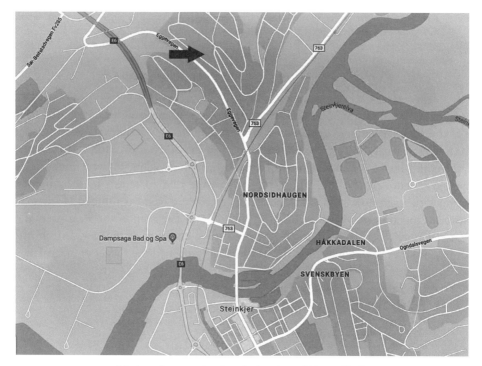

Modern-day map showing the location of Hegge Gård.

Meanwhile, after getting off the train in Steinkjer, I was to rendezvous with the NORSO I Group who were now in the area. After retrieving my baggage, I changed clothes. My destination was the farm owned by Thoralf Lian. Lian had offered it as a base for the operation and it had been earlier designated as another operational base intended for NORSO II. It was located in the hills, just outside Steinkjer.

The farm itself is quite a legacy of Norway's past. A newspaper article appeared in February 1929 stating that it was originally called Heggvin, or Heggin, and is described in old texts dating as far back as 1255. However, the farm is probably much older, going back to the first buildings of the Viking age, or perhaps earlier. It was owned by the King in 1703. Then, in 1747, it was handed over to the church and clergyman Jakob Hersleb, a priest in Stod (1721–1758). When he died in 1758, his daughter Margrete Hersleb owned it until she passed away in 1777. Her brother, priest Johan Taobis Hersleb, who was a chaplain in Stod from 1758 to 1775, had the farm briefly from 1775 until 1777 when it was sold to tax collector Knud Andreas Sommer for 3,300 riksdaler. After Sommer was transferred to the Drammen area in 1798, he sold the farm to Captain Georg Fredrik Coldevin for 6,050 riksdaler. His only son, Eilert Rosenvinge Coldevin, took over in 1833 for the sum of 1,800 spesidaler (the new currency at the time). Coldevin, who was married but had no

Thoralf and Marthe Lian with their daughter, Signe Elisabeth. (Courtesy Signe Elisabeth Lian)

children, died in 1868, and his two unmarried sisters each got a piece of Hegge where they lived until they passed away. In 1879, District Vet. Casper Lian bought Hegge from Fredrikke Coldevin for NOK 32,000. Lian died in 1889 and Hegge Gård has since been owned by the Lian family.[1]

By now it was apparent the war was winding down quickly and it was highly unlikely NORSO II, still in England, would be needed for any further sabotage operations and, thus, would not be joining us right away. Well, the Lian farm was still at our disposal since the invitation was extended by none other than our very valuable inductee, Thoralf Lian himself.

When we met at the farm, Mrs. Lian was one surprised lady! Her husband came home much sooner than she had anticipated, bringing in a rough, tough band of ruffians with him. Also, for good measure her train partner, the once former spy "Gerhard Sandmoen" was now transformed into a U.S. officer with more U.S. soldiers appearing as if by magic.

---

1 The author is indebted to Claus Lian for this information.

Thoralf Lian was an exceptional Norwegian patriot. He married Ingeborg Ree Lindstad (nicknamed "Dudde") from Stange, which is just outside the town Hamar, some 60 miles north of Oslo. They had seven children together: Carl Peter, Signe Elisabeth (nicknamed "Sissabeth"), Thoralf Jr., Claus, Marthe, Dag and Caspar.

OSS .30 cal. M1A1 Carbine used in the field by Thoralf Lian. (Courtesy Claus Lian)

OSS Remington Colt .45 cal. used by Thoralf Lian. (Courtesy Claus Lian)

IMPENDING VICTORY • 221

Colby was glad to have him attached to NORSO I when they attacked the Nordland railroad. Later on, when the rail lines at Lurdal were attacked, Colby split the group up into eight teams. Lian went in with Langeland and Rusdal to take out several sections of the rail.

Immediately after the war, William Colby wrote on a certificate to the OSS regarding Operation *Rype* and Thoralf Lian:

> This is to certify the Thoralf Lian of Steinkjer, Norway served as a member of this unit from 24 March to 20 May, 1945. His experience in living and working in the mountains of North Trondelag was of invaluable assistance to this unit in the accomplishment of its mission. No effort was ever too great for him to make if it would assist the unit in its task, or make the labor of its members easier. Though without special military training, Thoralf Lian showed himself the equal of the regular American troops in courage, resourcefulness and discipline.
>
> This certificate is intended to commend Thoralf Lian for his extremely arduous, but excellently performed work for the liberation of Norway. It is also intended to express, in the name of the Army of the United States of America, the deep appreciation felt by every officer and man of this unit for the invaluable assistance given them by him. (Signed William E. Colby, Major, FA)

For his bravery, Lian was awarded the Medal of Freedom by the United States War Department and the King Haakon VII Norwegian War Medal:

Thoralf passed away in 1982 and Ingeborg in 1997. During the war, the town of Steinkjer was heavily bombed and the result was a huge shortage of housing.

German Walther Model PP 7.65 mm taken from the German patrol killed at the Jaevsjo farm. (Courtesy Claus Lian)

Medal of Freedom/Norwegian War Medal, the accompanying citation noted that "Mr. Thoralf Lian performed meritorious and heroic services at great personal risk and of direct benefit to a United States force near Snassa [sic], Norway from 14 March 1945 to 8 May 1945. He volunteered to assist and give security on the ground during the dropping of this force and after its arrival joined it to enable it to carry out its mission. He participated in the attacks on the Nordland Railway at Tangen Bridge and Lurdal and made many dangerous and difficult marches through the German patrolled mountains. Mr. Lian's action reflect great credit upon himself and the Norwegian peoples engaged in attacking the German invader." (Courtesy Claus Lian)

Since Hegge was close to the town, in cooperation with authorities, the farmland was leased out for housing projects. However, the farm buildings at Hegge Gård still exist today, and the current owners are restoring them to their original condition, which date back to the early 1700s. The leased-out land around the buildings was later taken over by joint ownership of the Lian and Benum families. Three of the Lian brothers, namely Casper, Dag and Claus, then bought out the 50 percent ownership of the Benum family so now the land surrounding the farm building is solely owned by the Lian family.

While at the farm, my mind kept dwelling on the personnel lost on Plukkutjørnfjellet Mountain. Upon consulting a map and locating the coordinates, 10 kilometers northwest of Jaevsjo Lake, I was determined to visit the crash site. The trip would be about 40 miles as the crow flies east-northeast from the Lian farm. Twelve men, Army Air Force airmen and Office of Strategic Services (OSS) paratroopers, were buried there. I decided to take Hans Liermo with me since he was a very good skier and led NORSO I on very successful escapes from pursuing Germans after the sabotage operations. We set out in very short order.

By now news of the impending German capitulation had reached even the remote parts of Norway, thus we felt no need to be secretive about our journey. Along the way we reached a farmhouse and inquired about resting up for a bit. The farmer warmly greeted us at the door and invited us in. News that Allied forces were in the area had quickly spread throughout the local community and he was elated to welcome men who represented the liberators.

We had no sooner had removed our outer gear and sat down, but who should come walking down the stairs? The very girl on the train that had saved my life with a kiss! I don't know who was more shocked, her or myself. After getting over the incredible coincidence, I began to relate to her father how his heroic daughter had saved my life after I let my rage get the better of me on that German soldier. At first his brow furrowed, but gradually his demeanor changed as I revealed the details of that encounter in broken Norwegian. His daughter chimed in at appropriate times. By the time we finished, you could see look of pride in his eyes towards his daughter in how she had aided an Underground spy. I also took the time to tell her a little more about myself, in very general terms of course, as to what I was doing in Norway; something I could not do on that train. My parting words to her were, "Of all the heroic deeds by Norwegian citizens during the war, you can be counted among them."

At the crash site, it was a very somber experience for Hans and myself. I had seen others who lost their lives on the battlefields of D-Day. Somehow, however, for these men lost in the battle for Norway's freedom under the shrouds of secrecy, it was very different. It is hard to put into words, perhaps because they died not on well-known battlefields, but in an obscure way where their true heroics may never be known.

After returning to the Lian farm, we enjoyed a few days relative quiet and rest, demolishing much of the Lian food stores. We then commandeered two fairly good-sized trucks, loaded them and struck out for our eventual destination, Trondheim. It was quite a distance and a slow trip. We were definitely playing it by ear. The colors were shown to everyone possible en route.

On May 13, Borge Langeland, by then a second lieutenant by battlefield commission, sent a message to London in which he reported that all the Americans were in place at Steinkjer, that the German commander had been contacted and was cooperative, that the Home Front forces were in contact with *Rype*, and that Major Colby was going to Trondheim. Langeland also told London that the party had received a sensational welcome in Steinkjer and to please send coffee, cigarettes, candy and American flags. Ah yes, once again there would be coffee in Norway! He also said that the estimated 6,000 garrisoned German troops were under perfect discipline. It appeared to me that NORSO presence had a sort of relief factor to it to the Germans who were still in the area. Perhaps this was because NORSO acted

Gerhard Bolland and Hans Liermo at the crash site on Plukkutjørnfjellet Mountain. Since this visit, memorials and recognition have been established at the crash site by a grateful Norwegian nation for the men lost. (Author's collection)

as a deterrent to possible revenge by local Norwegian citizens and the now freed Russian prisoners.

On May 14, Langeland sent another message to London to report there were 32 in the *Rype* party, including Lieutenant Hoel, and that morale was high. The Jaevsjo base had just been closed and the men remaining there had departed. The word spread. Yanks were in the area!

On the same day, a final transmission was sent:

> May 14: Following from Commander Vetlesen. Glad to hear you are in Steinkjer. You are now under command of Colonel Holterman and you are close to /T station. All /T equipment is to be delivered to Milorg district leader in Trondheim.

I arrived in Steinkjer with my team. As we approached the northern edge of town, we were greeted by the mayor and a welcoming committee. The trucks were stopped and the mayor approached me with a most enthusiastic welcome. "Will your men march through town so we can all see them, and would you be as kind as to say a few words to the assembled people at the bandstand along our route?" I didn't answer immediately but turned to Herbert Helgesen and asked him to do the honors. After all, this was his old stomping ground. He flatly refused. There we were, with the mayor's party at the bandstand which also served as our reviewing stand and a platform for the least adept speaker of the day, namely myself. The NORSO groups and I marched to the bandstand. There was an opposite stand facing it. "This is going to be one lulu of a speech," I thought. I sensed the NORSO group felt the same.

"Now, you shall hear very poor Norwegian!" was my opening remark. The speech, if one could call it that, was as brief as I could make it. It outlined the group's exploits emphasizing that modest as our efforts were, we intended to ever increase them until they, the Nazis, had a stomach full. That brought the house down with hurrahs. They were giving vent at long last to their vast reservoir of pent-up emotions. We were all carried away in the intensity of the moment. The city, incidentally, was still crawling with German soldiers. NORSO marched right on by them, glowering eyes and all, throughout the city. At the southern end, NORSO boarded the trucks again.

The mayor also told me he had some men nearby that he wished me to see. We walked not too far to an assembled group of Russians. They were captured soldiers, TODT

Lieutenant Colonel Gerhard Bolland and Lt. Herbert Helgeson on the reviewing stand in Steinkjer. (Author's collection)

(the German engineering organization) workers that were free once again. These workers were forced into labor in German-conquered territories. It was a vital part of the German economic exploitation. The organization was named after its founder Fritz Todt, an engineer and senior Nazi figure. I sensed the mayor's point. He wished to reach them by building their morale. Again, I was approached to meet the leader, shook his hand and gestured that he was a fine group leader and looked on approvingly. Suddenly, a single word of Russian popped into my mind. Isn't it amazing how highly charged emotional scenes can bring out the human capacity to recall? Here was a word that I had heard once in a lecture on Russia 12 years ago at the Academy. So I popped off loud and clear "*Nechivo*." That brought down the house again. The closest translation offered is simply, "To hell with it, or let it ride." Again, the wall of tension melted. A local photographer caught Helgesen and myself on the reviewing stand. The tensions of war were quite apparent on our faces. Helgesen sent me a copy of the photo about a year later.

We probably spent about an hour at the parade and it was a great feeling of victory. I was informed by the NORSO I Group that Major Colby had gone to Trondheim to report to the district commander there, a Colonel Hans Reidar Holterman.

The next day, I sent a party down to meet with the mayor and deliver a concise message that, if the German troops caused him any trouble, he was to just call on us at the American flag. Colby returned on May 15 and briefed me that he had made arrangements to participate in the Syttende Mai (Seventeenth of May) parade.

Capturing the German Airfield at Trondheim Fjord

Meanwhile, as we continued on our journey, another thought crossed my mind. Hadn't my map studies shown that there was a large German aerodrome just east of Trondheim Fjord? I was quite certain this was the field from which sorties flew out to attack Allied shipping bound for Russia via the North Cape. At times this ranged as far out as Iceland and all the way to Murmansk. The hamlet nearby was called Værnes. A quick check of the map showed it was only about 90 kilometers from Steinkjer. It was just east of Hell, yes Hell, Norway. Hell is actually higher than Værnes. It is a fjord-side village with only a few hundred inhabitants. Before the war it was visited by thousands of British and American tourists, simply because of its name. The Americans especially liked to send postcards home that were postmarked from "Hell." Train tickets from Trondheim to Hell also made for humorous souvenirs. Later, on the same day, the Norwegian Special Operations Group was to go through Hell; this time, figuratively speaking, although it had already been through it literally.

The Trondheim airfield bothered me, yet at the same time excited me. Was this German aerodrome plum ready for picking? Several thousand troops must be stationed there. I decided to take Colby and Sather with me to check it out. I had the trucks (all two of them) stop at a farm north of Værnes. The Norwegian farmer there was loyal to the King and could be trusted. We gleaned every bit of information pertinent to the field that he could furnish. I forget whose advice I sought, Colby's or Sather's. My question: "Think the commanding officer will buckle in to us?" Some brows furrowed. "Let's give it a whirl!" A final adventure, one last chance to taunt the master race! The plan was daring.

We enlisted the farmer to find as many locals as he could. We would stage a mock convoy. Anyone with a tractor, truck, automobile or even a mule cart would be stationed just over the ridge on the outskirts of the airport. It was not very hard to find several locals anxious to participate. Five years of pent-up frustration under Nazi occupation and they were more than willing to help. We had them drive, ride, pull whatever they had back and forth on the dirt roads in order to raise a cloud of dust visible on the horizon. In addition, I placed several powerful, impressive-looking soldiers that struck an aggressive pose at one point on the crest of the ridge. The remainder of the men remained out of sight near some trucks and a few other vehicles we had acquired. They, along with some locals were to put on an "audible show." They revved up the engines, slammed hoods, shouted, and even swore a little, thus creating at least the impression of a considerable force.

I selected Colby and Sather to go forward with me to the gate to accost the sentry. We hopped into the two trucks and pulled up just defilade of Gate Number One, which was beside the road near the western end of Trondheim Fjord. We dismounted from the trucks. Tom was fluent in German and acted as my interpreter. "I'm going to insult the SOB. He should see this empty pistol holster and maybe he'll get the message." "Let's go," were my comments on advancing toward the gate.

We pulled up to the lone sentry and caught him by surprise. He saluted. We refused to acknowledge. I motioned to Tom for help. "Tell him to have his commanding officer report here immediately with extra jeeps for our use. We are inspecting his base now." Tom translated this to the sentry and got a nervous acknowledgement. He picked up the telephone, letting out a fast stream of German. The listener at the other end sensed his worried predicament. Tom told me the commanding officer was coming out immediately. In a relatively short time, the German version of two jeeps came out to the gate. Colonel Steifel stepped out and limped up to our position and saluted. He received a scowl in answer. I told Tom to tell him, "We can do this the easy way, or we can do this the hard way." Pointing to the dust cloud in the horizon, I continued, "I have two tank battalions[1] just waiting to level this place if we encounter any resistance." Gutsy, yes, but he bought the bluff! "Colonel, I wish to see your command immediately," I said. "You take me to Operations. I want all your available data for use by our aircraft in the future." Turning to Major Colby I said, "Colby, select some men to disarm the Nazi personnel. And then hop in one of the jeeps and run up and down the runways to see if they are mined." Then to Tom, "Come with me and see what you can find out about aviation fuel, storage, amounts, octane, etc."

We jumped into our respective vehicles and got off on our appointed rounds. Our data was secured quickly and we prepared to leave. After our inspection we left Colonel Steifel with these words: "Prepare to receive airborne troops here in a few days. They will be air landed. Have your drivers take us to Gate Number One. That will be all at this time." He seemed sad and acknowledged by a salute, which was unanswered. We departed and the drivers were dismissed where we had first met them.

Thus, we successfully seized Værnes airfield which was still occupied by a significant German military force, disarming a large number of SS troops that were there. We

---

1 At the time a tank battalion (squadron for cavalry units) usually had four companies of tanks, each with 14 tanks.

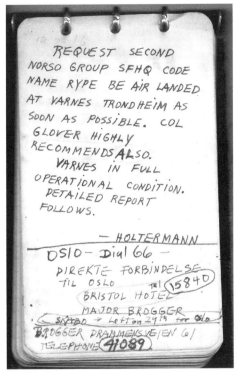
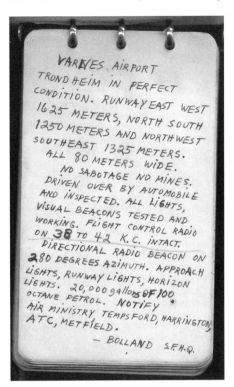

Excerpts from Lt. Col. Bolland's notebook from the captured German airport. (Author's collection)

returned to our unit and left without detection as to our actual strength. Slapping each other on the back we relished at what we had just pulled off, taking the surrender of a thousand garrisoned Germans without firing a single shot.

Once I returned to my party and the trucks, we started rumbling down the road once more, final destination, Trondheim. Levanger, a city of considerable size also happened to be on the way.

Meanwhile on May 8, Bernt Balchen had his own reception at Bodø. He commanded a flight of ten American C-47s from Kirkenes to the airfield at Bodø. The German in the tower radioed Balchen permission to land. A Luftwaffe truck with a "Follow me" sign met the C-47s to marshal them to their parking area. While taxiing, the aircrews observed German Ju88s and other aircraft all neatly lined up on another taxiway. Upon shutting down his engines, Balchen was met by a *Luftwaffe* staff car driven by the German base commander. He saluted Balchen and Balchen returned the salute. Afterwards, messing and quarters arrangements were made. The German commander then turned his fleet of staff cars over to the aircrews for their use.

CHAPTER 21

NORSO's Final Days

Travelling on, I now had a communication problem to deal with. Our suitcase radio could not raise London. The crystals did not bounce the radio signals properly at this distance, although the actual distance was shorter. I'd have to have that explained to me a little better someday by the Signal Corps.

Passing through Levanger, the mayor and his party insisted we stop and break bread with them. It was a joyous meal. We represented liberation to them. A telephone message had preceded us and the table was set upon our arrival. A better meal no one could ask for. It was from the heart. The fare was a simple meal of sardines and bread. We would never forget it.

My team arrived in Trondheim on the evening of May 15. We were the first Allied troops to reach the second largest city in Norway. Most of the men were released and pursued their own designs. It was still daylight during most of the nighttime hours this time of year. My men commandeered a couple of noisy motorcycles, attached an American flag to the lead cycle and roared up and down Trondheim's streets. This happened simultaneously with the emptying of the movie crowd from Folkelshus, a large community center showing the first film since the war. Did we show the colors! The Yankees had arrived! The response was electric. *Rype* had stolen the show! Later on, when the first fleet disembarkment of support forces arrived, in a manner of speaking, it was anticlimactic.

Only one minor incident left a blemish on the festivities in this Old Norse City of Kings. A first sergeant and a Norwegian attached to the Norwegian Special Operations (NORSO) Group had an altercation with another Norwegian non-military citizen. A little too much alcohol and celebration was going on. Weapons were fired into the air. At one point, First Sergeant Eliassen along with Thoralf Lian, the attached Norwegian, got into an argument with the local citizen that ended up with the inebriated sergeant shooting out a tire on the citizen's automobile. I did not find out about it until the next day. That did it! I was furious. I busted Eliassen down to private right then and there. A visit to the Norwegian court and the mayor's office were necessary with statements from both the men and the complaining party. In the back of my mind I wondered if Eliassen had agreed earlier with Lian that he would claim 100 percent responsibility when they stood in front of the court, which is exactly what happened. After all, he had already taken the hit when I busted him down. My demotion of Eliassen was upheld as suitable punishment and, despite his hospitality earlier at the family farm, Mr. Lian was removed from the NORSO Group immediately and sent home in order to appease the locals. Even though the incident was quickly resolved and smoothed over, I still reported it to London. The Norwegian people had been through enough during the war. Unruly behavior during post-war celebrations was insolent and senseless. NORSO's reputation did not need to be tarnished in this manner.

Wandering down to the fjord, a most welcome sight greeted my eyes. A British cruiser was lying offshore. There's my radio contact back to London, I thought. We will get NORSO II to fly into the Trondheim airfield. The significance of that Royal Navy vessel was not lost on me and reminded me once again of that inevitable "sphere of influence." Out there in the fjord was a symbol of that. Allied occupation of northern Norway, including *Rype*, was not allowed by Supreme Headquarters Allied Expeditionary Force. Lower latitudes had been assigned to others.

On May 16, the Norwegian police forces, commanded by Colonel Holterman, came in. They were made up of exiles that had settled in Sweden. The minute they crossed the border they became, as if by magic, Norwegian Army troops. The colonel picked up a new hat and was called the District Kommander of Trondheim. The Norwegian Government-in-exile had organized and planned it that way. Underground troops were emerging everywhere with rifles slung, often in makeshift uniforms and invariably in ski boots although it was now approaching the season of poor skiing, known in other parts of the world as summer.

Unfortunately, many Germans refused to surrender to them since they had not been legally recognized as the enemy. The Quisling-oriented businessmen went out of business in a hurry. Their stores were ransacked and windows smashed. Russian TODT workers, who had been captured by the Germans to work on engineering projects in occupied countries, were now wandering outside their compounds at will. German troops held fast to their encampments. Curiously, the now free workers would steal from the populace to sell to others to get enough money to purchase liquor to celebrate their new-found freedom. They did present a problem since their food supply was cut off by the Germans, just like that, which now made it our problem. As just one example of the enormity of the situation, there were approximately 72,000 Russian TODT slave laborers who had been assigned to road construction projects between Trondheim and Bodø. When Bernt Balchen arrived in Bodø, he found 15,000 of them close to starvation and living in work camps, crowded into quarters that normally would have held less than half that number.

May 16 was spent, among other things, "spooning up" for the day of days, Syttende Mai, the official Norwegian holiday celebrating the birth of the nation and commemorating the dissolution of the Calmar Union when Norway broke away from Sweden. Colonel Holterman honored us by letting *Rype* lead the parade. We carried both Old Glory and the Norwegian flag. We were a truly composite group. Who surprised us before the parade but none other than Karl Berre, who had been shot when the Germans attacked the cabin and had to be taken to Sweden on a jelka. Berre was in uniform and strong enough to march with his old buddies. King Haakon VII and Crown Prince Olav were in the reviewing stands in Oslo. They had arrived from London to take command of the Norwegian forces.

CHAPTER 22

Liberation

These were indeed happy times. Oslo, Trondheim and many other cities, towns and villages were alive with music and dancing. Liberation was celebrated without regard into the wee hours of the morning. The evenings were enjoyed by the men, girlfriends, sisters, relatives and, yes, even some parents managed to get there somehow. Small children were busy waving their little flags. They waved them all day and long into the evening hours. The next morning they were still waving them, or what was left of them. In many cases, by now they were just frayed, tattered strings on a stick. They had literally worn them to shreds with their waving.

There was a concentration camp in Grini that housed over 5,000 patriot inmates. Starved and tortured, they wore the scourges of war on their bodies. Quisling and his followers were quickly rounded up and tossed into these prisons, taking the place of the patriots and awaiting trial. In other countries, collaborators were strung from lampposts or met other gruesome fates at the hands of merciless crowds. It was not so in Norway. The Norwegian people as a whole had an intense loyalty to their institutions and respect for law. Essentially, nobody had been condemned without a fair trial in open court, not even Quisling himself.

Vidkun Quisling's trial itself made headlines throughout the world. He went before the bar of justices to answer a string of charges including theft, murder and treason. Interestingly, even in the last days, he clung stubbornly to his position as minister (president) of Norway with hopes of eventually ruling over the independent country of Norway once more. A meeting with Hitler in January 1945 seemed to give him a false hope this would happen. During his trial, Quisling stated Hitler told him, "Germany will restore the complete liberty and independence of Norway after victory." He further testified that, "When I talked to Hitler for the last time, at the end of January, I asked him precisely what the situation was and he replied that Germany would get by. I believed the Germans based their expectation on over valuation of the German offensive on the Western Front at Christmas, and partly on secret weapons that were not ready."

With the return of their beloved King, now almost 73 years old, the people felt as if their nation had been restored. There was a sense of national pride as well. Norwegian citizens who had performed deeds of great valor and self-sacrifice resembled the boldness of their Viking ancestors.

During the time of Norway's liberation, the German Army made no move to disrupt the ongoing celebrations and no statement was forthcoming either. They were still stronger militarily. Their stores of ammunition and arms were still intact. Except for guarded supply truck movements, they were not out among the populace.

I attached Norwegian Special Operations (NORSO) Group I to District Kommander of Trondheim (DKT) Colonel Holterman and suggested bringing in NORSO II immediately with more than 1,000 carbines still in existing Office of Strategic Services (OSS) stocks back in England. Holterman was anxious to further strengthen his position and the Underground because the Germans were still armed at Trøndelag. Their mission would be to have Colonel Steifel stack arms at Værnes aerodrome. I was pretty sure he would buckle all the way without any problems. After all, he had already been directed to prepare to receive airborne troops. No mention of the numbers had been made, but it would be best handled by Colonel Holterman's formal request. I wrote the following radio message on behalf of Holterman with his approval:

> REQUEST SECOND NORSO GROUP SFHQ CODE NAME RYPE BE AIR LANDED AT VAERNES TRONHEIM [sic] AS SOON AS POSSIBLE. COL. GLOVER HIGHLY RECOMMENDS ALSO. VAERNES IN FULL OPERATIONAL CONDITION. DETAILED REPORT FOLLOWS. HOLTERMAN

It was cleared and promptly sent to London. Then I composed another message for the Army Air Force's benefit:

> VAERNES AIRPORT IN PERFECT CONDITION. RUNWAY EAST WEST 1625 METERS, NORTH SOUTH 1250 METERS AND NORTHWEST SOUTHEAST 1325 METERS. ALL 80 METERS WIDE. NO SABOTAGE NO MINES. DRIVEN OVER BY AUTOMOBILE AND INSPECTED. ALL LIGHTS, VISUAL BEACONS TESTED AND WORKING. FLIGHT CONTROL RADIO ON 18 TO 42 K.C. INTACT. DIRECTIONAL RADIO BEACON ON 280 DEGREES AZIMUTH. APPROACH LIGHTS, RUNWAY LIGHTS, HORIZON LIGHTS. 20,000 GALLONS OF 100 OCTANE PETROL. NOTIFY AIR MINISTRY, TEMPSFORD, HARRINGTON, A.T.C., METFIELD. BOLLAND SFHQ

This was also cleared quickly and sent. So then, Hans Skabo, you will soon see your dearly beloved land of your birth, if I don't miss my guess. It was in the works. The rest was up to London.

Reports were coming in to Colonel Holterman that the German Navy was acting up in the Namsos area and could use a little sobering up. Well, NORSO I was available, although small. I had previously bragged a little to Holterman that the men weren't afraid of the devil himself. Holterman: "Well, how about using them?" What could I say but, "Okay."

I ordered Colby and NORSO I to Namsos, some 60 miles up the coast from Trondheim. They were to bolster the chief of police in the surrender of the German forces there and participate in garrison duty for disarmament procedures. There was a slow Allied buildup of occupation troops in the North Trøndelag area and Norwegians there perceived the proud German Army and Navy personnel could present problems. Namsos wanted visible evidence the war was over. Major Colby's showing of the colors at Namsos had a sobering effect on the still aggressive attitude of the sailors. The date for complete German disarmament there was set for May 23. Ten thousand German troops were in the area and 30 members of the NORSO I Group were going to supervise them! On the way to Namsos, they rode over the very rails they destroyed earlier. The Germans had an abundance of forced labor at their disposal since thousands of Russian prisoners were in the area and quickly repaired the railroads. The Germans were ordered to disarm themselves, but they did so slowly at first.

Their navy was far more reluctant to disarm than their army. Major Colby was instructed to inspect at will, but not to detain or arrest German personnel. The *Rype* men had reported brushes with German troops on narrow streets. It culminated when five German ships cruising the harbor with their crews began chanting "*Sieg Heil*" (Hail Victory). The next morning, Colby called the German commander to say he would be inspecting the ships at 9am. Reluctant crews were silent as Colby's inspections were made. The German crews received word from Colby that the war was over. It was their final "*Sieg Heil.*"

Meanwhile, I was awaiting the word on NORSO II, which was not long in forthcoming. NORSO II would arrive May 20 at the Værnes aerodrome. We were notified by radio. The message was received on the 19th.

I rustled around for a ride out to the field the next day. It was some 30 miles, and a dusty ride at that. A small reception party of Underground Home Guards was also arranged for. The next morning, some delay in getting a vehicle was experienced. We got off to a late start and, to make matters worse, a German truck ahead of us was churning up dust. We made repeated efforts to pass but he just wasn't going to let us by. We were getting later by the second. I looked at my watch anxiously. NORSO II was due in at that very moment and we were not yet there! Finally, my driver saw a chance to get by. I waved the driver down and stopped him. There wasn't the slightest doubt in our minds that his actions were deliberate. We were both ready to teach him respect for duly constituted authority. My driver said, "Should I work him over?" I read him the riot act and said, "I guess not. We're late enough already." I suspect he thought we were simply Norwegian citizens.

When we pulled up to the Værnes gate, there was a B-24 down with doors open. We had missed the landing. Various Home Guards were around the plane and I noticed Lieutenant Roger Hall standing there. It was supposed to be Major Olmstead in command. I later found out the major had been scratched for a mission

NORSO II on their way to Norway. Lieutenant Roger Hall standing, second from right. (Courtesy Linda Hall)

NORSO II enroute to Norway. Lieutenant Hall front left. (Courtesy Linda Hall)

back to Belgium after I had left England. Nobody had informed me. But where were the other planes?

Hall had been down for over half an hour already. NORSO II was busy unloading and securing billets, etc. An hour later and what did we see off to the east at last? Yes, it was another B-24 making a low turn on the base leg and then a final approach. Colonel Steifel bravely maneuvered a lead vehicle with me following in a jeep to bring it in for a tie down. About this time, Steifel sent me a message he received from Bergen. One B-24 down there, engine trouble, also a blown tire on landing, personnel okay. When our second latecomer finally came to a stop, upon seeing my men deplane I knew Hans Skabo was on the one that landed at Bergen.

The Germans at Værnes now had the dubious pleasure of seeing up-close the very airplane that had been unleashing untold furry upon their homes and fatherland, the B-24 Liberator. When the hatches were opened, out came over 700 carbines, US .30 caliber. These gave us 700 more armed Home Guards. We were catching up. The Germans were given the order: Stack arms.

Several Norwegian junior officers also arrived on this second Liberator for Colonel Holterman. These men had escaped to England and were trained for commissions there. Space was still available because the Nor–Greek contingent was left back in England. The Norwegian Government-in-exile sent along a case of penicillin, which was unmarked. I thought the case had been scrounged and sent by the commander, a gesture so typical of him. So, by error, an article was released to that effect to the Trondheim Press. The plane unloading was finally completed and contained five-in-one rations as had been requested. What a welcome sight. We had been short on rations, especially NORSO I, for quite some time. There was even powdered coffee in the shipment. The Home Guard rustled up some voluntary Norwegian women to do the cooking and KP. Colonel Stiefel was ordered to deliver rations in appropriate ratio to our needs, enhanced by the skills of our lovely new culinary staff. Our mess was in full operation.

The next day, lo and behold, who arrived but Lieutenant Colonel Hans Skabo with all of plane number three's personnel. He related that over the North Sea one engine went out and, before landfall, a second engine started showing a serious loss of power. After considerable evaluation, the decision was made not to challenge the mountains from southern Norway to Trondheim on two-and-a-half, instead of the normal four, engines. So, what to do? Land, of course. Where? Why not Bergen? "I think it has a small airfield," someone on the plane volunteered. "But where is it?," the crew asked. Finally, an ex-Norwegian seaman said, "Fly us back to the ocean and I'll lead us in." So they found the Bergen strip, a generous 1,100 yards long. After landing and blowing the tire, another rugged delivery was chalked up. Hans and the crew got the LORAN radio guidance system yanked out of the plane and abandoned one sad-looking bird. Down to the harbor they went. Hans commandeered a boat and had a lovely trip up the fjord region to Trondheim.

Incidentally, the personnel from the hour-and-a-half late second Liberator at Værnes gave me a funny, but also serious, account of their navigation difficulties upon arriving. It seems as the gear was grinding down, which one of the NORSO personnel correctly interpreted as a preparation to land, he anxiously peered out a window. He saw a Swedish flag on the hangar of the field and wasted no time going to the pilot. "You're not going to land here, are you?" "Yes," was the reply. "But this is Östersund, Sweden!" Well, the airport at Östersund is on the north side of a lake in Sweden. Værnes aerodrome is at the very eastern end of Trondheim Fjord. A 100 kilometer error on as bright and sunny a day as you could want. The NORSO man got him located over a railroad which the pilot "straddled" all the way to Trondheim. After a nice fly-by, he finally came in for a landing. If it were not for his innocent crew and my men, I think we would have been tempted to shoot him down on the fly-by ourselves. I questioned the pilot on his difficulties and asked him about his maps. Maps? He hadn't bothered to take them along. Maybe it's a good thing the air force broke away from the army. Hopefully more emphasis is put on navigation these days. One can certainly get lost in a big hurry, especially at jet speeds. Air-to-ground identification must be a terrific problem.

On May 24, Commander G. Unger Vetlesen radioed to Borge Langeland at Namsos to close down Langeland's station. That was the last transmission Operation *Rype* received. *Rype* then turned its equipment over to Milorg. The mission was over and all the men of NORSO took leave to visit relatives in Norway. One particular visit ended on a sad note. One of the members of *Rype* found his family had collaborated with the enemy and they were under arrest. Crushed by this, he became an American citizen, never to return to Norway.

Hans Skabo wrote a detailed report to Commander Vetlesen describing his activities from about May 20 to June 4 once he got into Norway:

S.O. Branch O.S.S. (main)
Subject: Report
To; Commander Vetlesen, Chief, Scandinavian Section
1. Departed from Harrington Airfield 0900 hrs. 20 May 1945 for Peterhead, Scotland where refueling of the plane took place. Party consisted of 3—three—Liberators. Took off at 1300 hrs. for Vaernes Airfield near Trondheim. Planes flew in formation. Weather excellent, sea calm. About ½ hour before arrival over the Norwegian coast, the outboard port engine in our plane conked out. However flight was continued. After arrival over Norway, location north of Signefjord, the inboard engine on the port side lost oil pressure. Pilot realized impossibility of reaching Vaernes and asked where landing could be made. I told him there was a field near Bergen but had no idea of length of runway. Radioed other planes to continue flight and our plane turned around headed for Bergen. Radioed Bergen both in English and Norwegian, however no reply. Eventually located airfield at Herdla approximately 15 miles north of Bergen. Runway extremely short for Liberator, however of necessity had to land. The pilot—Lt. Pittman—made an excellent landing. Only damage to plane: right wheel and tail skid. Plane was examined after landing and the two port engines found unserviceable.

2. No allied forces at Herdla. German Commander however placed all facilities at our disposal. Tried to contact Vaernes airfield to inform Col. Bolland or Lt. Hall. However found it impossible to get through. Contacted by phone, Col. Chew, a British Officer of the allied command in Bergen, and informed him of our mishap. The time approximately 1645 hrs. Col. Chew advised he would send a ship to pick us up, and transport the pilot, navigator and myself to Bergen. By 2000 hrs. no transport had arrived, so the German Commander was ordered to place at our disposal a speedboat located on the island. This was done immediately and Lt. Pittman, the navigator and I proceeded to Bergen. When approximately 5 miles from Bergen, we met a British minesweeper headed for Herdla. This was signaled, advising we were on board, and this was the ship sent to pick us up, we transferred from the German speedboat to the minesweeper.

3. Upon arrival in Bergen we were met by Squadron Leader Saunders who had been sent to receive us. We explained our desire to send a message to U.K. stating our position and requirements. This was arranged for by Squadron Leader Saunders and message was transmitted from a British destroyer at once. I was then informed that the British naval officer in charge of the Bergen district, Capt. Nicholson, wished to see me at Terminus Hotel. Capt. Nicholson was extremely courteous and helpful, however advised me that he did not want any allied forces on Herdla for the time being. Arrangements were made to return to Herdla the next morning by minesweeper to unload the ship and transport men, equipment and supplies to Bergen.

4. Departure for Herdla was made at 1000 hrs. 21st May. Upon arrival we learned that one Liberator had returned from Vaernes to pick up and take us to Vaernes. Due to the short runway at Herdla however (3000 ft) the pilot would not take a chance of loading our equipment and supplies. As it was useless for us to proceed without the same, I ordered the pilot to return to U.K. We decided however to strip the disabled ship of all secret navigational equipment and this together with parachutes and other loose equipment was loaded in the second plane which then took off for Harrington. The engineer on our plane accompanied the crew of the second plane so that he could make full report upon arrival at Harrington. All our equipment and supplies were loaded on the minesweeper and we proceeded to Bergen. Arrived Bergen approximately 1800 hrs.

5. Had a conference with Capt. Nicholson that evening, who informed me that he would place a minesweeper at our disposal for transportation to Trondheim. In view of the fact that the Germans were sweeping the Bergensfjord for mines the following day, he did not wish to proceed before Wednesday 23rd May.

6. A message was received at 0300 hrs. 23rd May, ordering the pilot and the crew of our Liberator to abandon the ship and proceed by first available transportation to Stavanger, where transportation to U.K. would be furnished. Departure of our detachment of the Norso Group was made at 0300 hrs. 23rd May for Trondheim. Arrived Trondheim at 1830 hrs. 24th May. I ordered my men to stand by and proceed to report to N.O.I.C. in Trondheim. He had departed for the day, however, his secretary furnished transportation to Britannia Hotel where I contacted Lt. Sather. Lt. Sather reported there were no quarters available in Trondheim and that the rest of our men were comfortably located at Vaernes airfield. Arrangements had been made for trucks to transport men and equipment. We returned to dock where all was loaded and the trucks then proceeded to Vaernes. I then contacted Col. Bolland at Müllers Hotel. Arrangements were made for a conference between Col. Holterman, Col. Bolland and myself the following morning.

7. I returned to Trondheim 1000 hrs. 25th May and met Col. Bolland. We discussed all Norso problems. Col. Bolland informed me that Major Colby and his men had moved from the field first to Steinkjer and afterwards at Col. Holterman's request to Namsos. Col. Bolland had received information however that there was very little for the men to do in Namsos and he was desirous of having all of Norso Group consolidated and to reorganize the same. I asked him if he had informed Col. Holterman of his desire. However, this he had not done. Col.

Holterman was not available in the morning and we met with him about 1400 hrs. I explained the situation to Col. Holterman who requested that I proceed to Namsos to investigate the conditions and determine whether or not there was any necessity for our men remaining there. Col. Bolland concurred. Departure for Namsos was made that evening, party consisting of Lt. Sather, driver and myself.

8. Arrived Namsos at 0400 hrs. 26th May and after a short rest we met with Major Colby and his officers. All morning was taken up with discussions of field operations as a whole, in particular signals received in London by us from Rype. Certain mistakes were pointed out to Major Colby who informed me, however, that it had been his understanding that all signals from Rype were received by us direct and that no signals passed through the British. This of course accounts for his insistence on suggested operations in Lierne etc. He was very sorry this had happened, however it was without any bad intention on his part. I found both officers and men in excellent condition and in high spirit, but restless. There was nothing for them to do and they had received strict orders not to contact any of the German camps in the vicinity. The only reason for their presence in Namsos was the fact, that the chief of Police was nervous on account of having a rather large contingent of Russian ex-prisoners and Germans in Namsos. I had both the German Commander and the Russian Commander meet with me and after personal investigation, I felt confident that there was no necessity for our men remaining in Namsos. I informed Major Colby that my recommendation to Col. Holterman would be that the group be transferred to Trondheim in order that reorganization of the entire unit could be made. Lt. Sather, Lt. Hall, driver and myself departed for Trondheim at 0800 hrs. 27th May. On account of several break-downs due to motor trouble we did not arrive at Vaernes until 1700 hrs. same day. Col. Bolland was informed of our return by telephone and arrangements were then made for a meeting with Col. Holterman the following morning.

9. After discussions with Col. Bolland in the morning of 28th May, we met with Col. Holterman where I was pointed out the facts as I saw them. Col. Holterman agreed that the men should be returned from Namsos to Vaernes for reorganization and reassignment. At this time he informed Col. Bolland that there were three jobs to be performed:

    1) Disarmament

    2) Guard duty in Trondheim

    3) For the group to be held in reserve in case of trouble within the district.

Col. Bolland told Col. Holterman that he did not wish for the group to partake in disarmament, however agreed to perform any other duty which. Col. Holterman might wish to have done, and also agreed to place himself and his men under the direct command of Lt. Col. Gjedde who is Col Holterman's executive officer. I also suggested to Col. Bolland that he make arrangements for ten days leave for the men having families in Norway at as early a date as possible. Upon completion of our discussion I returned to Vaernes to obtain my equipment and transportation for my trip to Oslo.

10. Departed at 0900 hrs. 29th May for Oslo with Lt. Sather and Lt. Dahl, a Norwegian officer. Encountered motor trouble on the way down and did not reach Lillehammer until 2030 hrs. in the evening. Stayed overnight and departed for Oslo the following morning. Arrived in Oslo in the afternoon. Could not locate Major Brøgger that evening. Called at Drammensveien 105 following morning where S.F.H.Q. Officers are located. Was informed that Major Brøgger was out of town and would be away all day.

11. Contacted Major Brøgger in the morning of June 1st at which time I gave him my verbal report. The Commander was to arrive that afternoon. Arrangements were made to contact Sunday 3rd and Monday 4th June.

12. Met with Commander Vetlesen and Major Brøgger at which time discussion regarding the future duties of the Norso Group were held. I recommended that Col. Bolland be relieved as

Chief Norso Group and that Major Colby reassume command of the field forces, the reason being I could see no necessity for having two field officers in Norway and furthermore that I felt Major Colby was entitled to command the men under peace conditions as he had so ably led them in operational period. Commander Vetlesen and Major Brøgger agreed with my proposal and the Commander requested that I furnish a written report of all happenings since our departure from England. Herewith the report.

13. It is recommended that definite arrangements be made for proper disposal of the bodies of 4 members of the Norso Group and also members of the crew of the plane which crashed in Trøndelag.

14. It is recommended that investigation be made of the encounter between a German patrol of five men and our Rype party at Saevsjøen where Germans were killed.

15. For information only: Observation was made in Trondheim that all vehicles used by the British had superimposed on and within the five-pointed white star painted on each side of a vehicle, a Union Jack. This, in my opinion does not denote an <u>allied</u> force.

16. Upon acceptance of this report I expect to obtain a leave for a period of 10 days.

(signature)

HANS H. SKABO

Lt. Col. C.E.

When NORSO I was ordered to proceed back to Trondheim, they were elated that soon the entire *Rype* group would be together again as a unit, despite some obvious empty spaces sprinkled throughout their formation.

An interesting event occurred when Colonel Skabo made his visit to the Værnes airport. Lieutenant Hall reported a lack of cooperation on the part of Colonel Stiefel. Skabo had Stiefel report to him immediately. Stiefel proceeded to complain bitterly about Hall insulting him during the surrender proceedings. He then began to rant on about how the Third Reich will rise again. Hall was smiling, but it quickly faded when Stiefel said, "I demand an apol—" That did it! Hall pulled the ivory-handled knife from the sheath of the ranting officer, threw it on the ground and broke the handle from the blade by stomping on it with his boot. Skabo slammed his clenched fist on the table and with the cold steel of his eyes fixed on Stiefel, he spat out, "No German will demand anything for a very long time!"

Later in life, Hall wrote a highly dramatic and very humorous account of life in the OSS. In it, he includes this incident in detail. His book, *You're Stepping on my Cloak and Dagger*, is a very good read. The son of a U.S. Navy captain, Hall was born in Baltimore and grew up in Annapolis, Maryland. From the University of Virginia he joined the army, and was then recruited by the secret service. He kept a personal journal of the Værnes affair and, according to his widow Linda Hall, retained the broken Nazi ceremonial dagger as a souvenir.

And speaking of souvenirs, at one point during inspection of the airfield, the trunk of a German automobile was opened to reveal about 100 German toggle-locked, recoil-operated, semi-automatic Luger pistols. With about 50 men in the ranks, I told each they could have two Lugers apiece. I did not, however, bother to keep any for myself.

Lieutenant Hall leading the NORSO II group at the captured airfield in Værnes, 1945. (Courtesy Linda Hall)

Lieutenant Hall in front of a German Dornier Do17 bomber at the captured airfield in Værnes, 1945. (Courtesy Linda Hall)

Lieutenant Hall with a German Type 82 Volkswagen Kübelwagen at the captured airfield in Værnes. His men painted the American star on it and Hall jokingly called it his "One Star General." (Courtesy Linda Hall)

After Colby and NORSO I returned to Steinkjer from assisting the chief of police in Namsos, at the request of Colonel Skabo, I then instructed Colby to march NORSO through the towns of Verdal, Levanger and Stordal on their way to Trondheim. Colby and NORSO received tremendous ovations as they passed from town to town. Norwegians on both sides of the street, from windows and from the rooftops, would cheer them on. Norwegians usually do not show much emotion, but the quick Allied presence, especially in North Trøndelag, changed all of that. They cried tears of joy. The noise of the crowds could be heard all the way to Oslo. Some chanted the call "reepah, reepah" in honor of *Rype*, who had chosen the white grouse that changed its color to brown in the summertime, as its code name. The marching men of *Rype* wore silk scarves made out of parachutes. That trick really left an impression on the crowds.

At Værnes we had unlimited transportation. We used the little Volkswagen jeeps as needed. The motor vehicle gasoline was gone, but we had unlimited supplies of aviation gas. Unfortunately, it was burning out valves because of the high octane. This problem was solved by mixing one gallon of lubricating oil to five gallons of gasoline. We gave Tom Sather a jeep plus fuel and let him go see his ailing father in Tromsø. This was the last time I was to see him alive.

In Trondheim, the civic leaders set up a dinner dance in the Hotel Britannia for British naval officers, the DKT officers of Colonel Holterman and our *Rype* unit. It was a truly festive occasion of joyous people. The pent-up emotions of all those years of occupation were released.

After dinner speeches were made, some being quite lengthy. I was told that a few words would be forthcoming from me. This caught me totally unprepared. An Englishman was giving a fine, very precise talk. I was to be next and last. My course of action followed the philosophy of a man who explained what an after-dinner speech should be like. The parallel was drawn to a woman's dress length. It should be just long enough to cover the subject and just short enough to be interesting. The point was made that we were symbolic of all Americans of Norwegian extraction, which oddly enough numbered a figure equal to the population of Norway. I, for one, was not about to let them down. Spontaneously, I started my gang singing "Mairzy Doats" and another equally ridiculous song, "Let's pick up the pieces where we left off, when so rudely interrupted by Hitler." The dancing began. The party was unforgettable.

Lieutenant Helgesen invited us to another party a few days later. This was a party set up by the Underground Home Front. Now seasonal fishing was picking up. We feasted on salmon caught the day before, with potatoes swimming in melted butter as well as other gourmet delights. We had cocktails galore. I asked how they were able to get liquor during the occupation. It wasn't too difficult. The Norwegians found a way to make alcohol from wood. Wait a minute, wood makes wood alcohol, doesn't it? They swore the alcohol they made from wood was not wood alcohol. It was a little rough, though, according to explanations I heard.

We had a speaker, none other than Professor Gjonde of Trondheim High School (High means "College" in Norway). His faith in the alcohol refining of occupied Norway was considerably more than mine. In fact, when he maneuvered himself into a chair to support his stance in order to speak, he opened with this remark: "You must pardon me if I'm a little deep into my cups tonight." The rest of his speech was quite interesting. He explained how getting arms to Underground teams north of Trondheim was difficult. Aircraft had to operate at extreme ranges and poor visibility. The problem was to move the arms from Trondheim northward. Professor Gjonde struck upon an ingenious solution. The master race as such would certainly be a patron of the arts. The professor suggested that because of anticipated bombing in the future, statues and other works of art should be moved by rail to safety in the north. The Germans approved the plan. Crates were prepared and loaded with weapons and ammunition instead of artifacts and moved northward with German help and blessings.

On my last trip out to Værnes, the German arms had been laid out on the hangar floors, cleaned and oiled. They were impeccable. Colonel Steifel issued all new uniforms and shoes to his men for their future use. They were already wearing them. He was under orders to proceed down to the beaches for movement back to Germany. He requested permission to take a portable generator for the staging area. You can imagine his morale problem. Soft-hearted me said to him, "Go ahead. Take the portable generator."

At this point it became apparent we would now have to protect our captives from the wrath of the Norwegians. One local told me he personally intended to work over a Nazi before they got away. The emotions and scales were tipping furiously. At Snåsa we heard shots ringing out at night. Germans were committing suicide. Comments coming from the locals were, "Isn't that sweet music!" This was a severe conflict period for sure. After a few weeks we kind of felt sorry for the poor devils. In the huddled, miserable darkness of the cold North Atlantic weather, many more Germans would choose Der Führer's way out.

After the capitulation and the formal conclusion of Operation *Rype*, it was now time for some personal ventures during my short time left in Norway. The Norwegian people were free to travel once again, without fear of the Third Reich watching their every move.

In Trondheim, the first post-war newspaper edition on the 17th of May had a little vignette concerning the fact that my grandfather, Gulbrand, a practicing master carpenter, had worked building the Nordland railroad. And just recently, his grandson had been instrumental in wrecking it! This story brought a phone call to me at DKT headquarters with an invitation to a Sunday dinner at the Bolland Estate near Flå, some 20-odd miles south of Trondheim. Needless to say, the invitation was accepted and the following Sunday was eagerly awaited. These were happy days and I didn't want to lose a precious second of it. Of course, always lurking in the back of our minds was the ominous picture of a future operation, Operation *Olympic*, the name given to the conquest of Japan proper.

So off I go to visit my relatives living south of Trondheim. This would be of great interest to my mother and father back in my hometown of Madison, Minnesota. It was a warm reception and they enjoyed hearing all the news I could share from home.

After our brief reunion was over, they asked me to return again in the not-too-distant future. Of course, at that time I did not know my future military endeavors would require me to serve in Korea and Japan as well.

In the meantime, *Rype* personnel had more or less established squatter's rights at the best spots in Trondheim. The most impressive was certainly at the Hotel Britannia. It had a modest bar and a splendid ballroom available and in use almost exclusively by *Rype* men and their friends. After the British cruiser's crew came ashore, the decision was made to establish a British Officers Club there. We were informed of this in a most unusual way. One fine evening a few *Rype* men plus girlfriends were dancing to a phonograph on the ballroom floor, enjoying themselves immensely, when what should happen to change it all? A small British ensign walked over to

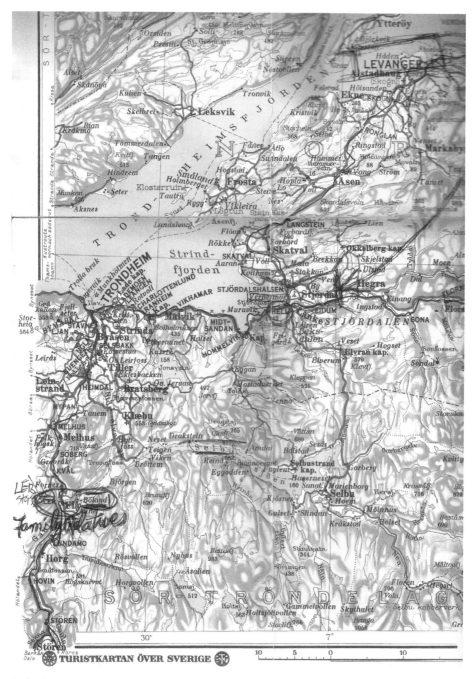

Gerhard retained this map he had marked up showing the location of family relatives in the Böland district, near Flä, south of Trondheim, along with the two family photos. (Author's collection)

Gerhard with his relatives. Caption on back of photo: "From left: Even Bolland's three children, Anna, Andreas and Anders Soerflaa."

a *Rype* man and started talking. His message was that in the future our people would kindly remove themselves and guests from the premises since this had now been designated a British Officers Club and Headquarters. He was talking to Odd Anderson, a former Purdue football tackle, now a sergeant. One glance down at the ensign, a quick grab of the ensign's ankle and he was suddenly transformed into a curling iron and sent sliding over to the bandstand, which fortunately happened to be vacant. The ensign marched off, never to return.

Well, after that incident, for some "strange" reason *Rype* was ordered to Namsos to keep the Germans in line there. A total of 26 men, including three officers, departed on May 18. The ballroom incident came to me by hearsay a few days later but, needless to say, not from any British personnel. While in Trondheim, Lieutenant Sather, knowing that disbandment would not be far off, had arranged for Colby to take both NORSO Groups to Schrøder's professional photo studio for pictures. An article in the November 1945 issue of *National Geographic* magazine has a full-page picture of the unit passing in review (p. 634 in the magazine). The same edition also carries a photograph on page 638 of a much more somber tone; the men who paid the supreme price on that mountain top plane crash near Jaevsjo.

Down in the Oslo area, the British moved in an airborne division commanded by a Major General Urquhart. This unit had fought a hard and bloody fight at

Bolland with his relative. Caption on back of photo: "Grandchild to Even Bolland, Klara Kyllo (born Soerflaa)."

Arnhem on airborne attacks across the lowlands in Belgium and Holland. My old division, the 82nd Airborne, also fought there with the performance you could always depend on. As the French would put it, *Noblesse oblige*. Noble things are expected of those nobly born. The 82nd Airborne's commander had been promised transportation to Norway in a large British flying boat, a Sunderland, but they left without him. He quickly arranged an airlift to Gardermoen airfield in Oslo in an

NORSO I

NORSO II

Combined NORSO I and NORSO II

American C-47. The movement of the 10th Mountain Division under General Edwin Walker was expedited.

The commander ordered me to report to the Oslo area. Fortunately, a flight was arranged in a Canadian Norseman. It took off from a steel mesh runway in Trondheim, about the first peacetime flight along this route. The trip was spellbinding. Bright sunshine with green in the valleys, yet snow lying on the permanent glacier between the cities just off to the right. Part of the emotion adding to the scenes below me was knowing that Norway had once again been returned to the peace filled, joyous nation it had been before.

Suddenly, over a mountain pass, the jewel Oslo with its fine harbor came into view. Even yachts were unfurling their sails once again. I was picked up upon landing and whisked away to report to the commander. His headquarters were located in the just recently disposed German consul's quarters. It had all the trimmings of the Victorian era, i.e., grand piano, vintage lamps and lavish dark drapes with heavy cloth shades and tassels.

By the time *Rype* completed its move to Oslo, the 10th Mountain Division was on occupation duty in and around the city as well. Preliminaries for the formal return ceremonies of King Haakon VII and the Government-in-exile were completed. These were detailed even down to the moment of stepping ashore on June 5, exactly five years to the day from his departure from Norwegian soil. We were able to draw fresh new uniforms called "Ike" jackets for the forthcoming gala event. This was an occasion beyond description. Although not as uninhibited as Syttende Mai in Trondheim, it carried with it a joyous reverent feeling the Norwegians have always had for their royal family and now even more so after five long years of absence. A very special niche in the hearts of all Norwegians. It seemed as if all of Norway gathered in Oslo to welcome their king.

They arrived by train, in wagons, by automobile and even on foot. They slept in the public parks, side-streets or hotel lobbies, wherever they could find room. Dancing and wandering around continued all night. The actual parade for the King and Royal Family lasted five hours. A king in any monarchy is a symbol, but King Haakon was loved by his people as an individual as well. It was certainly one of the greatest days in Norway's history.

By this time I had turned the entire command of NORSO I and NORSO II over to Colby. The King sent Crown Prince Olav up to Trondheim immediately after arrival. On the 9th of June, the whole unit had been sent up and had the special honor of being honor guard for the prince upon his arrival at Værnes. They participated in the parade in his honor in Trondheim on June 10 as the city celebrated.

There were pleasant trips on our own about the city. I took in views of quite well-preserved Viking ships in the harbor. I also visited Holmenkollen, the world-famous ski jump, and even got in a visit to a legitimate theater. To my complete surprise, there was an American girl playing a part. She spoke without any noticeable accent. The leisure time afforded me a chance to see more of my cousins for the first time. They were approximately my age. Doctor Sverre Ophus had a clinic in Oslo and lived near Bryn Station. The view was wonderful. It overlooked the city with its myriad of lights once again ablaze. His brother Alf lived nearby. Their father and mother were there when I met them. Sverre's wife arranged a dinner party to get acquainted. I had managed to save a five-in-one ration and took it along for the evening. Of all things, what do you suppose made the biggest hit? You guessed it, the powdered coffee! The doctor quite graciously prescribed for his tired but happy cousins some "medicine" for the occasion, Sykke Brandevine, shall we say, a medicinal brandy; a lot smoother than what we had experienced earlier.

During my time in Oslo, I wrote a chronological report detailing the NORSO Group Operations from May 8 to June 6 and submitted it to the Chief of the Scandinavian Section (see Appendix 1).

I must relate a touching experience while quartered in the consul's abode. We were on British rations there. Some small round sour ball candies were included. Any individual who did not take their allotment would toss them into a bowl on the table in the lounge for use by anyone who wanted them. Before venturing out on a stroll, I would grab a handful and dispense them to the children who had not had any candy for five long years. I became an eagerly anticipated pedestrian to the youngsters. One day a little girl queried me, "Mister soldier, do you have any candy today?" At that instant a very dignified, stately looking elderly woman

Norwegian newspaper dated June 7, 1945. Headline reads: "The Whole of Norway Greets Their King." (Author's collection)

was also passing by. She stopped to admonish the child. Little did she know that I understood what she was saying. "Young lady, do you want the American soldier to go back to America and say that little Norwegian girls beg?" At this, the youngster shamefacedly turned from me and walked away. I was proud to know these fine people. They instilled national pride, even in their children.

On June 14, orders were given to send us back to London for eventual movement back to the United States. In the not-too-distant future, an airplane was arranged for and, as many bodies as the war-weary old C-47 could carry were flown across the North Sea bound for England. It had an auxiliary gas tank mounted in the passenger compartment, taking up much of the cargo space. Like all long over-water hauls, we detected little erratic noises from the engine. The co-pilot sauntered back and surprised me by picking up a long broom. A very democratic crew, I thought, willing to clean up a bit. But no, wait a minute. He unscrewed the cap on the top of the barrel and pushed the broom handle down to the bottom of the auxiliary tank. He was measuring our remaining fuel in much the same manner we used to do on old Model T Fords. Fortunately, we ran out of miles before we ran out of fuel. We landed safely in England, back where we started our adventure from.

One of my final duties for the now fairly disbanded OSS offices was to write a summary report for Operation *Rype*, which I did on October 1 (see Appendix 1).

CHAPTER 23

Bon Voyage, Back to the United States

After the orders were given on June 14 directing the combined Norwegian Special Operations unit back to England, soon thereafter we were on standby for transportation back to the United States. The Office of Strategic Services (OSS) headquarters was collapsing rapidly. Many had already left for the States. It was even difficult to find someone to whom we could turn in property. Orders and assignments were big question marks. My supposed superiors were missing. I had a strange feeling I had been doing business with an unreliable firm. The broker in civilian life, who had headed up the OSS section I was assigned to, was long gone back to the States, busy, I imagined, with his stocks and bonds.

On June 23, as one of his last official duties as Chief of the Special Operations Branch for the OSS, Gerald Miller wrote me, as well as other officers, a letter of commendation. Attached to his letter was a form letter from General Eisenhower. They read, respectively:

HQ & HQ DETACHMENT
OFFICE OF STRATEGIC SERVICES
European Theater of Operations
United States Army
(Main)
APO 413
23 June 1945
SUBJECT: Letter of Commendation
TO: Sections Chiefs, SO Branch, OSS ETO,
            Attention: Lt Col Gerhard L. Bolland, 019565, Inf

The attached letter from the Supreme Commander of the Allied Expeditionary Force, has been received by the Commanding Officer, Office of Strategic Services, European Theater of Operations. I know that the receipt of such a letter of commendation will give you as much pleasure as it has given me. I am, therefore, attaching sufficient copies of the letter in order that each officer and EM in the SO Branch may be able to retain a copy for his personal use.

I should like, at this time, to express to each one of you, and to every member of your staff, my very sincere appreciation for the manner in which you have supported me in my capacity as Branch Chief. There was never an occasion when I called on any of you that I could not be certain that I would receive your wholehearted support. For this I am extremely grateful. I have always been proud of the manner in which each of you has carried out his duties. Those of you who are men and women of the Armed Forces have conducted yourselves with dignity and credit to the United States Army or Navy as the case may be. Those of you who have served in a civilian capacity have acquitted yourselves honorably in the execution of your duty.

It is with profound personal regret that our association now draws to a close. I hope that one day we shall meet again in the States. To all of you I give my heartfelt thanks, and I wish you the very best of luck in your new endeavors.

GERALD E. MILLER
Chief, SO Branch

Supreme Headquarters
ALLIED EXPEDITIONARY FORCE
Office of the Supreme Commander

31 May 1945

Dear Colonel Forgan,
Before the combined staff of Special Force Headquarters disperses, I wish to express my appreciation of its high achievements.

Since I assumed the Supreme Command in January 1944, until the present day its work has been marked by patient and far-sighted planning, flexible adaptation to the operational requirements of Supreme Headquarters, and efficient executive action during operations. In no previous war, and in no other theatre during this war, have resistance forces been so closely harnessed to the main military effort.

While no final assessment of the operational value of resistance action has yet been completed, I consider that the disruption of enemy rail communications, the harassing of German road moves and the continued and increasing strain placed on the German war economy and internal security services throughout occupied Europe by the organized forces of resistance, played a very considerable part in our complete and final victory. In DENMARK and NORWAY the Commanders concerned have already reported on the great help which they have received from resistance forces in maintaining law and order during the early stages of liberation.

The combination of certain sections of your two organizations, first established as Special Force Headquarters under the joint command of Brigadier Mockler-Ferryman and Colonel Haskell, was the means by which these resistance forces were so ably organized, supplied and directed. Particular credit must be due to those responsible for communications with occupied territory. I am also aware of the care with which each individual country was studied and organized, and of the excellent work carried out in training, documenting, briefing and dispatching agents. The supply to agents and resistance groups in the field, moreover, could only have reached such proportions during the summer of 1944 through outstanding efficiency on the part of the supply and air liaison staffs. Finally, I must express my great admiration for the brave and often spectacular exploits of the agents and special groups under control of Special Force Headquarters.

I would be grateful if you would convey, as a personal message, my thanks to everyone at Special Force Headquarters for their work. And through you I would like to express my gratitude to the two parent organizations, without whose cooperation and help the great success of Special Force Headquarters could not have been achieved.

Sincerely,
/s/ Dwight D. Eisenhower

Colonel W. R. Forgan,
Director OSS, UK Base,

ETOUSA.

For the trip back, being a small unit, we were able to fit into odd spaces available. Colby took half the NORSO group on the USAT *J. W. McAndrew* (AP-47), a troop ship. They departed on June 28, 1945. The trip took 11 days and eventually a huge sign came into view on the bluffs just outside Fort Hamilton. It read, "Welcome Home-Well Done." They disembarked in Newark and reported to Fort Hamilton in the borough of Brooklyn before being released to return to their respective homes.

I took the other half when, in early July, 1945, we reported to a Victory ship at Barry, Wales. Since the ship's guns were no longer needed, the gun crew quarters became available for our return passage to the good ol' USA. We expected to sail in a day or two. Anticipation and spirits were high but none of the ship's crew seemed in a hurry or particularly anxious. The ship itself was ready as far as we could tell. My men started familiarizing themselves with the workings of the ship. Several were

Left to right: Roger Hall, two unidentified men, Tom Sather, William Colby, Borge Langeland, unidentified, on board the *J. W. McAndrew* (AP-47) en route to the United States. (Courtesy Linda Hall)

ex-sailors of the Norwegian merchant fleet. We were wondering if there wouldn't
be some way to prod the ship's complement into pulling anchor. But how could we
without a captain aboard? Ten days passed with us living and waiting on board at
Barry. The answer for the delay was finally forthcoming. As long as the ship remained
there, the crew was drawing extra hazard pay. The captain finally showed up, a little
shaky but ambulatory. He announced our ship would be unable to sail our tenth
day on board since that fell on the 13th of July. Who in his right mind would want
an ill omen to haunt us on the return voyage? Our gang was ready to run the ship
by themselves by this time and, in fact, that is pretty much what happened once we
pulled anchor. Besides the jittery captain who spent most of his time in his quarters,
our fortunes and fate were in the hands of a brand-new ensign just out of the
Merchant Marine Academy. Soon one of our own members was operating the ship's
radio, showing the young ensign how to read the sextant on the rolling seas, and
advising him generally, whenever he asked. I ate at the captain's table at his request.
That pleasure was a dubious one, however, since we were all keyed up and struggling
to relax as best we could. A word or two from his quaky voice was no help at all,
believe me. He showed no noticeable improvement as the voyage lengthened either.

Since wartime had produced many jobs totally different from civilian pursuits, he
told me what his peacetime vocation was. It seemed he busied himself writing love
stories for a magazine that reputedly were all supposed to be true life experiences.
I asked him, "Wouldn't that be a difficult task for a man?" He said it really wasn't
difficult at all. All the writer had to do was make the man the S.O.B. in the first
couple of paragraphs and the female patrons of such "true story" magazines would
buy it.

It didn't take long on board the ship for everyone to soon know everyone else.
If only out of boredom my gang busied themselves about the ship. It turned out to
be a real take charge operation. Everyone worked together harmoniously except for
one particular crew member who did little, or nothing anyway, but yak and squawk.
His selfish nature became apparent to everyone. The ship's crew already knew his
reputation and we were quick to learn it too. He told me he was very selective in
his jobs. Whenever a rough run, like a trip to Murmansk in the Barents Sea was
in the works, he played it cool and stayed away from the hiring hall. He had been
able to get gravy runs like this one for the most part. He kept telling my men of
these "wise moves."

One day out of the clear, he obnoxiously blurted out to my men, "You guys
can have your medals. I'll take the moolah." The air became tense. Not a word in
reply. He sensed the mood and moved away uncomfortably. Fortunately, I heard
it and called a meeting of *Rype* immediately on the spot. My message: "I expect
to see —— answer roll call every morning and step safely ashore at Boston. Any
questions?" There were none. The message was understood by all, including the
obnoxious crew member who was listening from the back.

Boston harbor finally loomed up. We disembarked in jig time and finally stepped ashore at Boston. "Rocky" (Lieutenant Farnsworth) was with me. We both rushed to telephones and made long-distance calls back home to inform and comfort our loved ones that we were safe and sound back in the States. I could hear the relief in my mother's voice. Soon afterward we were mingling with the great American

Lieutenant Colonel Bolland, Washington, D.C., October 1945. (Author's Collection)

public. We didn't make much progress before Rocky grabbed a pretty girl (or was it the other way around) and gave her a big hug and a kiss. Off we both went to an American drug store. Malted milks, ice cream and more milk were the order of the day. The waiter questioned Rocky if there would be anything else. "Yes, just throw a quart of milk in my face for good measure."

We both proceeded to Washington, D.C., and reported to OSS Headquarters for debriefing. While at Area F, I was interviewed on July 26 regarding the OSS and post-Operation *Rype*. From what I saw in England and the goings on now in Washington, I felt the OSS had completed its tasks during the war effort and was quickly becoming a unneeded entity. Evidence was everywhere that the organization was winding down as a whole. I had a premonition that it would soon be deemed no longer necessary by the powers that be. At this point, I felt my best option would be to request separation and look for further opportunities in the regular army.

After the interviews, I ended up picking up a lovely 30-day leave and transportation at government expense. For Rocky to get home it was only a trip to Baltimore. I had to travel to Minnesota where my recently widowed mother anxiously awaited the return of her only son.

A trip to Japan was always lingering in the back of our minds, so relaxation was still a difficult task. Some irritations to our edgy frame of mind would bring verbal, if not a physical, response. Fortunately, I could vent my feelings in a salty language with no offense to anyone. It was all kept in Norwegian. During my leave to Minnesota, flash came the message: Hiroshima and the atomic bomb! There goes Operation *Olympic*. There goes several "isms": fascism, nazism and shintoism. My mind went back to Commander Vetlesen's words back in England. "There's a lot more trouble ahead, even after this one." We're still belabored by "ism" trouble.

CHAPTER 24

Closing Military Endeavors—Korea and Japan

In 1947, Lieutenant Colonel Bolland went to the Air Training Command Center at Randolph Field Sub-Base in San Marcos, Texas, and completed a course training to become a liaison pilot, graduating on April 5.

He then received orders to report for military duties in Korea and, afterwards, in Japan. Although he did not detail any of these activities in his manuscript, we get a brief glimpse of that time period from excerpts of personal letters he wrote, along with some documents, photos, memorabilia and news articles he retained.

Korea, November 1947–October 1948

Gerhard Bolland was first assigned to Camp Taejon in South Korea with the responsibility of protecting all dependents and dependents' housing. Later, he was ordered to Chuncheon, located on the 38th Parallel between North and South Korea to command the 2nd Battalion, 31st Infantry.

CAMP TAEJON
2 January 1948 … One neat trick the Russians are doing however is to push a lot of undesirables out of their zone (the lazy, infirmed, old) and they have created a real refugee problem in our sector. I talked to the Major in Seoul this morning. He said that normal population was 900,000 but was now over 1,600,000 for this reason.

9 January 1948 … Oh, would you send me a pair of 7-1/2D work shoes for my houseboy, Mr. "E" right away. He is about barefooted and he has to pay about 1-1/2 months wages for a Korean pair.

2 February 1948 … My Battalion is responsible for one and a half of the ten districts, or 15% of Korea. The only military forces in that area. We patrol constantly and have a great deal of guard, besides routine training, working out plans for future plausible action.

26 February 1948 ... I'm teaching Mr. "E" some English—he's smart, picks up new words every day. He's about Tom's age. I want to tell you how he got to be a houseboy. There were a bunch of tough city kids in Seoul (like any big city the world over—street urchins is a better term) who picked on "E". "E" was selling flowers to get money to eat with. He had come down from the Russian zone with his sister. The gang picked on "E" to put him out of business. Mr. "E" came up all beaten and bruised—<u>but HE STILL HAD HIS FLOWERS</u>! An officer saw the episode and said he'll make a good houseboy and took him to camp. He is good too—always builds his fire in the morning and never has stolen a single thing. He gives all his pay to his sister each month. He blushes when I tease him about girls. He has some hellish nightmares at times. Maybe a reaction to his Seoul life.

4 March 1948 ... I see where the U.N. decided to hold elections in Korea as far as possible and to leave open seats for representatives from North Korea if Russia will not let the Commission north to the 38th parallel. That's progress anyway. Maybe we can get out six months after elections.

19 March 1948 ... Don't let these stories about Korea upset you. I can assure you nobody here is too excited about the election fuss, nor about the Russians. Russians have reduced their troop strength in North Korea. This business of digging foxholes along the parallel is certainly a lot of hooey. Russia is in no position to strike now anyway. They're not in a position for using atomic warfare—I guess it will take 5 years. Northwest Airlines alone would evacuate all dependents in 48 hours. The trouble here is like any new country. They never campaign with "soapboxes" and words entirely for the first time. Koreans are just convincing each other, sometimes with bullets. We're letting them decide their fate without interference, as long as it is within bonds of reason. Otherwise it wouldn't be a "free election".

30 March 1948 ... I asked Mr. "E" should I take you and "aggie" (baby) to Korea. His eyes opened wide and his face lit up with a big "Yes!". I asked him if he'd be a babysitter—same answer "Yes!". He gets a big bang out of the snapshots. After picking out the best ones I let him take one for himself. He is very loyal and honest and he takes his job seriously. We have mutual confidence and trust in each other. We had quite a discussion on political prisoners the other night. It ran something like this. I said, "Maybe after elections, Number One Korean (President) puts bad men (Communists) in jail"—(we have been arresting these people endlessly of course). Mr. "E" said, "Oh, no goods Suh. No puts in jail—makee dead—no more troubles!" That ended that!

About Ike not wanting to be President? Let's wait until after the Conventions. He may decide that a crisis exists and he is needed. By the way—a few sensible orders are starting to come down since Omar has been boss.

4 April 1948 … Thank you for the package! I invited Mr. "E" to the "opening" saying "Maybe shoes". He was shaking with excitement, and then the <u>shoebox</u>. His eyes were bulging, "Oh, thank you suh!" They fit well. I made him apply several coats of shoe preservative before wearing and gave him a couple cans to use for the life of the shoes. He was the envy of all other houseboys—as happy as I would be with a new "Bonanza" or you with a new mink coat, I imagine.

11 April 1948 … In my area 93% of the eligible Koreans registered for the election. We should be able to run a good one. What the Russians will do is not known yet. So far they have been quiet. But look for them to set up an all Korean government in North Korea shortly after you receive this letter. They are opposing the election of course.

Mr. "E" with Lt. Col. Allen Walker. (Author's collection)

Soon I will move out of my Quonset into a Japanese building (old Japanese officer's quarters). Our camp used to be a Japanese airfield during the war. At least I'll see straight walls for a change. Just as I wrote this sentence, in walks Mr. "E" with some cherry blossoms.

13 May 1948 … Well the elections went off in good style—no trouble here. My guard functioned well. All American dependents and property unharmed. To dispel all these stories of danger, tension, and etc, I'll let you in on a little secret. I didn't even keep a weapon in my quarters at night. My guess is there will be no incidents involving American troops because the Russians do not want us to have any reasons for prolonging our stay here.

15 May 1948 … I saw Colonel Hunter off yesterday—he gave me another good report. I believe Operation "Vamoose" is coming up. Indications: 1. More and more dependents are being moved out of Korea—only those having signified that they will remain for at least one year are remaining and will probably be reassigned to the Far East Command. 2. The 17th Infantry goes to a paper status (no personnel) day after tomorrow. My Battalion becomes the 3rd Battalion of the 31st Infantry—no change except a redesignation as far as I know now. I'll still be in command.

We are busy making crates & boxes and moving families now. Two big shipments are on the 7th and 17th of June.

I may have to close Camp Taejon as the next senior to Col. Hunter, Lt Col. Scalan leaves with his family on the 7th of June.

16 May 1948 … I leave Taejon with reluctance to a new job with new people—but I'm going up to the Parallel determined to do a good job for the Division. I also leave behind a rather impressive record of accomplishments here. All tactical and training missions accurately fulfilled. Morale lifted. No venereal cases, no malaria, no fires, no officers in trouble, the best consolidated mess hall in Korea, a marked improvement in the area (living conditions), higher standards of performance of duty by subordinates, all with their complete cooperation and many expressed feeling of loss at my departure.

20 May 1948 … I have been given a position of trust by General Coulter himself. He briefed me yesterday. My new job is command of the right half of our line facing the Russians (the 38th parallel).

Chuncheon

21 May 1948 … Well I've gotten my first glimpse of Chuncheon. It's a lovely spot—a little valley surrounded by high mountains. There is less dust, practically

no nasty smells, less mosquitoes and it's cooler than Taejon—all around more healthful. I'm king up here—I'm the Tactical Commander and also Post Commander (wish my queen was here). There is a lot of work to be done however, and the job carries a great deal of responsibility with it. I have to care for Military Government Personnel also. Right now my concern is preparing for the rainy season—laying in adequate supplies because we will be cut off from our suppliers for quite a while.

About the big picture. The Army wants to pull out as soon as we lose sovereignty. The State Department wants the Army to stay—stay in such strength so that if the strength to stay were interned upon an attack by the North Korean Army it would cause the USA to declare war—thus the force would act as a deterrent to the Soviets in ordering an attack by their North Korean forces. They (State Department) considered that just military advisor groups would not be of enough significance if captured to get the USA to fight or stop Soviet orders.

Now Dr. Rhee Syngman winner of the election wants U.S. troops to stay but not at the expense of him losing even a temporary period of sovereignty.

He wants sovereignty at the expense of security if necessary. The new South Korean Government will no doubt ask for U.S. troops as soon as they can.

There are several questions. Can the National Assembly elect a chairman? Will they be able to set up a legislature, etc? Will their government be able to function? If it fails will General Hodge refuse to give up military control and disband the new Korean Government?

The State Department is cold-blooded about their calculations. The truth is we're giving up and trying to get out gracefully.

30 May 1948 … I received a letter from Alf Ophus in Oslo, Norway. The rationing is worse there than it is in England. Meat is almost unobtainable—they use chiefly fish. He said it is even worse in Finland however.

13 June 1948 … Well it's still raining—started Wed am (it's now Sunday)—it lets up occasionally but never clears up. However the rail line to Seoul is still open. Col. Griffin leaves today. I'll move into his quarters maybe tomorrow.

I laid down the law to the Battalion yesterday—read them the riot act and told them what I wanted.

I have a symphony of a thousand frogs croaking away just a hundred yards distant—they're a noisy bunch. One good thing about the rains—it keeps a lot of people from Higher Headquarters out of one's hair. They stay in Seoul.

Professionally I am betwixt doing my job and still preventing any of our soldiers from getting captured or interned—because this would force us to do business with an outfit we don't recognize- which would be "recognition in fact" whether formally or not, you see.

12 July 1948 … Corps HQ and everybody in the U.S. Army are absolutely in the dark on our future plans. This is wise however because secrecy is the only weapon Gen. Hodge has in his hands beyond his troops. Once he announces his plans he can no longer keep the Russians guessing and also I believe it will keep down the thievery of the Korean people on our property and equipment. I can imagine that we won't be able to close an eye just before we go. It will be the "last chance to get some American article" you see. That stealing is really something here.

14 July 1948 … Yesterday I made the trip to our farthest outpost—57 miles one way—it takes all day. We had 2 flat tires on the jeep which gives you an indication of the road conditions.

27 July 1948 … This is one of those days that try men's souls. I just received word that one of my trucks overturned 24 miles away in the mountains injuring 4 soldiers—one possible skull fracture, one possible broken leg, the other two not so bad. The ambulance is enroute now. There were 64 days without an accident on the board today—compared with 5 for the last month it's not bad—and considering the incessant rain and bad roads and increased traffic since the ambush in the other sector. Also the last two nights I've been receiving calls all during the night reporting imaginary things. These soldiers are new, green. They fired shots at absolutely nothing last night. I'm shaming 'em a little today and trying to steady them down. What luck I've had time will tell.

8 August 1948 … The South Korea Labor Party (Communist) have been raising hell the last couple of nights. This will probably continue off and on til election time—if there is an election. We are alerted. The Korean police are coping with the situation—so don't imagine me in a cross-fire of bullets.

14 August 1948 … Well, the Corps inspection team has left. The senior officer told me not to worry—so I gather we did well. The report will be down later. I was told our vehicles were about as good as any unit in Korea. Better than excellent which is rarely passed out here. Considering the fact we operate over the worst possible road conditions in Korea all the time, I consider it an achievement.

We are cut off on the main road to Seoul by a mountain slide that will take about a week to get rid of. The train runs ok and it is possible to get to Seoul by route over a circuitous route, so we're ok.

Gen. McArthur & wife are coming to Seoul for Korea's big day (Hodge should be very unhappy—he'll be standing to the left of McArthur and there'll be a woman too!). We are on alert here for any opposition by communists of course.

15 August 1948 … Today was Korean Independence Day, the birth of this new nation. I stood in the reviewing stand with the Governor of this Province, Kangurando—the

largest Province in Korea and watched the South Korean Constabulary Battalion march by—yes battalion—you see, we haven't been asleep here exactly. We've been working with them a good deal and helping them organize and train. Although forces in the South are not as large as up North, they are better trained and equipped. I can't tell you numbers. The National Police are a well-trained organization also. They also passed in review.

I wore my same paratrooper boots that I had when I saw the King return to Norway, incidentally. There is much celebrating here today. We are all staying in our compound—no parade, no nothing. This is their day. We're leaving it up to them entirely here. A soldier's reward is not material. But it is days like these that reward us in a different way, I guess.

16 August 1948 … The Koreans certainly had a wonderful day (weather) for their Independence Day—not a cloud in the sky and not too warm—just a cool tinge in the air. We had no sabotage or incidents in our area here in Chuncheon. Everything went off very nicely.

My troubles at present are a jittery Regimental Commander. He's catching hell from all directions and is very uneasy. I'm trying not to add to his troubles. There's a rumor out he may be relieved of the Regiment. I believe he's getting less trouble from us than from elsewhere however. Let's hope so anyway.

McArthur put on quite an act yesterday I hear. So my Lieutenant down there tells me anyway—a speech "Hamlet style" too.

17 August 1948 … I must tell you about an incident in Seoul at the "Big Doings" Sunday. McArthur took his cap off and gave it to some Korean constabulary officer to hold, then mounted the ceremony platform. The sun was warm. Soon Mrs. McArthur is seen giving "Doug" the signal for "put your cap back on". McArthur sees it and immediately complies with the order (now you know who runs the Far East Command). Doug to Hodge "Get my cap". Hodge to a Major General "McArthur's cap". The Major General to a Brigadier General. The Brigadier General to a couple of Colonels—alas not a Major in sight! So off they go on a cap hunt not having the slightest idea where it is. Then they finally locate it. But the Korean entrusted with the honor of holding McArthur's cap isn't about to give it up. But after much persuasion and an interpreter, the cap goes to the Colonels—then it goes being passed up the line of rank until if finally rests on McArthur's head again (that's what we call a chain of command).

9 September 1948 … The news commentators probably got you down by saying "there are no definite plans for immediate withdrawal of troops from Korea and anyone who says so is spreading Communist propaganda". I wouldn't feel too badly. Don't you think we're working up a bargaining point with the U.N.—putting this

idea up to them "Well what are you (U.N.) going to do about Korea? We're not getting out until you people take care of them". Just have faith.

17 September 1948 … A very tragic accident happened in Korea, fortunately from a personal point of view, no men from my Battalion were involved.

At 2000 hours 15 Sept a train, north of Taejon enroute to Seoul crashed into another parked train, killing 24 Americans instantly, injuring 82 and I believe the dead are close to 40 now. Many were from the Taejon Camp—first the fire, then this. Lt. Col. Walker is having more hard luck recently! The trains are not only expensive toys but also dangerous ones in the hands of the Koreans.

I had a jeep stolen last night and it was overturned—3 GI's took it—not badly damaged—we're trying to find the culprits—we have the jeep—we'll fingerprint it before moving it.

Col. Baird made a very quick trip through—left on this morning's train (Doodlebug). He seemed very pleased. He should have been—we were sharp.

I go this afternoon for the second and last lecture on Korean and American relations. Hope to return tomorrow night—so I can get my mail.

19 September 1948 … Returned from Seoul last night. I attended the funeral for the soldiers killed in the train wreck—the memorial services I should say, very impressive. President Syngman Rhee and General Coulter spoke. The count now is 35 dead. None were from my Battalion, 6 were from the Regiment—(3 from Taejon)—only 2 knew one soldier slightly.

I have the malaria licked here now. I'm about the lowest in rate and number in Korea, I guess.

My trip had some good news also. It seems I'll be able to retain enough personnel to maintain the identity of my units in future plans. All my work, our "spirit de corps" will not be thrown away.

2 October 1948 … I feel like a well inspected individual! The Inspector General stayed from Sunday night to Thursday afternoon. Then General Piburn arrived at noon Thursday and left this morning. We passed with "Flying Colors"! The General made complimentary remarks when he left this morning. My reputation in the Division is now well established and since the Division is remaining intact, I will not have to go through all that again with strangers.

I expect to stay in Seoul about one month—just a guess, that's all. The shipping strike (water transportation) will slow up some. How much I do not know. Expect I'll be eating cured meat (ham) until I squeal.

The move is coming along nicely. One more week and all my responsibility (tactically) ceases.

8 October 1948 ... I was relieved of the ammunition dump Guard today. Outpost 24 (my last) is relieved tomorrow and that's it—except for closing out my last company area and moving to Seoul on Sunday morning. My houseboy here "Hong" gave me a small present—a silk piece of handkerchief with different colored silk thread used to print "Chuncheon, Korea" on top, a flying dragon in the middle and "Gerhard Bolland" on the bottom—touching. I start packing this afternoon. I cleared my office out this morning. Really feel a big sense of relief these days.

31 October 1948 (To Aunt Ardie) ... These are happy days for me because in just two days I'll be enroute to my new home—where Eileen and Eric join me before too long. They should be receiving alert notices for overseas very shortly if they haven't already been alerted.

It should be a very fine experience for Eileen. Her life will be quite different from what she has lived in the States. In many ways it will be like a lapse back in time to the days of Ladies, Lords and Manors. She will have a complete retinue of servants—as many as she likes, maybe more than that, as the effort is to provide employment to the Japanese.

The length of stay is nice too—about a year and she'll be on her way back to the United States, better for the experience.

As the wife of a Regimental Executive Officer, she will find her social life lively and full, I can assure you. The recreational facilities are numerous and varied—on a country club scale. To say the picture is over drawn, one need only point out that officers leave reluctantly and many extend their tours. The things they enjoy there would be financially impossible elsewhere.

1 November 1948 ... I'm happy to leave Korea. I feel like I've been at grips with the devil—brother against brother! What a despicable, depraved segment of humanity, professing man to be the highest and ultimate, and his material gains the final goal! I also thank God that I was given the strength to come out the victor in my task here. I am not preaching a sermon, nor am I fanatical but the issues are that basic: God or atheism—and the entire world is falling into one or the other camp right now. May our own camp be the stronger.

Japan (Sendai and Sapporo) November 1948–February 1950

Lieutenant Colonel Bolland was assigned to command the 17th Infantry Regiment A1 07 Unit in Japan, first in Sendai and then in Sapporo. On February 12, 1949, he completed the Air Transportability Staff Course at the Eighth Army Training Center for Troop Carrier Aircraft. Also, during this tour of duty, their second child, Judith, was born in Sapporo on December 20, 1949.

5 November 1948 … Well here I am in Japan, just arrived last night and tonight I take a train for Tokyo (get there Sunday morning). I am now at Hakata, Kyushu, the Southern Island. It's remarkable what a hundred miles can do! I can hardly accustom myself to such a difference- stuffing myself with fresh pears, apples, etc—which we didn't dare eat in Korea.

Korea is a great deal like living in the "Wild West." They've got guns & ammunition now so everybody is running around trying to see who's champion. The National Police hate the Constabulary—the Constabulary hate each other. As I was passing through Taejon enroute south the Constabulary had a fight amongst themselves—almost another revolt like at Yoshu. At Pungsan some hoodlum heaved a stone through the window opposite me. It's like Jimmy Durante says, "Everybody wants to get in on the act." All in all a Wild West atmosphere. We moved out quietly at night—a sneak move. Korea for the Koreans—that's my motto.

7 November 1948 … Spending the day in Tokyo before proceeding up north to Sendai where I'll be working at Camp Schimmelphenning [Schimmelpfennig]. Arrived at 8:30 this morning. Took a nap til noon. Spent about two hours "delousing" myself from Korea—wore out a cake of soap in the shower.

Tokyo is a lot like any large city in the world. The Japanese people live way below our standards, but by comparison with Korea …

Lieutenant Colonel Bolland leading the troops in Sendai, Japan. (Author's collection)

10 November 1948 … You are going to Camp Schimmelphenning APO 468 UNIT 1 At Sendai Japan, about 250 miles north of Tokyo.

7 December 1948 … It looks like the old seventh is catching it again. They must be running quite a gauntlet to the coast. That outfit always had a miserable service—almost cursed.

I've got an idea to settle the Orient problem. Arm the Japanese, send them to Formosa. Then they'll prod Chiang and send him to China. He'll prod the Red Chinese and send them to Korea. Then the Koreans can swarm Japan. Now we've got a nice little circle going. We'll stay alongside the circle and when the ones we like go by, cheer em' and when the ones we don't like go by, give them a crack on the fanny. When the speed gets going fast enough, we'll bend the traffic into ever decreasing circles until they finally disappear on their own!

In the field with the 17th Infantry, Sendai, Japan. (Author's collection)

Reunited with his family at the dock in Yokohama, Japan, January 27, 1949.

UN Should Quit Korea at Once, Byrd Declares

'Situation Hopeless,' Senator Believes

DRIVER, VA., Dec. 5—(AP)—Senator Byrd (D-Va.) called tonight for the immediate evacuation of United Nations troops from Korea, "now that the situation is hopeless."

Of the three alternatives the United Nations faces—to stand and fight, to go on the defensive or to evacuate—Byrd declared:

"I am not an appeaser, but I say that we should evacuate now that the situation is hopeless and wait for a better day."

Byrd lashed out sharply at the decision to cross the Thirty-eighth Parallel in Korea in what he termed a "sideline war."

"We can't go about the world making democrats out of people who do not want to be democrats," he asserted.

Newspaper clipping attached with letter of 7 December 1948. (Author's collection)

Easter 1949, Hokkaido, Japan.

Saying goodbye to his children before returning to Korea, February 28, 1950.

Oh, a banker friend of Cmdr Gordon was visiting him in the hospital and I expressed myself on the oriental problem. The banker is a very good friend of Senator Byrd and evidentially expressed the idea to Byrd and my own words came back at me in the paper (see clipping).

10 December 1948 ... Dearest, I received the good news—and hope you get your port call for New York, Dec 27th! You will be increasingly better off embarking there—although the time on the water will be longer. There are compensations of seeing different ports besides the Canal. You may see Honolulu. Don't forget your camera to document your trip—you'll enjoy it later. "SAI" means Sendai—you still dock at Yokohama. The change was only to notify the 2nd medium port Bn there to make arrangements for you to travel *to Sendai & I'll be there doing that arranging.*

After Eileen and Eric joined him in Japan, the personal letters obviously ceased.

Brief Return to Korea in 1950

9 November 1950 ... I heard Truman last night. I'll swear he was "tight"—couldn't even read his script. I guess he had a right to after the assassination attempt. George introduced Stassen. Missed the introduction but heard most of Stassen's speech. It had a lot more dignity.

Korea must be a logistic hell. Those dammed radios will not support all our divisions in North Korea. All we need now is some snow! I'm certain that Inchon can't handle the needed supplies (Seoul's port city). That means stuff had to come up from Pungsan—with the 7th division moving south from Seoul to Pungsan for their amphibious loading. It must have been something.

24 November 1950 ... You can't bargain with Orientals. You just simply dominate them or you've lost (who's no. 1 man?—that's what they want to know). Bargaining is only interpreted as fear and weakness. A note of sadness. Lt. Engh was killed. Remember the rawboned blonde "norski" from North Dakota in Capt. Hertle's Company?

Don't move. I want to get at Colonel Ford. If I can get him on my side I can probably get back and finish that flying course. I'm going to be perfectly fine for flying when I get out of here. I'm as certain of that as I was certain I could have never made it from Japan directly.

Pass over or not I think I'll ask for a reassignment and it may as well be the Flying School. Don't announce my plans or even intentions. Do you think Ford can be bent? We both owned private planes—we have that in common anyway.

December 5, 1950 … Well, we'll have to pull out of Korea I fear—they're swarming over the lands like locust. White man's supremacy in the Orient is fast coming to a close. We're being challenged every time we turn around.

Back in the United States

Later, in the spring of 1950, Bolland left Korea for good and was once again reunited with his family.

During his time in Korea, several of his personal letters described a slow, deteriorating health condition with several complications. Upon returning to the United States, he was subjected to medical tests and evaluations at the military complex in Denver, Colorado. The Physical Evaluation Board report dated April 3, 1951 cited, "Sclerosis, multiple, chronic, severe; manifested by reflex changes and marked cerebral deterioration as shown by impaired abstract thought, adaptability and powers of concentration." The diagnosis confirmed a debilitating disease with relapses and remissions possible. Faced with the uncertainty of good physical health, he reluctantly realized retirement was inevitable, although not by choice. Records of interviews by medical professionals show his desire was to continue on in military service. "I'm not a quitter!" as he exclaimed on one report.

However, at the age of forty-one, Lt. Colonel Bolland was forced to end his military career due to his deteriorating health. He retired on a 100 percent physical disability benefit.

After retirement, he first moved his family to Riverside, California, where they had three more children, Anita, Andrew and Matthew. Then, eventually, to his hometown of Madison, Minnesota, where their sixth and final child, Eileen Jr. was born. Finally, in 1960, they moved to Stoughton, Wisconsin, where he spent the remainder of his life.

During his retirement years, his love for flying never abated. At one time, when his health condition was in remission, he enrolled in a Federal Aviation Administration Airframe Mechanics and Powerplant Program, completing all course work in 1967.

Lieutenant Colonel Gerhard Bolland passed away on November 9, 1999, at the age of 90, leaving a legacy for generations of Bollands to be proud of. In his honor, the Bolland family dedicated a bench to the local Veterans Memorial Park in Stoughton, Wisconsin.

Conclusion

D-Day changed the course of history. It gave us a perspective on humanity we may never witness again. General Douglas MacArthur, who played a prominent role in the Pacific theater, gave his farewell speech on April 19, 1951, to a Joint Session of Congress. In his closing remarks, he delivered his soul, if you will:

> I am closing my 52 years of military service. When I joined the Army, even before the turn of the century, it was the fulfillment of all of my boyish hopes and dreams. The world has turned over many times since I took the oath on the plains at West Point, and the hopes and dreams have long since vanished, but I still remember the refrain of one of the most popular barrack ballads of that day which proclaimed most proudly that, "old soldiers never die; they just fade away."

There is something about age and experience that offers these kinds of perspectives. Perhaps we will never again see a generation such as this. To a great extent, sovereign nations must now deal with "invisible wars," those which are fought, not with the sounds of weapons being fired and strategies drawn out on pieces of paper, but an insidious war, fought from within the culture for the hearts and minds of its citizens. Perhaps the greatest danger of these wars is complacency, because just around the corner from complacency is apathy.

Those counted as "among the firsts," paratroopers of the 82nd and 101st Airborne Divisions that dropped from the sky behind enemy lines on that fateful day, June 6, 1944, played no small part in the liberation of Europe from Hitler's Third Reich. Although badly scattered at first, they attacked the enemy from behind with ferocity and courage, paving the way for the Allied landing forces on the beaches to gain a foothold on the European Continent.

On the 75th anniversary of D-Day, June 6, 2019, President Donald J. Trump gave a speech at the site of Omaha Beach in France. As his speech made clear, to the generations that have followed, this historic event remains forever as the legacy of that greatest generation that sacrificed so much:

> We are gathered here on freedom's altar, on these shores, on these bluffs, on this day 75 years ago, 10,000 men shed their blood, and thousands sacrificed their lives for their brothers, for their countries, and for the survival of liberty.

Today we remember those who fell and we honor all who fought right here in Normandy. They won back this ground for civilization. To more than 170 Veterans of the Second World War, who join us today, you are among the very greatest Americans who will ever live. You are the pride of our nation. You are the glory of our republic. And we thank you from the bottom of our hearts.

Our debt to you is everlasting. Today we express our undying gratitude. When you were young, these men enlisted their lives in a great crusade—one of the greatest of all times. Their mission is the story of an epic battle and a ferocious eternal struggle between good and evil. On the 6th of June, 1944, they joined a liberation force of awesome power and breathtaking scale....

Seven decades ago, the warriors of D-Day fought a sinister enemy who spoke of a 1,000-year empire. In defeating that evil, they left a legacy that will last, not only for a 1,000 years, but for all time. For as long as the soul knows for duty and for honor, for as long as freedom keeps its hold on the human heart.

To the men who sit behind me and to the boys who rest in the field before, your example will never, ever grow old. Your legend will never die, your spirit, brave, unyielding and true, will never die. The blood that they spilled, the tears that they shed, the lives that they gave, the sacrifice that they made, did not just win a battle. It did not just win a war. Those who fought here won a future for our nation. They won the survival of our civilization, and they showed us the way to love, cherish and defend our way of life for many centuries to come.

Today as we stand together upon this sacred earth, we pledge that our nations will forever be strong and united. We will forever be together, our people will forever be bold, our hearts will forever be loyal, and our children and their children will forever, and always be free. May God bless our great Veterans, may God bless our allies, may God bless the heroes of D-Day, and may God bless America.

Several decades have passed since these "firsts" appeared as part of America's military strategy and strength. These "paratroops" and the men and women of the Office of Strategic Services (OSS) were the first to take up operations and carry out missions to protect freedoms and liberties throughout the world from the would-be oppressors. Both Special Forces and paratroopers in today's military can be found in various branches. The roots of these modern-day units run deep, and their beginnings can be traced back to World War II.

5307th Composite Unit insignia.

One of these groups is particularly noteworthy. They carried out their operations in the jungles of South-East Asia, including China, Burma and India. "Merrill's Marauders," as they became known to journalists at the time, were simply referred to as Shipment 1688 by the shipping planners. Officially they were named the 5307 Composite Unit or Unit Galahad.

The Marauders demonstrated the capabilities of long-range penetration, conducting their warfare mostly as an improvised force of American soldiers. Attacks were conducted after seemingly impossible marches through mountainous jungles and taking on the far superior Imperial Japanese Army by surprise. Numerically outnumbered and despite scarce supplies, jungle diseases, and on the brink of exhaustion, they gained and held their objectives. This unit, which was originally intended to last for only a single 90-day combat mission, became the heritage of today's Army Rangers. The Marauders, and of course the OSS as the original soldiers from the sky, are counted among those that forged today's Special Forces and paratrooper units.

There is also a Special Forces branch of today's army known as the Green Berets. The *Ballad of the Green Berets* is a song about them, made popular by Sergeant Barry Sadler in the 1960s. Its lyrics describe the grit, determination and courage of today's paratroopers:

> *Fighting soldiers, from the sky.*
> *Fearless men, who jump and die.*
> *Men who mean, just what they say.*
> *The brave men, of the Green Beret.*
> *Silver wings, upon their chest.*
> *These are men, America's best.*
> *One hundred men, will test today.*
> *But only three, win the Green Beret.*
> *Trained to live, off nature's land.*
> *Trained in combat, hand to hand.*
> *Men who fight, by night and day.*
> *Courage take, from the Green Beret.*
> *Silver wings, upon their chest.*
> *These are men, Americas best.*
> *One hundred men, will test today.*
> *But only three, win the Green Beret.*
> *Back at home, a young wife waits.*
> *Her Green Beret, has met his fate.*
> *He has died, for those oppressed.*
> *Leaving her, this last request.*
> *Put silver wings, on my son's chest.*
> *Make him one, of America's best.*
> *He'll be a man, they'll test one day.*
> *Have him win, the Green Beret.*

Even the Carpetbaggers have direct descendants. They are the 492nd Special Operations Wing of the United States Air Force stationed at Hurlburt Field in Florida. The original 801st Bombardment Group (Provisional) was replaced by the 492nd Bombardment Group, and the group performed special operations missions throughout the remainder of the war in Europe. It was inactivated on 17 October 1945. Later, the Air Force Special Operations Air Warfare Center was formed at Hurlburt in 1962 to train and deploy some of the first special operations airmen, known as Air Commandos. This unit was replaced by the current 492nd Special Operations Wing which was activated in May 2017 and retains the heritage of the original Carpetbaggers.

The Consequences of OSS Operation *Rype*

In June 1945, *Rype* completed its mission in Norway. Even then, the Allies were concerned the Germans might make a last ditch stand in Norway with its remaining forces there. If this was to happen, *Rype* had orders to train and supply local resistance groups. Otherwise, if Germany surrendered with no further attempts at resistance, *Rype* had orders to help restore order in northern Norway.

William Colby summarized the operation in his report dated June 30, 1945, to the commanding general of the OSS offices in Washington, D.C.:

> This operation was characterized by most severe climatic and physical obstacles which were overcome by the spirit and determination of the men comprising the unit. The results of this operation consisted in slowing down the German evacuation in Norway, as its military result, and through the chance that these were the only Allied uniformed troops operating in Norway prior to the capitulation, a political result of considerable favorable reaction viz-z-viz the United States upon the people of Norway. This last result was brought about to some extent by the extensive publicity in Norwegian papers given the unit before its departure from Norway.

Rype carried out its mission of unconventional warfare with skill and bravery against one of the strongest conventional armies of its time, the German *Wehrmacht*. Lieutenant Colonel Gerhard Bolland was proud to be Commanding Field Officer of both NORSO I (Norwegian Special Operations) and NORSO II teams consisting of brave American soldiers and Norwegian Nationals. *Rype* was unique in having been the only Norwegian–American operation to "invade" Norway. The OSS NORSO Group was the only paratrooper-ski unit in the U.S. Army to be on Norwegian soil. The *Rype* operation remained highly classified until the Freedom of Information Act in 1975 deemed it unclassified.

In the world of secret intelligence, usually only the failures of special operations, such as *Desert One*, the ill-fated rescue attempt of American hostages from Iran in 1980 under the Carter Administration, make the headlines. The successful ones remain shrouded in secrecy. *Rype* is a story of one of those highly successful missions that occurred back in World War II, when covert operations were a fledgling endeavor.

In carrying out unconventional warfare deep behind enemy lines, the *Rype* mission serves as a classic example to military planners of an unqualified success. Yet, in retrospect, the costs were high in order to deliver and support it. Of the 80 men trained for the mission, 36 were chosen to parachute into Norway. The initial penetration into Norway started out badly. Five were accidentally dropped into neutral Sweden. Ten other paratroopers and 14 airmen were killed on the initial flights. Aircrews had little experience flying in the far north and, in winter operations over Scandinavia, they encountered unfamiliar mist and cloudy obstructions over the drop zones. Besides, they discovered the view from an aircraft over Norway in winter with white landscape conditions caused everything on the ground to look the same.

Given the high uncertainty, the field operations of the *Rype* mission went quite well. The drop on the snow-covered frozen Lake Jaevsjo was accomplished as planned on March 24, 1945. Although broken ankles and legs were high risk injuries on such drops behind enemy lines, the 16 members of NORSO I parachuted down to the lake without major injuries. Resupply and reinforcement attempts by air were unsuccessful due to foul winter weather. This eliminated the mission's primary target for destruction, the formidable railroad bridge over the Grana River. Instead, *Rype* destroyed the bridge at Tangen. To reach Tangen, the men had to ski as far as 75 miles to their target, each taking turns pulling 60 pounds of plastic explosives on toboggans. *Rype* also destroyed two-and-a-half kilometers of rail lines in a remote area in the Lurudal Valley. Upon completion of these sabotage operations, the men had to outski the pursuing German ski patrols. The *Rype* mission was an unqualified success in meeting OSS criteria for successful strikes. That is, approach the target undetected, destroy the target, incur no casualties and successfully escape capture by the pursuing enemy. *Rype* thus slowed German troop movements along the Nordland railroad from one battalion a week to, at the very most, one battalion a month. To understand why *Rype*'s achievements were important, one must study the strategic environment of which it was a part.

After the Allies won the Battle of the Bulge from December 1944 through January 1945, Supreme Headquarters Allied Expeditionary Force (SHAEF) perceived Nazi Germany was about to collapse. SHAEF was nonetheless concerned German High Command might decide to bring back to Germany, from Norway, several hundred thousand troops, including 150,000 crack mountain troops, to defend the Fatherland. Impassable snow-covered roads in northern Norway and British control of the high seas would dictate German use of the Nordland railroad to transport these troops southward. SHAEF consequently ordered missions like *Rype* to repeatedly damage this and other infrastructure. In one night alone, combined Allied saboteurs and Norwegian Underground units damaged Norwegian transportation networks in 750 places. The Allied teams of saboteurs had radios and wireless contact with Special Forces Headquarters (SFHQ) in London to report their accomplishments and to pinpoint the locations of German units.

Because Norwegians, from 1940 on, pleaded with the Allies to stop bombing raids on Norway, sabotage was the only allowed alternative. Neutral Sweden's role during World War II should also be considered. When Norway and Denmark were occupied by German troops on April 9, 1940, Sweden feared she might also be occupied. Sweden behaved cautiously and its policy towards Norway was one of unfriendliness. Norway and Sweden share a long border across which many Norwegians fled the *Gestapo*. When the tide of war was beginning to turn against Nazi Germany in 1943, Swedish fears of German occupation subsided. The Norwegian Government-in-exile in London, with the approval of Swedish authorities, established "health camps" for Norwegians in Sweden. These were actually Underground outposts to give military-age Norwegians two to three weeks of military training. These then evolved into "police reserves" and eventually into regular Milorg units. In 1944, the British made an agreement with Sweden and Milorg to establish "weather stations" in Sweden next to the northern frontier of Norway. In reality, they were "little Gibraltars" that housed Milorg personnel, weapons and supplies to be used in operations against the enemy in Norway. The British *Woodlark* party, located in Jagthytta, Sweden, near Lake Jaevsjo in Norway, aided in the reception of the *Rype* party on March 24, 1945. Milorg couriers, carrying written correspondence that could not be transmitted by wireless, shuttled between Stockholm and Lake Jaevsjo for the *Rype* mission. This form of communication with Milorg in Stockholm, and eventually with SFHQ in London, was excellent. No mail was intercepted by alien agents.

Operation *Rype* taught the OSS that air support must be delivered accurately and on time, in spite of the elements. Less than a 50-percent delivery rate was unacceptable. New navigational technologies, aircrew training procedures and maintenance support systems had to be developed for future covert activities by the Army Air Force. Fortunately, resupply by land from Sweden made the *Rype* operation a success. But resupply procedures from Sweden should have been developed by the OSS, even before the *Rype* party dropped into Norway. For *Rype*, the biggest problem was food. The advantage of resupply from a neighboring country became most obvious to the OSS only after air support failed. In short, the *Rype* mission became vulnerable to the oldest law on the books, "Murphy's Law." Future planners of Special Forces operations must anticipate the worst in difficult missions and be cautious before committing brave men to them.

Enlistment of patriots within an occupied country is critical. The resistance forces in Norway during World War II, often in small groups of hunted, sleepless and nameless men, fought against incredible odds, yet their impact cannot be overestimated. Operating only within their own group, they did not know the members of other groups or higher officers from whom orders came for sabotage jobs. Life-long friends could be working in different groups and knew nothing of the other's activities. In fact, some may have suspected their neighbors were cooperating with the Germans. After the capitulation, old neighbors learned of, and were amazed by, the activities of those they had known for so long. These patriots, who knew the countryside so well, were invaluable in aiding the Americans and British in locating secret German installations.

One such story was a resistance group learning of a country hotel at Lillehammer that served as a German staff headquarters. Many secret documents were concealed there and the staff officers that resided there were almost always perpetually drunk. The group had acted on information from a German deserter who had joined the Norwegian Underground.

Covert operations behind the lines is a silent war, so to speak. There are no big campaigns, no frontal assaults with hundreds of thousands of men and machines.

There is only a battle in the shadows, clandestine intelligence, spies and sabotage. Landing in the dead of night in inhospitable terrain in the middle of a winter blizzard, a handful of white-clad figures began the first Allied assault inside Norway. Lonely and hunted men, their mission was secret, their capture meant certain death by firing squad and their citation would simply read: "Missing ..." They had been hand-picked for their perilous assignment. General Eisenhower had warned that the half a million Germans in Norway must be prevented from shifting to the Western Front. A David and Goliath task carried out by American paratroopers and Norwegian patriots. These were the specially trained men of America's top secret intelligence agency, the OSS.

The Legacy of OSS

The OSS takes its place in history as the first coordinated spy agency ever created by the United States Government. The 13,000 members from all walks of life were the "firsts" in that legacy.

An article that appeared in the October 13, 1945, edition of *Collier's* summed it up best:

> The story of the OSS is a fabulous one. It is the story of hundreds of units, thousands of ordinary, everyday Americans. Its scenario follows no pattern, its action occurs in dozens of places at once, its plot weaves an intricate web over Africa, Europe, Scandinavia and Asia. But always, at the center of the web, a group of tireless research experts and analysts sit in obscure Washington offices sifting intelligence that comes from scattered sources in the field, comparing seemingly unrelated facts and figures, fitting all the pieces of the jigsaw puzzle together.
>
> An OSS undercover operator in Sweden, for example, reports to Washington headquarters that German agents are frantically buying up ball bearings of all sizes from local factories, hardware stores and junk dealers. Another agent deep in Czechoslovakia radios that 500 precision-instrument technicians are being recruited by the Nazis to be rushed to a Focke-Wulf accessories plant in Austria. From an OSS operative in Abbeville, word comes that only twenty percent of Goering's [sic] crack Yellow-Nose Fighter Squadron was able to get aloft against the latest Allied bombing mission, due to a shortage of replacement parts. Word is flashed to the Eighth Air Force of the newest enemy shortage, and the bombing of all ball-bearing factories in the Reich is redoubled. Another Luftwaffe bottleneck is corked.
>
> Often these infiltration teams ran onto "targets of opportunity". Word of these fleeting objectives- a body of troops particularly vulnerable for a few hours, a convoy of ammunition trucks halted overnight on an exposed section of road- would be flashed to Tactical Air Force headquarters, sometimes even to aircraft in flight. From Romania, an operator reported a suspicious looking big-inch pipe leading from the silo of a group of newly constructed farm buildings in a rich oil area. A flight of Liberators blasted the farm buildings the following day.

History closed the chapter on the OSS shortly after the war ended. General Donovan addressed a final gathering of OSS employees on September 29, 1945:

> Men and Women of OSS,
> We have come to the end of an unusual experiment. This experiment was to determine whether a group of Americans constituting a cross-section of racial origins, of abilities, temperaments

and talents could meet and risk encounter with the long-established and well-trained enemy organizations.

How well this experiment has succeeded is measured by your accomplishments and by the recognition of your achievements. You should feel deeply gratified by President Truman's expression of the purpose of basing a coordinated intelligence service upon the techniques and resources that you have initiated and developed.

This could not have been done if you had not been willing to fuse yourselves into a team—a team that was made up not only of scholars and research experts and of the active units in operations and intelligence who engaged the enemy in direct encounter, but also of the great numbers of our organization who drove our motor vehicles, carried our mail, kept our records and documents and performed those other innumerable duties of administrative services without which no organization can succeed and which, because well done with us, made our activities that much more effective.

When I speak of your achievements that does not mean we did not make mistakes. We were not afraid to make mistakes because we were not afraid to try things that had not been tried before. All of us would like to think that we could have done a better job, but all of you must know that, whatever the errors of failures, you have done an honest and self-respecting job. But more than that, because there existed in this organization a sense of solidarity, you must also have the conviction that this agency, in which each of you played a part, was an effective force.

Within a few days each one of us will be going to new tasks whether in civilian life or in government work. You can go with the assurance that you have made a beginning in showing the people of America that only by decisions of national policy based upon accurate information can we have the chance of a peace that will endure.

The OSS was officially disbanded on October 1, 1945, by order of President Harry S. Truman. Truman indicated that most OSS components would be transferred to the State and War Departments. One of William Donovan's major goals was to have the OSS continue to thrive as a valuable agency for the United States Government after the war ended. It did not. This was a terrible disappointment to Donovan. However, many of his ideas survived. Ultimately, the OSS served as a precursor to the development of the Central Intelligence Agency (CIA). In a sense, the OSS was the petri dish of experiments for the later agency. Unconventional thinking, daring risk taking, even the delusion that all covert operations would result in a magic bullet with spectacular results later infected much of the thinking in the fledgling CIA.

Today's United States military reflects the OSS roots in its various branches. The Navy SEALs grew out of the Maritime Unit of the OSS, however the United States Coast Guard was in existence before then. The *Jedburghs* led to the eventual formation of the Army Special Forces. The Air Force Special Operations Command owes its beginnings to the 801st/492nd Bombardment Group (the Carpetbaggers). The Marine Special Operations Command are the result of the Marines who served in the OSS.

Even after the OSS was disbanded, the United States Government did come around and entually realized the need for a permanent, formal intelligence gathering and spy agency. For those who lived through the scourges of the war, major impetuses, such as the unforeseen attack on Pearl Harbor, necessitated the creation of such a permanent agency.

Thus, two years after the dissolution of the OSS, on July 26, 1947, the CIA was created when President Truman signed the National Security Act into law. Roscoe H. Hillenkoetter became its first director. He served from 1947 to 1950. As mentioned earlier, William Colby, who led the NORSO I team, eventually became its director and served from 1973 to 1976.

The years that Colby was Director of the CIA were also eventful ones for the agency on the world stage. Shortly after he assumed leadership, the Yom Kippur War broke out. This surprised not only the American intelligence agencies but also the Israelis. This reportedly affected Colby's credibility within the Nixon administration. Colby participated in the National Security Council meetings that responded to apparent Soviet intentions to intervene in the war by raising the alert level of U.S. forces to DEFCON 3 and defusing the crisis.

Then, in 1975, after many years of involvement, South Vietnam fell to communist forces in April, a particularly difficult blow for Colby, who had dedicated so much of his life and career to the American effort there.

***

In 1974, our family took a trip over the Easter holiday to Richmond, Virginia, to visit my sister and her husband, who was doing graduate work at the Medical College of Virginia. It was at this time our father took a day trip up to Washington, D.C., for a pre-arranged visit with William Colby during his tenure at the CIA. Since the location of the CIA's headquarters was still not officially made known to the public at that time, agents met him at the bus depot and, per standard protocol, blindfolded him and drove him around the city before taking him to CIA headquarters. Correspondence between my father and William Colby during this time period is located in Appendix 4. Interestingly, the letterhead from Colby's letters only states: "CENTRAL INTELLIGENCE AGENCY; WASHINGTON, D.C. 20205." No physical address appears on either the stationery or envelopes.

That same year, on October 10–12, 1975, William Colby attended a 30th reunion gathering of the OSS in Minneapolis, Minnesota. Due to health conditions, Lieutenant Colonel Gerhard Bolland was not in attendance.

Epilogue: Congressional Gold Medal

The date is March 21, 2018, the place is the United States Capitol in Washington, D.C. A Nor'easter snowstorm of major proportions hits Washington and the government is shut down. ... well, with one exception. Those specifically invited to attend the Office of Strategic Services (OSS) Congressional Gold Medal Ceremony were allowed into the U.S. Capitol. I guess even a major snowstorm could not prevent the long overdue recognition of those 13,000 hardcore OSS members that so faithfully served their country many years ago. These included 16 surviving members, some from the Carpetbaggers group that flew into the respective operational areas; tough guys even to the end, with most of them well into their nineties.

This author, Matthew Bolland, and his wife Nancy were among those invited to attend along with other family members.

The Congressional Gold Medal is the highest civilian honor Congress can bestow. It is the expression of national appreciation for distinguished achievements and contributions to a particular individual, institution or event. Only 163 such medals, including this one, have ever been awarded in the entire history of the United States. The first one dates back to March 25, 1776, when Congress bestowed one upon George Washington. Back then, it was called the Continental Congress Medal.

It was indeed an honor to attend on behalf of my late father. Even though I grew up watching patriotic movies and television shows that graced the airwaves with battles of World War II, 1945 still seemed like such a long time ago. My father had already lived a lifetime of experiences by then, something that came alive to me every time he shared numerous stories about those days. He made a significant contribution to the OSS's Operation *Rype* in Norway during World War II. Just one more soldier, as part of that greatest generation, making personal sacrifices for the sake of the common good.

The OSS Society has noted that for many years the heroic contributions of their members, which included some of the most daring covert operations of World War II, remained shrouded in secrecy. Their contributions were largely unknown to the American public.

Senate Bill 2234, co-sponsored by 73 Senators, including all 15 members of the Senate Intelligence Committee, was passed and signed into law by the president, authorizing the presentation of the Congressional Gold Medal to the OSS Society on behalf of the 13,000 men and women who so bravely served their country. After all these years, they finally got the recognition they deserved. This medal is a fitting tribute to those heroic members, including my own father, who took great risks and whose stories can now finally be told.

The medal itself was designed with OSS code names used for some of the most secret operations. These appear on the back of the medal. Among them is *Rype*. Thus, the very operation under field command of my father is now a permanent part of the Congressional Gold Medal. In this respect, my father, Lieutenant Colonel Gerhard L. Bolland left a fitting legacy for future generations of Bollands to be proud of.

Reports on NORSO and *Rype*

Report on NORSO Group Operations, May 8–June 6

Oslo, Norway
13 June 1945
Subject: Chronological Report of Norso Group Operations from 8 May to 6 June in Trøndelag, Norway

TO: Chief, Scandinavian Section
THRU: Chief, Norso Group

1. On May 8 1945 I proceeded to the Metfield Air Base to secure transportation for Stockholm, Sweden, on my journey to the Norso Group in the field. My verbal orders were to take command of the Norso Group in the field and direct all its future operational activities. At Metfield, I found Sergt. Joa and his five men whom I also escorted on their way to join the Group in the field. On 10 May we left by air for Stockholm, arriving in the afternoon.

2. On 11 May I contacted Vaudeville and arranged an interview immediately with the guide to the Norso Group base—Mr. Gaundal. After my conversation with him I was alarmed to find that the present strength of the Norso Group was approximately 60 people. I became concerned over the food situation. The alarm was partially substantiated by a message to London before I left from Major Colby, leader of the Norso Group in the field, to the effect that it would be necessary for him to move to a road net, preferably Lierne, for the reason of obtaining food and supplies. I also knew that transportation difficulties, due to melting snow and ice, were setting in. Together with the assistance of Vaudeville, I immediately arranged a re-supply air mission by Colonel Balchen to the base in the field. Mr. Gaundal, however, stated to me that the group had moved from its location at the Javesjø farm to a place on the Swedish side of the border. In view of this I had Mr. Gaundal telephone the nearest farm and to send instructions immediately to the Norso Group for Lieut. Sather to come to the farm the next morning at 1000 hours with specific

information as to the exact pinpoint for the planned dropping of supplies. On May 12 at 1000 hours a telephone reply was received from the farm stating the message had been delivered to Major Colby, and his reply was that the Group was moving to Steinkjer immediately after midnight 11-12 May, which I later learned was on orders from Chief, Norso Group, by radio. I then decided to move to Steinkjer by the quickest means possible, rather than proceed through the route usually used by the guide, because melting snow conditions would make this a slow and difficult trip. I was still concerned over the food situation so 225 emergency rations were picked up to be moved with me en route and I arranged for 700 rations to be sent as early as possible to Steinkjer.

3. Arrangements were made to leave by train for myself and Sergt. Joa's group at 2200 hours, 12 May. The rest of the day was spent examining letters written by Major Colby to Vaudeville, talking to Mr. Gaundal and trying to secure certain comfort articles, like tobacco for the Group. In one letter from Major Colby to Vaudeville, I was surprised to find out that Major Colby was trying to open the Waxwing Inter-communication Plan through Stockholm, which was in violation of our radio message to him from London, stating this should not be done. Before leaving I also obtained an operational fund of 20,000 Norwegian krone and 2,000 Swedish kroner from the American Legation in Stockholm.

4. We left by rail as planned, arriving in Trondheim in the evening of 13 May on the first civilian train since V-day. The supplies were moved to a train leaving for Steinkjer the same night and we proceeded to Steinkjer on this same train, arriving at 0400 hours 14 May.

5. I found the Group to be in high spirits and not in any way, as far as I could see, suffering from a lack of food or malnutrition. The unit was living at a large farm called Hegge, on a hill on the outskirts of Steinkjer, which was owned by a Norwegian attached member of the Group,—a Mr. Thoralf Lian. The Group then numbered 38 men, Major Colby having already released about half the Group to return to their homes. He left four men at the Javesjø farm base to receive myself and Sergt. Joa's group. Some members of the Woodlark party were still integrated with the unit, and had apparently never left the Norso Group base. They were also present with the group at Steinkjer.

6. Major Colby was not present upon my arrival. I was informed that he had gone to Trondheim to report to the District Commander, Trondheim (DK/T)—Colonel Holterman. He returned to Steinkjer early in the morning of 15 May and I talked with him later in the day.

7. In the morning of 15 May the reception party which had been left at Javsjø farm, arrived at Steinkjer. I decided to release them from the unit and did so that day.

By conversation with them before being released, I found that they found many attractive features in their service at the Norso Group base,—not the least important being the fine food and tobacco available except during the last few days, when variety had become meager. This was all in sharp contrast to their life in Occupied Norway. I was also informed that three cows had been killed at Javesjø farm and used for food. Immediately steps were taken to contact the owner of Javesjø farm,—Mr. Alfred Andersen,—for an agreed settlement of the damage and loss to his property caused by the Group.

8. Upon talking with Major Colby I found that he had arranged for the participation of the Norso Group in a parade in the 17 May Celebrations at Trondheim, and that he had also arranged to march through the towns of Verdal, Levanger, and Stjørdal enroute. I approved the plan, and transportation was immediately secured for the trip to Trondheim.

9. The presence of the group in Steinkjer had a good effect, inasmuch as there were 3,000 to 4,000 Germans present in the town. It had a good effect on both the Germans and the local Norwegians, because it brought to them the realization that there were already, at this early date, Allied Troops in Nord-Trondelag. I believe the same fine effect was secured in the towns of Verdal, Levanger and Stjørdal also.

10. I instructed Major Colby to be Commander of the Troops and march the Group through the various towns. They received a tremendous ovation by the town's people who were jammed on both sides of the streets along the entire route of march through the towns. Short expressions of gratitude by the town dignitaries and replies for the group were also made at some central meeting place in the three towns.

11. At Stjørdal I discovered that the Vaernes airport lay just outside the city, under command of a German force. I decided to examine the field to determine its condition, especially to find out if the Field was useable, and what type of aircraft it could handle. The Field was found to be in first class condition, no mines or apparent sabotage, except on certain German planes around the field. After gathering technical data and driving over all runways to satisfy myself as to their condition, we proceeded to Trondheim, arriving about 1900 hours, 15 May.

12. On 16 May I reported to the DK/T for orders. He decided to use the Group as his reserve, keeping it in Trondheim temporarily and also gave me orders for the parade next day. I received authorization from DK/T to incorporate the Woodlark party members in the Norso Group. I also informed the DK/T of possibilities of air landing the remainder of the Norso Group still in England, at the Vaernes airport. He was anxious that this be done so he wired London for the group to be sent, if possible. I also wired to London all technical data collected during inspection of the field.

13. Lieut. Sather was appointed to act as publicity officer and he was instructed to handle the story of the Group's activities for publication in the newspapers and to handle any pictures or news reels to be taken of the Group. On the parade the following day the DK/T's Police Troops, a detachment of the British Navy, the Home Front, and our Group participated. They were enthusiastically received. Major Colby again acted as Commander of Troops. Colonel Holterman invited me along with other Allied representatives to be with him in the reviewing stand.

14. An unfortunate incident occurred early on the morning of 17 May which I was not informed of until the following day. The First Sergeant of the Group—Sergeant Eliassen, and Mr. Lian, an attached Norwegian, under the influence of liquor, had discharged their pistols several times, damaging some property, which included the tire of an automobile. I called for an investigation in the Norwegian Courts and received sworn testimony from our two men and the accusers. As a result of the testimony it was decided to reduce Sergeant Eliassen to the grade of Private and to dismiss Mr. Lian from the Group immediately. The incident was hushed up and no far-reaching damage to the Group's reputation was noticeable.

15. The scarcity of Allied troops and the attitude of the Germans in Trøndelag at this time made further arming on Milorg in Trøndelag highly desirable. An attempt to receive arms from Stockholm failed. I told Colonel Holterman that I would try to secure more weapons for him as soon as possible. A wire was sent later, requesting the remaining OSS stocks in England to be flown in by air. At this time it was also decided to move the entire Group to Namsos as there were large numbers of German troops there, especially German Navy personnel, whose attitude was anything but healthy. This was done because of a request for help to Colonel Holterman from the Police Chief at Namsos. The Group was moved to Namsos by rail on the evening of 18 May under the command of Major Colby. I established an office in the DK/T headquarters, Trondheim.

16. The request for additional Norso men in England was approved and on the afternoon of 20 May, two planes landed on Vaernes airfield with fourteen men, under the command of Lieut. Hall. This had a good effect on the Germans and caught them by surprise, as they were notified only a few minutes before the arrival of the planes. Lieut. Hall was ordered to garrison Vaernes immediately.

17. A third plane with Lt. Colonel Skabo and seven men failed to reach Vaernes that day but landed instead at Herdla Airfield in the vicinity of Bergen, with motor trouble. On 21 May, the two planes at Vaernes returned to England. One was sent back with a sample of German aviation gasoline for analysis. The other one was sent to Bergen in effort to pick up Colonel Skabo and his Group and have them taken to Vaernes. However, this was not deemed advisable by Colonel Skabo and

the plane was sent back to England from Bergen. Colonel Skabo arranged for the transportation of his Group by minesweeper to Trondheim, and arrived in Trondheim the evening of 24 May, taking the group directly to the Vaernes Airfield.

18. About this time the situation began changing. It had been a question in the minds of everyone as to whether the Germans in Trondelag would comply with their disarmament orders,—namely, to disarm themselves. 23 May was the deadline set for the beginning of the disarmament. The Germans started disarming slowly at first; the Navy showed more reluctance than the Army in complying, but they also began the disarmament procedure. The Russian prisoners were, by this time, behaving themselves quite well. The mission of the group was gradually changing from operational to that of a token force. The Namsos Group became an agency for passing on instructions from the Allied Disarmament Commission, and an agency for making administrative decisions for the German Commanding Officer in the Namsos area.

19. The Group at Vaernes (now numbering 22 men) under the command of Lieutenant Hall, were instructed to act as an information agency, keeping close watch on the German activity at the field. They were also instructed to prevent looting by Russians and the local population, which they did. The Group also prepared for the reception of arms from the UK and for the accommodation of the air crews flying them in.

20. On 25 May, Colonel Skabo proceeded to Namsos to gather information for his final report as Chief for the Norso Group. He agreed to give me his recommendations as to how long the Group under command of Major Colby, would be needed in the Namsos area, upon his return. His recommendations were that the unit was no longer needed in Namsos, and he also further recommended that the two groups be consolidated and brought together at one base.

21. On 28 May a conference was held with DK/T,—Colonel Skabo being present,—and the decision was made to move the Namsos Group to the Vaernes Airport and consolidate both Groups and place the Group under the command of Group II DK/T, which was garrisoning the vicinity of Trondheim. I then told the Chief of the Norso Group that I intended to maintain Major Colby's identity with the proposed new Group as far as possible.

22. The Namsos Group was moved by boat to Trondheim, arriving at 2300 hours, 1 June, thence by truck to Vaernes. I put Major Colby in charge of the reorganization of the Group into a single unit of three sections. The Group was instructed to act as a reserve for the DK/T. I endeavored to keep the Force from any prolonged mission in the disarmament program, and also from prolonged guard duty. This was, in effect, accomplished.

23. On 2 June, the first contingent of Allied Occupation Troops (one Battalion) arrived in Trondheim, and DK/T was placed under the command of Brigadier Smith,—Zone Commander, Trondheim area, Allied Forces.

24. Just before reporting to Oslo, plans were made for the participation of the Norso Group in the events connected with the proposed visit of Crown Prince Olav to Trondheim on 9 June. This included participation in the Guard of Honor for the arrival of the Crown Prince to the Vaernes Airport around noon, and also participation in a large parade to be held later in the city of Trondheim.

25. There being no anticipated future operational use of the Norso Group, I was ordered to Oslo to turn in a report on its activities for the period of 8 May–6 June 1945 inclusive. On 6 June, I turned over the command of the unit and all remaining operational funds (see enclosure #1) to Major Colby, and proceeded to Oslo by air, reporting to the Chief of Scandinavian Section the same day.

(signature)
Gerhard L. Bolland
Lt. Col. Inf. 0-19565
  encl:1.

Report on Operation *Rype*

Several reports of certain phases of the "RYPE" operation have been submitted to the Office of Strategic Services but it is believed that no overall picture of the nature, purpose and ultimate goal of the operation has been given to date. Because of this, and also because the Office of Strategic Services will cease to function as such as of today, this brief report is submitted.

Two years ago a group of Norwegian-American bilingual soldiers volunteered for parachute missions in Norway. This group was recruited from the 99th Mountain Battalion—a Battalion of Norwegian-Americans training in the mountains of the Western United States at that time.

As Africa, instead of Norway, was chosen for the initial landing, missions in Norway were not forthcoming and the group was used in small parties behind the lines in France, practically destroying its identity. In late 1944 the group was reconstituted again in hopes of use in the theatre for which it had been originally intended. At this time the group was interviewed by Lt. Col. Hans Skabo (C.E. Reserve) who carefully selected about half the group for an Operation in Occupied Norway.

He carefully sifted the group trying to find those men who sincerely wanted to work for Norway and who could ski well. Fifty men were selected and transferred from Operational Groups to Special Operations Section of O.S.S. and sent to

Scotland for intensive training. Major William B. Colby (FA Res.) was put in charge of the initial group.

Due to political considerations the Operation was limited to the area north of Trondheim. Upon advice from the Air Corp (U.S. Army), the operation was deemed feasible.

In January 1945, Lt. Col. Gerhard L. Bolland (019565), (Infantry, Regular Army) was taken off a proposed operation called "HUSKY" in North Cape, Norway, again due to political considerations. Col. Skabo had him assigned to Operation "RYPE," initially for the detailed planning and mounting of the operation, and finally for the overall field command as the operation progressed.

The plan was briefly this: 1. To have two groups of approximately 35 men each, both commanded by a Major, and an overall command by a Lt. Colonel commanding both groups and the operational and supply bases.

Major Colby was selected to command the first group called "NORSO I," Major Olmsted (who incidentally never got into Norway) to command the second called "NORSO II," Colonel Bolland to have overall field command and Colonel Skabo as Chief of "NORSO GROUPS" to run the Operation from London until the invasion or occupation of Norway by the Allied Forces.

The initial mission was to retard the movement of German troops in northern Norway on their movements south over the NORDLAND RAILWAY, by repeated cuts on the rail line in accordance with SHAEF Directives. The operation was planned with flexibility to accommodate changes in mission from one of sabotage to others like; arming, organizing and training the Underground in NORTHERN TRONDERLAG, running an avenue of escape to Sweden of Norwegian nationals in trouble with the Germans, or fighting on an initial penetration of Occupied Norway from Sweden in Tronderlag. These of course within the limitations imposed by SHAEF and the charters of operation for OSS.

The supply problem was an extremely difficult one. The plane loads were made up in self-contained units of men and supplies, each capable of independent operation in the field, on skis, at sub-zero temperatures for forty days without any help; completely self-sufficient units. A base near the Swedish border was to be established and stocked by courier service from Stockholm. Emergency supplies were to be dropped by air by Col. Bernt Balchen, A.T.C., on call. Resupply from the United Kingdom was to be tried if found practical.

The success of the operation was predicated on the use of better men and better skiers than the Germans could put into the field against them in the area chosen for the Operation.

The area selected for the parachute drop was Jaevsjo Lake, east of SNASSA in nord-Tronderlag (64° 7'N–13° 02' 00" E), this being solidly frozen in winter.

What was actually accomplished in the field will be explained by reference to lists "A," "B," "C" and "D" attached to this report. The operation was mounted and waiting from 29 January 1945 but the Air Corp reported repeatedly that flying conditions were not suitable until 24 March 1945.

On the night of 24 March 1945, list "B" dropped on or near Jaevsjo Lake to a Reception Party of several Norwegians. Eight planes started, four dropped at the target, one dropped personnel and loads in Sweden thinking it was over the target, three planes returned to the U.K. unsuccessful. On 31 March a second try to get Norso Group I in the air was made, all planes unsuccessful, one crashed in the ORKNEY ISLANDS on the return trip, killing six of our personnel listed on list "A" and marked with an asterisk (*).

These six men were interned at Cambridge, England together with Air Corp personnel. The co-pilot was the only survivor, he stated that two motors had failed on the four-engine Liberator used. On 6 April 1945 the third and last attempt by air was made with the misfortune again of having "Norso Group I" killed as the Liberator crashed into the mountain just 8 kilometres from the actual target. Our personnel, marked by a cross (x) on list "B," were killed together with the entire crew of the Liberator. They are now buried on the scene of the crash on the side of PLUNKETTFJELL MOUNTAIN, ten (10) kilometres NORTHWEST OF JAEVSJO LAKE (64° 07' 22" North) 13° 02' 00" East.

The crash was found some time later by the Group in the field and they were given a military burial on PLUNKETTFJELL where they still rest.

Major Colby was ordered to begin attacking the Nordland Railroad which he did during the entire month of April. These attacks included the destruction of the TANGEN BRIDGE and also 3 Kilometres of rail between LURUDAL and AGLE Stations. German patrols were eluded successfully except for one, which the Group accidentally met and annihilated at a cost of only one wounded loyal Norwegian, a KARL BERRE of Trondheim, who had been recruited by the Group in the Field. However, with the aid of PENICILLIN and by quick evacuation by sled with skiing to Sweden, his life was saved. He had been shot in the intestines.

"RYPE" in conjunction with a small group of NORIC men at WOODLARK, lying a little farther north, managed to keep the railroad in a state of continual confusion by a staggering and coordination of their attacks through SFHQ in London.

Because of the repeated failures of getting the operation into the field by air (17 sorties flown—4 successful) and the short periods of darkness now becoming a hazard to flying that far north, this method had to be abandoned for something else. Colonel Bolland took the remainder of "Norso Group I" by air to Sweden, then by courier to the Operational area. These men are listed on list "C"—the enlisted men having made unsuccessful attempts to get in by plane and parachute on 24 March, 31 March and 6 April 1945.

There was some question whether the Germans would make a "last ditch stand" in Norway if Germany surrendered. It was our personal feeling that they would—so we carried out our plans for what might be a prolonged operation in Norway.

But after VE day, the Germans in Norway also capitulated. Colonel Bolland moved the Group down from Steinkjer, inspected the VAERNES AIRPORT, (Stjordal) near Trondheim, found it in good condition and immediately wired Col. Skabo in London to take NORSO II in by air and land it to reception at VAERNES AIRPORT. (Germans still occupied the Air Field).

NORSO I was sent to NAMSOS to bolster the Chief of Police because of the arrogant attitude of German Navy personnel there.

NORSO II was air-landed at VAERNES AIRPORT on 20 May 1945 under the escort of Col. Skabo, who then proceeded to Oslo. Lt. Hall was given the mission of seizing and occupying VAERNES AIRPORT and later helping in the disarmament of the German Military personnel in that area.

Colonel Holterman, District Commander Trondheim, (Norwegian Army) was anxious to further strengthen his position and the underground because the Germans were still armed in Tronderlag. Col. Bolland suggested to Col. Holterman that it might be possible to bring in more arms for MILORG if desired, to which Col. Holterman enthusiastically agreed. The UK was wired for rifles, and approximately a thousand U.S. carbine rifles from OSS stocks in the UK were sent immediately to Col. Bolland for Holterman and delivered by air to the VAERNES AIRPORT. They were promptly turned over to MILORG by Col. Holterman. On 1 June 1945 NORSO I was moved from Namsos and consolidated with NORSO II at VAERNES and operated under orders from Col. Holterman, DKT for a short while.

On 5 June Col. Bolland turned the troops over to Major Colby and reported to the Chief of the Scandinavian Section (Cmdr G. Unger Vetleson) OSS in OSLO. Plans were made to evacuate the Group by air to the UK. The entire group was back in England by the end of June 1945 completing the Operation "RYPE".

LT. Colonel Gerhard L. Bolland
Filed Commander, Operation RYPE

6th

1 October 1945

OPERATION "RYPE"

Several reports of certain phases of the "RYPE" Operation have been submitted to the Office of Strategic Services but it is believed that no over-all picture of the nature, purpose, and ultimate goal of the operation has been given to date. Because of this, and also because the Office of Strategic Services will cease to function as such as of today this brief report is submitted.

Two years ago a group of Norwegian-American bilingual soldiers volunteered for parachute missions in Norway. This group was recruited from the 99th Mountain Battalion - a Battalion of Norwegian-Americans training in the mountains of Western United States at that time.

As Africa, instead of Norway, was chosen for the initial landings, missions in Norway were not forthcoming and the group was used in small parties behind the lines in France, practically destroying its identity. In late 1944 the group was reconstituted again in hopes of use in the theatre for which it had been originally intended. At this time the group was interviewed by Lt. Col. Hans Skabo (C.E. Reserve) who carefully selected about half the group for an Operation in Occupied Norway.

He carefully sifted the group trying to find those men who sincerely wanted to work for Norway and who could ski well. Fifty men were selected and transferred from Operational Groups to Special Operations Section of O.S.S. and sent to Scotland for intensive training. Major William B. Colby (FA Res.) was put in charge of the initial group.

Due to political considerations the Operation was limited to areas north of Trondheim. Upon advice from the Air Corps (U.S. Army), the operation was deemed feasible.

In January 1945, Lt. Col. Gerhard L. Bolland (O-19565), (Infantry, Regular Army) was taken off a proposed operation called "HUSKY" in North Cape, Norway, again due to political considerations. Col. Skabo had him assigned to Operation "RYPE", initially for the detailed planning and mounting of the operation, and finally for the overall field command as the operation progressed.

The plan was briefly this: 1. To have two groups of approximately 35 men each, both commanded by a Major, and an overall command by a Lt. Colonel commanding both groups and the operational and supply bases.

-1-

-2-

Major Colby was selected to command the first group called "NORSO I",
Major Olmstead (who incidentally never got into Norway) to command the second
called "NORSO II", Colonel Bolland to have overall field command and Colonel
Skabo as Chief of "NORSO GROUPS" to run the Operation from London until the
invasion or occupation of Norway by the Allied Forces.

The initial mission was to retard the movement of German troops
in Northern Norway on their movements south over the NORDLAND RAILWAY, by
repeated cuts on the rail line in accordance with SHAEF Directives. The
operation was planned with a flexibility to accomodate changes in mission
from one of sabotage to others like: arming, organizing and training the
Underground in NORTHERN TRONDERLAG, running an avenue of escape to Sweden
of Norwegian nationals in trouble with the Germans, or fighting on an
initial penetration of Occupied Norway from Sweden in Tronderlag. These
of course within the limitations imposed by SHAEF and the charters of
operation for OSS.

The supply problem was an extremely difficult one. The plane
loads were made up in self-contained units of men and supplies, each capable
of independent operation in the field, on skiis, at sub-zero temperatures
for forty days without any help; completely self-sufficient units. A base
near the Swedish border was to be established and stocked by courrier
service from Stockholm. Emergency supplies were to be dropped by air by
Col. Bernt Balchen, A.T.C., on call. Resupply from the United Kingdom was
to be tried and used if found practical.

The success of the operation was predicated on the use of better
men and better skiers than the Germans could put in the field against them
in the area chosen for the Operation.

The area selected for the parachute drop was Jaevsjo Lake, east
of SNASSA in Nord-Tronderlag (64^0 7' N-13^0 02' 00" E), this being solidly
frozen in winter.

What was actually accomplished in the field will be explained
by reference to lists "A", "B", "C" and "D" attached to this report. The
operation was mounted and waiting from 29 January 1945 but the US Air
Corps reported repeatedly that flying conditions were not suitable until
24 March 1945.

On the night of 24 March 1945, list "B" dropped on or near Jaevsjo
Lake to a Reception Party of several Norwegians. Eight planes started, four
dropped at the target, one dropped personnel and loads in Sweden thinking it
was over the target, three planes returned to the U.K. unsuccessful. On
31 March a second try to get Norso Group I in by air was made, all planes
unsuccessful, one crashed in the ORKNEY ISLANDS on the return trip, killing
six of our personnel listed on list "A" and marked with an asterik(*).

These six men were interned at Cambridge, England together with
Air Corps personnel. The co-pilot was the only survivor, he stated that two
motors had failed on the four-engined Liberator used. On 6 April 1945 the
third and last attempt by air was made with the reinforcements for Norso
four more of "Norso Group I" killed as the Liberator crashed into a mountain just 8 kilometres from the actual target. Our personnel, marked by
a cross (x) on list "B", were killed together with the entire crew of the

-3-

Liberator. They are now buried on the scene of the crash on the side of PLUNKETTFJELL MOUNTAIN, ten (10) kilometres NORTHWEST OF JAVESJO LAKE (64° 07' 22" North) 13° 02' 00" East.

The crash was found some time later by the Group in the field and they were given a military burial on PLUNKETTFJELL where they still rest.

Major Colby was ordered to begin attacking the Nordland Railroad which he did during the entire month of April. These attacks included the destruction of the TANGEN BRIDGE and also 3 Kilometres of rail between LURUDAL and AGLE Stations. German patrols were eluded successfully except for one, which the Group accidentally met and annihilated at a cost of only one wounded loyal Norwegian, a KARL BERRE of Trondheim, who had been recruited by the Group in the Field. However, with the aid of PENICILLIN and by quick evacuation by sled with skiing to Sweden, his life was saved. He had been shot in the intestines.

"RYPE" in conjunction with a small group of NORIC men at WOODLARK, lying a little farther north, managed to keep the railroad in a state of continual confusion by a staggering and coordination of their attacks through SFHQ in London.

Because of the repeated failures in getting the operation into the field by air (17 sorties flown - 4 successful) and the short periods of darkness now becoming a hazard to flying that far north, this method had to be abandoned for something else. Colonel Bolland took the remainder of "Norso Group I" by air to Sweden, then by courier to the Operational area. These men are listed on List "C" - the enlisted men having made three unsuccessful attempts to get in by plane and parachute on 24 March, 31 March and 6 April 1945.

There was some question whether the Germans would make a "last ditch stand" in Norway if Germany surrendered. It was our personal feeling that they would - so we carried out our plans for what might be a prolonged operation in Norway.

But after VE day, the Germans in Norway also capitulated. Colonel Bolland moved the Group down from Steinkjer, inspected the VAERNES AIRPORT (Stjordal) near Trondheim, found it in good condition and immediately wired Col. Skabo in London to take NORSO II in by air and land it to reception at VAERNES AIRPORT. (Germans still occupied the Air Field).

NORSO I was sent to NAMSOS to bolster up the Chief of Police because of the arrogant attitude of German Navy personnel there.

NORSO II was air-landed at VAERNES AIRPORT on 20 May 1945 under the escort of Col. Skabo, who then proceeded to OSLO. Lt. Hall was given the mission of seizing and occupying VAENES AIRPORT and later helping in the disarmament of the German Military personnel in that area.

-4-

Col. Holtermann, District Commander Trondheim, (Norwegian Army) was anxious to further strengthen his position and the underground because the Germans were still armed in Tronderlag. Col. Bolland suggested to Col. Holtermann that it might be possible to bring in more arms for MILORG if desired, to which Col. Holtermann enthusiastically agreed. The UK was wired for rifles, and approximately a thousand U.S. carbine rifles from OSS stocks in the UK were sent immediately to Col. Bolland for Holtermann and delivered by air to the VAERNES AIRPORT. They were promptly turned over to MILORG by Col. Holtermann. On 1 June 1945 NORSO I was moved from Namsos and consolidated with NORSO II at VAERNES and operated under orders from Col. Holtermann, DKT for a short while.

On 5 June Col. Bolland turned the troops over to Major Colby and reported to the Chief of the Scandinavian Section (Cmdr G. Unger Vetleson) OSS in OSLO. Plans were made to evacuate the Group by air to the UK. The entire group was back in England by the end of June 1945 completing the Operation "RYPE".

The Carpetbaggers

In 2019, the author attended a Carpetbaggers reunion and had the privilege of interviewing surviving members of Operation *Carpetbagger*, four in person and one by phone:

Hewitt Gomez, navigator, and William Becker, top turret gunner (via phone interview), both from the Jere Davis flight crew

Hewitt Gomez tells a humorous story of his attempt to become a pilot. The minimum height requirement was 64 inches. He happened to be 63 inches. Well, he was always

Left to right: Robert Holmstrom, Hewitt Gomez, Howard Pollari and Eugene Polinsky, Carpetbaggers' Reunion, Minneapolis, Minnesota, October 21–25, 2019. William Becker was not present but was interviewed by phone.

at the local YMCA, so he would hang from his knees and hold on to some 50-pound weights to try to "stretch" himself up to the minimum requirement. Then, at home he built a noose in his garage and he was on a ladder when his younger brother came running up thinking Hewitt was trying to kill himself. "Try explaining that one!," he said. "I just wanted to be a pilot and was trying to make myself one-inch longer, which of course didn't work." He thought to himself, "What the (blank) does a one-inch difference make?" Well, enough of a difference to not allow him to reach the pedals in the aircraft. After not being able to meet the minimum height requirement, the military gave him the choice between becoming a bombardier or a navigator. He chose navigator.

As a navigator, then 19-year-old Gomez was responsible for the entire flight path and safe return of his crew. He was the only one on the plane that knew where they were headed. Not even the pilot was privy to that information. Upon take-off, he would give the pilot an initial heading and then, as the flight progressed, supply additional bearings as needed. The tools for Carpetbagger navigators included celestial navigation, maps, landmarks and radio beams.

He recalls one particular flight where the older Pioneer compass had been replaced in the B-24 with a newer, modern compass. He was used to adjusting the older

Standing: Paul Fluhart (co-pilot), Jere Davis (pilot), Irving Adams (bombardier), Hewitt Gomez (navigator). Kneeling: James Mazzoni (engineer), William Becker (top turret gunner), Joseph Alfes (radio operator), Carl Shaw (gunner), James Stafford Sr. (gunner), Eugene Wells (gunner).

compass to read true north instead of magnetic north. He truly got scared when he came realize that the newer compass had already been adjusted for that. To remedy the situation, he told the pilot to head straight south. That way he had a fixed point to re-correct the new compass and re-calculate all his bearings.

There was one phenomenon with these types of flights that Hewitt recalled. It was a round ball of light that appeared on the wing tips. The first time he saw this he told the pilot, "Turn 90 degrees!" It's still there. "Turn another 90" ... still there! It followed the aircraft wherever it went. They were worried it was something the Germans sent up to track them in order to knock them out of the sky. Later on, they learned it was actually light reflecting off the engines. It became known as the "foo-foo ball" to flight crews. "We sure got fooled by the foo-foo ball."

On one particular mission into Norway, Gomez navigated the plane into the mouth of a waterway that ran between the fjords. Since the mouth was the widest part, Gomez took them down the middle, figuring that would be the safest and the furthest away from any ground fire. Intelligence had provided the locations of German anti-aircraft emplacements. Although they made it through successfully, the two British planes following them were shot down. Both Hewitt Gomez and William Becker remember this mission well. After they flew deep into the fjords, they heard the bombardier yell to the pilot, "Pull up, pull up!" He was startled to see that they were just a few feet above the tree line. From that point on, the bombardier had the best view from within the plane. So he began to direct the pilot. "Two degrees left, now a half-degree right!" After this mission, when they returned to the base, they found tree branches sticking out of the wing's ailerons! "It must have been a tree growing sideways out of the fjords," Hewitt said. A few feet closer to that side and they would not have made it.

Pilots were allowed only 20 minutes to search for the operational area and then had to high tail it back to the U.K. before the fuel gave out. "We often flew lower than 2,000 feet in those mountainous areas," he said. "Sometimes as low as 500 feet. We weren't looking for a factory or a city. We were looking for a couple of guys with signal fires or flashlights. It was night and you could only see about a mile-and-a-half at that level." As with all Carpetbagger missions, the navigators had the last word to continue or abort the mission.

When asked about whether or not they encountered any night fighters, Mr. Gomez recalled one incident where a German plane came straight at them from a lower altitude. They held their breath because they thought it would open fire, but it flew right under them without incident. He believes that since it was near the end of the war and the German *Luftwaffe* was critically low on fuel, the plane was headed back to base before the fuel ran out. He learned later that the Germans resorted to using oxen to pull the planes out to the runway in order to save on taxying fuel.

Upon asking Hewitt what his most vivid memory was, without hesitation he mentioned flights where he was assigned to bring back dead bodies. One of those was to retrieve the bodies of a plane that had been accidentally shot down by the citizens of that occupied country. They thought it was an enemy aircraft. The grief and remorse of the population was profound. Another involved retrieving the bodies from the *Rype* operation aircraft that crashed in the Orkney Islands. "The horrific smell is something you never forget," he said. "The bodies had been there for five days." He ended up on this flight because his name was picked out of a hat for navigational duties for these recovery missions.

On a more positive note (if there ever can be one during a time of war), Hewitt recalled the time he saved the life of his bombardier, Irving Adams. With such tight quarters, the navigator and bombardier flew pretty much with their backs resting against each other. After a while he realized Irving had not moved for some time. That seemed strange so he turned around and saw Irving slumped over. He noticed his oxygen line had become disconnected, so he immediately hooked it back up. After a few minutes, Irving regained consciousness and began functioning normally as if nothing had happened. "That would have been a wonderful way to die!" was Hewitt's last comment.

William Becker was only 18 years old at the time when he remembers training in the States. As mentioned, he was also assigned to Jere Davis's flight crew along with Hewitt Gomez and served as the top turret gunner. As was the case, this crew would remain together throughout the duration of the war. The U.S. Army Air Force was busy flying training missions out of the newly created Chatham Field in the vicinity of Cherokee Hill, which was one of the highest elevations near Savannah, Georgia. During practices, they would fly from Savannah to Cuba and back at night. At the time, Becker did not understand why they trained at night. It later became apparent when they flew "by the light of the moon" dropping sabotage personnel and supplies behind enemy lines. Today, such activities are known as Black Ops.

On one particular mission, Becker recalled encountering enemy ground fire. He radioed the pilot to drop the left wing. He then followed the tracer rounds back down to the ground and gave it a couple of bursts. To this day he still does not know if he killed anybody or they just ceased after he returned fire from his twin .50 caliber M2 Browning machine guns.

Much later in life, Bill Becker, who served from 1939–45, became the first Carpetbagger to receive the Norwegian Defense Medal, on behalf of King Harald V, from the defense attaché at the Norwegian Embassy. Rear Admiral Ole Morten Sandquist presented the award and said to Mr. Becker, "You have participated in the liberation of Norway. Norway thanks you for your invaluable contribution in the struggle for freedom."

While serving as the air arm of the Office of Strategic Services (OSS) and flying in the Norwegian Special Operations Group, radio silence was maintained at all times. The crew could only talk to each other on the intercom. Although there were other missions flown by the Jere Davis crew into other countries, a summary of Carpetbagger operations from the Harrington Museum database in the UK records a total of ten attempts/missions by the crew into Norway. Note: some entries into the Harrington database lack the pilot's name, so it is unknown if additional operations by this crew were carried out in Norway:

Legend for load dropped designations:
J = Joes (personnel)
C = Drop containers in bomb bay
P = Packages
N= Nickels (propaganda leaflet bundles)

Date	DZ Codename	Coordinates (if known)	Load Dropped	Reason NC
1/2Sep44	Leather 3	62d 52' 25" N 11d 25' 30"E	Not completed	no reception seen
3/4Sep44	Leather 3	62d 52' 25" N 11d 25' 30"E	Not completed	bad weather
12/13Sep44	Reins 2	59d 23' 40" N 10d 03' 26"E	12C	
14/15Sep44	Leather 3	62d 52' 25" N 11d 25' 30"E	12C, 5P	
19/20Sep44	Crupper 9	60d 25' 25" N 09d 54' 05"E	Not completed	engine failure
22/23Sep44	Crupper 6	60d 22' 40" N 10d 17' 30"E	Not completed	bad weather
17/18Apr45	Bit 31		12C, 7P	
19/20Apr45	Bit 10		Not completed	enemy action
22/23Apr45	Crop 21		Not completed	no reception seen
25/26Apr45	Crupper 47		Not completed	no reception seen

Eugene Polinsky, navigator, Neil Ellis flight crew

Eugene Polinsky was born on September 11, 1920, in Manhattan, New York, grew up in New Jersey and attended Rutgers University. In 1942, he enlisted in the Army Air Force. After receiving navigator training at various bases out west, at the age of 23 he found himself stationed at Station 179 (Harrington) airfield as a first lieutenant. According to Polinsky, he was the navigator on 35 secret missions piloted by Neil Ellis. All were flown in the dark between March 6 and mid-August 1944. He is the last living person from his crew. The plane, of course, had very tight quarters. In fact, Mr. Polinsky recalls he sat on a gun case for all their missions.

A summary of Carpetbagger operations from the Harrington Museum database records 34 of these Carpetbagger attempts/missions by the Ellis crew into France and Belgium:

Standing: Neil Ellis (pilot), Glen Stanislaus (co-pilot), Eugene Polinsky (navigator), Herbert Goff (bombardier, Goff did not have a regular crew and flew with a number of other crews). Kneeling: Ray Green (engineer), Ray Orwasky (radio operator), Pedro Pereda (tail gunner), Cecil Waters (dispatcher). Not Shown: Salvatore Luciano (gunner, orphaned), Louis Harman (bombardier), Roy Koons (engineer, KIA).

Date	DZ Codename	Coordinates (if known)	Load Dropped	Reason NC
France:				
10/11Apr44	Newsagent 2	45d 33'N 04d 03'E	Not completed	no reception seen
11/12Apr44	Pimento 50	43d 58'N 01d 24'E	12C, 6P, 6N	
11/12Apr44	Pimento 52	44d 29'N 01d 22'E	Not completed	missed check points
27/28Apr44	Wheelright 100	44d 55'N 00d 43'E	Not completed	no reception seen
29/30Apr44	Stationer 63	45d 41'N 01d 39'E	Not completed	code not legible
30Apr/1May44	Bob 174	47d 35'N 05d 20'E	12C, 8P, 3N	
6/7May44	Peter 79	44d 58'N 03d 20'E	Not completed	bad weather at target
10/11May44	Tom56A	49d 24'N 03d 11'E	12C, 8P, 6N	
29/30May44	Bob 165		12C, 8P, 12N	

2/3Jun44	Marksman 34		12C, 6P, 4N	
12/13Jun44	Stationer 121		Not completed	no reception seen
14/15Jun44	Harry 21		12C, 10P, 2N	
22/23Jun44	Historian 15		12C, 6P, 1N	
25/26Jun44	Fireman 12A	46d 25'N 01d 22'E	12C, 2P, 4N	
31May/1Jun44	Percy 1A		Not completed	code not legible
1/2Jul44	Fireman 12	46d 25'N 01d 22'E	12C, 7P, 5N	
3/4Jul44	Scientist 103		12C, 7P, 3N	
4/5Jul44	Donkeyman 66A		12C, 8P, 3N	
6/7Jul44	Stationer 159		12C, 7P	
8/9Jul44	Stationer 110D		Not completed	bad weather at target
10/11Jul44	Wheelright 156		12C, 8P	
13/14Jul44	Digger 38		Not completed	lost way
15/16Jul44	Hamish 2A		12C, 8P, 3N	
16/17Jul44	Minister 12		Not completed	no reception seen
18/19Jul44	Fireman 14B		12C, 8P	
19/20Jul44	Ian 8		12C, 7P	
25/26Jul44	Historian 24		12C, 7P	
26/27Jul44	Felix 4		12C, 7P	
29/30Jul44	Stationer 164E		Not completed	bad weather at target
8/9Aug44	Messenger 29A	46d 57'N 05d 45'E	12C, 9P	
9/10Aug44	Ventriloquist 56		3J, 12C, 10P, 8N	
Belgium:				
7/8May44	Tybault 29		12C, 3P, 4N	
28/29May44	Osric 29	50d 40'N 04d 42'E	12C, 3P, 13N	
6/7Aug44	Osric 98		12C, 5P	

Polinsky recalled one mission where they flew under RAF bombers that were flying a night raid at a much higher altitude. As the ground fire was coming up, he heard his radio operator, who didn't know what it was, say, "Well, that's pretty." He exclaimed back, "That's flak!" The radio operator dived under his seat … as if that was going to help. If it hit the plane, being under his seat would not help one iota.

The pilot, Neil Ellis, was considered the old man on their crew since he was all of 25 years old. Eugene said he was an excellent pilot and his skills were a main reason their crew survived the war.

On an earlier mission, while flying in supplies to resistance groups, Eugene recalls an incident when they were coming back. They had just crossed over into English airspace when they took friendly fire. He immediately took a reading. After they landed, he reported it the headquarters as required. He was met with shrugged shoulders. Apparently, some trigger-happy gunners were a bit nervous with the D-Day invasion just around the corner.

On their 35th and final mission, the Ellis crew played a key role in liberating Antwerp in Belgium. Four Carpetbagger aircraft attempted to drop limpet mines to help the Resistance save the harbor from destruction. The plane they used for this mission was nicknamed "Red Ball Express." Flight crews were not assigned to one particular plane but had to take what was available at the time. The crew then had to adjust the equipment, including navigational instruments. Three of the aircraft didn't make it back, but the fourth B-24, navigated by Mr. Polinsky, completed its mission and survived. This last mission must have happened after August 10, 1944, since the 34th mission, code-named *Ventriloquist 56* over France, is recorded on the Harrington database as having happened on that day. This author could not confirm the exact date of the Antwerp drop for the Ellis crew's 35th and final mission.

It was not until much later in life, almost 60 years, at a reunion of former Resistance fighters in Belgium in 2001, that Mr. Polinsky learned this very mission was a major turning point. It allowed the Underground to free the city and harbor. At the time, he had no idea what was being dropped out of the Joe Hole. It has been said the greatest mistake in the war was the endless stalemate over Antwerp Harbor. Those that controlled the harbor, controlled the progress of the war. Four weeks later, all of Belgium was freed from Nazi occupation. Polinsky gives credit to General Donovan and his insight as to the importance of the harbor. Indeed, ending this stalemate was instrumental in shortening the war.

Reflecting on his time with the 801st/492nd Bombardment Group at Harrington, he recalled some of the more pleasurable moments; that would be enjoying dances with the local girls. "It was just splendid!" For his heroic deeds, Mr. Polinsky was decorated with the Distinguished Flying Cross, and Air Medal with three Oak Leaf Clusters, along with Belgium and French accolades.

Incidentally, when the B-24 Liberator crashed in the Orkney Islands on March 31, piloted by Henry L. Polansky, his name was misspelled and, due to the similarity, Eugene Polinsky was reported as dead. Having seen the error on the mission's report board back at Harrington, Eugene exclaimed, "As you can see, I'm still quite alive."

Later in life, Eugene Polinsky went on to become a Grammy-winning producer/writer/actor. He was also a famous concert pianist. After the war, he met up with Lee Strasberg and got involved with the American Theater Wing, acting and directing. He went on to write theater reviews, something he did even back in college, but later, more professionally, under the pseudonym Eugene Paul.

Robert Holmstrom, tail gunner, James Bingham flight crew

The Bingham Carpetbagger crew flew missions primarily into occupied Europe. Being the tail gunner, Robert Holmstrom had a unique responsibility. Although the main hatches and bomb bays were used to drop main cargo and personnel, there was also a smaller hole near the back of the plane. This was used to drop propaganda leaflets or other smaller packages. Since Holmstrom was located in the back, it was his responsibility to drop those packages. He said the most unusual packages he ever dropped were "Passenger (Homing) Pigeons" in cardboard oatmeal boxes. There were three pigeons per box and it was fitted with a small parachute with a barometric fuse set to open at 100 feet. There was enough food inside to last the pigeons for three days. These packages were dropped with false information in case they fell into German hands. Otherwise, when the Underground got hold of them, they would write messages and send them back to England. They always included code words in their messages in case the Germans tried to do the same and deceive the Allies. He remembers doing this on two separate missions. One was a load of 15 pigeon boxes while flying down the Danube River.

Holmstrom explained there were so many unique drops for very different purposes that the guys at these reunions were surprised to learn what the others

Standing: James Bingham Jr. (pilot), William Michael (co-pilot), James Mallor (bombardier), Richard Billings (navigator). Kneeling: Robert Holmstrom (tail gunner), Richard Ecker (ball turret gunner), John Reinhold Jr. (radio operator), Paul Kovah (NT gunner), Everette Mitchell (engineer).

actually dropped during the war. Successful Carpetbagger missions supplied the Underground with the tools they needed to disrupt the Germans. The Underground even used explosives to blow up telephone poles, causing the Germans to resort to radio communications which could be easily intercepted.

Howard Pollari, flight engineer, Lloyd Jones flight crew

Howard Pollari's crew also flew missions primarily into occupied Europe, although he did state they made three flights into Norway in April 1945. As flight engineer, he kept his eyes on the instrumentation during take-off and while in flight.

Pollari recalled one incident when pilot Jones had completed his pre-flight checks, taxied onto the runway, pushed the throttle forward and began heading down the runway. They had picked up a good head of steam when Pollari noticed the manifold pressure on engine number three was down which meant that engine was low on power. He tapped the pilot on the shoulder and pointed to the gauge. In his words, "We burned up a lot of rubber but Jones was able to stop the plane before we skidded off the runway."

Standing: Crew chief, asst. crew chief, Paul Werner (radio operator), Vernon Key (bombardier), Howard Pollari (flight engineer). Kneeling: Don Bennett (co-pilot), Dan Wilcher (navigator), Lloyd Jones (pilot).

Upon asking him about the most frightening event he encountered, he related this story. They were on their way back from a mission and the pilot radioed he was having trouble with the controls for the back of the plane. He asked Pollari to check it out. On the B-24, as was typical with aircraft construction in those days, the control cables and hydraulic lines ran along the inside of the fuselage. Pollari got back to the forward bomb bay area and discovered a mechanical malfunction. One of the seven-foot-long supply canisters did not eject completely and had hung up on the cables. There was also a second canister just above it that had not released at all. There was only one way to get to it. He had to crawl out and straddle the catwalk between the open bomb bay doors to try to dislodge it. He reached the lower canister and began pushing and kicking. These canisters weighed about 700 pounds when fully loaded. What happened next occurred in a split second. The top canister dislodged, hit the bottom one and both dropped out the opening, taking one of the bomb bay doors with it. Pollari himself almost ended up in the North Atlantic with them. After he gathered himself from the harrowing experience, he went back to the cockpit and reported to the pilot that they had just launched two packages and a bomb bay door.

The 492nd Bomb Group alone flew more than 3,000 sorties out of Harrington. They averaged about 15 night flights a month with about 40 to 50 planes each night, flying only during favorable moon periods.

Ground crew loading canisters and supplies into a B-24 at Harrington.

The actual OSS/SOE (Special Operations Executive) container packing station for the aircraft was about 50 miles from Harrington and simply known as Area H. The supply effort was massive since it supplied aerial deliveries for resistance groups in Belgium, Denmark, France, Poland and Norway. France alone had some 300,000 resistance fighters before D-Day that were supplied by airdrop. Ten officers and 350 enlisted men worked long hours to get the operational materials ready for the sorties.

Supply requests from the resistance forces would come into London, be worked out and then sent to the packing station to load ammunition, weapons and whatever else was needed for that particular drop. There were, of course, different-size canisters. The typical "H" canister was about five feet tall, and weighed between 300 and 320 pounds when fully loaded. It had five individual compartments that could be loaded separately and had shock absorbing material on the end opposite the parachute harness. Longer equipment, such as Bren guns, was wrapped in burlap bags and placed into longer "C" containers. The bomb bays of the Carpetbaggers' B-24s were modified to carry twelve of these canisters. Carpetbagger missions were flown without fighter protection and the drops increased in volume as the Underground forces grew in numbers during the course of the war.

One noteworthy person associated with the Carpetbaggers was Colonel Clifford Heflin. He started his military career in 1938 with the Air Cadets. When World War II broke out, he flew anti-submarine missions. Later, he was assigned to the OSS and became commander of the Carpetbaggers. Because of his extraordinary work, it got him the attention of the military commanders in charge of the Manhattan Project, the top-secret operation that developed the atomic bomb. He was assigned to the 216th Army Air Forces Base Unit Special Airfield along with Paul Tibbets, who commanded the 509th Composite Group. Together, these groups shared parallel chains of command at Wendover and were responsible for dropping the atomic bombs on Hiroshima and Nagasaki. He was awarded the Legion of Merit by General Eisenhower and the Croix de Guerre by the French Government.

APPENDIX 3

Documents Relating to Operation *Rype*

Bolland's assignment to O.S.S. and Scandinavian Section

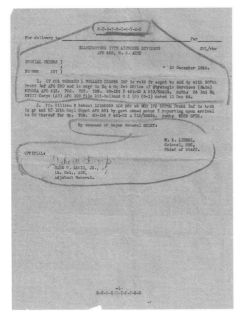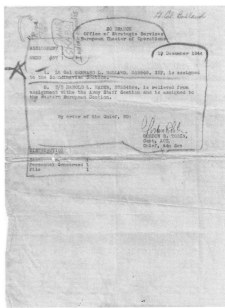

O.S.S. Assignment to Special Operations Branch

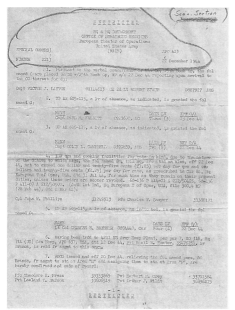
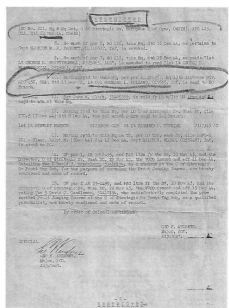

O.S.S. Assignment to Parachute Duty

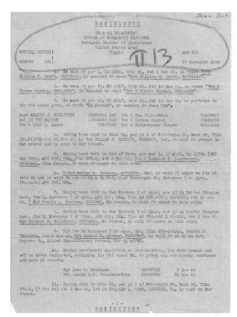
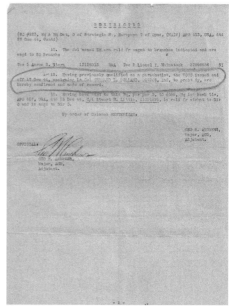

O.S.S. Assignment to NORSO Section

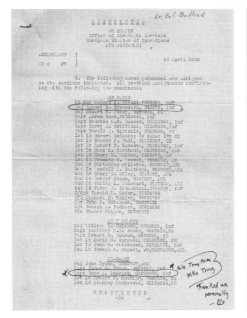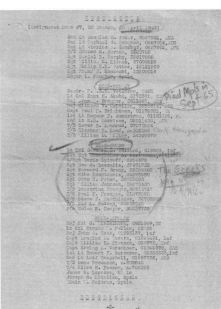

Lt. Colonel George Brewer assigned to O.S.S. Scandinavian Westfield Section

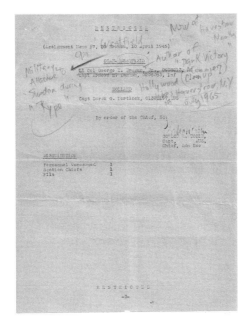

O.S.S. Assignment of personnel from Area "H" to Area "P"

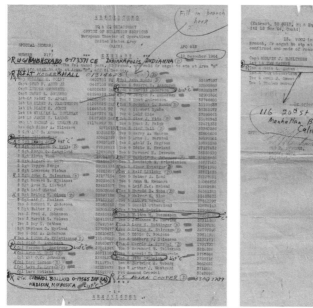
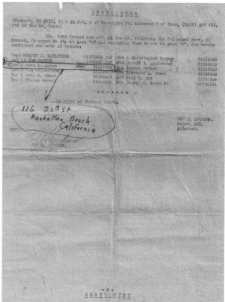

O.S.S. ordering personnel to a secret destination

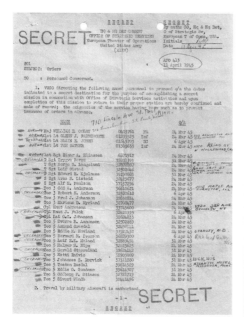
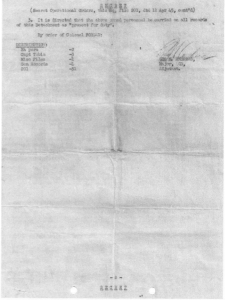

O.S.S. NORSO Group squad assignments

O.S.S. list of NORSO personnel still in the UK

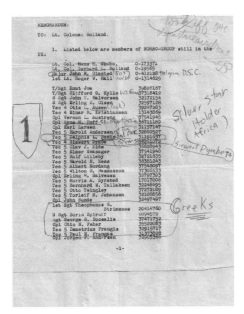

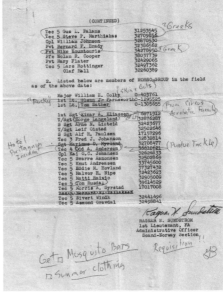

Commendation letter from General Eisenhower

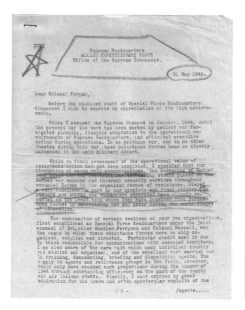

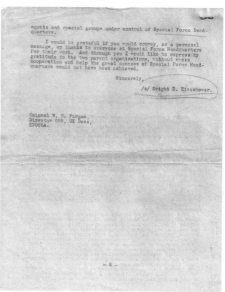

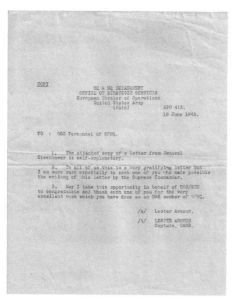

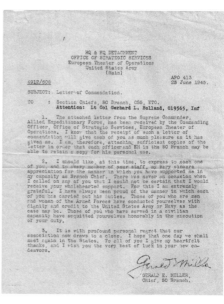

Status and home addresses of O.S.S. NORSO personnel

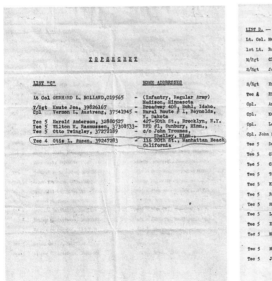

1 October 1945

TOP SECRET

LIST (A)

KILLED IN OPERATIONS	HOME ADDRESSES
X 1st Lt Blain H. Jones, 01645703, SC	- McClay St., Milroy, Pa.
* T/Sgt Trygve Berge, 39031393	- 1528 B 31 St., Oakland, California
* S/Sgt Edward E. Kjelness, 39230883	- 631 Josse Ave., San Francisco, California
X T/3 Robert W. Anderson, 32580618	- 409 James Ave., Jamestown, New York.
X Cpl Knut J. Falck, 32421335	- 4156 E G St., New York.
X T/5 Bernard N. Iverson, 36209300	- Richland Center, Wisc.,
* T/5 Leif E.K. Meland, 32869494	- 9209-215 PO Queens Village, New York
* T/5 Gerald Ottersland, 32624142	- 4204-8th Ave., Brooklyn, New York
* T/5 Johannes S. Rorvick, 37311880	- Inek, Wisconsin
* T/5 Eddie O. Sondeno, 39614907	- Martinsdale, Montana

LEGEND: "X" (cross) marks men now and still interred on the side of PLUNKETTFJELL MOUNTAIN - just 10 kilometres Northwest of Jaevsjo Lake. (64° 7' 22" North - 13° 02' 00" East.) in North Tronderlag, Norway. (Killed 6 April 45)

"*" (asterisk) marks the men interred at the U.S. Army cemetery in Cambridge, England. (Killed 31 March 45)

LIST B. — NORWAY

Major WILLIAM E. COLBY, 0425761, FA	710 Lincoln Ave., St. Paul, Minn.
1st Lt GLENN J. FARNSWORTH, 01295525, INF	723 Newington Ave. Baltimore, Md.
1st Lt TOM SATHER, 01305655, INF (Capt.)	11110 Kling St., N. Hollywood, California
1st Sgt Einar A. Eliassen, 6871912	5005 8th Ave., Brooklyn, N.Y.
T/Sgt Borge O. Langeland, 32876287	8115 3rd Ave., Brooklyn, N.Y.
T/Sgt Leif Oistad, 32502646	6628 Trit St., Linda Vista San Diego, California
S/Sgt Arne W. Listeid, 32423677	556 - 40th St., Brooklyn, N. Y.
S/Sgt Alf E. Paulson, 17157296	Rural Route #1 Alamo, North Dakota
Tec 3 Odd A. Anderson, 36610621	2013 Maple Ave., Evanston, Ill.
Tec 3 Fred J. Johansen, 32832814	24 Harrison St., Jamestown, N. Y.
Tec 3 Marinus D. Myrland, 32708477	475 - 55th St., Brooklyn, N.Y.
Cpl. Knut Andreasen, 33745600	7520 3rd Ave., Brooklyn, N.Y.
Cpl. Kai O. C. Johansen, 32621833	575 - 52nd St., Brooklyn, N.Y.
Tec 5 Sverre B. Aanonsen, 32502869	768 - 45th St., Brooklyn, N. Y.
Tec 5 Amund Gravdal, 32498841	579 - 84th St., Brooklyn, N.Y.
Tec 5 Eddie N. Hovland, 37327432	Stanley, North Dakota
Tec 5 Halver N. Hipe, 32423623	877 - 59th St., Brooklyn, N. Y.
Tec 5 Matti Raivio, 32905009	759 - 40th St., Brooklyn, N. Y.
Tec 5 Tosten Rundal, 39614529	Atlantic Hotel Missoula, Montana
Tec Oddberg F. Stiansen, 32721719	839 - 57th St., Brooklyn, N. Y.
Tec 5 Sivert Windh, 32441496	1423 Cropsey Ave., Brooklyn, N. Y.

TOP SECRET

LIST "C"

	HOME ADDRESSES
Lt Col GERHARD L. BOLLAND, 019565	- (Infantry, Regular Army) Madison, Minnesota
T/Sgt Knute Joa, 39826167	- Broadway 408, Buhl, Idaho.
Cpl Vernon L. Austreng, 37541945	- Rural Route # 1, Reynolds, N. Dakota
Tec 5 Harold Anderson, 32680527	- 427-50th St., Brooklyn, N.Y.
Tec 5 Milton M. Rasmussen, 37308533	- RFD #1, Sunbury, Minn.
Tec 5 Otto Twingley, 37272189	- c/o John Trounes, Shelley, Minn.
Tec 4 Otis L. Ausen, 39247283	- 116 20th St., Manhattan Beach California

LIST D. — Air Landed VAERNES

	Home Addresses
Lt. Col. Hans H. Skabo, 0173371 GK	Indianapolis, Indiana
1st Lt. Roger W. Hall, 01314625 INF	11 Murray Ave., Annapolis, Md.
M/Sgt Clifford G. Kyllo, 37318412	McCanna, North Dakota
S/Sgt John I. Halvorsen, 32172154	c/o N.T. Morris 230 Park Ave., N.Y.
S/Sgt Erling M. Olsen, 32597128	61 Crampton Ave., Woodbridge, N.J.
Tec 4 Einar F. Kristiensen, 13143869	5906 - 5th Ave., Brooklyn, N.Y.
Cpl. Arne M. Hoff, 36711189	5030 N. Kenneth Ave., Chicago
Cpl. Karl Larsen, 31157147	Middle St., 198 New Bedford, Mass.
Cpl. Lars S. Larsen, 32259479	81 Court House Place, Jersey City, N.
Cpl. John Sunde, 32497497	629 - 56 St., Brooklyn, N. Y.
Tec 5 Delphis L. Bonin, 31191637	854 Main St., Willimantic, Conn.
Tec 5 Olav J. Eide, 36628943	3211 W. Evergreen Ave., Chicago
Tec 5 Olaf Hall, 32260389	53-09 6th Ave., Brooklyn, N.Y.
Tec 5 Torleif R. Johansen, 32108856	915 - 56th St., Brooklyn, N.Y.
Tec 5 Elmer Kvassager, 37541940	Route #2, Grand Forks, N. Dak.
Tec 5 Ralf Lilleby, 32721635	628 - 78th St., Brooklyn, N.Y.
Tec 5 Harold K. Ness, 36381243	1302 W. 5th St., Duluth, Minn.
Tec 5 Lars N. Rottinger, 32497632	655 - 56th St., Brooklyn, N. Y.
Tec 5 Erling K. Salvesen, 32797393	421 - 43rd St., Brooklyn, N. Y.
Tec 5 Morris A. Byrstad, 17017008	666 N. Minnesota Ave. St. Paul, Minn.
Tec 5 Nolan Cooper, 38037739	Henderson, Texas
Tec 5 Jorgen F. Anderson, 32905366	Fulton Hotel, 42nd St., NYC

APPENDIX 4

Postwar Correspondence

Post-war correspondence with James Gavin

September 2, 1974
Lt. Gen. James Gavin, Ret. U.S. Army
25 Acorn Park
Cambridge, Massachusetts 02140

Dear "Slim Jim",
There are advantages to being slender. Reflect on the angry bullets that went cracking by instead of providing a backstop for the same.

You and General Omar Bradley gave us some anxious moments when Bradley pinned the D.S.C. on you at Porterie Ridge at a front-line presentation. The Ridge had just recently been captured and was hopefully secure. This same Ridge was to become the highlight of my service in Normandy later on. I had the privilege of conducting the last attack of the 82nd in Normandy which captured the last half-mile from Porterie Ridge to the road, thus cutting the last remaining road from Cherbourg to Saint Lo.

Since we were decimated, I was given extra personnel from Lt. Col. Smith's 3rd Battalion which made it a composite effort of two battalions. I heard the glider regiment was pulling out of the line, so I latched onto all of their 81mm mortar ammunition which was very effectively used by Lt. Young. The objectives were captured without a single casualty and the enemy was propelled with sufficient velocity to not make a meaningful stand until they reached the Saint Lo area. Incidentally the map of areas captured by the 82nd was made too early to show this last half-mile. When I met Col. Raff he was profusely laudatory of our successful attack.

Early in Normandy I had been the Executive Officer of the 507th. My main duties then consisted of monitoring the regimental phone at night and going with the attacking battalions of the 507th. Many days were spent tramping the front-line battalions from flank to flank, a duty not particularly conducive to longevity. When the attrition of battalion Commanders came, I was given the Second Battalion.

After the night attack we were pulled out of line and sent back to England to retrain. The personnel of the 507th were hoping daily Col. Millet would reappear and assume command of the 507th again. This was probably a source of irritation to Col. Raff and upon release of the 507th from the 82nd he was to assert his authority in a very dramatic way.

He summoned an officer's call. There was the organizational chart. He stood to the front, pulled every company Commander's name from the chart and arbitrarily assigned them different companies on the spot. He also changed every one of his staff: S-1, S-2, S-3 and S-4. We all left officer's call stunned in disbelief. In one sweep of his hand, he had created a green regiment. Now the men no longer knew their Company Commander nor did the Company Commander know his men.

Shortly thereafter, to compound the crisis, General Brerton alerted us for a combat mission in France. I then went up to Regimental Headquarters and asked if Raff would not rescind his orders or at least hold in abeyance until after the next combat mission. The answer was "no". From then on, our relationship became frosty.

After several more alerts General Patton kept overrunning our objectives and we were to settle down to routine training again.

The OSS were looking for an officer fluent in Norwegian, who could ski to go on a mission for the King. I volunteered, was immediately accepted and left the 507th for the OSS assignment. Now I was to feel Col. Raff's wrath for the last time. He gave me a "Satisfactory" efficiency report. This was to give me no end of embarrassment in future assignments. I learned later it was used to block my promotion to full Colonel for my service in Korea.

I eventually ended up with a general hospital discharge with a prognosis of five years to live. The doctors didn't realize they were dealing with a tough, ex-paratrooper.

Respectfully,
Lt. Col. Gerhard L. Bolland, Ret. U.S. Army, 0-19565

JAMES M. GAVIN
25 ACORN PARK
CAMBRIDGE, MASSACHUSETTS 02140

September 12, 1974

Lt. Col. Gerhard L. Bolland (Ret.)
508 S. Van Buren Street
Stoughton, Wisconsin 53589

Dear Colonel Bolland:

Thank you for your letter of September 4. It has been very good
to hear from you after these many years. I remember you very well. As I
recall, you were somewhere near the bottom of my stick the night we jumped
into Normandy.

I always felt very sorry for the extra battalion commanders that
were sent over. Their position was an extremely difficult one. Until they
had their own commands and became well worked into the operations, their
situations were quite difficult.

I recall very well the pinning-on affair on Porterie Ridge. General
Ridgway particularly wanted to have it done there. General Howell and Ben
Vandervoort were both there as well.

I did not know of your attack that you describe as the last attack
of the 82nd, and I was interested to learn of it. I do not quite understand
"I respectfully submit these facts to you for your consideration and the
recognition you believe they deserve." I have been out of the Service almost
eighteen years and I am not in a position to make awards, if this is what you
have in mind. If, as you say, the Army has a section set up to evaluate
situations such as that that you describe, I would think that you would get
in touch with them.

I was interested to learn that you had volunteered for service in
Norway. Incidentally, I had heard of that famous Officers" Call when all
company commanders changed positions. I agree, it was an incredible situation.
I never heard of such a thing.

Thank you for writing to me. It has been particularly good to hear
from you.

With best regards,

James M. Gavin

(Author's collection)

Post-war correspondence with William Colby

CENTRAL INTELLIGENCE AGENCY
WASHINGTON, D.C. 20505

1 April 1974

Lt. Col. Gerhard L. Bolland
U.S. Army Retired
508 South Van Buren Street
Stoughton, Wisconsin 53589

Dear Colonel Bolland:

It was nice to hear from you after all these years. I would indeed be glad to see you if my rather hectic schedule will permit it. Perhaps the best solution would be for you to call my office, Area Code 703, 351-6363, after you get to Richmond and we will see what the schedule looks like.

Thanks again for the note and I do hope we can see each other.

Sincerely,

W. E. Colby
Director

508 S. Van Buren Street, Stoughton, Wisconsin 53589   July 31, 1974
Mr. William Colby, Director Central Intelligence Agency
Washington, D.C.

Dear Bill:

I was pleasantly surprised with the Parade Section of our Sunday paper (The Wisconsin State Journal, Madison) feature article written by Lloyd Shearer. I thought it was splendidly done. I am enclosing a copy so you may add it to your collection from around the country.

My visit with you last April was the highlight of our trip. My morale took a definite boost which has been evident even to the family. I wish to thank you for your efforts on my behalf.

In these days of political turmoil in Washington you are bringing to your agency a high degree of STABILITY. Here in the Midwest, I find that both you and the CIA are held in high regard. There were no attempts at vilification when you first took over the directorship of the agency. I would suspect the incidents mentioned in the article were the doing of those desirous of a weak CIA.

In Madison, Minnesota, a Mr. Jon Willand is writing a history of Lac Qui Parle County. It should be published in about a year. It will become a part of the Minnesota Historical Society archives. I sent him your name and Norway exploits because I believe they should be included in the book. This reminds me of our takeover of the Luftwaffe Air Base at Vaernes (Trondheim). Your group performed magnificently and exuded confidence and complete mastery of the situation to the point where Colonel Steifel was convinced we were an advance party of a larger unit. He turned over his small arms leaving him impotent. I left him with these words. "Prepare to receive troops from the United Kingdom in a few days".

Fortunately you will always have high morale in any unit you command since you live by the fundamental precept of leadership summed up in the words, "Never ask a man to do anything you wouldn't do yourself".

I wish you good fortune in your retirement program, comparable to those of the armed services.

In a few years I expect to hear that Colby is to the C.I.A. what Hoover was to the F.B.I.

Sincerely,
(signature)
Gerhard L. Bolland, Lt. Colonel, 0-19565, U.S. Army, Retired

CENTRAL INTELLIGENCE AGENCY
WASHINGTON, D. C.

OFFICE OF THE DIRECTOR

7 August 1974

Lieutenant Colonel Gerhard L. Bolland, USA (Ret.)
508 South Van Buren Street
Stoughton, Wisconsin 53589

Dear Colonel Bolland:

Thank you so much for your nice note of July 30th and the extra copy of <u>Parade</u> Magazine. It was good to hear from you, and it was particularly good to see you during your recent trip here. Your very kind words give me a challenge to meet in the future, but I will try to reflect some of the spirit we had in the NORSO Group. Meanwhile, my very best wishes to you, and I will hope to be seeing you again one day.

Sincerely,

W. E. Colby
Director

CENTRAL INTELLIGENCE AGENCY
WASHINGTON. D. C. 20505

December 5, 1975

Lt. Colonel Gerhard L. Bolland, USA (Ret.)
508 S. Van Buren Street
Stoughton, Wisconsin 53589

Dear Colonel Bolland,

Thank you so much for your nice note. You were very thoughtful to think of me at this time, and I deeply appreciate your sentiments. I am relieved to say that the Brigadier General Joseph M. Colby, who died in October, was not my father, who is still with us here. Thank you for your nice comments about him in any case.

I read with much interest your reminiscences about your involvement in our Norwegian effort. I remember well your joining us, and I much appreciate the support you brought to us. I particularly remember how considerate you were in those days after we got together in Steinjer and in Trondheim. You made a substantial contribution to our mission in Norway, and you should indeed be proud of the service you rendered to our country at a difficult period.

Thank you again,

Sincerely,

W. E. Colby
Director

Gerhard Bolland's Army Career

Regular Military

WAR DEPARTMENT
THE ADJUTANT GENERAL'S OFFICE
WASHINGTON

IN REPLY
REFER TO
A.G.201. Bolland, Gerhard Leroy   June 12, 1934.
(6-12-34)Off.

SUBJECT: Appointment as second lieutenant
in the Regular Army.

TO: Cadet Gerhard Leroy Bolland,

United States Military Academy.

     1. The President has appointed you a second lieutenant of
Infantry, Regular Army, with rank from June 12, 1934.
Your serial number will be O-12565.

     2. Forward to this office at an early date a recent photograph
of yourself, taken in uniform. The photograph should be unmounted,
not exceeding 8 inches in width and 10 inches in height, and should
show upon the back thereof your name, rank and organization, plainly
written or printed, and as nearly as possible the date when taken.

     By order of the Secretary of War:

Adjutant General.

WAR DEPARTMENT,
Washington, June 12, 1934.

SPECIAL ORDERS)
No. **139**)

1. The appointment as second lieutenants in the Regular Army of the United States, with rank from June 12, 1934, and the assignment to arms of the following named cadets, graduates of the United States Military Academy, Class of 1934, are announced:

*   *   *   *

INFANTRY.

*   *   *   *

218. Gerhard Leroy Bolland.

*   *   *   *

By order of the Secretary of War:

Official:
JAMES F. McKINLEY,
Major General,
The Adjutant General.

DOUGLAS MacARTHUR,
General,
Chief of Staff.

PLEASE PRINT - PEN OR PENCIL OR TYPEWRITER MAY BE USED

019565

A. OFFICER REPORTED UPON: BOLLAND? Gerhard L., 1st Lieut., 16th Inf.
   A's official status with respect to you Plat. Ldr., 16th Co., AC., NYWF
B. PERIOD COVERED BY THIS REPORT ~~5~~ Months, from 2/1/39 to 6/30/39
C. STATIONS AT WHICH HE SERVED
D. CONSIDER CAREFULLY THESE DEFINITIONS, KEEP THEM IN MIND WHEN RATING. TAKING
   INTO CONSIDERATION HIS LENGTH OF SERVICE AND THE OPPORTUNITIES AFFORDED HIM,
   WHICH MIGHT HAVE A BEARING UPON HIS PERFORMANCE OF DUTY, PERSONAL CHARACTER-
   ISTICS, OR PROFESSIONAL QUALIFICATIONS.

   UNSATISFACTORY: Performance of the particular duty reported upon or personal characteristics or professional qualifications below minimum standard
   --inefficient.

   SATISFACTORY: Performance of the particular duty reported upon or personal
   characteristics or professional qualifications up to minimum standard---
   passably efficient.

   VERY SATISFACTORY: Performance of the particular duty reported upon in an
   efficient manner. Personal characteristics, professional qualifications
   or efficiency above that acceptable as SATISFACTORY.

   EXCELLENT: Performance of the particular duty reported upon in a very
   efficient manner. Personal characteristics, professional qualifications,
   or efficiency above VERY SATISFACTORY but below SUPERIOR.

   SUPERIOR: Outstanding and exceptional performance of the particular duty
   reported upon. Personal characteristics, professional qualifications,
   or efficiency above that considered EXCELLENT.

   UNKNOWN: To be used in all cases in which the reporting officer has had
   insufficient opportunity during the period covered by this report to
   observe the officer reported upon to permit a rating as to the performance of the particular duty, his personal characteristics, or professional
   qualifications.

E. DUTIES HE PERFORMED: (State separately. Where possible show duration of each
   in months. Example: Co. Comdr. ordinary garrison training, 8 mos. Summary
   Court, 6 mos., Brig. Adj. prepared training schedules, Supply Officer.)
   In describing the manner of performance of duty, use one of six classifica-
   tions as given under D, and consider carefully the obstacles encountered by
   the individual in the performance of each duty listed. The opinions expressed in this report are based on intimate daily contact, ~~frequent or~~
   ~~infrequent observation of the results of his work, or academic ratings.~~
   (Line out inappropriate words or amplify under "Remarks" according to circumstances.)

Duty	:Months:	Manner of Performance
Platoon Leader	: 5 :	Supervisor
	: :	
	: :	
	: :	
	: :	

F. What degree of success has be attained: G. Enter on lines below any out-
   under the following headings: ENTRIES: standing specialties of value in the
   BASED ON PERSONAL OBSERVATION OR   military service. MAKE NO ENTRIES
   OFFICIAL REPORTS DURING PERIOD   EXCEPT WHERE STATEMENT IS BASED ON
   COVERED BY THIS REPORT. (See par. D   PERSONAL OBSERVATION OR OFFICIAL RE-
   above.)   PORTS DURING PERIOD COVERED BY THIS
                                               REPORT. Show pilot and/or observer
                                               ratings of Air Corps Officers.

	Unknown	Unsatisfactory	Satisfactory	Very satisfactory	Excellent	Superior	
1. Handling officers and men						X	
2. Performance of field duties	X						
3. Administrative and executive duties					X		
4. As an instructor						X	
5. Training troops					X		
6. Tactical handling of troops (units appropriate to officer's grade).	X						

- 1 -

O. How well do you know him? *Intimately*

P. Remarks (including entry required by par. 11a. AR 600-185)
Suited for duty with civilian components

Q. In case any unfavorable entries have been made by you on this report, were the deficiencies indicated hereon brought to the attention of the officer concerned while under your command and prior to the rendition of this report? *None* If yes, what improvement, if any, was noted? _____

If no improvement was noted, what period of time elapsed between your notification to him of his deficiencies and the rendition of this report?

R. Based on your observation during the period covered by this report, give in your own words your estimate of his GENERAL VALUE TO THE SERVICE.
Of high present and very high potential value to the service

S. I certify that to the best of my knowledge and belief all entries made hereon are true and impartial and are in accordance with AR 600-185.

(Signed) *M. L. C. Smith Jr.*
(Name typed)
(Grade and Org. *Capt 14th Inf*
(Comg. what? *Prov Co 14th Inf*
(Place) *Camp George Washington*
(Date) *July 5*   Incls. _____

THE
PRESIDENT
OF
THE UNITED STATES OF AMERICA

E PLURIBUS UNUM

To all who shall see these presents, greeting:

Know Ye, that reposing special trust and confidence in the patriotism, valor, fidelity and abilities of _____ Gerhard Leroy Bolland _____,

I do appoint him, temporarily, a Captain _____ *in*

The Army of the United States

to rank as such from the _____ ninth _____ *day of* _____ September _____, *nineteen hundred and* _____ forty _____. *He is therefore carefully and diligently to discharge the duty of the office to which he is appointed by doing and performing all manner of things thereunto belonging.*

And I do strictly charge and require all Officers and Soldiers under his command to be obedient to his orders as an officer of his grade and position. And he is to observe and follow such orders, and directions, from time to time, as he shall receive, from me, or the future President of the United States of America, or the General or other Superior Officers set over him, according to the rules, and discipline of War.

This Commission to continue in force, during the pleasure of the President of the United States, for the time being, under the provisions of section 127 a, National Defense Act, as amended.

Done at the City of Washington, this _____ first _____ *day of* _____ October _____, *in the year of our Lord, one thousand nine hundred and* _____ forty _____, *and of the Independence of the United States of America, the one hundred and* _____ sixty-fifth _____.

By the President:

H. C. Holdridge

Adjutant General.

W. D., A. G. O. FORM No. 0662.
OCTOBER 1, 1940

2665

WCM-wsb-mgr-1509

WAR DEPARTMENT
THE ADJUTANT GENERAL'S OFFICE

In reply
Refer to   WASHINGTON
         AG 201-Bolland, Gerhard L.   April 4, 1942.
            (4-2-42)OD

         SUBJECT: Amendment of Orders.

         Thru: Commandant,
                       The Infantry School,
                          Fort Benning, Georgia.

         TO: Captain Gerhard L. Bolland, Infantry

                    So much of paragraph 23, Special Orders 54, War Depart-
         ment 1942, as pertains to Captain Gerhard L. Bolland 019565,
         Infantry, is amended to relieve him from the First Infantry
         Division, Camp Blanding, Florida, and temporary duty at the
         Infantry School, Fort Benning, Georgia, and assign him to
         further temporary duty as student the Parachute Course at the
         Infantry School, Fort Benning, Georgia, effective upon com-
         pletion of his present course of instruction.

                              By order of the Secretary of War:

                              s/W.C. McMillion

201-Bolland, Gerhard L. (Off)   · 1st Ind.
    (4-4-42) Amendment of Orders.
THE INFANTRY SCHOOL, Office of the Commandant, Fort Benning, Georgia,
April 6, 1942. TO: Captain Gerhard L. Bolland, (THRU: Commanding
Officer, 1st Student Training Regiment, ISSC), Fort Benning, Georgia.

                              s/P. H. D.

A TRUE COPY:

                   William V. Zandri
                   WILLIAM V. ZANDRI
                   2nd Lt., Infantry
                   Adjutant.

COPIED:

         4-10-42, 13th Trg. Bn.
         WVZ/lac

The Infantry School
United States Army

This is to Certify That:

Captain GERHARD L. BOLLAND   O19565

has satisfactorily completed the prescribed course in Parachute Packing, Ground Training, and Jumping from a plane in flight. He is, therefore, entitled to be rated from this date, July 4, 1942 , as a qualified Parachutist.

For the Commandant

H. B. Wheeler

Colonel of Infantry
Secretary

D-Day

E X T R A C T

HEADQUARTERS 507TH PARACHUTE INFANTRY
Office of the Regimental Commander
A.P.O. #230 U. S. Army

GENERAL ORDERS)
              :
NUMBER   9   )   7 August 1944

     1. Pursuant to the provisions of WD Circular No 186, 11 May 1944, the following named Officers, Warrant Officer, and enlisted men are awarded the Combat Infantryman Badge for exemplary conduct in action against the enemy in the Normandy, France, campaign, 6 June 1944 to 9 July 1944:

           ***   ***   ***   ***

         Lt Col Gerhard L. Bolland   019565

          ***   ***   ***   ***

By Order of Colonel RAFF:

                              GEORGE J. ROPER
              Captain, 507th Parachute Infantry,
OFFICIAL: Adjutant

 (War Department
    OFFICIAL
The Adjutant General

     Seal)

       /s/ George J. Roper
       GEORGE J. ROPER
       Captain, 507th Parachute Infantry,
       Adjutant

                          A CERTIFIED TRUE COPY:

                            J. C. PHILLIPS
                            Major, AGD

R E S T R I C T E D

HQ & HQ DETACHMENT
OFFICE OF STRATEGIC SERVICES
European Theater of Operations
United States Army
(MAIN)

80 BRANCH

Lt Col
Bolland

200.6/5-AMS

APO 413
23 June 1945

SUBJECT: Award of Bronze Service Arrowhead.

TO   : Personnel Concerned.

In accordance with the provisions of War Department Circular No 465, dated 9 December 1944, and letter, Hq, European TO, file AG 200.6 OpGA, subject "Individual Service Award of Bronze Service Arrowhead", dated 9 May 1945, the following named officer who served with Hq, 82nd Airborne Division, is authorized to wear the Bronze Service Arrowhead:

Lt Col GERHARD I. BOLLAND   019565   Inf

By order of Colonel FORGAN:

GEO H. ANDREWS,
Major, AGD,
Adjutant.

DISTRIBUTION: "B", "D" & "P"

R E S T R I C T E D

Post-war reassignment from the OSS back into the Regular Army

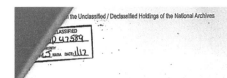

SHP:jah

15 October 1945

SUBJECT: Reassignment of Lt Colonel Gerhard L Bolland, 019565, Inf.

THRU: Commanding Officer, Headquarters and Headquarters Detachment, 2324 F Street, NW, Washington, D. C.

TO: The Adjutant General's Office, Room 2402, Munitions Building, Washington 25, D. C. ATTENTION: Lt Colonel Ruth.

1. It is requested that above subject officer be assigned to Inf RTC, Ft McClellan, Ala, as requested by Commanding General, Army Ground Forces (Major Meyer).

2. It is further requested that EDCMR be 17 October 1945.

FOR THE DIRECTOR:

S. H. PARKINS,
Major, Inf,
Personnel Branch.

cc: Security
Statistical
CG, AGF (Maj Meyer)

201-Bolland, Gerhard L. (0)   1st Ind   CVC/ok

WD, OASW, Hq & Hq Det, SSU, Rm 21, 2324 F St, NW, Wash 25 DC., 15 Oct 45.

TO: The Adjutant General, WD, Wash, DC. ATTN: Lt Col Ruth, 1046 Munitions.

Approved.

FOR THE COMMANDING OFFICER:

CARL V. CASH
1st Lt, AC
Asst Adjutant

SPECIAL ORDERS)

No 248   :

WAR DEPARTMENT
Washington 25, D.C., 17 October 1945

*   *   *   E X T R A C T   *   *   *

10. The following changes in asgmts and duties are directed. WP. TDN. TPA. PCS. 601-31
P 431-02,03,07,08 A 212/60425. All dates are 1945 unless otherwise indicated.

Name	EDCMR	Relieved from	Assigned to
*****		*****	*****
CAPT ROBERT J. BOEHM 0440257 MC	18 Oct	OASW WD Strategic Services Unit, Washington, DC.	5th SvC Newton D. Baker GH, Martinsburg, W Va.
LT COL GERHARD L. BOLLAND 019565 Inf	17 Oct	..........do..............	Inf RTC Ft McClellan, Ala.
*****		*****	*****
CAPT JAMES R. BREECE 0562605 AC	17 Oct	OASW WD Strategic Services Unit, Washington, DC.	AAF Redistribution Sta No 6 San Antonio, Tex. Delay en route of 15 days is auth chargeable as lv. Par 1c C 2 AR 605-115 13 Dec 1944 requires officers to keep a record of lv used.

*   *   *   *

BY ORDER OF THE SECRETARY OF WAR:

G. C. MARSHALL
Chief of Staff

OFFICIAL:

EDWARD F. WITSELL
Major General
Acting The Adjutant General

A TRUE EXTRACT COPY: _____

Documentation for Bronze Star

```
                        ʼAR DEPʼRTʼENT
            OFFICE OF THE ʼSSISTʼNT SECRETARY Oʼ ʼʼʼR
                     Hq. & Hq. Detachment
                     STRATEGIC SERVICES UNIT
              2324 F Street, N.W. Washington 25, D.C.


                                            15 January 1946


   SUBJECT:  Authorization for Bronze Star "Ground Combat Norway".

   TO:       Personnel Concerned.


             Under the provisions of Section I, General Order 105, War
   Department, 19 November 1945, and in accordance with paragraph 7 b (2),
   Circular 195, War Department 1944, the personnel listed herein, all
   present or former members of this organization, are authorized a Battle
   Participation Award, Ground Combat Norway, to the European-African-Middle
   East Theater Ribbon, for action in enemy occupied territory. Per Auth
   contained in 1st Ind, TAG, AGPD-C 200.6 (12 Sept 45).


        RANK        NAME                    ASN

   Lt. Col.  BOLAND, GERHARD L.          O-19565
   1st Lt.   BLAIN E. JONES              O-1645703
   T/Sgt     Berge, Trygve               39 031 393
   T/Sgt     Joa, Knute                  39 826 167
   S/Sgt     Kjelness, Edward E.         39 230 883
   T/3       Anderson, Robert N.         32 580 618
   T/4       Ausen, Otis L.              39 247283
   Cpl       Austreng, Vernon L.         37 541 945
   Cpl       Falk, Knut J.               32 421 335
   T/5       Anderson, Harold            32 880 527
   T/5       Iverson, Bernard K.         36 389 300
   T/5       Melund, Leif E.K.           32 869 494
   T/5       Ottersland, Gerald          32 624 142
   T/5       Rasmussen, Milton M.        37 308 533
   T/5       Rorvick, Johannes S.        37 311 880
   T/5       Sondeno, Eddie O.           39 614 907
   T/5       Twingley, Otto              37 272 189


        BY ORDER OF MAJOR CARINI:


                                        CARL V. CASH
                                        1st Lt., AC.
                                        Adjutant
```

WAR DEPARTMENT
THE ADJUTANT GENERAL'S OFFICE
WASHINGTON 25. D. C.

8 October 1947

AGPD-C 201 Bolland, Gerhard L.
(4 Sept 47) 019 565

SUBJECT: Letter Orders

TO: Lieutenant Colonel Gerhard L. Bolland
        (In Care of Adjutant General)
        Fourth Army Headquarters
        Fort Sam Houston, Texas

    1. By direction of the President, under the provisions of
Executive Order 9419, 4 February 1944, (Sec II, WD Bul. 3, 1944),
a Bronze Star Medal is awarded to Lieutenant Colonel Gerhard L.
Bolland, 019 565, 507th Parachute Infantry Regiment, for ex-
emplary conduct in ground combat against the armed enemy from
6 June 1944 to 9 July 1944 during the Normandy Campaign in the
European Theater of Operations.

    2. Authority for this award is contained in Par 15.1e
AR 600-45 and is based upon General Orders No. 9, Headquarters
507th Parachute Infantry Regiment, dated 7 August 1944.

    3. The Commanding Officer, Philadelphia Quartermaster Depot,
will forward an engraved Bronze Star Medal direct to the recipient
at the address shown above.

    BY ORDER OF THE SECRETARY OF THE ARMY:

Adjutant General

World War II Ground Force Casualties Report, January 10, 1946

ARMY GROUND FORCES CASUALTIES IN WORLD WAR II

Source of Information: Memorandum for Chief of Staff,
U.S. Army, from Commanding General, Army Ground Forces,
dated 10 January 1946

CASUALTIES IN DIVISIONS
(7 Dec 41 thru 31 Aug 45)

DIVISION	KILLED IN ACTION	WOUNDED IN ACTION	MISSING IN ACTION	TOTAL CASUALTIES
AIRBORNE DIVISIONS (Auth Strength 8558)				
11th Airborne	1011	4073	40	5124
13th Airborne	9	3	1	13
17th Airborne	1119	4214	87	5420
82nd Airborne	1581	5544	552	7677
101st Airborne	1731	5584	273	7588
TOTAL	5451	19418	953	25822
ARMORED DIVISIONS (Auth Strength 10752)				
1st Armored	1671	6158	1609	9438
2nd Armored	1447 *incorrect*	5550	122	7119
3rd Armored	7206	7206	179	9620
4th Armored	1448	4669	90	6207
5th Armored	735	2498	46	3279
6th Armored	1222	4263	45	5530
7th Armored	1109	3886	283	5278
8th Armored	333	1137	24	1494
9th Armored	702	2292	205	3199
10th Armored	901	3300	80	4281
11th Armored	617	2559	21	3197
12th Armored	636	2289	117	3042
13th Armored	115	370	11	496
14th Armored	538	2097	108	2743
16th Armored	0	14	0	14
20th Armored	43	130	0	173
TOTAL	13752	48418	2940	65110
CAVALRY DIVISION (Auth Strength 13747)				
1st Cavalry	1612	7236	35	8883
MOUNTAIN DIVISION (Auth Strength 14108)				
10th Mountain	783	3128	219	4130
TOTAL CASUALTIES OF AIRBORNE, ARMORED, CAVALRY AND MOUNTAIN DIVISIONS	21598	78200	4147	103945

-1-

Casualties in Divisions Cont'd)

DIVISION	KILLED IN ACTION	WOUNDED IN ACTION	MISSING IN ACTION	TOTAL CASUALTIES	
1st Infantry	4295	15457	1241	20893	
2nd Infantry	3239	11757	212	15208	
3rd Infantry	6571	24650	2326	33547	HIGH
4th Infantry	4581	16311	313	21205	
5th Infantry	2479	8997	178	11654	
6th Infantry	1542	7272	37	8851	
7th Infantry	3237	11887	55	15179	
8th Infantry	2617	9748	277	12642	
9th Infantry	4474	16961	750	22185	
24th Infantry	2275	9145	98	11518	
25th Infantry	2159	7680	26	9865	
26th Infantry	1978	7611	236	9825	
27th Infantry	2273	6753	370	9396	
28th Infantry	2323	9324	943	12590	
29th Infantry	4612	14475	279	19366	
30th Infantry	3464	12888	286	16638	
31st Infantry	502	1853	52	2417	
32nd Infantry	3235	10711	178	14124	
33rd Infantry	699	3493	136	4328	
34th Infantry	3281	14165	3460	20906	
35th Infantry	2843	11032	304	14179	
36th Infantry	4265	18874	3579	26718	
37th Infantry	1834	8218	18	10070	
38th Infantry	1251	5562	92	6905	
40th Infantry	1245	4833	68	6146	
41st Infantry	968	4632	24	5624	
42nd Infantry	416	2165	273	2954	
43rd Infantry	1966	8637	47	10650	
44th Infantry	1079	3697	123	4899	
45th Infantry	4030	19415	3762	27207	
63rd Infantry	911	3239	80	4230	
64th Infantry	229	917	36	1182	
65th Infantry	800	636	15	1451	
69th Infantry	375	1110	9	1494	
70th Infantry	617	1832	46	2545	
71st Infantry	157	506	13	676	
75th Infantry	922	3159	37	4118	
76th Infantry	726	2143	55	2924	
77th Infantry	3037	10531	133	13701	
78th Infantry	1565	5918	125	7608	
79th Infantry	2306	11253	331	13890	
80th Infantry	3116	11486	344	14946	
81st Infantry	500	1992	251	2749	
83rd Infantry	3276	10857	210	14343	
84th Infantry	1394	4974	138	6506	
85th Infantry	1390	6583	1440	9413	
86th Infantry	123	594	36	753	
87th Infantry	1171	4170	144	5485	
88th Infantry	1810	10173	3118	15101	
89th Infantry	266	662	50	978	
90th Infantry	3883	13914	302	18099	
91st Infantry	1216	6795	1016	9027	
92nd Infantry	338	2242	620	3200	

Casualties in Divisions Cont'd)

DIVISION	KILLED IN ACTION	WOUNDED IN ACTION	MISSING IN ACTION	TOTAL CASUALTIES
93rd Infantry	43	133	18	194
94th Infantry	894	4709	292	5895
95th Infantry	1307	4788	126	6221
96th Infantry	3135	13246	453	16834
97th Infantry	199	701	33	933
98th Infantry	0	0	0	0
99th Infantry	1010	4080	254	5344
100th Infantry	916	3656	180	4752
102nd Infantry	1027	3527	75	4629
103rd Infantry	706	3256	182	4144
104th Infantry	1445	4801	111	6357
106th Infantry	326	1299	1023	2648
? Americal Combat ? ? Team ?	1529	5190	99	6818
TOTAL	122562	474099	31208	627860

TOTAL ALL DIVISIONS   *Killed* (144,160)   *Wounded* (552299)   *Missing* (35268)   (831314) *TOTAL*

LIST OF DIVISIONS IN ORDER OF NUMBER OF CASUALTIES ARMY GROUND FORCE.

1..........(3rd) Infantry
2..........45th Infantry
3..........36th Infantry
4..........(9th) Infantry
5..........(4th) Infantry
6..........34th Infantry
7..........(1st) Infantry
8..........29th Infantry
9..........90th Infantry
10..........96th Infantry
11..........30th Infantry
12..........(2nd) Infantry
13..........(7th) Infantry
14..........88th Infantry
15..........80th Infantry
16..........83rd Infantry
17..........35th Infantry
18..........32nd Infantry
19..........79th Infantry
20..........77th Infantry
21..........8th Infantry
22..........28th Infantry
23..........(5th) Infantry
24..........24th Infantry
25..........43rd Infantry
26..........37th Infantry
27..........25th Infantry
28..........26th Infantry
29..........3rd Armored
30..........1st Armored
31..........85th Infantry
32..........27th Infantry
33..........91st Infantry

34..........1st Cavalry
35..........(6th) Infantry
36..........82nd Airborne   (*ABN. are Light Divisions*)
37..........78th Infantry
38..........101st Airborne   *P.R.O. DIVISION*
39..........2nd Armored
40..........38th Infantry
41..........Americal
42..........84th Infantry
43..........104th Infantry
44..........95th Infantry
45..........4th Armored
46..........40th Infantry
47..........94th Infantry
48..........41st Infantry
49..........6th Armored
50..........87th Infantry
51..........17th Airborne
52..........99th Infantry
53..........11th Airborne
54..........7th Armored
55..........44th Infantry
56..........100th Infantry
57..........102nd Infantry
58..........33rd Infantry
59..........10th Armored
60..........63rd Infantry
61..........103rd Infantry
62..........10th Mountain (*Light Div.*)
63..........75th Infantry
64..........70th Infantry
65..........5th Armored
66..........98th Infantry

-3-

(Casualties in Divisions Cont'd)

67............11th Armored		78............66th Infantry
68............9th Armored		79............65th Infantry
69............12th Armored		80............89th Infantry
70............42nd Infantry		81............97th Infantry
71............76th Infantry		82............86th Infantry
72............81st Infantry		83............71st Infantry
73............14th Armored		84............13th Armored
74............106th Infantry		85............93rd Infantry
75............31st Infantry		86............20th Armored
76th I........69th Infantry		87............13th Airborne
77............8th Armored		88............98th Infantry

////////////

Service in Korea

HEADQUARTERS
THIRD BATTALION, 32ND INFANTRY
APO 7, c/o Postmaster
San Francisco, California

10 October 1948

Lt Col. Gerhard L. Bolland
2nd Bn, 31st Infantry

Dear Bolland:

As you depart from Chunchon I wish to take this opportunity to thank you for your cooperation and to assure you that I consider it a distinct honor to Command the unit that is to replace you and your troops. The turn over has been most pleasant because of the spirit of cooperation that has been examplified by both yourself and your staff.

It is sincerely hoped that we may successfully carry out those plans and project which you have so ably iniatiated, and further that you will continue to think of this as your Korean home and to visit us at any opportunity.

Most Sincerely,

/s/ Robert B Jones
/t/ ROBERT B JONES
Lt Col., Inf
Commanding

A TRUE COPY:

J. E. TORGERSON
Capt   Cav
Actg Asst Adj Gen

201-Bolland, G.L. (Off)   1st Ind   EWP/gd

Headquarters Seventh Infantry Division, Office of the Commanding General, AFO 7, c/o Postmaster, San Francisco, California, 13 October, 1948.

TO: Lieutenant Colonel Gerhard L. Bolland, 2nd Battalion, 31st Infantry, AFO 7, c/o Postmaster, San Francisco, California. (Thru Commanding Officer, 31st Infantry.)

    I am glad to have this letter brought to my attention. I wish to add my appreciation of the splendid manner in which you performed your duty in command of the Outpost Battalion at Chun Chun, Korea.

                            /s/ E. W. Piburn
                            /t/ E. W. PIBURN
               Brigadier General United States Army
                 Assistant Division Commander

201 - Bolland, Gerhard L (Off)   2nd Ind   WJB/dm

Headquarters, 31st Infantry Regiment, AFO 7   15 October 1948

TO: Lt Colonel Gerhard L Bolland, Commanding Officer, 2nd Battalion, 31st Infantry Regiment, AFO 7

    1. Attention is directed to 1st Indorsement.

    2. I wish to add my appreciation and thanks for a job well done.

                            /s/ W. J. Baird
                            /t/ W. J. BAIRD
                          Colonel, 31st Infantry
                          Commanding

A TRUE COPY:

J. E. TORGERSON
Capt   Cav
Actg Asst Adj Gen

201-Bolland, G.L. (Off)   1st Ind.   EWP/gd

Headquarters Seventh Infantry Division, Office of the Commanding General,
APO 7, c/o Postmaster, San Francisco, California, 13 October, 1948.

To: Lieutenant Colonel Gerhard L. Bolland, 2nd Battalion, 31st Infantry,
APO 7, c/o Postmaster, San Francisco, California. (Thru Commanding Officer,
31st Infantry).

    I am glad to have this letter brought to my attention. I wish to add
my appreciation of the splendid manner in which you performed your duty in
command of the Outpost Battalion at Chun Chun, Korea.

                                 E. W. PIBURN
                    Brigadier General United States Army
                        Assistant Division Commander

201 - Bolland, Gerhard L (Off) 2nd Ind.   WJB/dm

Headquarters, 31st Infantry Regiment, APO 7   15 October 1948

TO: Lt Colonel Gerhard L Bolland, Commanding Officer, 2nd Battalion,
31st Infantry Regiment, APO 7

    1. Attention is directed to 1st Indorsement.

    2. I wish to add my appreciation and thanks for a job well done.

                        W. J. BAIRD
                        Colonel, 31st Infantry
                        Commanding

Retirement from active service

```
Symbols:  DP  - By direction of the President
          TDN - Travel directed is necessary in military service
          WP  - Will proceed to
          TPA - Travel by officer by privately owned automobile is authorized,
                DS for officer's travel is authorized, par. le, AR 605-180
          AD  - Active duty
        TDPFO - Temp duty pending further orders
        EDCMR - Effective date of change on morning reports
        DDALV - Days' delay en route auth chargeable as lv
       DDALVP - Days' delay en route auth chargeable as lv provided it does not
                interfere with reporting on date specified and provided indi-
                vidual has sufficient accrued lv
```

```
SPECIAL ORDERS)                       DEPARTMENT OF THE ARMY,
NO.       96)                         Washington 25, D. C., 15 May 1951.
```

E X T R A C T

***   ***   ***

37. LT COL GERHARD L. BOLLAND (Maj) O19565 Inf having been determined to be
perm unfit for dy by reason of phys disability of 100 percent incurred while
entitled to rec basic pay is ret from active svc 31 May 1951 with grade and ret
pay of LtCol as prov by Secs 402 and 409 Act Congress approved 12 Oct 1949 (PL
351 81st Cong). He is rel fr asg Medical Holding Det Fitzsimons AH, Denver,
Colo, 31 May 1951 and at proper time WP his home. PCS. TDN. 2110425 1-22-222
P 431-02, 03, 07 S99-999.

***   ***   ***

BY ORDER OF THE SECRETARY OF THE ARMY:

OFFICIAL: J. LAWTON COLLINS
   EDWARD F. WITSELL   Chief of Staff, United States Army
   Major General, USA
   The Adjutant General

A TRUE COPY

J. SILVERSTEIN
Major,   AGC

Bibliography

Publications

Bank, Aaron, *From O.S.S. to Green Berets; The Birth of Special Forces*, Presido Press, Novatno, CA, 1986.

Bascomb, Neal, *The Winter Fortress*, Houghton Mifflin Harcourt Publishers, New York, NY, 2016.

Bearden, Bob, *To D-Day and Back: Adventures with the 507th Parachute Infantry Regiment and Life as a WWII POW*, Quarto Publishing Group, London, England, October 2007.

Beayan, Colin, *Operation Jedburgh*, Viking Adult Publishers (a division of Penguin Group, Canada), Toronto, Canada, May 4, 2006.

Booth, T. Michael, and Spencer, Duncan, *Paratrooper: The Life of Gen James M Gavin*, Simon & Schuster Inc., New York, NY, 1994.

Borden, Louise, *Ski Soldier, A World War II Biography*, Calkins Creek, An Imprint of Highlights, Honesdale, PA, 2017.

Burgett, Donald R., *Currahee!*, Houghton Mifflin Publishing Co., 1967.

Butalla, S. Fabian, *Warbirds in the Cloak of Darkness*, Hellgate Press, Ashland, OR, 2018.

Brokaw, Tom, *The Greatest Generation*, Random House Publishers, New York, NY, 1998.

Brown, Anthony Cave, *Wild Bill Donovan, The Last Hero*, Times Books, a division of Quadrangle/ The New York Times Book Co., Inc., New York, NY, 1982.

Bruce, David K.E., *OSS Against the Third Reich, The World War II Diaries*, Kent State University Press, Kent, Ohio and London, England, 1991.

Bryant, Arthur, *The Turn of the Tide*, London, William Collins & Sons Co. Ltd., 1957, pp. 700–701.

Capa, Robert, and Barry, John, "D-Day, Eyewitness to the Invasion," *Newsweek Magazine*, May 23, 1994.

Chalou, George C., "The Secrets War: The Office of Strategic Services in World War II," *Mazal Holocaust Collection*, National Archives and Records Administration Publishers, Washington, D.C., 1992.

Claffy, Reidar, *How Norway Resisted*, The American Scandinavian Foundation, New York NY, 1945.

Colby, William, *Honorable Men / My Life in the CIA*, Simon & Schuster Publishing, 1978.

Colby, William E., *OSS Operations in Norway: Skis and Daggers*, FOIA, https://www.cia.gov/library/ center-for-the-study-of-intelligence/csi-publications

Conant, Jennet, *A Covert Affair: Julia Child and Paul Child in the OSS*, Simon and Schuster Publishers, New York, NY, 2011.

Cowley, Robert, and Parker, Geoffrey, *The Battle of Britain, The Reader's Companion to Military History*, 1996, Houghton Mifflin Harcourt Publishing Company.

Cromarty, Monica, "Hitler and Falconry," *Falcons Canada*, https://www.falconscanada.com/ Hitler_and_Falconry.html

Dietrichson, Professor of Philosophy Paul, *Norwegian Resistance During WWII*, University of Washington, Western Viking Publishers, June 16, 1995.

Dreux, William B., *No Bridges Blown, With the OSS Jedburghs in Nazi-Occupied France*, University of Notre Dame Press, Notre Dame, IN, 1971.

Dunlop, Richard, *Donovan, America's Spymaster*, Rand McNally & Company, August, 1982.

Earl, David W., *Almost Home: The Story of the B-24 Crash at Walliwall Orkney*, Hanover Publications, Stalybridge, United Kingdom, June 25, 2011.

Fjellgård, Gjefsjøen, *The Plane Crash on Plukkutjønnfjellet*, June 21, 2021, https://gjefsjo.no/flyulykken-pa-plukkutjonnfjellet/?fbclid=IwAR2VUnosTRO4sfgecWitC1UTN8aOXmB1qllKR-gAkSQB8nqiiobL5eZ7ZttM

Ford, Lt. Col. Corey, and Mac Bain, Maj. Alastair, "Cloak and Dagger," *Collier's* Magazine; Crowell-Collier Printing Press, Springfield, OH, October 6 and 13, 1945.

Ford, Corey, "Donovan of OSS," *Mazal Holocaust Collection*, Boston, Little, Brown and Company Publishers, 1970.

Francois, Dominique, *507th Parachute Infantry Regiment*, Casemate Publishers, Havertown, PA 19083, 2010.

Gabel, Kurt, *The Making of a Paratrooper: Airborne Training and Combat in World War II*, University Press of Kansas, Lawrence, Kansas, 1978.

Gallagher, Thomas, *Assault in Norway: Sabotaging the Nazi Nuclear Program*, Lyons Press, Guilford, CT, 2002.

Gavin, Gen. James M., *On To Berlin*, Bantam Books/published by arrangement with Viking Press, New York, NY, August 1978.

Gjefsjo, Nils Christian, *Gjefsjoen Fjellgard, The History and Cultural Landscape on Gjefsjøen*, www.gjefsjo.no/historie/

Gralley, Craig R., "A Climb to Freedom: A Personal Journey in Virginia Hall's Steps," *Studies in Intelligence*, Vol 61, No. 1, March 2017,

Haugen, Einar, *Norway and the War*, The American Scandinavian Foundation, New York NY, May 17, 1940.

Heimark, Bruce, O.S.S. *Operation RYPE: Cutting the Nordland Rail Line in Occupied Norway at Two Points in the North Töndelag Area, April, 1945*, Thesis presented to the University of Nebraska Department of History, May, 1990

Heimark, Bruce H., *The OSS Norwegian Special Operations Group in World War II*, Praeger Publishers, Westport, CT, 1994.

Henry, Thomas R., *The White War in Norway*, National Geographic Society, Washington, D.C., November, 1945.

Herrington, Ian, *Special Operations in Norway, SOE and Resistance in World War II*, I.B. Tauris & Co. Ltd; London, England, 2019.

Hollinshead, Martin, *The Last Wolf Hawker, The Eagle Falconry of Friedrich Remmler*, The Fernhill Press, Staffordshire, United Kingdom, 2006.

Hollinshead, Martin, *German Eagle*, The Fernhill Press, Staffordshire, United Kingdom, 2008.

Hoppe, Jon, "The Attack on the USNS Card," *U.S. Naval Institute Blog*, October 7, 2015, https://www.navalhistory.org/2015/10/07/the-attack-on-the-usns-card

Howarth, David Armine, *Across to Norway*, William Sloan Associates, New York, NY, 1952.

Insall, Tony, *Secret Alliances, Special Operations and Intelligence in Norway 1940–1945*, Biteback Publishing, London, England, November 12, 2019.

Irving, David, *The German Atomic Bomb*, Simon and Schuster Publishers, New York, NY, 1967.

Irwin, Will (Lt. Col. Ret.), *The Jedburghs, The Secret History of the Allied Special Forces, France 1944*, Public Affairs Book Publishers, New York, NY, October 10, 2006.

Johnson, Major Kim M., *An Analysis of the Norwegian Resistance During the Second World War*, Research Paper AU/ACSC/0146C/97-03 presented to The Research Department Air Command and Staff College, Maxwell AFB, March 1997, http://www.dtic.mil/dtic/tr/fulltext/u2/a394028.pdf

Jones, Benjamin F., *Eisenhower's Guerrillas—The Jedburghs, The Marquis & The Liberation of France*, Oxford University Press, Oxford, England, February 3, 2016.

Katz, Barry, "Foreign Intelligence; Research and Analysis in the Office of Strategic Services, 1942–1945," *Mazal Holocaust Collection*, Harvard University Press, Cambridge, MA, 1989

Kauffmann, Henrik de, *A Free and United North*, address given at the Seventh Annual Scandinavian–American Day Gathering in Des Moines, Iowa, July 28, 1940, *The American-Scandinavian Foundation Newspaper*, New York, NY.

Keegan, John, "D-Day, History's Greatest Invasion," *U.S. News & World Report*, May 23, 1994.

Kittredge, Eleanor, "Norway, A Country That Waited Until It Was Too Late," *New York Times Book Review*, November 30, 1941.

Koht, Dr. Halvdan, *Norway, Neutral and Invaded*, Macmillan Publishing Company, New York, NY.

Lee, Raymond Eliot, *The London Journal of General Raymond E. Lee, 1940-1941*, Hutchinson Publishers, London, England, 1971.

Lindgjerdet, Frode, "Operation Rype," *Journal of Military History*, Gjefsjøen Fjellgård, March 25, 2015, https://gjefsjo.no/2015/03/artikkel-om-operasjon-rype-i-tidsskriftet/

Lindgjerdet, Frode, *The Battle for the Nordlandsbannen 1945—Operation Grouse and the Attacks on the Railway in Nord-Trondelag*, ARK Books, 2016.

Lulushi, Albert, *Donovan's Devils*, Arcade Publishing, New York, NY, 2016.

Macintyre, Ben, *Rogue Heroes, The History of the SAS*, Crown Publishing/Penguin Random House Publishers, New York, NY, 2016.

McIntosh, Elizabeth P., *Sisterhood of Spies, The Women of the OSS*, Naval Institute Press, Annapolis Maryland, 1998.

Melton, H. Keith, *OSS Special Weapons & Equipment*, Sterling Publishing Company, Inc. New York, NY, 1991.

Miller, Russell, *Behind the Lines: The Oral History of Special Operations in World War II*, St. Martin's Press, New York, NY, 2002.

Morgan, Martin K. A., *Down to Earth, The 507th Parachute Infantry Regiment in Normandy*, Schiffer Publishing Ltd., Atglen, PA, 2004.

Nelan, Bruce W., "Ike's Invasion," *Time Magazine*, June 6, 1994

Nordyke, Phil, *All American All the Way: The Combat History of the 82nd Airborne Division in World War II*, Zenith Press, 2005.

Nyquist, Gerd, *99th Battalion: The Long Way Home*, Aperture Press, LLC, 201 Washington Street, Suite 533, Reading, PA 19601, March 31, 2014.

O'Donnell, Patrick K., *Operatives, Spies and Saboteurs, the Unknown Story of Men and Women of World War II's OSS*, Free Press, a Division of Simon & Schuster, Inc, New York, NY, 2004.

Pearson, Judith L., *Wolves at the Door, the True Story of America's Greatest Female Spy*, The Globe Pequot Press, Guilford, Connecticut, 2005.

Persico, Joseph E., *Roosevelt's Secret War: FDR and World War II Espionage*, Random House Publishers, New York, NY, 2001.

Peterson, Jeffrey G., *The United States' Changing Attitude Toward Norway, 1940–1943*, The Viking Press, New York, NY, April 1966.

Preisler, Jerome, *First To Jump*, Penguin Random House LLC, New York, NY, December 2014.

Public Affairs, Central Intelligence Agency, "The Office of Strategic Services: America's First Intelligence Agency," United States Central Intelligence Agency Public Affairs Office, Washington D.C., 2000.

Robuk, Erika, *The Invisible Woman*, Berkley, New York, NY, February 2021.

Ross, Robert Todd, *U.S. Army Rangers and Special Forces of WWII: Their War in Photographs*, Schiffer Publishing, Limited, Atglen, PA, 2002.

Ryan, Cornelius, *The Longest Day*, Fawcett Publications Inc., Greenwich, CT, 1959.

Sacquety, Troy J., "The OSS: A Primer on the Special Operations Branches and Detachments of the Office of Strategic Services," *Veritas*, Vol 3, No. 4, 2007.

Scandinavian Ships in the Battle of the Atlantic, The American Scandinavian Foundation, New York NY, July 15, 1941.

Smith, Bradley F., *The Shadow Warriors: O.S.S. and the Origins of the C.I.A.*, Basic Books Publishers, New York, NY, 1983.

Smith, Steven Trent, "Surprise, Kill, Vanish: Operatives Take on Nazi Forces in Norway," *World War II Magazine*, February 2018.

"SOF Editor," "OSS Office of Strategic Services Special Operations," *Soldier of Fortune* magazine, November 9, 2019, www.sofmag.com/oss-office-of-strategic-services-special-operations/?fbclid=I-wAR2l3P-A40Fz9lnxtVmg0k0wj5RZugMXwEnsNXpGIxOa_s-jaHFQ6ZZOgEY

Soley, Lawrence C., "Radio Warfare: OSS and CIA Subversive Propaganda," *Mazal Holocaust Collection*, Praeger Publishers, New York, NY, 1989.

Sons of Norway, *Hidden Heroes: World War II in Norway*, District 5; Lulu Press, 2016.

Sonsteby, Gunnar, *Report From #24*, Barricade Books Inc., Fort Lee, NJ, 1999 (Original Publication by Lyle Stuart), 1965.

Stevenson, William, *A Man Called Intrepid*, Harcourt Brace Jovanovich Publishers, New York/London, 1976.

"The North," *Scandinavian Times Newsmagazine*; Vol 2, No. 2, Sydney, Australia, May 1965.

The Resistance Movement In Norway: World War II, The Viking Press, New York, NY, June 1966.

United States, Office of Strategic Services, *Assessment of Men: Selection of Personnel for the Office of Strategic Services*, Rinehart Publishers, New York, NY, 1948.

Waller, Douglas, *Wild Bill Donovan, The Spymaster Who Created the OSS and Modern American Espionage*, Free Press, Simon & Schuster, New York, NY, 2011.

Waller, Douglas, *Disciples, The World War II Missions of the CIA Directors Who Fought for Wild Bill Donovan*, Simon & Schuster Publishers, New York, NY, 2015.

"War Report of the OSS (Office of Strategic Services)," *United States War Department/ Strategic Services Unit/History Project*, Walker Publishers, New York, NY, 1976.

Wilber, Brig. Gen. W. H., "Infantrymen—The Fighters of War," *National Geographic Magazine*, Washington D.C., 1944.

Wildman, Sam, "One of the heroes of the Second World War visited the site of his former base in Harrington," *Northhamptonshire Telegraph*, September 4, 2019.

Unpublished and archival materials

Bolland, Lt Col. Gerhard L, Personal memoirs, transcribed 1966.

Bolland, Gerhard L, OSS Personnel File, Box 66, Locations 230/86/27/05, https://www.archives.gov/files/iwg/declassified-records/rg-226-oss/personnel-database.pdf

Carpetbagger Photographic Archives & 801st/492nd BG-London OSS Data Depot, http://www.801492.org/HonorRoll/Honor%20Roll.htm

Colby, William, OSS Personnel File, https://archive.org/details/WilliamColbyOSSPersonnelFile

Colby, William E, OSS Personnel File, Box 133, Locations 230/86/28/07, https://www.archives.gov/files/iwg/declassified-records/rg-226-oss/personnel-database.pdf

Farewell Address at Gathering of OSS Employees; G. Edward Buxton and General William J. Donovan; September 29, 1945, http://www.ossreborn.com/files/buxtonspeech.pdf

National Archives, Records of the Office of Strategic Services, https://www.archives.gov/research/guide-fed-records/groups/226.html

National Archives Records, OSS Papers, https://search.archives.gov/search?query=O.S.S.+Papers&submit=&utf8=&affiliate=national-archives

OSS, "OSS Activities, December 1944," Memorandum to the Director from Reports Officer W.B. Kantack, Captain A.C. dated February 28, 1945, Washington History Office, Box 124, Folder 1.

OSS Archives, Special Operations Branch, Norwegian Section, NORSO, Operation RYPE, London, England, Office of Strategic Services Operational Groups:
http://oss-og.org/norway/norso_01.html
http://oss-og.org/norway/norso_02.html
http://oss-og.org/personnel.html

Office of Strategic Services (OSS) Organization and Function, Schools and Training Branch, June, 1945, https://www.ibiblio.org/hyperwar/USG/JCS/OSS/OSS-Functions/index.html

"OSS Operational Group Command Manual," prepared by William J. Donovan OSS Director, December, 1944. Declassified December 3, 2013 (authority NND 843099).

"OSS Operational Groups Field Manual," Strategic Services Field Manual No. 6 prepared by William J. Donovan OSS Director, April 25, 1944. Declassified December 3, 2013 (authority NND 843099).

"OSS Special Operations Field Manual," Strategic Services Field Manual No. 4 prepared by William J. Donovan OSS Director, February 22, 1944. Declassified December 3, 2013 (authority NND 897161).

Roosevelt Letter dated July 11, 1941, creating Coordinator of Information, http://www.ossreborn.com/files/COI_EO.pdf

Roster, 507th PIR, April 1, 2009, http://www.usairborne.be/Roster/ROSTER-507PIR.pdf

30th Reunion of the O.S.S. held October 10–12 in Minneapolis, Minnesota; Newsletter produced October 25, 1975.

War Department: Adjutant General's Office; Official Army Register; January 1, 1945, https://ia801409.us.archive.org/34/items/officialarmyregi1945unit/officialarmyregi1945unit.pdf

"World War Two Special Operations and Code Words," OSS, April 16, 1945, (https://archive.org/details/SOBranchOSSETOCodeWordsAndOperations)

Online resources

A Look Back… The Office of Strategic Services, Operation Rype, Central Intelligence Agency Article; 2010, https://www.cia.gov/news-information/featured-story-archive/2010-featured-story-archive/oss-operation-rype.html

Aviation Research Group Orkney and Sutherland; www.crashsiteorkney.com

"Chef-du-Pont (Manche), The Cities of Normandy During the 1944 Battles," D-Day Overlord, https://www.dday-overlord.com/en/battle-of-normandy/cities/chef-du-pont

"Clifford Heflin," Atomic Heritage Foundation, Washington D.C., https://www.atomicheritage.org/profile/clifford-heflin

National Museum of Nuclear Science and History, Albuquerque, NM, https://www.nuclearmuseum.org/

National Museum of the United States Army; Fort Belvoir, VA, https://armyhistory.org/

Operation Carpetbagger, Carpetbagger Aviation Museum, https://harringtonmuseum.org.uk/operation-carpetbagger/

"OSS Operation RYPE/NORSO," 99th Infantry Battalion (Separate), https://www.99battalion.org/index_files/rype.htm

"Plukktjønnfjellet Memorial Pyramid," Snåsa Naeringsforum Organization, Wordpress Smart Media, www.snasa.no/besok-oss/museer-og-historiskesteder/plukktjonnfjellet-minnepyramide/

"Special Operations Executive (SOE) and the Intelligence Corps, Background History," British Intelligence Museum, 2019, http://www.militaryintelligencemuseum.org/

The Carpetbagger Photographic Archives and Historical Research Center, http://www.801492.org/MainMenu.htm

"The First Into France, 'Pathfinders' of the Normandy Invasion," August 21, 2015, https://militaryhistorynow.com/2015/08/21/first-in-the-fight-11-fascinating-facts-about-d-days-airborne-pathfinders

"The Office of Strategic Services: America's First Intelligence Agency" Government Publishing Office, Library of the Central Intelligence Agency; https://permanent.access.gpo.gov/websites/www.cia.gov/library/publications/intelligence-history/oss.htm

Audiovisual resources

Air Warriors: B-24 Liberator, Smithsonian Channel Production, Series 9 Episode 5: B-24 Liberator by Sturm der Liebe, March 27, 2021, https://www.dailymotion.com/video/x8085yh

Distinguished Service Award Presentation to William Becker, William Donovan Award Dinner, October 22, 2016, https://youtu.be/r2fyqybrdk8

"Operation Carpetbagger: B-24s Drop Agents and Supplies into Occupied Europe in WW2," *YouTube*, May 29, 2013, https://www.youtube.com/watch?v=UhwrAAhGM-A

Original Carpetbagger links, 492nd Special Operations Wing heritage to WWII mission, May 10, 2017, https://youtu.be/PGZeAbwVOpA

"Operation Carpetbagger Trailer (3 of 3)," *YouTube*, October 25, 2018, https://www.youtube.com/watch?v=tkasNRXGS0U

"World War II; Causes and Timeline," *History Channel*, A&E Television Networks, https://www.history.com/topics/world-war-ii

Index

References to images are in *italics*.

Abwehr (German Intelligence), 46
Adams, Irving, 306
air crashes, 175–8, 222–3, *224*, 305–6
aircraft, British, 47
    Mosquito, 179
aircraft, German, 123
aircraft, Norwegian, 57
aircraft, U.S., 14–15
    B-24 Liberator, 154–6, 159, 239
    C-47 Skytrain, 26, 28, 32, 37
    CG-4 Waco Glider, *27*, 28, 37
    Horsa gliders, 28
Albertsen, Jon, 204
Alderdyce, Maj Joe, 108
All American Soldier, The (song), 44
Alms, Col, 131
Anderson, Maj Gen F., 122, 127–8
Anderson, T/5 Harold, 207, 210
Andersson, Alfred, 167
Andreasen, Cpl Knut, 164
Arbenz, Jacobo, 91
Armour, Cmdr Lester, 122, 127–8
Atlantic Ocean, 75
Atlantic Wall, 26, 30
Ausen, T/4 Otis L., 207, 210
Austreng, Cpl Vernon, 207, 210
Austreng, T/5 Wilton, 207

Balchen, Col Bernt, 120–2, 123, *124*, 229
Ballad of the Green Berets (song), 279
Baltic States, 1, 2
bank notes, 72
Barnett, Patricia, 88
Batchelor, Lt Col Herbert, 39
Battle of Britain (1940), 45–6
Baungstead, Maj, 150

Baxter, James P., 88
BBC (British Broadcasting Corporation), 73, 98, 119, 132, 134, 152
BCRA (Bureau Central de Renseignements et d'Action), 95
Becker, William, 303–7
Bedell Smith, Gen Walter, 90
Belgian Army, 25
Belgium, 2, 46, 49, 56, 310
Berg, Mo, x
Berg, Paal, 59
Bergen, 50, 239
Berre, Karl, 197, 233
Bessarabia, 2
Bingham, James, 310–12
Bismarck, Otto von, 68
black propaganda, 91
Bletchley Park, 70
Blood Upon the Risers (song), 15, 17
Bodø, 55, 229
Boehm, Lt Gen Franz, 215
Bolland family, 63–6, 247, *248–50*, 253
Bonin, T/5 Delphis L., 145
Borden, Louise: *Ski Soldier, A World War II Biography*, 105
Boström, Wolmar, 60
Bradley, Lt Gen Omar, 24, 29
Brand IV (hospital ship), 67–8
Bräuer, Dr. Kurt, 49–51, 52, 73
Brewer, Lt Col Charles, 134–5
Brewer, Lt Col George S., 165–6
Britain, *see* Great Britain
British Army, 1, 25, 125, 249–50
    21st Army Group, 23
    21st Independent Parachute Co., 30
    see also SAS
British Empire, 88
Brogger, Capt A. W., 134

Brogger, Lt Col Charles E., 151
Brokaw, Tom: *The Greatest Generation*, 24–5
Bromstad, Alf, 128–9
Brooke, Gen Sir Alan, 23
Bruce, David, 83
Buchenwald concentration camp, 69
Bulge, Battle of the (1944–50), 281
Burget, Donald, 19
    Currahee, 11
Burke, Mike, 88

Camp X (Canada), 108
Canada, 72
Canadian Army, 25, 30
Carpetbaggers, 153–6, 279, 303–14
Casey, William Joseph, 92
Chamberlain, Neville, 45
Cherbourg, 31–2
Child, Julia, x
Christian X of Denmark, King, 51, 54
Chuncheon, 266–71
Church of Norway, 58–9
Churchill, Winston, 1, 23, 29, 47
    and Balchen, 121
    and Battle of Britain, 45, 46
    and Donovan, 83
    and Finland, 53
    and Norway, 103
    and nuclear weapons, 148
    and Royal Navy, 112
    and SOE, 101
CIA (Central Intelligence Agency), x, 90–1,
    92–3, 284, 285
Claffy, Reidar, 54–5
clothing, 137–9, 187–8, 208, 209
code breaking, 69–70
code letters, 132, 134, 135–6
COI (Coordination of Information), 81–6
Colby, William, xi, 92–3, 221, 237, 245, *259*
    and Britain, 202–4
    and CIA, 285
    and drops, 161, 163–4, 167–8, 175–7
    and equipment, 138
    and German surrender, 215, 216
    and Lapps, 170
    and NORSO, 117–18
    and post-war correspondence, 326–9
    and railroads, 171–3, 174–5, 179–80,
        184–5, 187, 188, 192–3

and *Rype*, 144, 147, 149–50, 159
and Trondheim, 227–9
and Vetlesen, 180–1, 197–200
and *Woodlark*, 201
communism, 81, 92
Congressional Gold Medal, 287–8
Cotentin Peninsula, 31–2, 37
Cox, Capt Al, 108
Croft, Maj Andrew, 125
Cromarty, Monica, 69
Cuba, 91
Czech Army, 25, 30

D-Day, xi, 21–6, 28–32, 34–42, 277–8
Dahl, Oblt A. H., 105
Dalnaglar Castle (Scotland), 109, *110–11*, 115,
    143, 149–50
Dalton, Hugh, 46, 47
Davis, Jere, 306, 307
De Gaulle, Gen Charles, 96
Denmark, ix, 1–2, 46, 49, 60–1
    and invasion, 53–4
    and surrender, 51
Devorchak, Pvt Leonard, 31
Dietrich, Marlene, x
Donovan, Gen William, ix–x, 81–7, 283–4,
    310
    and Dulles, 90
    and OGs, 109
    and OSS, 88, 93
    and Scandinavian Section, 98
    and Sweden, 121, 205
Douglas, Maj, 151
Dowding, ACM Hugh, 46
drop zones, 30–1, 35, *38*, 47
DuBois, Cora, 88
Dulles, Allen, 83, 88, 90–1
Dulles, John Foster, 83, 90
Dunkirk, 60
Dutch Army, 25

Eastern Front, 23
Eden, Anthony, 121
Eisenhower, Gen Dwight, 23, 25, 26, 28–9, 41
    and Boehm, 215
    and commendations, 257–9
    and presidency, 90
Eliassen, 1Sgt Einar A., 144, 162–3, 231–2
Ellis, Neil, 307–10

England, *see* Great Britain
English Channel, 21, 25, 26
Enigma machine, 69–70
equipment, *9*, 101–2
  and espionage, 208, 209
  and *Rype*, 137–40, 144–5
Erickson, John, 209
espionage, ix, 46, 54, 84–5, 91
  and Sweden, 189–91, 205–13
explosives, 140–3, 189

Fairbairn, Maj W. E., 108
falconry, 68–9
Falkenhorst, Gen Nikolaus von, 54, 148
Farnsworth, Lt Glenn J., 118, 144, 149, 162,
  186–7, 261–2
fascism, 1, 51, 81, 262
FBI (Federal Bureau of Investigation), ix, 83, 86
Finland, 1, 49, 53, 127
FIS (Foreign Information Service), 86
Fleming, Ian, 108
food supplies, 78, 139, 140, 180
Ford, John, x, 88
Fort Benning (GA), 5–8, *9*, 10–11, *12*, 13–15,
  17–20
France, 1–2, 5, 46, 54, 95
  and capitulation, 45, 56
  and OSS, 89–90
  see also D-Day
Free French Army, 25, 30
French Army, 206
Frihagen, Anders, 72

Gause, Maj Gen Alfred, 24
Gavin, Maj Gen James, xi, 24, 32, 35, 37
  and D+1 Day, 40–1
  and Pathfinders, 30, 31
  and post-war correspondence, 323–5
  and promotion, 42, 44
GC&CS (Government Code and Cypher
  School), 46, 70
German Air Force, *see Luftwaffe*
German Army, xi, 21, 201, 232
  and Norway, 123, 124
  and Norway evacuation, 129–30, 133
German Army (units):
  17th SS Waffen Panzergrenadier Dvn, 41
  91st Infantry Rgt, 24
  Grenadier-Rgt 1057, 39

German Navy, *see Kriegsmarine*
German–American Society, 59–60
Germany, ix, x, 1–2
  and Britain, 45–6
  and D-Day, 31
  and Denmark, 53–4
  and Eastern Front, 23
  and Norway, 3–4, 49–53, 54–60
  and *Rype*, 158
  and surrender, 215–16, 223
  and torpedoes, 67–8
Gestapo, 69, 103, 204
Godfrey, Adm John H., 81
Goethe, Lt James H., 30
Goillot, Paul, 90
gold, 71–2
Gold Beach, 30
Goldberg, Arthur, x
Gomez, Hewitt, 303–7
Göring, Hermann, 45, 69, 103
Great Britain, ix, 1–2, 45–6, 83, 123–4
  and Dunkirk, 60
  and *Ibrox*, 146
  and Norway, 52–3, 54, 55–6, 67, 73, 75–6,
    79
  and OSS, 87–8, 89
  and psychological warfare, 94–5
  and *Rype*, 201–4, 215–17
  see also SOE (Special Operations Executive)
Greeks, 169, 208
Green Berets, 279
Greene, Agnes, 88
Grini concentration camp, 235
Guatemala, 91
Gubbins, Brig Colin, 47
guerrilla warfare, 94–5

Haakon VII of Norway, King, xi, 3, 50–2, 98,
  121
  and exile, 54, 56
  and German surrender, 216
  and return, 233, 236, 252–3, *254*
Hahn, Otto, 147
Hall, Lt Roger, 237, *238*, 239, 243, *244–5*, *259*
Hall, Virginia, 89–90
Hambro, C. J., 50
Hansteen, Gen, 129
Hare, Jaqueline, 89
Haugen, Einar, 60

Haugland, Lt Knut, 119, 147–9
Hayden, Sterling, x, 88
heavy water, 147–9
Hefrin, Lt Col Clifford, 153, 164
Hegge Gárd, *217*, 218–22
Helgesen, Herbert, 118, 146–7, 168, 184, 246
   and Steinkjer, 224, 225
Helms, Richard McGarrah, 91–2
Hemingway, John, x
Heroes of Telemark (film), 148–9
Hillenkoetter, Roscoe H., 285
Himmler, Heinrich, 69
Hitler, Adolf, ix, 1, 2, 91, 206
   and Britain, 45, 46
   and D-Day, 25
   and Denmark, 53–4
   and falconry, 68, 69
   and Norway, 67, 103
   and nuclear weapons, 149
   and Quisling, 235
   and suicide, 215
Hjelmtveit, Nils, 52
Hoel, Lt Hans, 118, 157, 168, 180, 224
Holland, *see* Netherlands
Holmstrom, Robert, *303*, 310–12
Holterman, Col, 74, 232, 233, 236
Hoover, J. Edgar, ix, 83
hospital ships, 67–8
Hovland, T/5 Eddie, 164

Imperial Eagle (*Reichsadler*), 68–9
intelligence, ix–x, 2, 31, 73, 128–9
   and USA, 81–6
   see also CIA (Central Intelligence Agency);
      OSS (Office of Strategic Services); SOE
      (Special Operations Executive)
Iran, 91, 92
iron ore, 2, 56, 103, 206
Italy, 1, 2, 46, 90, 208

J. W. McAndrew, USAT, 259–60
Japan, ix, xi, 2, 46, 247, 262
   and Bolland, 271–3, *274*, 275
   and *Magic*, 86
   and *Ultra*, 70
Jedburgh teams, 95, 284
Jenkins, Sgt Kenneth, 20
Jews, 1

Joa, T/Sgt Knute, 207, 210
Johansen, Cpl Kai, 161, 162–3
Johnson, Hershel, 122
Johnson, Lyndon B., 92
Joint Chiefs of Staff (JCS), 85–6
Jones, Lt Blaine E., 144
Juno Beach, 30

Kanin, Garson, 88
Kauffmann, Henrik de, 60
Kellam, Maj Fred, 39
Kennedy, John F., 91
Khrushchev, Nikita, 91
Kittredge, Eleanor, 49
Kjelness, Edward E., 115
Knox, Frank, 83
Kohlt, Dr. Halvan: *Norway, Neutral and
   Invaded*, 49
Koht, Dr. Halvdan, 60
Kompani Linge, 79
Korea, xi, 263–71, 275–6
Kriegsmarine, 67–8, 236–7
Kristiansand, 50
Kroona, 1Lt John, 200, 208

La Fière, 38–9, 40–1
La Graignes, 41
Lang, Capt Helmut, 25
Langeland, 2Lt Borge O., 115–17, 162–3, 184,
   240, *259*
   and drops, 174, 175–6, 177
   and Steinkjer, 223, 224
Lapps, 137, 169–70, 172
Larsen, Lt Harold (Hans), 118–19, 158
Larson, Maj H. P., 129, 184, 206
League of Nations, 1, 49
Leigh-Mallory, AM Sir Trafford, 23
Leisteid, S/Sgt Arne, 162–3
Leksvik, Jens, 184
Lian, Marthe, 210–12, 219
Lian, Thoralf, 210, 218, 219–21, 231–2
Lie, Trygve, 121
Liermo, Hans, 161–2, 171, 194, 196, 222–3
Lierne, 150, 200, 201
Lindquist, Col Roy, 39
Linge, Capt Martin, 79
loading manifest, *33–4*
Lorentzen, Öyvind, 76

Luftwaffe, 45–6, 52, 123, 305
Luleå, 56
Luxembourg, 2, 46, 49

MacArthur, Gen Douglas, 87, 268, 269, 277
McGinitry, Maj Jim, 39
Mackesy, Maj Gen P. J., 206
MacLeish, Archibald, ix–x, 85
Magruder, Brig Gen John T., 88
Maloney, Lt Col Arthur A., 40
Manhattan Project, 148
Marshall, Gen George, 23
Märtha of Norway, Crown Princess, 53, 56
Mendez, Lt Col Louis G., 39
Merderet River, 37, 39–40, 42
Meredith, Capt R. L., 69
Merli, Sgt Gino, 25
Midtskogen, 57
Miller, Gerald, 257–8
Millett, Col George V., Jr., 20, 37, 39
Milorg (Norwegian Underground Army), 73–4,
    103, 104, 189, 204
    and *Rype*, 161, 200, 240
    and Sweden, 208, 281–2
mines, 24–5, 56
Minnesota, 63, 64–6
Mockler-Ferdman, Brig Gen, 131
Montgomery, FM Bernard, 23, 215
Morgenstierne, Wilhelm, 60–1
Mosaddeq, Mohammad, 91
Mosjøen, 206
Munthe-Kass, Oblt, 105
Murphy, Jim, 85
Murphy, Robert, 31, 81
Murphy, Lt Thomas A., 30
Mussolini, Benito, 1
Myrland, T/3 Marinius, 162–3

Namsos, 236–7
Nao, Lam Son, 116–17
Napoleonic Wars, 49, 60
Narvik, 50, 56, 103, 206
Nasjonal Samling, 51, 58
Netherlands, 2, 46, 49
New York National Guard, 83
newspapers, 79
Nielsen, Lt Col R. Rosher, 50
Nilssen, Bjarne, 148
Nimitz, Adm Chester, 87

Nixon, Richard, 92
Nordland rail line, 104, 112, 127–31, 133–4
    and reconnaissance, 182–6, 193–4
    and sabotage, 171–3, 179–80, 186–9,
        191–3, 200–1
    and targets, 143–4, 151–2
Nordlie, Maj J. E., 129–31, 151
Normandy, *see* D-Day
NORSO (Norwegian Special Operations
    Group), 5, 19, 104–9, *110–11*, *251–2*
    and beginnings, 123–6
    and departures, 157–9
    and drops, 159–63, 167–8, 173–4, 175–9
    and final days, 231–3
    and Namsos, 236–7
    and personnel, 113–22
    and recruiting, 168–9
    and reports, 289–94
    and Skabo, 189–91
    and Steinkjer, 223–6
    and Sweden, 164–7, 207–8
    and victory march, 245
NORSO II (Norwegian Special Operations
    Group), 237, *238*, 239–40, 243, *244*,
    251–2
North, Lt Henry Ringling, 88
North Africa, 87
Nortraship, 76–7
Norway, ix, xi, 1–4
    and *Abwehr*, 46
    and Bolland family, 63–6
    and church, 58–9
    and exile government, 52–3
    and hospital ships, 67–8
    and invasion, 49–52, 54–8, 59–60
    and liberation, 235–6, 245–7, 249, 252–3
    and merchant fleet, 75–7
    and OSS, 97–9
    and resistance, 71–5, 78–80
    see also NORSO (Norwegian Special
        Operations Group); *Rype* operation
        (1944)
Norwegian Army, 25, 56–7; *see also* Milorg
Norwegian Underground, 101, 118–20, 123–5,
    151
    and *Rype*, 136–7, 143, 149
    see also Milorg
nuclear weapons, 147–9

Obolensky, Serge, 144–5
Oechsner, Fred, 91
Oien, Lt Col, 147, 149, 150
Oistad, T/Sgt Leif, 105, 164–5
Oksnevad, Torlay, 72
Olav V of Norway, Prince, xi, *51*, 52, 56, 121
    and return, 233, 253
Omaha Beach, 22–3, 29, 30, 277–8
operations:
    Carpetbagger (1944–5), 153–6, 303–14
    Husky (1944), 99, 101–2, 104
    Ibrox (1945), 146
    Jupiter (1942), 79, 103
    Neptune (1944), 21–2
    Overlord (1944), 21–6
    Sonnie (1943), 121–2
    Squatter (1941), 87
    Torch (1942), 87
    see also Rype operation (1944)
Oslo, 50, 57, 71, 72, 252–3
Oslo Gang, 191
OSS (Office of Strategic Services), x, xi, 86–90,
    95–6, 283–5
    and Carpetbaggers, 154
    and commendations, 257–9
    and Donovan, 84, 85
    and employees, 93–4
    and Helms, 91–2
    and *Rype*, 105–8, 127–8, 129, 132–3
    and Scandinavian Section, 97–9, 101–2
    see also NORSO (Norwegian Special
        Operations Group)
Ostberg, Lt Col Edwin J., 40

Pacific Theater, 87
paratroopers, ix, x–xi, 44, 277–8
    and Britain, 87
    and D-Day, 24, 26, 28–9, 30–2, 34–42
    and "Merril's Marauders," 278–9
    and OSS, 92, 95
    and *Rype*, 130–1, 145
    and training, 5–8, *9*, 10–11, *12*, 13–15,
        17–20
    see also NORSO (Norwegian Special
        Operations Group)
Pathfinders, 30–1
Paulsen, S/Sgt Alf, 108, 162–3, 194–5
Pearl Harbor, 83

Pearson, Judith: *Wolves at the Door*, 89–90
Pétain, Philippe, 2
Petersen, Maj Axel, 3–4
Phelps, Julia, 89
Poland, ix, 1, 46, 50, 70
Polinsky, Eugene, *303*, 307, 309–10
Polish Army, 25, 30
Pollari, Howard, *303*, 312–14
Powers, Francis Gary, 91
Procopé, Hjalmar, 61
propaganda, 91, 92
psychological warfare, 94–5

Quebec Conference (1943), 23
Queen Maud (hospital ship), 68
Quisling, Vidkun, 3, 51, 52, 57–8, 60
    and followers, 186, 196
    and resistance movements, 73
    and trial, 235

radio, 30, 86, 94
    and Carpetbaggers, 155, 306–7
    and merchant fleet, 75–6
    and NORSO, 119–20, 123–4, 159–61,
        163–4
    and Norway, 56, 78, 79
    and *Rype*, 135–6, 189
Raeder, Genadm Erich, 67, 103
RAF, *see* Royal Air Force
railroads, 206; *see also* Nordland rail line
Raivio, T/5 Matti, 161, 162–3
Ramsay, Adm Bertram, 23
Rasussen, Wilton, 210
rationing, 78
Reagan, Ronald, 22–3, 92
Red Cross, 67–8
refugees, 131–2
reindeer, 137, 169–70
Reistad, Col Ole, 53
Reitter, Leopold, 69
Rejewski, Marian, 70
religion, 58
Resistance movements, 46, 47, 310
    and Norway, 57–8, 71–5, 78–80
    see also Norwegian Underground
Rockefeller, Nelson, 86
Romania, 2
Rommel, FM Erwin, 24, 25

Roosevelt, Franklin D., ix, 2, 23, 34–5, 188
and intelligence, 81–3, 86
and Norway, 56, 71
and nuclear weapons, 148
Roper, Capt George, 97
Royal Air Force (RAF), 26, 45–6, 47, 153–6
Royal Navy, 45–6, 54, 112
Ruge, Gen Otto, 56
Rusdal, T/5 Tom, 164
Rusdal, Torsten, 117
Russian Army, 23
Rype operation (1944), xi, 5, 19, 181–2, 240–3
and Britain, 201–4, 215–17
and Carpetbaggers, 154–6
and consequences, 280–3
and German defense, 195–7
and inception, 103–9, 112
and Lapps, 169–70
and preparations, 127–52
and railroads, 171–3, 174–5, 179–80, 200–1
and reconnaissance, 182–6, 193–4
and reports, 294–7
and sabotage, 186–9, 191–3
and Vetlesen, 197–200
and victory, 245–6
see also NORSO (Norwegian Special Operations Group)

sabotage, 73–4, 79–80, 104, 205–6
and heavy water, 147–9
and OSS, 94, 95
and railroads, 150, 171–3, 179–80, 186–9, 191–3, 200–1
Saint-Sauver-le-Vicomte, 32
Sainte-Marie-du-Mont, 32
SAS (Special Air Service), 87
Sather, Carl, Sr., 114–15
Sather, 1Lt Tom, 114, 133, 157–8, 163, *259*
and railroad, 184, 186
and reconnaissance, 194–5
and Trondheim, 227–9
Savoldi, Joe, 88
Scandinavia, *see* Denmark; Norway; Sweden
Scherbius, Arthur, 69
Schlesinger, Arthur, Jr., x
Schwartzwalder, Capt Floyd, 38–9
Seibert, Pete, 105

SFHQ (Special Forces Headquarters), 124–5, 135, 147, 207–8
SHAEF (Supreme Headquarters Allied Expeditionary Force), 129–31, 132–3, 200, 201, 281
Shetland Islands, 75
Skabo, Lt Col Hans, 104, 113–14, 147, 151, 240–3
and espionage, 205
and NORSO, 189–91, 239
and *Rype*, 132–3, 134–5
skiing, 57, 104–5, 109, 139, 170–1
and Finland, 53
and Minnesota, 64–5
and training, 125
Skouras, George, 88
SOE (Special Operations Executive), 46–7, 73, 79, 95–6, 101
Soederman, Harry, 122
Sons of Norway (*Sönner av Norge*), 59–60
Sonsteby, Gunnar, 72, 191
Sørkedal Ski Company, 57
Sörlie, Kjell, 136–7, 168, 189, 202
Sörlie, Odd, 136–7
Soviet Union, 1, 2, 91, 127, 225
and Korea, 264, 265, 266, 268
Spaatz, Gen Carl, 122
Speidel, Maj Gen Dr. Hans, 24
spies, *see* espionage
Stagg, Grp Capt J. M., 26
Stalin, Joseph, 29, 91
Stapel, Wilmer, 153
Station XII, 47
Stavanger, 50
Steen, Gunnar, 128–9
Steffanson, Viljalmar, 125
Steifel, Col, 228, 236, 239, 243, 246–7
Steinkjer, 118, 210, 213, 217–22, 223–6
Stephenson, Sir William, 1, 81, 108
Stimson, Henry, ix, 23]
Stirling, David, 87
supplies, 123–4; *see also* food supplies
Sweden, 49, 92, 121, 131–2, 133
and drops, 164–7
and iron ore, 2, 56, 103, 206
and Milorg, 281–2
and spies, 189–91, 205–13
and *Woodlark*, 135, 152, 202

Sword Beach, 30
Syttende Mai (Seventeenth of May) parade, 66, 226, 232–3

Tangen Bridge, 183–9, 191–3
Terboven, Josef, 58
Thor, Vilhjalmur, 61
Timmes, Lt Col Charles, 37
TODT, 225, 232
Tolischus, Otto, 59
Toronto Island (Canada), 53
tower jumping, 10, 11, 12, 13, 15
Tripartite Pact, 46
Tromsø, 52, 114
Trondheim, 50, 206, 227–9, 231–2
    and liberation, 247, 249, 253
Tronstad, Leif, 148
Truman, Harry S., 90, 284, 285
Trump, Donald J., 277–8
Turing, Alan, 70
Twingley, T/5 Otto, 207, 210

Ukraine, 2
Ultra, 70, 86
United States of America (USA), ix–x, 2, 46, 60–1, 259–62
    and D-Day, 22–3
    and gold, 72
    and intelligence, 81–6
    and Norway, 56, 59–60
    see also CIA (Central Intelligence Agency); Minnesota; OSS (Office of Strategic Services); Roosevelt, Franklin D.
U.S. Air Force, 279
U.S. Army, 22–3, 25, 93, 263–73, 275
U.S. Army (units):
    10th Mountain Dvn, 97, 105, 114, 115, 252

82nd Airborne Dvn, xi, 5, 24, 31–2, 42
101st Airborne Dvn, 26
507th Parachute Infantry Rgt (PIR), 20
99th Mountain Btn, 3, 4, 104–9
U.S. Army Air Force (USAAF), 28, 93
U.S. Navy, 284
Utah Beach, 24, 30, 31, 32

Værnes, 227–8, 236–7, 239–40, 243, 246–7
Vandervoot, Lt Col Ben, 39
Vemork Hydro-Electric plant, 147–8
Vetlesen, Lt Cmdr G. Unger, 53, 98–9, 101, 125–6, 147
    and Britain, 201–2
    and Colby, 172, 180–1, 193, 197–200
    and OSS, 129
    and Skabo, 132–3, 135, 240–3
    and supply drops, 124
    and Sweden, 167
Vichy France, 2
Vietnam War, 92–3, 116–17, 285

Walker, Gen Edwin, 252
weather conditions, 26, 137–9
whalers, 137–8
What Every Soldier Should Know About Airborne Troops (pamphlet), 24
Williamson, Emmy Lou, 89
Wilson, Hugh, 88
Windh, T/5 Sivert, 164
women, 88–90, 117
Woodlark, 127, 131, 133, 134–5, 150, 152, 172
    and Britain, 202
    and Colby, 201
    and Milorg, 200
World War I, 49, 54

Yom Kippur War, 285